ANALECTA BIBLICA

INVESTIGATIONES SCIENTIFICAE IN RES BIBLICAS

99

"Do This as My Memorial"

**The Semantic and Conceptual
Background and Value of Ἀνάμνησις
in 1 Corinthians 11:24-25**

ROMAE
E PONTIFICIO INSTITUTO BIBLICO
1982

FRITZ CHENDERLIN, S.J.

"Do This as My Memorial"

The Semantic and Conceptual
Background and Value of Ἀνάμνησις
in 1 Corinthians 11:24-25

ROME
BIBLICAL INSTITUTE PRESS
1982

TYPIS PONTIFICIAE UNIVERSITATIS GREGORIANAE — ROMAE

Preface

This book, except for a few minor additions and alterations, is a doctoral dissertation successfully defended in late 1980 at Claremont Graduate School before a board consisting of Drs. James A. Sanders, Burton Mack and Chan Hie Kim. My interest in the subject of Eucharistic memorial dates from the time of my theological studies in India. I hope eventually to unfold the implications of the conclusions here reached in another mainly theological study.

Much of the material in the dissertation was included in papers submitted to my various professors in the doctoral program at Claremont: Drs. James M. Robinson, Hans Dieter Betz, Kathleen Wicker, and Burton Mack. To them and to my director Dr. Sanders I offer sincere thanks for their expertise, direction and encouragement during the pleasant time I spent at Claremont. Dr. Mack was especially kind and helpful in listening and responding to my early formulations of the dissertation material.

I would also like to offer special thanks to the Very Rev. William Barry, pastor, and to the priests, nuns and parishioners at Our Lady of the Assumption Church in Claremont, for their generous and prayerful support while I was a resident there. And finally, to the Provincials and members of the Patna and Detroit Provinces of the Society of Jesus, and the Darjeeling Region of the Calcutta Vice-Province, who made different kinds of sacrifices to enable me to bring this project to successful completion.

Santa Barbara, California, May 1, 1982.

Table of Contents

List of Abbreviations and Expressions

ad finem	at or near the end
Antiq.	Antiquities of Josephus
Apoc.	Apocryphon or Apocrypha; Apocalypse
As. Mos.	Assumption of Moses
B. C.	Before Christ
B. C. E.	Before the Christian Era
C	Corinthians
c.	circa—about
C. E.	Christian Era
cf.	confer—compare
Ch.	Chronicles, Chapter
C. I. C.	Commander in Chief
Clem.	Clement
col.	column
Cor.	Corinthians
Dan.	Daniel
De Conf. Ling.	De Confusione Linguarum (Philo)
De Cong.	De Congressu Quaerendae Eruditionis Gratia (Philo)
De Mem.	De Memoria (Aristotle)
De Mig.	De Migratione Abrahami (Philo)
Deut.	Deuteronomy
Dial.	Dialogue
DMP	Demotic Magical Papyri
Eccl.	Ecclesiastes (Qoheleth)
Ecclus.	Ecclesiasticus (Sirach)
ed.	editor, edited, edition
Est.	Esther
et al.	et alibi—and elsewhere
Euthyd.	Euthydemus (Plato)
Exod.	Exodus
Ezek.	Ezechiel
Gal.	Galatians
Gen.	Genesis
Gk	Greek
Gl.	Galatians
Gosp.	Gospel
Hab.	Habacuc
Heb.	Hebrews
ibid.	ibidem—in the same place
i. e.	id est—that is
introd.	introduction
Isa.	Isaiah
JBC	Jerome Biblical Commentary
Jer.	Jeremiah

Jn	John
JTS	Journal of Theological Studies
Jub.	Jubilees
Jud.	Judith, Judah
Judg.	Judges
Kgs	Kings
LCL	Loeb Classical Library
Lev.	Leviticus
L. & S.	Liddell & Scott
LXX	Septuagint
Mac.	Maccabees
Mal.	Malachi
Matt.	Matthew
N	Nomen—[insert] name
n. d.	no date
Nm.	Numbers
NN	Nomina—[insert] names
NT	New Testament
Num.	Numbers
OT	Old Testament
Par.	Paraphrase
para.	paragraph
Phil.	Philippians
Plat.	Plato
Pr. Azar.	Prayer of Azariah
Preis.	Preisendanz
Prov.	Proverbs
Ps., Pss.	Psalm, Psalms
1 QS	Manual of Discipline
R	Romans
R.	Rabbi
Rabb.	Rabbinical
rev.	revised
Rev.	Revelations
Rom.	Romans
RSV	Revised Standard Version
Sam.	Samuel
Sir.	Sirach (Ecclesiasticus)
subst.	substantive
s.v.	sub verbo—under the entry
T.	Testament
Teach.	Teachings
Thess.	Thessalonians
Tim.	Timothy
trans.	translated or translated by
v.	verse
v. g.	verbi gratia—for example
Wisd.	Wisdom of Solomon
Zech.	Zechariah

Chapter I: **Text, Thesis, Methodology** [1]

The Text

1. Let us state our text in Greek and English [2] in compartmented form, as a working basis for reference and comparison, assigning appropriate letters for the verse subdivisions.

23b.	. . . ἔλαβεν ἄρτον	… [he] took bread,
24a.	καὶ εὐχαριστήσας	and when he had given thanks,
24b.	ἔκλασεν καὶ εἶπεν·	he broke it, and said,
24c.	τοῦτό μού ἐστιν τὸ σῶμα	"This is my body
24d.	τὸ ὑπὲρ ὑμῶν·	which is for you.
24e.	τοῦτο ποιεῖτε	Do this
24f.	εἰς τὴν ἐμὴν ἀνάμνησιν.	in remembrance of me."
25a.	ὡσαύτως	In the same way
25b.	καὶ τὸ ποτήριον	also the cup,
25c.	μετὰ τὸ δειπνῆσαι, λέγων,	after supper, saying,
25d.	τοῦτο τὸ ποτήριον	"This cup
25e.	ἡ καινὴ διαθήκη ἐστιν	is the new covenant
25f.	ἐν τῷ ἐμῷ αἵματι·	in my blood.
25g.	τοῦτο ποιεῖτε,	Do this
25h.	ὁσάκις ἐὰν πίνητε,	as often as you drink it,
25i.	εἰς τὴν ἐμὴν ἀνάμνησιν.	in remembrance of me."

And Paul adds:

26a.	ὁσάκις γὰρ ἐὰν ἐσθίητε τὸν ἄρτον τοῦτον	For as often as you eat this bread
26b.	καὶ τὸ ποτήριον πίνητε,	and drink the cup,
26c.	τὸν θάνατον τοῦ Κυρίου καταγγέλλετε,	you proclaim the Lord's death
26d.	ἄχρι οὗ ἔλθῃ.	until he comes.

---

[1] The arabic numbers to the left of each paragraph designate the paragraphs serially throughout the work. These numbers will be used to locate cross references, the reference being initiated by the appropriate number placed within round brackets in the body of the text. This will avoid a proliferation of footnotes due to the frequent references that will have to be made to texts assembled in our survey of the literature, as well as to various arguments and conclusions. Other lettering and numbering will be restricted to material within the text itself and will be kept to a minimum. The Table of Contents may be used to locate the parts within the totality whenever that should seem desirable.

[2] Unless otherwise noted, English biblical texts used in this work will be taken from *The Bible, Revised Standard Version*, 2nd ed. (New York: American Bible Society, 1971).

2. Willi Marxsen notes at the beginning of his study of the Lord's Supper as a christological problem that it is a consensus of scholars today that "The four so-called accounts of the institution of the Lord's Supper... may be described as 'cult formulas' or as communion 'liturgies,' even if here and there they have been given a literary reworking. The *Sitz im Leben* in any case is cultic." [3] We shall accept this estimate without discussion; as we proceed, our own investigations will repeatedly corroborate it.

The Thesis

3. As its title indicates, this study's focus will be the term and concept of ἀνάμνησις as it occurs in 24f and 25i. It will be our thesis that in understanding and translating this term, special care must be taken to leave within it all the potentialities for memorial significance, by way of denotation and connotation, that the evidence tells us would probably have attached to the term at the time and in the context in which Paul used it; and that the only English translation that fully satisfies this requirement plus the exigencies of the Greek ἐμήν, here found in combination with ἀνάμνησιν, is "Do this as my memorial."

The Method

4. In the positive demonstration of the validity of this thesis, the main task will be to show what the potentialities in question actually are. To this end we shall undertake in Parts III and IV a study of the relevant concepts and terms, first in the literature that was either directly available to Paul and his readers, or that represents thinking and language that was available; and then in Paul himself. The present reader may refer to the closing lines of these Parts and their various sections for summaries of the conclusions reached in them, and a listing of the potentialities. In general, we may say here that both the term ἀνάμνησις and its near synonym μνημόσυνον signify "reminder", and that in the pertinent literature these and associated words, both verbs and nouns, refer to man's [4] reminding God as often as they do to man's reminding men. More specifically, the terms, in conveying the technical meaning of "cultic reminder", recall a group of types and particular examples from both Greek and Hebrew sources that are applicable to the Christian cultic situation each in its own way even while they share the quality of reminding God and/or reminding man.

---

[3] Willi Marxsen, *The Lord's Supper as a Christological Problem*, trans. Lorenz Nieting from *Das Abendmahl als christologisches Problem* [Gutersloh: Gerd Mohn, 1963] (Philadelphia: Fortress Press, 1970), pp. 4-5.

[4] Unless otherwise evident, the word "man" and substitutive pronouns, in their various cases and numbers, will be used throughout this study with the generic English meaning of "human being" without exception of race or sex.

5. Part I will conclude with a presentation of the principal positions taken by various scholars who have concerned themselves directly with our question. This should provide a certain perspective in which to view the thesis and its development. Additional perspective will be given by Part II. That will explore four conceptual areas that are inevitably entered upon by anyone concerning himself with traditional cultic materials, and particularly with specifically memorial ones. The areas are interpretation, history, time-space and sacramentalism. Our investigations into these areas will each be initiated by discussions of certain modes of thought that may have influenced scholars and schools either to shy away from our debate entirely or to place on the understanding and translation of the text restrictions that the evidence, considered extensively and in depth, does not seem to warrant. In effect, Part II will provide a hermeneutical background as well as some theological reflections in reference to which the reader may focus his own vision both of the problem and of the material to be treated and conclusions to be reached in Parts III and IV. Part II will also demonstrate a good probability that Paul and his readers would have adopted attitudes in these conceptual realms that are in agreement with positive conclusions we shall reach in the Part, conclusions that in turn are attuned to more specific ones relating to cult and memorial that we shall reach about Paul and his Christians in Parts III and IV. In other words, a set of general probabilities will match a set of more particular ones, so that Part II will serve as both an introduction to and corroboration of the succeeding development. The independence of the provenance of the argumentation used in Part II from that used in Parts III and IV make the combination an argument from convergence. Finally, a fifth Part will round out our study. In it, key scholarly positions sketched out in Part I and elsewhere will be assessed from the vantage point provided by the positive results of the first four Parts. This will both locate our work better in the spectrum of scholarship and throw additional light on those results and the argumentation leading to them.

6. The term "probabilities" used ten lines above is advisedly chosen. We shall not claim to present absolute proofs in this work—the nearest we may come to that may be proof that absolute proofs are not possible here. The clause we shall recommend for the translation of the Greek " εἰς τὴν ἐμὴν ἀνάμνησιν ", "Do this as my memorial", will be recommended because it expresses a sum of real possibilities and likelihoods, whereas alternative translations are unwarrantedly exclusive.

7. Part II will serve two ancillary functions as well. It will encourage the reader to ask himself whether his own views in the four areas mentioned predispose him in any way. It will also give him a glimpse into the mind of the present writer. This is not without advantage. If the reader, for example, were addressing himself to a work by Bultmann or

Cullmann, he would have a fair idea already of the writer's hermeneutic, and would automatically read what the author had to say with that in mind. It would be important: one does not always get the same meaning from a given phrase occurring in both Bultmann and Cullmann. In the present case, the reader must start from this study itself, and so both deserves and needs some notion of its author's views on interpretation and history, the more so because of the nature of our text. Brevard Childs, in his important work on memory and tradition in the Old Testament (see 182ff), puts his discussion of these matters at the end. It seems preferable here to put ours in large part at the beginning and refer back to it either verbally or mentally as the work proceeds. Certainly, Childs' discussion is not grounded solely on the word study with which he prefaces it.

CHAPTER II: **Key Figures in the Debate**

8. In his book on the Eucharistic words of Jesus, Joachim Jeremias asserts, in regard to the command for repetition, that the more common kind of translation, which shows the disciples being told to remember Christ, should be dropped in favor of a translation like "This do, that God may remember me."[1] The exclusiveness of this reading is evident: human remembering is excluded as an element of the explicit injunction. Jeremias was undoubtedly reacting against exclusiveness in the other direction, which had been the usual scholarly attitude until his time, and has been reaffirmed by various scholars since he made his statement, partially in reaction to *it*. We shall see later what it is that God remembers, in Jeremias' view. His argumentation is based in part on some of the same materials that we shall see in Parts III and IV; we shall conclude that his reading of those materials was one-sided, though accurate as far as it went, which was something less than halfway.

9. Jeremias was not the first to suggest that reminding-God[2] is involved in the Eucharistic ἀνάμνησις, but he was the first to bring to the fore the wide extent of the evidence for reminding-God; the only real debate on the subject has revolved around his work. In a short but influential article written in 1958, Douglas Jones remarks that "The attempt is made from time to time to show that the words which St. Paul understood Jesus to have used to order the repetition of the Eucharist have not merely a sacrificial association but a more precise Jewish liturgical origin."[3] Jones takes particular aim at Jeremias' reminding-God contention as put forward in the second German edition of *The Eucharistic Words*. Jones' conclusion is that "the objection to the usual translation of I Cor. xi. 25 does not withstand scrutiny; that common usage would suggest the usual translation while analogies for the alternative are found to be inadequate; that the Passover context would at once suggest the usual

---

[1] Joachim Jeremias, *The Eucharistic Words of Jesus*, trans. Norman Perrin from *Die Abendmahlsworte Jesu*, 3rd ed. [Göttingen: Vandenhoeck & Ruprecht, 1960, with author's revisions to July 1964] (New York: Charles Scribner's Sons, 1966), p. 255.

[2] This hyphenated form of this phrase or the parallel one, "reminding-man", will be used whenever the two words are used as a gerund couple, as distinct from other syntactical arrangements whether involving gerunds or not.

[3] Douglas Jones, " ἀνάμνησις in the LXX and the Interpretation of 1 Cor. XI. 25," JTS 6 (1955): 183.

translation and require explicit redirection to permit any other." [4] But Jones' argument has serious deficiencies of its own, and he introduces a theme that recurs in later commentaries on our text when he appeals to "common usage" and makes statements such as "The most obvious meaning of our Lord's words is the straightforward one 'to call me to remembrance.'" [5] This 'straightforwardness', understood as Jones understands it to carry a note of exclusiveness, would, I am sure, puzzle a first century reader; and the puzzlement would be vastly deepened by his awareness of all kinds of possible meanings for "ἀνάμνησις" that might not be part of the normal mental equipment of a twentieth century man, but would have been for him. He would admit that a "memorial" in the 1 Corinthians context would involve reminding the people about Jesus, but he would be able to see various other possibilities for it as well—a number of them involving reminding-God.

10. Both Jeremias and Jones demonstrate a kind of "either-or" thinking that we have already characterized as "exclusive". At the other pole from such thinking is the wild kind of imaginative simile typified by some patristic exegesis. We shall later discuss the qualities and implications of "exclusive" thinking. It seeks out dogmatic expressions limited to single species within the genus, and in this sense might also be called "specific" thinking. It reveals a tendency to oversimplification as against legitimate pluralism.

11. Another example of it in our text is the translation of the "ἐμὴν" as an objective genitive, giving in English either "of me" or some equivalent like Jeremias' simple "me". Whereas the translation "my", though subjective in form, allows for an objective *meaning* should the concept of "memorial" require that, the objective forms exclude the subjective meaning. This particular example of "exclusiveness" is very common with exegetes of our text, though not universal. We shall later conclude that it is an unjustifiable limitation on the text.

12. Reference is made above (9) to the "first century reader". It appears that from the second century C. E. onward, Christians were no longer inclined to associate the element of reminding-God with the term "memorial". The influence of Greek thinking was a main factor in this change, and we shall see how this influence operated, remarking here only that it did so in two ways, discouraging specific "reminding-God" terminology on the one hand, and providing as an alternative expression of "Godward" [6] orientation in the Eucharist the concept of sacrifice understood as identical with the Eucharist rather than merely referential to

---

[4] Jones: 191.
[5] Ibid.: 188.
[6] The term is used by Jones, though in hyphenated form; see p. 183 of his article.

the crucifixion event.[7] Writing of the liturgies in the West in the second and third centuries, Jean Paul Montminy says,

> At that period there appeared ... in the eucharistic prayer itself, at the moment of the anamnesis, an explicit sacrificial element. ... It occupied a very important place for Hippolytus, where the commemoration of the death and resurrection of Jesus moved on to the offering of sacrifice: "Memores ... offerimus tibi panem et calicem." The ἀνάμνησις, which responded to the Lord's command, included an oblation.[8]

"Anamnesis", of course, is the term used for that part of the Mass between the quotation of the words of institution, with the concluding expression "Do this...", and the communion. Thus, the word "respond" in Montminy's statement. He goes on to say, "It further appears that this mention of oblation had already existed [in the Eucharistic service, as distinct from merely outside it and in reference to it] at the time of St. Justin. In his forty-first chapter of the *Dialogue with Trypho*, the philosopher-martyr speaks of sacrifice and oblation made in the memory of the suffering of Christ and at his order."[9] The text in question clearly relates the term "sacrifice" to the "bread... and also the cup of the Eucharist."[10] The development of the sacrificial idea in the Oriental liturgies seems to have come somewhat later, but it is present in the Basilian Egyptian and Antiochene liturgies.[11]

13. The Reformers who rejected the notion that the Eucharist is a sacrifice did not, as might perhaps be expected, turn their attention to the reminding-God potentialities of ἀνάμνησις. They read the Pauline and Lucan texts in the "reminding-man" sense and in no other. For them as for the majority of their modern followers this was the "straightforward" way of interpreting the term and the texts. One reason for this was the fact that in spite of their emphasis on Scripture, they were in many ways quite as effectively cut off from Hebrew modes of thought as were their papist contemporaries. And they had a feeling that, as we shall see, was very Greek—the feeling that reminding-God is somehow a denigration of the Divinity. This feeling is explicit in some of the modern Protestant commentators. In 1960 Hans Kosmala wrote an influential article on Jeremias. He points out that his own view is traditional. "We have no different witness in the Christian tradition."[12] But his principal

---

[7] We shall henceforward generally use the term "Calvary" as synonymous with "crucifixion event", both for brevity's sake and to emphasize the historical quality of the event in Paul's eyes. This quality will be referred to several times as we proceed.

[8] Jean-Paul Montminy, "L'offrande sacrificielle dans l'anamnèse des liturgies anciennes," *Revue des sciences philosophique et théologique* 50 (1966): 389.

[9] Montminy, 389-390.

[10] Justin Martyr, *Dialogue with Trypho*, in *The Ante-Nicene Fathers*, ed. Alexander Roberts and James Donaldson, vol. 1 (New York: Charles Scribners Sons, 1899), p. 215.

[11] See Montminy, 392f.

[12] Hans Kosmala, "'Das tut zu meinem Gedächtnis'," *Novum Testamentum* 4 (1960): 81.

argument against God's being "reminded" is that "He always knows...." [13]
He calls Jeremias' interpretation of Hebrews 10:3, in which God is seen
as reminded of sin, a "theological short circuit".[14]

14. Kosmala's theological problem is explicated, though without reference to him, by Norman Hook. Denying that "the idea of the *azkarah*
is... present" in 1 Cor. 11, Hook adds, "Yet this very notion frequently
appears in theological writing, apparently without any consciousness of
the fact that the Christian doctrine of God is involved." [15] Putting the
discussion once more in the Passover setting, like Jeremias, he indicates
in a lengthy note on anamnesis that he is concerned not just with modern
theology: "...[O]ur particular concern is with the significance of the
word 'ἀνάμνησις' in 1 Corinthians 11:24-25." [16] He sees the *azkarah* as
"something to be done which would induce God to remember," [17] an "Old
Testament idea which has no place in the Christian doctrine of God." [18]
However, he does concede a legitimate Godward aspect to Passover memorial. "But the Passover ... was also a memorial before God, in the sense
that their remembrance represented their side of the covenantal obligation,
and was therefore something which God required to enable Him to fulfil
His side of the covenant relation. When they remembered, God was
enabled to respond with His gifts of grace." [19] Note that he says *before
God* and does not say "When they *reminded*". To "remind" is for him
equivalent to "try to induce."

15. Douglas Jones has his own problem with regard to reminding-
God; one that also best comes to light in his discussion of Jeremias on
Hebrews 10:3. Admitting that this text does involve reminding-God, he
denies a parallel with 1 Corinthians 11 because he thinks reminding-God
there would be "perilous in the extreme." [20] His idea is that when God
"remembers" sin in Scripture he punishes it—that there is no other possible Divine response to Divinely remembered sin.

16. At the end of his work Hook refers to Max Thurian's book on
memorial, closing with the remark that "it assumes uncritically that Old
Testament thought-forms can legitimately be transferred to the Christian
scene." [21] He means by "uncritically" that the legitimacy of such a
transferral is not proved. However that may be on the plane of her-

---

[13] Kosmala, 82.
[14] Ibid.
[15] Norman Hook, *The Eucharist in the New Testament* (London: The Epworth Press, 1964), p. 129.
[16] Hook, p. 147.
[17] Ibid.
[18] Ibid., p. 150.
[19] Ibid., p. 147.
[20] Jones: 186.
[21] Hook, p. 150.

meneutical principle, commentators like Daube, Schoeps and E. Sanders have in recent years underscored the fact that Old Testament thought-forms abound not only in the parts of the New Testament more favorable to perpetuating Jewish institutions, but in Paul.[22] In the area of analogy, Daube expresses a kind of rule that Paul and his contemporaries would undoubtedly have thought to be justified, when he says, "Certainly, no example from history could have more weight than one set by God." [23] The types that Paul does point to are meant to have their effect largely on the basis of this rule. However, it is patent that Paul was consciously open to influences from outside the Jewish sphere that other New Testament writers were closed to: he never excludes profane or non-Hebrew analogues or examples that might further his message. In 1 Corinthians itself he draws on the practice of prostitution as a teaching tool (6:15ff); the table of demons joins the table of God for the same purpose in chapter 10, though in a secondary role.

17. Hook's criticism of Thurian, all the same, is valid in that this author does not adduce sufficient evidence to show that the thought-forms with which he is *particularly* concerned would have been forms easily occurring to—indeed, inevitably occurring to—Paul and his readers. Thurian recognizes the importance of "reminding-God" in the Old Testament cultic literature, but does not show, for example, how widespread this notion was in the first century C.E., nor how easily it could be integrated into even Greek modes of thought once a more familiar psychology of relationship with the Divinity was established. The respect for the Old Testament literature and *its* availability would of course have been an important factor in the acceptance of the Hebrew analogues, but it should be shown (we shall do this) how often the analogues came to mind and use in the actual sphere in which Paul lived, wrote and was read. As for Hellenic analogues like memorial feasts related to heroes, memorial foundations of various kinds, and royal memoranda, Thurian ignores them.

18. The force of Thurian's conclusions is further diminished by his unquestioning acceptance of the exclusively objective meaning for "ἐμὴν". "The possessive ἐμὴν ... here takes the place of an objective genitive, and this is the only instance in the New Testament." [24] "The expression... is

---

[22] The fact of this influence on Paul is hardly contested today, in theory, at least; but the extent and weight of it is still simply not universally appreciated. Some idea of it can easily be got from a glance at the Pauline scriptural references in seminal books by these authors. V.g.: David Daube, *The New Testament and Rabbinic Judaism* (London: The Athlone Press, 1956); Hans J. Schoeps, *Paul*, trans. Harold Knight from *Paulus: Die Theologie des Apostels im Lichte der jüdischen Religions-geschichte* [Tübingen: J. C. B. Mohr, 1959] (Philadelphia: Westminster Press, 1961); and E. P. Sanders, *Paul and Palestinian Judaism* (London: SCM Press Ltd., 1977).

[23] Daube, p. 76.

[24] Max Thurian, *The Eucharistic Memorial*, in two parts, trans. J. G. Davies

to be understood to mean 'in memory of me, as a memorial to me'." [25] In
fact, the *combination* of the pronominal adjective with a term that was
commonly understood to have a number of technical cultic applications
in the literature (Thurian, like Childs and Schottroff, points out the main
ones in the Old Testament itself) would have been the principal factor
in alerting the first-century reader to the analogical potentialities of that
term, "ἀνάμνησις".

19. Carrying out an interpretation of Paul's and Luke's texts that he
undoubtedly feels their readers would have been able to make on the basis
of their knowledge of the Old Testament, Thurian builds up a plausible
memorial structure for the Eucharist incorporating the continuing intercessory function of the risen Christ in heaven [26] and on the Christian table.[27]
At one stage he states his position thus:

> The Eucharist is ... a sacrifice in so far as it is the memorial and sacrament
> of the unique sacrifice of the cross and of the heavenly sacrifice of the
> intercession of Christ. It is the memorial of the sacrifice of Christ because
> it presents it before the Father as a living and present intercession; it
> is the sacrament of the sacrifice of Christ because it makes it present
> before the Church as an effective and actual means of sanctification.[28]

Several points strike the reader here. The Eucharist is not only defined
in terms of sacrifice but is *identified* with it. Sacrifice itself is here
defined in terms of memorial and sacrament. As we shall emphasize,
the Pauline text in its context allows for a sacrificial reference by
"memorial", but even that is only one of the analogues "memorial" suggests.
Part of the reason for Thurian's focus on sacrifice is ecumenical: he is
trying to heal the wounds the issue has caused over the centuries. But
another is his subsumption under the term "sacrifice" of a number of
analogues and spiritual meanings that the first-century reader would
probably not have thought of when presented with the term "memorial",
even though he might have recognized them as "sacrificial" in a general
sense of the word.

20. Thurian bases his identification of Calvary [29] and sacrifice less on
an analysis of Paul's views than on the identification in *Hebrews*. This
hardly suffices for a study of a Pauline or Lucan text in its own right,
even though the conclusion might be correct. Thurian's interest in
memorial is subservient to his desire to show that the Eucharist is a

---

(Richmond, Virginia: John Knox Press; part I 1960; part II 1961), I, p. 46 (see also II,
p. 34). He refers to Blass-Debrunner, Lohmeyer and Jeremias as authorities on the
point.
   [25] Thurian, I, p. 46.
   [26] See Thurian, II, p. 13.
   [27] See ibid., pp. 13, 91, 108.
   [28] Ibid., p. 13.
   [29] See our own note 7 this chapter.

sacrifice as well as a sacrament, the argument being that it is a sacrifice because it was and continues to be a memorial and offering. The "once for all" of *Hebrews* is of course a problem for him, and he spends some time arguing the point that "the heavenly intercession of Christ... is the continual extension of the sacrifice of the cross." [30] Or, as he puts it earlier, "The uniqueness of Christ's sacrifice does not imply an isolated act in past history but an historical act with a continuing efficacy which is extended in the intercession of the Son of God: the unique sacrifice of Christ on the cross is an everlasting sacrifice...." [31] The fact is, he never really justifies the appellation "sacrifice" for the memorial aspect of the Eucharist in terms of the texts themselves. The question is, why, even if the action of Christ is in a true sense an "extension" of an action that was a sacrifice, should the term "sacrifice" be applied to the extension when the sacrifice was a "once for all" historical event. I am not saying that it could not be applied, as on a metonymical basis; but that he has not shown that the text justifies such an application.

21. The basis would still at least border on metonymical even if the real presence were assumed. The question of species intrudes here, of course. Would the realities believed present justify, and would the historical difference (the difference that would make the metonymy instead of total identification) with whatever that implies, allow the direct predication of the species "sacrifice" of the extension of the original act? At any rate, Thurian sees little value in a Eucharist in which there is no real presence. He says, "It is because of the real presence... that there can be a true memorial of the Lord", and "The Lord's memorial ... has no meaning unless the Lord himself is sacramentally present in the Eucharist; otherwise the memorial is no more than a symbolic performance, which may be moving but would have no ontological reality." [32] Even though real presence would add much to the force of the memorial, it seems necessary to reject this position, and do so on the very basis of the reminding-God significance that Thurian accepts. For by reminding God in a "new covenant" sense—reminding him of the death of his obedient servant Christ—the blessings of that event could be forthcoming (on both Paul's and Thurian's theological suppositions) even though Christ were not present on the Christian table. Christ would still be contemporaneously involved, taking up the plea as an advocate at the right hand of God. As for ontology, psychological acts and symbolic ones too do have their ontology; these would at the transcendent level be part of the Divine knowledge of them, and that in turn part of the Divine response to them; which again would terminate in very concrete blessings. In

---

[30] Thurian, II, p. 13.
[31] Ibid., p. 9.
[32] Both quotations from Thurian, II, p. 108.

such a memorial relationship what Thurian well says of the Eucharistic celebration could still be quite true: "The Eucharistic memorial is a recalling to us [i.e., a reminding-us], a recalling by us to the Father, and a recalling of the Son to the Father for us." [33]   Such a picture can be built up quite convincingly once the Eucharist is seen to refer to Christ's sacrifice and Christ is seen as interceding in heaven, with all the participants quite aware of what is going on at the different historical times and places as well as in heaven.   Thurian's focus on sacrifice and his strong emphasis on identification of Eucharist and sacrifice tend to obscure the fact that there are other memorials that are capable of revealing various aspects of this tapestry of relationships, adding and deepening meaning in a number of ways.   It is not the purpose of this study to show in every particular how they might do so, but to show that for Paul and his readers they were available to do so, and were of a general nature to do so—when, of course, the key words "my memorial" were published in their Pauline context.   Sacrifice was available too, and was of such a nature; and it was accepted by Paul's time as a memorial. But for sacrifice to contribute meaning to the Eucharist it does not have to be identified outright with it.   I think that if Thurian were to start again with the premises we provide, he might reach some of the same conclusions he reached the first time; but they would have a surer foundation and be less open to criticism as being unjustified.   And the other analogues of memorial that we shall acknowledge in this work could be explored too for the notes of meaning they might add to flesh-in the skeletal substructure of the Eucharistic celebration.

22. As far as the sacramental aspect of the Eucharist is concerned, Thurian does well to stress that sacrament looks to Divinely-produced effect.[34] We shall see Paul's own positive interest in gaining Divine blessings (see, for example, 188ff, 200, 421), and the implications for this of his tying-in the Eucharist with Divine judgement (383, etc.). Thurian's equation Eucharist = sacrifice = memorial + sacrament is, as noted above, misleading.   Even if the Eucharist is not called a sacrifice it can be a memorial. The memorial aspect then conforms in part with Christ's present intercessory action, in part with the celebration at the Christian table—these being memorial in the senses described above.   In terms of sacrifice, the whole action might then be seen as a "communion" of the sacrificial analogue, Calvary, the communion being realized precisely through the several kinds of memorial.

23. The Roman Catholic position on a number of the points mentioned above has usually been quite close to that adopted by Thurian. A notable

---

[33] Thurian, II, p. 36.
[34] See, for example, ibid., p. 108.

difference is the general failure to see reminding-God in Paul's " ἁ ἀμνησιν ". For example, the noted liturgist Josef Jungmann equivalently sees Paul's reference in 11:26-27 to proclamation of the death as a kind of interpretation of "ἀνάμνησιν".[35] We shall discuss this at more length after we have developed our own position, merely remarking here that his reading would mean an exclusion of a reminding-God meaning for "ἀνάμνησιν".

24. The force of the critique of Thurian made above should become more evident as we proceed. However, though Thurian has written at some length on our subject, it is really the positions of Jeremias, Jones and Kosmala that have been central in the debate up to now, and to them we shall give more attention once we have worked out our own conclusions. These writers are referred to as to authorities in the subsequent commentaries on 1 Corinthians, like those of Conzelmann and Ruef. Conzelmann abruptly dismisses "God's remembering"[36] when he dismisses Jeremias' version of it with the words, "But this interpretation is in contradiction to the plain wording. The meaning is: 'in remembrance of me.'"[37] He clearly means, "in the people's remembering me." Ruef comes to the same decision somewhat less abruptly on the basis of a distinction which he attributes to Jones. He says, "The idea of *remembrance* (Greek, *anamnēsis*) in the Bible has a fund of meaning peculiar to the biblical tradition. This meaning, however, is not in the word *anamnēsis* itself, but in the nature of the things remembered."[38] This is a notable example of how the issues in the area of memorial can be blurred. There is, of course, no sound justification for a sharp distinction between "the word *anamnēsis* itself" and "meaning ... in the nature of the things remembered." The knowledge of that meaning is often derived from nothing else than the uses of memorial words with the phenomena. In any case, the words distil phenomena's memorial aspect for later recovery. These are the real issues. First, *how much* does the term ἀνάμνησις (and, we might add, its synonym μνημόσυνον), in whatever context, say about things to be remembered; and even more basically, does it say anything about *who* remembers as well as what is remembered? Ruef's distinction may imply that if you did take the *word* seriously, you would have to consider the rememberer as such as well as the things remembered, and that would mean "God's remembering". If he meant this, his distinction does not sidetrack the issue. Mean it or not, he at least disregards the issue, moving on immediately to point out that the mighty acts of God for Israel (and by analogy,

[35] See Josef A. Jungmann, *The Mass*, trans. Julian Fernandes, ed. Mary Ellen Evans (Collegeville, Minn.: Liturgical Press, 1975), p. 16.

[36] Hans Conzelmann, *1 Corinthians*, trans. James W. Leitch from *Der erste Brief an die Korinther*, 1st ed. [Göttingen: Vandenhoeck & Ruprecht, 1969] (Philadelphia: Fortress Press, 1975), p. 198.

[37] Conzelmann, p. 199.

[38] John Ruef, *Paul's First Letter to Corinth* (Philadelphia: Westminster Press, 1977; first pub. Penguin Books Ltd., 1971), pp. 119-120.

for the Christian Church) are what is remembered. In this he seems to wish to generalize the New Testament applications of the biblical memorial analogues more than Paul or his first century readers would want to do, thus restricting the "how much" of our first point just above. But that is secondary to our main concern, his exclusion—practical, and in view of his reference to Jones probably theoretical as well—of God's remembering and a fortiori of reminding-God. In truth, the importance of "who remembers" appears in the very expressions he uses to show the importance of what is remembered. "What Israel remembered was what God had done for them.... What the church remembered was what God had done ...." [39] *If it is important to say that* Israel *remembers, it is important to say that* God *does.* And because this is so, it is important for any commentator to point out the potentialities of the text for conveying the meaning that God *does.* And just as important to point out its potentialities for conveying the meaning that the human rememberers are to *remind* the Divine Rememberer.

25. Another Catholic author whose views are occasionally cited is Johannes Betz. We may confine ourselves here to quoting his criticism of Jeremias, which he presents in a note.

> We must reject his exegesis. 1) As far as the syntax goes, it is best if one takes the subject of the clause, namely the ones celebrating the feast, as the ones remembering. 2) In point of fact, it is unusual in the New Testament for Jesus to ask prayers for himself. 3) Historically, all the liturgies from the beginning have understood the means of fulfilment of the memorial to be the people celebrating the Eucharist; v.g., the *"Unde et memores."* [40]

To comment on these points in order. 1) Betz thinks in terms of "remembering" only. If the people *remind* God, they are the subject just as much as in remembering or being reminded by what they do. And ἀνάμνησις, as we shall stress, involves reminding. 2) When the people remind God of Christ it is not to pray for him but to benefit from his saving acts. Again, like Jeremias himself, Betz presumes the objective meaning for " ἐμὴν". But "my memorial", both through the people's remembering and their reminding, can involve Christ's remembering *them* and reminding God of *them*, whether on Calvary or as heavenly advocate. This kind of involvement sees the Eucharist as metonymically related to both Calvary and Christ in heaven in such a way as to unite with the Savior in the functions related to both. It perceives that Calvary and Christ's heavenly advocacy are reminders and memorials in their own right—indeed, are the primary memorials in what we have already (see 21) called a "tapestry"

---

[39] Ruef, p. 120.
[40] Johannes Betz, *Die Eucharistie in der Zeit der griechischen Väter*, 2 vols. (Freiburg: Herder, 1961), vol. 1, p. 151, note 36.

of relationships. The Eucharist, by the memorial and other relationships it has with them, could be *called* "Calvary" or "Christ interceding for us" as the bread in the text itself is called "body"; and consequently could take part of its memorial meaning from their being memorials. 3) On this point see 490ff.

26. We may conclude the chapter with a reference to C. K. Barrett, who does take Jeremias seriously. However, Barrett has his own distinctions. "This [Jeremias'] interpretation may possibly be valid for an earlier stage of the tradition, though not, it seems for Paul; nevertheless Dr. Jeremias's conclusion at this stage may be right." [41] Barrett probably excludes God's remembering at the Pauline stage because he sees that there is definitely question of men's remembering, while, like Jeremias, not adverting to the possibility that ἀμάμνησις for Paul means *both* God's and men's remembering. His translation "as my memorial" is no doubt a recognition of the exigencies of the Greek. The same exigencies were recognized by James Kleist, the editor of Kaegi's grammar, when he made his translation of Luke in the forties. [42]

27. Barrett's remark that Jeremias' interpretation might be valid for an earlier stage of the tradition reveals something of the same kind of "specific" limitation we have spoken of already. (See 10-11.) He is thinking in terms of one interpretation or the other being simply right or wrong at any given stage. But the nature of the alternatives makes it quite conceivable that the exclusiveness Jeremias attaches to his interpretation can be dropped without the whole interpretation's being thereby rendered meaningless. In other words, he might be partly right, and his adversaries partly right too, and this at the Pauline stage of the tradition. If our thesis is correct, this is indeed the case.

28. Enough has been said to bring the main concerns of our thesis into a focus sufficiently clear for us to proceed with our investigation. As we stated earlier, we shall return to the cardinal positions sketched above, and other related ones, after reflecting on certain implications the first-century milieu has for our thesis, surveying the materials available to Paul, and developing our position. (Some of the elements of the latter have of course been adumbrated in the preceding paragraphs.) Familiarity with all this is a prerequisite for making a really well-founded judgement on the different scholarly opinions. Most general readers lack one or another or several elements of such familiarity, and there are aspects and implications of these matters that may not have been attended to even by those who have already devoted special thought to them.

---

[41] Charles Kingsley Barrett, *A Commentary on the First Epistle to the Corinthians* (New York: Harper and Row, 1968), p. 271.
[42] See *The New Testament*, trans. James A. Kleist and Joseph L. Lilly (Milwaukee: Bruce, 1956).

PART II: **SOME PROBABLE KEY QUALITIES OF THE PAULINE WORLD-VIEW, HERMENEUTIC, AND THEOLOGY**

CHAPTER I: **Interpretation, History and Essence**

Introduction

29. We have already stated the relationship of this Part to the others (see 5-7). As to the subject of this chapter, it may be useful to stress that by Paul's own admission, the text we are dealing with was for him a "tradition". This underlines something that, although it would be true even if Paul had written completely independently, is more obviously true when what he wrote centers around a received communication. The something in question is the multiple level of interpretation that must necessarily be involved in dealing with any text. Barrett's reference to "stages" of tradition (cited in 26), suggests the same multiplicity. There is the way Paul understood the received traditions, the way he treated them, the way his readers interpreted him at the time he wrote, and the way subsequent generations have interpreted the whole. Our present study is not directly concerned with the origins of the tradition Paul recounts; our main interest is in what he thought and made of it, and the reading of his statement that his addressees might have been expected to make. We are not, therefore, directly concerned with the question of the historical origins of the Eucharist as practised by Paul's churches—with whether or not it was in the beginning an eschatological fellowship meal or perhaps one of the Qumran type. We *are* directly concerned with what Paul and his readers *thought* it might have been originally, or said (and read) it was. This is not to deny the importance of the first question, or the possible relationship of Paul's and the others' views with that question. Indeed, we shall give some attention in this chapter to the *kind* of relationship they probably felt did exist. But the "kind" is more important to our thesis than the "did exist". The explicitly traditional nature of our text openly invokes the receivers' view of history; but in fact *any* received text requires the exercise of that view, for any text is a tradition. For our text, therefore, interpretation and historical viewpoint are inextricably linked in several ways.

30. The term "essence" is used in our chapter title. We could as well say "identity". By this we mean the principle of continuity of individual things and people as well as of societies. Without such a principle there is no basis for either interpretation or history. The chapter will include a discussion of the nature of the principle and its relationship to the historical exercise and to interpretation, the aim being to arrive at some estimate of Paul's attitudes towards the same. The point will also be made here that everyone *has* such attitudes, even though they may never be expressed reflectively.

31. The main conclusions drawn in the chapter are summarized in paragraphs 69-70. The reader might wish to use the conclusions as guide-posts and checks when perusing the argumentation that leads up to them.

History Interpreted

32. Nils Dahl begins his essay "Anamnesis" with the statement: "In times past history was considered one of the fine arts. It had its muse, Clio, and the muses were called daughters of Mnemosyne. According to this mythological allegory, history was born from memory."[1] Dahl goes on to say that history has become a "liberated young woman who looks quite critically upon her maternal ancestors, memory and tradition."[2] But he concludes that, even after criticism, "The historical enterprise makes sense only on the presupposition that there is something in the past that deserves to be preserved in memory or to be rescued from oblivion."[3]

33. Dahl's statement about history's self-criticism seems to refer to history more in the sense of a chronicle, a reconstruction of past events. The literal meanings behind mythological thinking and expression must be laid bare: we live in an age that though certainly not averse to mytho-logizing, prefers to do its own rather than to perpetuate the myths of previous eras, except when it writes histories of myth. Our dim view of other people's myths is a bequest from our scientistic forbears through the past several centuries.

34. But there has been a more radical criticism of history that tries to evaluate the function of such reconstructions in present experience. This criticism is reflected in the distinction between *Historie* and *Geschichte* made by Bultmann;[4] and in interpretational terms has probably been carried farthest by Hans Georg Gadamer in his *Truth and Method* and other writings. Let us briefly review Gadamer's position as a way to laying open our particular problem. We may follow the summary given

---

[1] Nils Alstrup Dahl, *Jesus in the Memory of the Early Church* (Minneapolis, Minn.: Augsburg Publishing House, 1976), p. 11.
[2] Ibid.
[3] Ibid.
[4] For a summary discussion of the distinction see William G. Doty, *Contemporary New Testament Interpretation* (Englewood Cliffs, New Jersey: Prentice-Hall, Inc., 1972), p. 22.

by a Gadamer expert, David Linge in the introduction to his selection from Gadamer's essays.

35. Linge begins with Schleiermacher and Dilthey, who both identified the meaning of the text or action with the subjective intention of the author, and thought that the interpreter could scientifically reconstruct the mind of the author.[5] Gadamer sees this as paying "homage to the Cartesian and Enlightenment ideal of the autonomous subject who successfully extricates himself from the immediate entanglements of history and the prejudices that come with that entanglement."[6] This is to negate "his own present as a vital extension of the past,"[7] and to make one's own historicity an "accidental" as distinct from "ontological" factor.[8] Revealing the phenomenological origins of Gadamer's position,[9] he says that present "prejudices... constitute the initial directedness of our whole ability to experience."[10] Understanding is not reproductive but productive, not reconstruction but mediation. "Understanding is an event, a movement of history itself in which neither interpreter nor text can be thought of as autonomous parts."[11] In the "mediation" the knower's present situation becomes "overcome and fused with future horizons."[12] We must not engage in "preliminary methodological self-purgations"[13] but enter a dialogue with the text, in which we let the text speak to us.[14] If we do this, we will go beyond the world view of the author and probe the "fundamental concern that motivates the text—the question that it seems to answer,"[15] looking not *at* the author but *with* him at what he attempts to communicate,[16] treating the text not as a cipher for something behind it (the author's view), but as a vital input into the present experience. In terms of meaning, "the customary way of defining the meaning of a text has been to identify it with the subjective act of intending of its author,"[17] so that the meaning is repeated (reproduced, reconstructed) by the correct interpretation.[18] Gadamer includes in meaning "excess of meaning" that goes beyond the author's intention "explicit or implicit."[19] This is the

---

[5] See Hans-Georg Gadamer, *Philosophical Hermeneutics*, ed. and trans. David E. Linge (Berkeley: University of California Press, 1976), editor's introduction, p. xiv. This work will subsequently be referred to as "Gadamer-Linge".

[6] Gadamer-Linge, p. xiv.

[7] Ibid.

[8] Ibid.

[9] See also Gadamer-Linge, p. xxxiii.

[10] Ibid., p. xiv.

[11] Ibid., p. xvi.

[12] Ibid., p. xix.

[13] Ibid., p. xxi.

[14] See ibid.

[15] Ibid.

[16] See ibid., p. xx.

[17] Ibid., p. xxiii.

[18] See ibid.

[19] Ibid., p. xxv.

"ontological possibility" of the work; [20] as for understanding, " 'One understands differently when one understands at all.' " [21]   Linge cites Ebeling: "Identity and variability belong inseparably together: interpretation is to say the same thing in a different way, and by virtue of saying it thus, to say the same thing." [22]   But Gadamer puts this in terms of "forgetting". "Only by forgetting does the mind have the chance of total renewal, the capacity to see everything with fresh eyes, so that what is long familiar combines with the new into a many-levelled unity." [23]   This "many-levelled unity" is of course the "fusion of horizons" remarked above.

36.   It is evident that Gadamer owes much to Hegel.   "It was Hegel who saw that knowledge is a dialectical process in which both the apprehending consciousness and its objects are altered." [24]   "In the *Phenomenology of Spirit* Hegel sought to show that every new achievement of knowledge is a mediation or refocusing of the past within a new and expanded context." [25]   This is taken by Gadamer to equivalate the "fusion of horizons". Yet, this does not mean accepting absolute Spirit.   "For Gadamer, however, this 'higher universality' remains finite and surpassable and is not to be equated with Hegel's absolute knowledge in concepts." [26]

37.   Gadamer also has a debt to Husserl, and sees the phenomenological slogan, "To the things themselves", as an expression of Husserl's "desire to gain access to the pre-reflective givenness of things in a way that would not be distorted by theories or anticipatory ideas of any kind"—by "theoretical objectifications." [27]   Linge says that some critics of Husserl accused him of overlooking the life-world as such, aiming rather at explicit objects of consciousness—things as they appear.   Gadamer says, rather, that he did not ignore the life-world as such but wanted to deal with the relativity that worried him in terms of variations of an essential structure, the transcendental ego.   But, says Gadamer, he failed, for the horizon of the life-world is unobjectifiable. [28]   Heidegger saw this, and it is Heidegger's approach that Gadamer accepts.   Heidegger's Dasein discloses itself not as the objectification of infinite Spirit [Hegel], nor as disclosive of the constitutive accomplishments of transcendental ego [Husserl], but "Dasein comes upon itself as radically finite and temporal 'being in the world'." [29]

---

[20] Ibid., p. xxvi.

[21] Ibid., p. xxv; citation from Hans-Georg Gadamer, *Wahrheit und Methode* (Tübingen: Mohr, 1960), p. 280.

[22] Gadamer-Linge, pp. xxvi-xxvii; cited from Gerhard Ebeling, *The Problem of Historicity* (Philadelphia: Fortress Press, 1967), p. 26.

[23] Hans-Georg Gadamer, *Truth and Method* (New York: Seabury Press, 1975), p. 16.

[24] Gadamer-Linge, p. xxviii.

[25] Ibid., pp. xxxix-xl.

[26] Ibid., p. xl.

[27] Ibid., p. xlii.

[28] See ibid., p. xliv.

[29] Ibid., p. xlvi.

Heidegger's thinking: "By concentrating on the beings that are disclosed to its gaze, metaphysical thinking forgot being itself as the event of disclosure or openness that allows beings to come forward into unconcealedness." [30] "This forgetting of being (of what Heidegger calls the ontological difference) opens the way to conceiving being in static, thing-like terms—as the underlying permanent substance of things, or their uncaused cause, eternal ground, and so on." [31] But being is ontologically "different", it transcends such modes of conceiving. Heidegger's effort is a "determination to interpret Dasein's mode of being out of itself and to make its finitude— its temporality ["Time", of *Being and Time*"]—the horizon for the question of being and truth." [32] Heidegger says that "Of course only as long as Dasein *is* (that is, only as long as an understanding of Being is ontically possible) 'is there' Being." [33] But this is no assertion of a priority of being over Dasein; if anything, it is an "inadequacy of Heidegger's language." [34] Gadamer perceptively distinguishes: "In *Being and Time* the real question is not in what being can be understood, but in what way understanding *is* being." [35] And of course, that is Dasein, "There-being".

38. I doubt if this is a concession that we cannot know being somehow without objectivizing, for to concede this would on Gadamer's terms be to remove the possibility of knowledge at the only level that can put us in contact with Dasein, the pre-reflective level. Rather, as meant, it involves an unjustifiable, reflective type of distinction, supposedly applicable at the pre-reflective level, between the manner of knowing and what only deserves to be called the dynamism of *being* known. That this distinction is unjustifiable is evident from the fact that Heidegger and Gadamer find it necessary to re-attribute to the dynamism as such (i.e., to Dasein), active knowing propensities. It becomes not just "being understood" but "understanding". Order mystically comes to be ordered awareness. "Dasein is open to beings because it has already construed being in some way as the horizon against which they appear. The mode of access to being is through this understanding of being that Dasein already has—the understanding of being in light of which it discloses the beings with which it is directly involved." [36] And, "Dasein continually projects itself" into the future; it "*is* thrown... by the past *as a heritage of funded meanings that Dasein takes over from its community*." [37]

---

[30] Ibid., p. xlix.
[31] Ibid.
[32] Ibid., p. 1; square brackets the present author's.
[33] Ibid.; citation from Martin Heidegger, *Sein und Zeit* (Tübingen: Max Niemeyer, 1963), p. 212.
[34] Gadamer-Linge, p. li.
[35] Ibid., citation from *Wahrheit und Methode*, p. 49.
[36] Ibid., pp. xlvi-xlvii.
[37] Ibid., p. xlvii, italics by the present writer.

39. Actually, as the "against which they appear" would indicate, what Heidegger and Gadamer seem to do with the "fusion of horizons" is to presume without or with minimal acknowledgement a knowledge of a spacial [sic] set of inner-relationships constituting unified experience, while failing to note or at least to point out that the dynamism of the experience and the continuity of development that is experienced in it (its durationality) directly show that at least some of these relationships have directedness into the experience in the direction of its flow, while others, which are not presently dwindling into extinction, have directedness out of it in the same direction. In other words, they do implicitly admit a "how" for the experience in a spacial sense, but are reluctant to attribute this overtly to the experience qua knowing because they fail to see how it can apply to the experience as durational. In fact, *the experience involves durational as well as spacial perception "how"*; and this, in Gadamer's terms, at a pre-reflective level. Dasein is directly known, not only as "here-being" but as "into-here-being" and as "from-here-being". But there is more. First, when this perception is blended with a *memory experience* of the "input" experience, there is part of the wherewithal at hand for a direct intuition of inner-relationships as persisting—a pre-reflective knowledge of "essence", of "identity".

40. "First... part of the withdrawal". In fact, the analysis just made seems to describe an animal as distinct from a human experience in the sense that it lacks something of the full human one. Without something *still* more, identity, though present, will not be perceived as such. There is an awareness in human experience not only of the inner-relationships within the experience, but of the relationship of those parts to a unit whole of experience that is not merely a perception but a perception of the perception—a "reflection" in a completely fundamental sense of the psychological term. However this occurs, it is there. It finds its vocal expression in the first personal noun or pronoun.[38] Such reflection constitutes a kind of primally analogous essential meaning within any present experience. It is only by reference to this perception that other identities are seen *as* identities. And part of it, once again, is the memory of previous similar experience feeding into this experience. In truth, what is described

---

[38] That the non-human animal does not have this reflection seems evident from the fact that even the higher non-humans never say "I" unless they have been programmed for it like parrots. They can learn other human language in limited quantity and use it, and have a good deal of their own language. They respond by way of signs, vocal or otherwise—signs that show they have related the language to the appropriate things. But in spite of having the physical abilities to convey further meaning, they stop here. No normal human will allow language barriers to deter him from expressing his I-consciousness in communicative ways. It is an irresistible drive that comes from the very luminosity of the concept. There is compelling cause to conclude that other animals lack the concept. But in any case, humans have it, whether non-humans do or not.

hcre is the most basic case of the sense of history.[39]　In is the history of the historian himself.

41. *We have the wherewithal above to attempt a definition of identity or essence. It will be a durationally persistent set of relationships within unit limits—so, of "inner-relationships".* In particular, of certain notable and constituent relationships that persist within the limits of the unity and among each other in spite of changes in minor relationships and even the loss, from time to time, of one or another of the more notable ones. Such are the "I"—the same essential reflective perceptive experience extends durationally into this one—and any other "things" that are perceived along with it. "The statement of essence just given is an expansion of the rough definition of identity given in paragraph 30.

42. In locating the principle of identity, we have also partly located the character of becoming. The words "changes in minor relationships and even the loss, from time to time, of one or another of the more notable [persistent inner-relationships]" describes becoming in terms independent of relationships to *other* things than the particular thing that is the main question in any given case.

43. At times, Gadamer presents the appearance of derogating "things" even while he makes repeated use of them for argumentation. Of course, there is some basis for suspicion of philosophical speculation about "things", as distinct from popular views of reality and interpretation. Heidegger sees a trend in western philosophy that goes back to Plato's stable world of ideas and finds new life in the thinking of Descartes and scientism. Again, "This forgetting of being [in discredited metaphysics] opens the way to conceiving being in static, thing-like terms—as the underlying permanent substance of things, or their uncaused cause, eternal ground, and so on." [40]　One wonders how far "and so on" is meant to go. At any rate, while Gadamer was certainly right in abjuring Hegel's absolute spirit and Husserl's transcendental ego as modern examples of the ab-

---

[39] The animal experience, if we are correct, has no present or past I-consciousness to serve as a reference point, to make the experiential note of "input" significant. And as a result, the animal is not able to read other beings than himself as essences either—as "things"—while man is. What the animal reads is the material constituents of essential knowledge without the formal note of essence: the dog's master appears to the dog as a generalized concept or set of concepts that have been formed from multitudes of overlaid individual perceptions of the master maintained in memory, with the differences gradually forgotten but the main lines strengthened by repetition. The present perception of the present master blends smoothly with this if he does the normal things; it causes surprise if he does something new. And it causes grief if there *is* no present master to go with the present memory—the master-less surroundings being perceived, and perceived sharply, as against the master-full memory. The dog is sad because the master is absent from half of the present experience; the man may be sad additionally because the dog cannot tell him this in man-to-man terms!

[40] Gadamer-Linge, p. xlix.

solutizing tendency, he seems to have paid inadequate attention to the possibility (and in the minds of common people everywhere, the universally evidenced fact) of visualizing true "things"—beings that are changing and finite and "being in the world", even while they retain their identities. Indeed, it is only when "thingness"—essential identity through change and duration—is consciously underlined that meaning can be found in the flux that is present experience. Not that Gadamer reduces present experience to some sub-human experience; rather, without adequately investigating its sources, he appears simply to *presume* the perceptions of essential distinctions within that present experience. And past experiences as well.

44. The reference to cause-effect in paragraph 42 should not be taken to suggest that there is meaning only in identity as such. There is a sameness of every effect to its causes that is also a carrier of meaning through the flux. But this meaning is dependent on the fact of identity in the termini of the process. Given that, it can be extremely significant. Additionally, when causes and effects are considered in themselves, they will necessarily have their own identities.

45. If the above analysis is correct, a prime value must be placed on understanding things as they were and became and caused, in order fully to appreciate things as they are, are becoming, and are causing. A reader of a text will inevitably find special meaning in past events that the text expressly or implicitly shows to have an essential continuity of identity, and/or causality, from those events with the reader. *Person as such is the maximal bearer of essentiality and meaning, with societies of persons assuming an important and to some extent substitutive role; while the land and its features and other notably durable things, both natural and artifact, will have their own important places. Causation as such follows as an important second to identity.* So, the mediation that Gadamer talks of so often has to be a mediation between and by identities if it is to be meaningful. And these identities must to some extent be isolated from one another even as they are seen to be identical one with another or to affect one another. This first isolation is possible because they *endure*— are separated *within* themselves by stages of their own existence.

46. It is somewhat dangerous to put this into abstract temporal terms because we are likely to develop a container view of time and lose sight of the fact that there is nothing constitutive of time but the durational beings whose changes we measure in temporal terms. More of this problem presently. But if that fact be understood, we can justly say that in any experience, if we wish to probe its meaning, we must be aware of the present as present, as moving into the future, as developing from the past; and also of the past as its own present with the same kind of movement and development. In other words, we must distinguish the now-present and past-presents, and not just accept the (now) present results of those past-presents without distinguishing the identities and causations involved. As to the future presents, they are unknown except insofar as they are predictable on the basis of present and past directionalities; but by studying now-presents and past-presents we can add considerably to meaning by plotting future ones on the same basis as we perceive present ones and remember past ones.

47. The place of memory in this scheme is central. It is memory that enables us to place the various elements of meaning in their proper places in the present experience. In the scheme the past survives into the present without losing its own dignity and worth; it becomes a valued part of present experience, giving depth and perspective to one's perception of one's own and other present identities. Linge offers a citation from Merleau-Ponty that gives a totally different impression, and underscores the reality of the hermeneutical problem.

> ... the world as soon as he has seen it, his first attempts at painting, and the whole past of painting all deliver up a tradition to the painter—*that is,* Husserl remarks, *the power to forget origins* and to give to the past not a survival, which is the hypocritical form of forgetfulness, but a new life, which is the noble form of it.[41]

Linge calls this the "deeper achievement of understanding [which] beautifully confirms Gadamer's hermeneutics."[42] What is regrettable is that in this view the past is seen as forgettable *in any case.* We must insist that all the contributions of the past can be embraced in the present experience *without* forgetting the past *as past*; and that the remembering of it in this way adds a great deal to the present experience that could not be had otherwise. Indeed, as was noted above, only thus can the experience as "mediating" be understood *in the experience* as distinct from secondarily, which is how it appears that Gadamer gives us to understand it in his writings on the subject. All of us must value this kind of secondary knowledge. *But it is vitalized only by being incorporated in an experience that already has the primary kind.*

48. It is quite consistent that Gadamer can think that Heidegger's position "drives the concept of self-understanding—indeed, the entire notion of selfhood—from its central position in Western philosophy.... Thus, for Heidegger, the basic relation is not man's relation to himself (i.e., his 'self-consciousness,' his subjectivity) but his relation to and immersion in the event of being...."[43] Gadamer's descriptions of things as "static", "permanent substance", etc., would of course include the "I", and

---

[41] Gadamer-Linge, p. xxvii; citation from Maurice Merleau-Ponty, *Signs* (Evanston, Ill.: Northwestern University Press, 1964), p. 59.
[42] Gadamer-Linge, p. xxvii.
[43] Ibid., p. liv.

amount to a caricature of the reality, which as we have seen incorporates flux and change without detriment to essentiality. In particular, he fails to give due credit to I-consciousness as the very core of the human experience. If it *is* the core, "immersion" in the event of being as Gadamer recommends it is likely to become a de facto concentration on I to the detriment of other. A questionable "nobility".

49. The above appreciation of the importance of past as past finds common corroborative manifestations in human beings' sense of history, in their seeking of "roots", in love of geneology, in the honor paid to ancestors and heroes. The people and events that we locate in times past are not just constructs of qualities derived from our present surroundings; they are found by memory and located quite consciously in their own presents, which are our pasts. To a very real extent, the temporal separation from us protects their symbolic and other values for us from the vicissitudes of our present surroundings and makes it ever clear to us that these are more than present experience, that they can be imitated or not, heeded or not, as we choose. They may of course have very real effects on us, operating through chains of causality spanning the temporal gap: this is one aspect of what Gadamer calls "effective history".[44] But as we have seen (44ff), even this has a special meaning when the identities of the causes are known and kept noetically separate in our minds, on a temporal scale as well as a spacial one.

The Biblical Intuition of History

50. Both the Hebrew and the specifically Christian scriptures provide us with splendid examples of the value that men and women in general, and the ancients and orientals in particular, place on essence-identity. In the Bible the identity of God; of his individual servants like Abraham, David, Paul; of his people whether the old or the new Israel—all these are personal or societal identities of kinds that are literally essential to the whole. There are also at least partially inanimate identities like the land, the city, the temple; and situational ones like the continuing covenant relationship between God and his servants which in effect constitute a family with God as the paterfamilias. Each of these entities is met with on numerous occasions throughout the pages of the scriptures, occasions which individually and as a collection are seen by the sacred writers themselves as by us today as claims of encounters with God—of revelations that are guided by his hand to become "Revelation". The writings present themselves as man's memories of these encounters, and the modes of

---

[44] Gadamer-Linge, p. xxi. Non-human animals suffer effects just as humans do, of course. But they manifest no sense of history or love of geneologies. It is humans who boast of the pedigrees of dogs and colts, and write stories of the noble beasts of long ago: Hannibal's elephants and Robert E. Lee's Traveller.

access to an understanding of the identities involved in them. The main point to be made here is that when we speak of the appreciation Israel had, for example, for Israel as an individual or as a nation; or that Paul had for Christ and for the Church; we are speaking of identities remembered in their pastness as well as known in their presentness; when we talk of "Scripture" we are speaking, in part, of history composed of innumerable histories.

51. The Israelites' respect for personal identity recognized in its pastness and in its enduring is as it were symbolized by the term "name". "Name" stands for the desire that men of later times might remember. It is not just a human desire for fame (as in "Let us make a name for ourselves " in Gen. 11:4) but a Divine mode of benediction: "I will bless you, and make your name great, so that you will be a blessing." (Gen. 12:2). And the psalmist: "May his name endure for ever, his fame continue as long as the sun; may men bless themselves by him, all nations call him blessed." (Ps. 72:17). Everyone would like to become a legend— or at least to have a niche in history. But there is a societal aspect to the above statements that goes beyond this kind of hope. "He made Jacob glad by his deeds, and his memory is blessed forever," says 1 Mac. 3:7. This constitutes an acknowledgement that human beings have to have their heroes, that they rejoice in glorifying them and relive their exploits in imagination. Early men may also have felt that by recounting the ancients' deeds they somehow shared mystically in their prowess and strength, and few of us would be averse to sharing out ourselves in this way if we had such a belief. Certainly, too, cries like "Remember the Alamo" have had their real influence on later events, and it is possible that some of the participants in the battle may have been moved by awareness of *that* possibility. Cicero's hunger for fame may have been less societal, but it was no less real; and reality is after all what we are talking about.

52. The Israelites also saw themselves as somehow perpetuated by their physical descendents. Parenthood was the surest way of immortalizing one's name. Paul would have the Christians remember Abraham for his faith rather than for physical parenthood, but he takes it as axiomatic that that faith deserves remembrance, and uses the cipher of fatherhood to ensure that it will be so.

53. There was of course a tension in the Hebrew mind between the certainty of death and the desire for some kind of continued personal existence in the bosom of the clan. It is amazing, really, how the Hebrew religious thinkers of earlier times managed to maintain a trust in God's ways with men in spite of their evident assumption that death was the end of their subjective experience of living. It is a degree of faith that should warm the heart of any modern religious thinker who conceives it impossible to know whether God has anything in store for the individual after death, for it goes beyond mere doubt to near certainty that he has *nothing* in store. But this tension never moved over into a view of the experiencing [and, inevitably, the experiencer] as the ontological locus of a swelling wave of language. This was not the Israelite way. The question was sharpened, as in Job, to the point where something had to give; and what gave was the view that man's future was limited to the perpetuation of his name. The doctrine of immortality, particularly in the form of personal resurrection, gained strength, and by the Christian era was well enough established for it to become a basic assumption of the Christian position. The individual-in-society became the main focus of future Divine activity, and this raised the importance of remembering the individuals and societies of the past to a new plane. For it was now conceivable that there would be a family reunion, and an accounting might have to be rendered of how well the children had remembered the fathers, as well as how well the fathers had provided for the children. There is certainly something of this expectation in the unsophisticated early Christians' attitude towards Jesus. "Every one who acknowledges me before men, I also will acknowledge before my Father...", says Jesus in Q (Mat. 10:32). This was certainly taken in the perspective of the resurrection and second coming. It was a family expectation, concerned with all earthly finite being, but primarily with the family members: "For the creation waits with eager longing for the revealing of the sons of God... will be set free from its bondage to decay and obtain the glorious liberty of the children of God... as we wait for adoption as sons, the redemption of our bodies." (Rom. 8:19-23).

54. The Hebrew attitude towards clan was from one standpoint an attitude towards history. It looked not only outward in space but backward and forward through time. Further, the forward-looking had a part in qualifying the backward-looking, for the Israelite saw the relationship of the heroes of the past to himself partly in terms of his own hopes and expectations of the future: he wanted his own name to be glorified and could understand how David would want him to glorify the name of David. The example demonstrates how the historical attitude was built around a concrete recognition of the concept of accidentally fluxing essences summarized in paras. 41-42. "The Israelite" and "David" are essences. They are the essences of individuals. But as we have intimated, the same combination of essential notes may be found and recognized as same across a far wider spectrum than that of clan. Physical generation was seen by the Hebrews as the basis of such similarity among men, and this view fits perfectly with their emphasis on the durational. Recognizing the real essential sameness of all men, they extended the unity from generation back beyond Abraham to Adam. In these terms, Christianity was at one

with them. But Christianity looked outward even more emphatically than
it looked backward, and became a still greater promoter of universal human
essences than Israel. What Paul calls on mankind to do is to recognize
a universal shared identity: brotherhood and sisterhood admitted and
embraced, the essential sameness of individual essences throughout the
human race.

Recorded Identity as Meaning and History

55. A more exact conception of universal essence will be gained by
a further investigation of history and meaning. What we said when discussing Heidegger and Gadamer equivalently affirms the validity of a view
of history that sees meaning in authors' subjective understanding of their
material. We may remark of this statement that 1) "Authors'" is advisedly
plural, and that in a double sense. 2) The omission of the definite article
before "meaning" is also advised. In regard to the first point. "Authors"
is plural. By the power of memory, many more authors than one are
available to me at any time I am attempting to read a given author's text.
Yet (the second point) I retain only a *part* of the comprehension of the
subjective understandings that were revealed to me by the texts I have
read and now read, for I forget. Similarly, the text I now read contains
certain elements from other texts that its author read and partly forgot.
Some of these texts he may have reproduced in his own text without
understanding them, for once a text is in being it can be reproduced
without understanding—this is one of the marvels of language, that in
a very true sense it can exist without being comprehended, and may even
use a defectively comprehending mind as an agency of its own perpetuation.
(The word "use" here implies no world-mind or secret, mystic power; it
merely recognizes that the relationships among the bits of language that
the brain picks up and retains in quite material forms are not always
consciously perceived.) But when this author's text comes to me, until
I reproduce and develop it, my problem is to get as much of what *he* understands out of it as possible, and then to get at what the earlier contributing
authors understood of what they contributed, and so on as far back as
possible. Any such comprehension, in other words, involves the recorded
experiential elements of the text, each stage providing the record of the
then-author's own experience of the unification of the previous experiences.
It is accepted that the unification as such is not just a sum of parts, but
represents as well a contribution from the author that includes contextual
material like that now available from my own context to me, plus—and
this opens a new area of meaning—whatever of the author's other characteristics may be added to the mix. One of these characteristics is the knowledge that he may have from other *than* texts: if you will, from nature.
I include the scientific findings of archaeology in the category of "texts"

here, unless I as reader should happen to be the archaeologist. In fact, every reader is to some extent a recorder of natural facts, many of which may be visible to him alone.

56. There is much meaning, and much important meaning, that at any stage of the development of language (for that is what the sum of the recorded elements just listed describes) may be perceived but never recorded, and so never integrated into language. It is evident that even with a developed language in a society, the concept antedates the word that goes with it. The baby learns what a mother is whether or not the word "mother" is related to his knowledge. And you can say the word "mother" to him a million times so that he learns it parrotlike, and he may apply it to nothing more than a mental state, using it as an expletive; or to various things or to his porridge. He *will* apply it to something or some things, given time, for he perceives or feels all kinds of things that the circumstances in which he hears it suggest he apply it to.

57. Granted, once he has made the connection of a certain number of words and concepts, he can be taught *through* language without the direct perception of the things that was necessary in the beginning. This is another of the marvelous aspects of language, but though there is a great subtlety about the actual procedure, there is no real mystery. Let me quote here from an as yet unpublished paper on hermeneutics written some months ago.

> As the fund of concept-word pairs increases, it becomes possible to develop some concepts by analogy without the addition of further direct experience—though of course learning by [direct] experience will also continue as long as the infant lives and thrives. In the formation of "analogical" concepts, language already learned by the infant is used by the teacher, taking advantage of distinctions within the already-learned related pure concepts [i.e., pure concepts related to the language] to line out conceptually distinguishable portions of a number of those concepts— in every instance portions that show similarity to the new concept the teacher wishes the infant to form. The idea of combining the various portions-of-similarity is then indicated by linguistic sign, the presumption being that the concept related to this sign (namely, the concept "combining") is also present and has been previously linked to the linguistic sign used. It is up to the infant's native powers to achieve the actual fusion. The process is "definition", "description", "explanation", depending on the complexity of the conceptual material to be taught. Finally, the new concept [new to the infant] is assigned its own proper expressed and mental word, either by putting a new word to the definition or by calling attention to the fact that the definition fits an already-learned word.[45]

Clarity about the various steps of the learning process enables us better to assess and criticize statements like that made by Wilhelm von Humboldt:

---

[45] Fritz Chenderlin, "Towards a Realistic Hermeneutic" (typescript in possession of this writer), pp. 15-16.

"The interdependence of word and idea shows us clearly that languages are not actually means of representing a truth already known, but rather of discovering the previously unknown." [46]

58. The notion of "lining out"—what the seventeenth century Jesuit scholar Francis Suarez called "*praecisio intellectus*" [47]—is another way of stating the basic truth that essential characteristics are evident from the combination of present spacial concept with memory that we have previously discussed. Language can only work by first isolating and then combining various of the notes into essential quanta that are in most cases far less complex than the original events or things recorded, but because they deal with inner and external relations, absorb the unimportant changes and variations and give a valid outline of the phenomenon. This is the "reconstructive process" terminating in a true representation of "things" that Gadamer seems to strike rather blindly at. Blindly, because he does not appear to note that the things *as such* are moving with their accidentals, so that like a hunter failing to lead his bird he misses the mark. In fact, there is no other way in the world of finding what texts and nature have disclosed in the past than by reconstructing the various authored contributions in the analogical manner described above. The several authors are the teachers here. But if I want to get full meaning out of the text, I have to distinguish as well as I can what each author taught; distinguish too in each case between what he taught with understanding (using the same native powers he had to use as a babe) and what unwittingly, as a mere reproducer. Finally I must discover how much each used nature as his source.

59. Meaning may be lost because it is never recorded in language, or if recorded, is not passed on to posterity. Present experience is so valuable because it gets much of this not-to-be-recorded meaning. This is being, but it is largely unshared being. "Largely", for it colors the interpretation of language, and the use of language, so that in an *indirect* way it is mediated into language. Linge describes this partly in Gadamer's terms: "In every moment of dialogue, the speaker holds together what

---

[46] Gadamer-Linge, p. xxx; cited from Wilhelm von Humboldt, *Werke* (Darmstadt: Wissenschaftliche Buchgesellschaft, 1963), vol. 3, pp. 19-20.

[47] See Francisco Suarez, *Disputationes Metaphysicae* (Hildesheim: Georg Olms Verlagsbuchhandlung, 1965; reprinted from Paris edition of 1866); II, 2, 10ff. (p. 72). Suarez, whose work has not always been appreciated by other members of the Thomistic school he purported to embrace, was well ahead of his time in his understanding of the inherited notion of "abstraction", which was then generally explained in a manner that always seemed to the present writer to smack of philosophical sleight of hand. The mind "drew the universal out of" the sense representations. Of course, universal ideas do exist: the question is, how? "Abstraction" gives a false impression of the manner of their formation. Suarez had to retain the word in order to present the appearance of scholastic orthodoxy, but he added the alternative (really, the corrective) "precision".

is said and addressed to the other person with the 'infinity of the unsaid'." [48] "Infinity": a mystic word, and even if attributed solely to the speaker's unique experience, misleading. For that experience has definite limitations and definite inner-relationships. It is mysterious only by reason of the complexity of its elements and the relationship they bear to the unit perception of them. This latter is no magical holism, but a relationship to "I", however "I" be perceived. It is content held within and by a unique unicity; but the unicity recognizes itself as one of many such, and the content is anything but infinite. For the rest, a shading off into non-comprehension is no awareness of infinity, nor openness to it.

60. The impression I get from Gadamer is that language can convey the "holding together" that Linge speaks of (we shall not talk of "infinity") along with "what is said". As Linge puts it: "It is this ... relation to the whole of being that is disclosed in what is said...." [49] And he goes on: "The whole of being that is mirrored and disclosed in language... cannot be reduced to propositions." [50] Here is the crux. For the truth is that being canot be disclosed by one human being to another without being reduced to propositions, and all one can get out of propositions is what their inner-relationships and inter-relationships provide, as seen in the context the communicatee provides. If Gadamer wishes to change the definition of "language" to include the unique personal totality of view that is each one's experience, then he should begin with the new definition, for it is new. *But what is shared and "disclosed" of that totality is only parts of it, and these are shared through essential formulations, the processes we have described above.* Gadamer uses nothing other than these processes in presenting his position. He thereby makes me more appreciative of the value of present experience. But he leaves a false impression that what cannot be "reconstituted" from shared propositions is somehow passed on in other than essential forms. In truth, even the material that was passed on without ever being understood is in essential forms, except that here the essentials have gone unappreciated, their inner-relationships unexplored. They are unopened packages; but when opened, they do not spill out some amorphous, gelatinous mass; they disclose an intricate group of inter-related items that are mysterious only by reason of their complexity and their situation in the new knower. And what of the actual transfer? The reception of communication from another human being in any way is itself a unique happening. *But it is subjectively multiple, unique at both terms.* It is a unique *relationship*, a ratio, not a whole number. The author has his unique experience, the reader his. The only *link* is formal language *cum* nature. The "nature" is the nature

---

[48] Gadamer-Linge, p. xxxii; enclosure cited from *Wahrheit und Methode*, pp. 443-444.
[49] Ibid., p. xxxii.
[50] Ibid.

of the reader himself. Practically, that adds up to his present perceptions: what is held in memory and presently activated; and what in other perceptions presently active, including the perception of the author and the circumstances of the communication. *Unless one includes some kind of extra-sensory perception, that is all there is.* And we should discuss the value and interpretation of language within these parameters.

61. Gadamer leaves one with a sense of unease about scientific method. It is unfortunate, since the mediation he values so highly has so much of its value from communicated attempts to grasp the past " in itself". And because those attempts involve essential thinking, *it is possible to reconstruct again and again, in one thinker after another, an understanding of the material that though never the same qua total experience in any two of the understanding subjects, is nevertheless immediately recognizable to all of them as the representation of the phenomenon that was experienced by the original author.*

62. This of course suggests that without the solution of the epistemological problem—or unawareness of it—there can never be a feeling of ease with meaning. Popular thinking does not concern itself with distinctions between phenomena and noumena, and indeed speaks as though the latter were directly known. It *is* unaware of the problem, and *is* at ease with meaning, justifiably or not. It is not "philosophical", then. And yet, it may be for all practical purposes right, if phenomena do somehow accurately represent noumena, even though philosophical reflection may not show how it is right. If you are right, and do not worry about "ifs", you are indeed at ease and in fact safe. I have myself in the above discussion several times referred to "things" when a phenomenologist might refer to "phenomena". I have left the instances uncorrected, because I think they do not really need correction—think that phenomena do accurately represent noumena. This is not a "naive" conclusion, but an involved philosophical one that there is no space or need to detail here. What does merit note, however, is that when the element of accurate noumenal representation is added, a relatively satisfactory term is found for the various examples of reconstruction that different experiences of a text, and the original perception, can point to as identical. The phenomenal stage offers just twice as many possibilities for instability as the noumenal.

63. There is one element of cognitive "coloring" that is extremely important for appreciating a view of history like that of Dilthey. It is the emotional element: anger, fear, etc. These are mixed sensations that contain conceptual elements like "I am threatened"—elements that because of the deep involvement of the "I" trigger physiological changes which themselves are perceived and become part of the total sensation. In an attempt to reconstruct an emotional experience, it may be possible and desirable to leave out much of the physiological part of the experience in order to consider the other elements more carefully. This would be more "abstract" thinking. On the other hand, an actor, or a historian like Dilthey who aimed at reliving the event as it was, might think the experience inadequate without the physiological part.

64. The reference to an actor in the previous paragraph recalls a statement Patrick Gardiner makes about Benedetto Croce: "What the artist and the historian have in common is the task of comprehending things and happenings in their unique particularity: unlike the scientist, they do not treat individual events as instances of universal laws." [51] We might reflect on this for a moment.

65. Reflect, for example, that universal laws were in existence long before modern times, and in other than Western milieus. "The north wind brings forth rain," says Proverbs 25:23. How did those who formulated this statement get this idea of the north wind? Patently, by seeing and hearing about many individual north winds, which by report and observation operated in a manner that eventually was seen to justify the universal statement. It was by induction that they came to be universal, just as happens with the scientist today. We should not let the scientific liking for hypotheses distract us from the parallel. The modern scientist formulates hypotheses in order to localize his inductive exercises; but it is the results of the induction that justify or fail to justify the *laws*. On the other hand, we must not let the fact that the scientists of old—they would have preferred to be called "philosophers"—got many of their bits of wisdom in finished form from their colleagues and ancestors, distract us from the fact that someone had to compose the formulation first. If it was a legitimate statement, it was very probably got by genuine induction: the collecting of individual instances on a scale that justified the eventual formulation of a law.

66. To return to Gardiner's statement. The scientist cannot logically be treating the individual instances that ground *his* statement of a law as instances of the law when he is gathering them. Instances that fit his hypothesis, yes; a law, no. The real problem is, what does he do with a law once he finds one? The question should be of interest to historians as well as to physical scientists. For in truth, the historian must be a scientist willy nilly. He can only "relive" by "reconstructing", and he can only reconstruct by combining essential notes ultimately got by induction, with or without the help of hypothesis. And he too formulates laws. "Washington suffered recurrent toothache" is a law about Washington quite as truly as "gases exert pressure" is about gases. Put enough Washingtonian

---

[51] Patrick Gardiner, ed., *Theories of History* (Glencoe, Ill.: The Free Press, 1959), p. 225.

laws together and work up an emotional sense of pain, and it becomes possible to relive a winter's night in the C. I. C.'s tent at Valley Forge.

67. Failure to recognize the communicational difference in experience we spoke of earlier (60); to admit the necessity and function of essential thinking in making use of historical evidence; to recognize the roles of native perception and analogy in the formation of ideas; to take account of distinctions like that between the evidential material in historical thinking and the emotional additives... ...such failures contribute in different ways to a disrespect for the autonomy of past as present in its own context, and sometimes for the now-present too. For such failures can lead to a kind of forgetfulness of the present, a nostalgia, a living in the past that means leaving the present. Dilthey may strike us this way. Or they may lead to an immersion in the present with or without the emphasis on mediation that Gadamer places. Dilthey's fondness for reliving the event is shared in a more intellectual way by Collingwood, with his "inside" approach; but Collingwood leans towards Gadamer's stress on the present when he himself stresses the critical aspect of historical thinking—the present capacity to appreciate rather than the past that is appreciated.[52]

68. The question of historical method seems to be reduced only too often to that of purpose: What does the "historian" want "history" to do for him, and what does he want to do with "history". As the inverted commas suggest, such considerations really beg the question of what history really is. The materials for its definition are mainly there in the nature of things and of man, and in the texts. Perhaps there is too much talk of historians and too little of history. For history is really language, and language is a fact because mankind is a fact. There is no true history without historians; but part of the truth about history is that every man is a historian—it is a question of amateur and expert. Probably the word "history" is best used to apply to a combination of ways of handling the material, and to a combination of purposes. It is my contention that the actual practice of most amateur historians in every age, as well as of the large majority of the experts, constitute such a combination. In particular, that the biblical view in both Old and New Testaments does; and within the New Testament, the Pauline view as well as the rest. What then are the elements of the combination?

A Working Definition of History

69. We may apply the word "history": a) To the gathering of individual facts by an inductive process and the reconstruction of the events they

---

[52] See Robin George Collingwood, *The Idea of History* (Oxford: Clarendon, 1946), pp. 215-216.

stem from, using hypothesis where that is helpful and stating laws where that is warranted, as an aid in understanding causal interrelationships and trends. b) To the reliving of the reconstructed event "from the inside", both for the dramatic experience of doing so, and for the significance of that experience for the future by its contribution of directionality and dynamism to the flow of events. c) In this incorporation of the reconstruction and reliving into present experience, to the retention of the clear distinction of now-present from past-present, in order firmly to retain hold on reality (as I-consciousness, memory, and hope for the future uniquely enable us to do) while giving other personal identity (and the otherness in my own identity that change induces) its true worth wherever it may be found in past, present or future. d) To the awareness of the uniqueness of the "now" vantage point on the forward edge of the wave of finite being, and of the capacity that gives for living an accumulated wealth of experience never before available [this is true for any "now" at any time of history] and for estimating and planning the future from a position never before reached.

70. The relationship between points "d" and "c" is one of the most haunting aspects of history. For while every later event in the durational flux ideally incorporates more past experience for the human participant than those before it, these earlier events are in their own contexts unique in that never again will just *that* stage in the flux be reached. I say "*are* unique." *That is what history can and must do: perpetuate past-present identities so that they are revitalized by becoming elements of the now-present experience of a self-conscious identity while remaining clearly different from it, clearly past.* This is the very core of true historical—*and memorial*—thinking and living. *The past retains its dignity while it blends with present experience.* Note that we are not speaking here of the *effects* of past events, but of the events as historically reconstituted. Of course, the reconstitution is one of the effects of the event in a purely material sense, for the event produces the evidence on which the reconstitution is based. But that is an incidental consideration here.

Chapter Close: Our Text a Paradigm

71. Paul in general, and our text in particular, could serve as a paradigm of respect for identity and history as we have described them, of their importance as sources of meaning, and of memory as the means to grasp them. We shall explain this statement in the following chapter as regards Paul in general; here we can point out that our text deals with his propositional report on a supposedly historical situation, with Christ's own then-identity, that of his then-listeners, and those of Paul's readers, as well as various non-personal identities, taking important parts in subsequent vital and onward-looking experiences that are related to the original one by a mandate that specifically includes memory. This thing that Christ did before his death remains especially meaningful precisely because of the situation in which it occurred and its relationship to what Christ is now —not dead but *having* died, and that *subsequent* to giving the mandate— and what he and the readers will be "when he comes". The meaning is much increased by the fact that Christ's identity endures independently of the minds of those who remember, and so does the corporate identity of his followers; but these things take much of their own meaning from the conscious relating of them to their past situation as well as the future one.

CHAPTER II: **Man's Perception of and Response to Patterns in History Divinely Planned**

The God-Man Tension in Historiography

72. Gardiner deals extensively with the common tendency of historical writers to find patterns in history. He distinguishes three main types of pattern: a) "...all that has happened or is going to happen has been (or is) preordained or intended by some 'hidden hand'—whether this hand be the hand of Providence or that of Hegel's 'cunning of Reason'...." [1] b) "[History's] course up to date has shown a trend in a certain direction...." [2] c) "...historical events conform to particular causal laws...." [3] The first type is similar to V. Gordon Childe's "theological historiography". Of this Childe says, "...the unifying principle cannot be demonstrated by history or deduced from it, but has to be imported from without." [4] The third type is Childe's "naturalistic theories of historical order". [5] Childe also proposes a third category of his own called "magical historiography", and distinguishes between magic and religion in describing it. "Magic is a system for assuring that men get what they want, whereas religion teaches them they ought to want what they get." [6] This thinking is the basis for his saying that this kind of historiography is still current in the "great man theory", whereby the course of history is moulded by human decisions. Childe says of this: "Plainly, if such personalities have mysteriously emerged from time to time and have 'changed the course of history', any conception of an historical order must go by the board." [7]

73. It seems clear that it is possible for some men to be conceived of as *instrumenting* the will of the gods, thus becoming "great"; so that a theological type of order can be associated with them. Rejection of such a view of history would follow from a rejection of the gods or of their ability or wish to use men as instruments. At least, the modern historian should recognize that some peoples who believed firmly in the gods (or God) have accepted such Divine instrumentality and had such a view of history. And he should study the evidence for instrumentality

---

[1] Gardiner, p. 7.
[2] Ibid.
[3] Ibid.
[4] Vere Gordon Childe, *What is History?* (New York: Henry Schuman, 1953), pp. 36-37.
[5] Ibid., p. 43.
[6] Ibid., p. 37.
[7] Ibid., p. 40.

with as open a mind as he would give to any other evidence. There *is* strong evidence for such a view in the Old Testament picture of Israel as the creation of God for definite purposes however obscure these might be in detail, and of the place of Israel and the other nations in the working-out of such purposes. The Lord has laid down "ways" for men and nations, and certainly knows where they lead, even if man does not. Paul too manifests such a view then he says things like "Necessity is laid upon me" in respect of his preaching the gospel. (1 Cor. 9:16). He as an individual had a historical call, and is committed by a provident God to historical encounters that will lead up to Christ's return. Paul's leaning towards a "theological historiography" is also evident in his treatment of the old and new Israels. Paradoxically, he also manifests a tendency towards the "great man theory", as when he says just after the passage quoted above, "I have made myself a slave to all, that I might win the more." (1 Cor. 9:19). The same paradox and tension recurs constantly throughout the Old Testament—Israel guided by God often in spite of itself, yet constantly urged to *choose* to go the way of God, to be *willingly* instrumental.

74. Childe's principal objection to the "great man theory" seems to reflect a bias against the second element of the paradox, free will. Presumably he sees the actual function of great men to be the experiencing of the meeting of various currents and riding on definably new surges; and this is to a certain extent a valid view. But it seems arbitrary to exclude the possibility of truly free choice just because one dislikes the idea of "Jack-in-the-boxes who emerge... from the unknown to interrupt the real continuity of history." [8] Whence the law that says history has to be predictable? In fact, Childe seems to accept that history may be unpredictable, but attributes this to factors "incalculable" [9] because of lack of data. If one had all the data, then, history *would* be perfectly predictable. This is an a priori law itself, and accords badly with the rationality of a statement like "The laws of history are just short-hand descriptions of the way in which historical changes do come about. They do not cause or govern those changes." [10] At any rate, Childe himself seems to fit in Gardiner's second category.

Divine Interventions as Material for History

75. What of "theological historiography"? Although philosophizing about history has been common with historians from the beginning, it does not seem true history to explain the process from without unless the intervention from without appears to be *part* of the historical process in some way. Theological historiographers make claims, sometimes, that

---

[8] Childe, p. 43.
[9] Ibid., p. 82.
[10] Ibid.

this is the case with their presentations. It is certainly not the case with purely philosophical assumptions like a rejection of free will. In the present work we shall make no judgement on the accuracy or falsehood of evidence for the fact of Divine interventions in human affairs; but we have already judged and shall judge further on whether the first century or earlier writers made such judgements. That is a valid exercise in the history of religion.

76. One must be continually alert to distinguish when one thinks as a historian and when as a theologian or philosopher. And as a historian, to distinguish one's own theological views from those of the persons one is studying, for their theological views are matter for history. Let us reflect on some attitudes that could predispose to an a priori rejection of Divine interest in and use of history. One sensitive area here is that of the knowledge or lack of knowledge of God. There is much modern thinking on this subject that is different from the ancient views, and the differences have to be consciously adverted to. William Doty says of Bultmann: "He... tries to show that the presence of seemingly mythic words like 'God' does not necessarily imply myth but may be understood anthropologically." [11] To get at our point we must see what Bultmann means by the final word. Doty develops Bultmann's view. "We must speak of God. But we should be clear that such speaking does not actually give us a grasp on God's being. At best we speak analogically: God's action is taken 'as an analogue to the actions taking place between men.'" [12] This seems to define "anthropologically". Doty concludes: "According to Bultmann's hermeneutic, therefore, we are not forced to speak of God as the necessary precondition to interpretation of texts that include religious language." [13]

77. I think it can be said that Bultmann would not concede that language ever gives us a "grasp" on *any* individual being. Soulen says of Bultmann's understanding of the term "myth": "Here myth is defined as a way of speaking about the Transcendent in terms of the immanent; the world beyond in terms of this world." [14] Since *anthropos* is in "this world" rather than "the world beyond", it would seem that the "mythic-anthropological" distinction is invalid, and that Bultmann ought forthrightly to say that God must be included in the realm of the mythic. But if he did not preach he occasionally practised this approach. In an article published in 1963 he speaks of a revelation that authorizes man "to understand himself as sustained by the transcendent power of God," [15] an under-

---

[11] Doty, p. 24.

[12] Ibid.

[13] Ibid.

[14] Richard N. Soulen, *Handbook of Biblical Criticism* (Atlanta: John Knox Press, 1976), s.v. "Myth, Mythology."

[15] Rudolf Bultmann, "The Idea of God and Modern Man," quoted in Robert Funk

standing that he describes several pages further on: "Readiness consists in openness in allowing something really to encounter us that does not leave the I alone...." [16] This "something" is the earlier transcendent "God", "veiled by the unknown future" [17]—and, one may say, by the analogical language of the present. "Something", of course, is still "thing", and one must logically question the propriety of excluding even this "something" from the genus "myth". What we must finally ask is whether there is a foundation in some phenomena directly perceived by man that justifies a statement of "input" even this vague. For it seems that not only are *we* open, but there is reason somewhere for speaking of "something that does not leave the I alone." Bultmann, when talking of the transcendent as occurring not "between" but "within" worldly events, ultimately puts the burden for justifying such language on "faith".

> The thought of the action of God as an unworldly and transcendent action can be protected from misunderstanding only if it is not thought of as an action which happens between worldly actions or events, but as happening within them ... The close connection between natural and historical events remains intact as it presents itself to the observer. The action of God is hidden from every eye except the eye of faith. Only the so-called natural, secular (worldly) events are visible to every man and capable of proof. It is *within* them that God's hidden action is taking place.[18]

78. It seems necessary to conclude that this faith in "something" is either a hypothesis or a dogmatic belief. Recourse to discussion of when it comes be in the believer—whether on the occasion of preaching or as a faculty at baptism or some other time—does not remove the dilemma, for we are speaking of a human understanding that results in statements about "something" supposedly other than the mind. Bultmann speaks of "an existential understanding of myself which is at one with and inseparable from my understanding of God and the world." [19] Gadamer might suggest that faith be seen as entering the world in language, particularly the language of revelation. But the problem still remains: how does it get over into our conscious perception and into language that reflects the "I"?

Which Way Analogy?

79. We heard Bultmann say God's action is taken "as an analogue to the actions taking place between men." (76). Most biblical writers would

---

(ed.), *Translating Theology into the Modern Age* (New York: Harper and Row, 1965), p. 98.

[16] Bultmann, "The Idea," p. 94.

[17] Rudolf Bultmann, *Jesus Christ and Mythology* (New York: Charles Scribner's Sons, 1958), p. 23.

[18] Bultmann, *Jesus Christ and Mythology*, pp. 61-62.

[19] Rudolf Bultmann, *Theology of the New Testament*, trans. Kendrick Grobel, 2 vols. (New York: Charles Scribner's Sons, 1951-55), vol. 2, p. 239. See Doty, p. 24, note 30.

probably have argued that this is only a superficial view, since man's action can itself be nothing more than an analogue of God's, just as man's idea of man is only an imperfect imitation of the idea of man that God had when he said, "Let us make man." If myth means seeing explanations for the naturally inexplicable in more fundamental, "supernatural" unexplainables, then the Hebrew God was the ultimate myth. In an age when it was simply accepted that gods *were,* few would have thought to question Yahweh's existence on the issue of his genus—that *was* no issue. Nor, given the basic later Israelite understanding that Yahweh was Israel's God, would it easily have been doubted that he could explain *himself* in any way he might think men capable of understanding; further, his actually explaining himself was sufficient guarantee that the manner of explanation was valid. Individual prophets were often questioned as to their authentication by Yahweh, but the institution of prophecy was generally accepted as making common sense. The questioning attitude of a man like the Preacher can be read to mean scepticism not about God's revealed ideas about himself, but about non-revealed human ideas on that exalted subject. I suspect that precisely such a reading was made by those who saw fit to publish his work in the company of other works that are free in expressing themselves on God and man's relationship with him. No doubt the question arose from time to time as the canon was being formed as to whether Qohelet's presentation undercut truths that were seen as actually having been revealed by God. But his book was useful as an expression of the need to be very careful about the facts of revelation. There are false prophets. Further, there is fallacious and foolish worldly wisdom, so that it is dangerous to say things about God other than the things he himself has said. Qoheleth seems also to suggest that the latter category was very limited in scope. But even he says things about God, taking as fact God's existence, his personal nature, his goodness, his transcendence. James Sanders says that much when he notes that for Qoheleth, "God is God, right enough, make no mistake about it." [20] There are identity-notes to that predicative "God", or the subject "God" means nothing. As for God's relationship to man, the basic possibility of revelation is implicit in the phrase that recurs throughout the Preacher's essay, "what God has given him". Finally, regarding the scope of revelation, it seems true to say that the last word in canon, as most Jews and early Christians saw it, was had not by the parts in isolation—not even by the last parts written—but by the whole, with each part interpreted in conscious relation with others, even though the number of the others and the manner of the relationship may not always have been clear.

---

[20] James A. Sanders, *Torah and Canon* (Philadelphia: Fortress Press, 1972), p. 115. Sanders attests to the Preacher's acceptance of the note of Divine goodness in the sentence previous to the one we have quoted. The qualities of personality, goodness and transcendence certainly say *something* about "God-ness".

The corporate entity's view of itself and of God accepted the Preacher's warning and put it with other views, but evidently saw it as compatible with far more statements about God and man's relation to him than the Preacher would have been willing to make.

Paul the Model

80. The New Testament, including St. Paul, follows this description and might almost be a model of it. Paul never thinks of denying that God gave the Mosaic law; his concern is to show that God has also given Christ, who at the finite level of law has fulfilled it as an integral system. Paul eschews the term "prophet" when speaking of his own mission, probably because he wishes to underline the once-for-all content of his message. But his gospel fills the requirements for a typical prophetic message in every other sense. "The gospel which was preached by me is not man's gospel. For I did not receive it from man, nor was I taught it, but it came through a revelation...." (Gal. 1:12). The point here is not whether Paul or Christ is the prophet; or both. It is that the gospel is prophecy. Basically its content is the kerygma, and in this Paul's gospel is the same as that of the other New Testament authors, and he can use traditional formulas, as in Rom. 3:24-25 and 4:24-25. So, Paul says to Cephas: "We ourselves... know that a man is justified by faith in Jesus Christ." (Gal. 2:16). Cephas knows this too. What makes Paul different is not the basic content of his gospel but his hammering at the significance of it and his intuition of its implications relative to the law. "If justification were through the law, then Christ died to no purpose." (Gal. 2:21). But the gospel says that Christ did die, and to a purpose. It is simply assumed that this is what *everyone* assumes who professes to be "Christian".

81. There is no question but that Paul was more interested in the truth of redemption through Christ than in its methods. The methods mean nothing if the main truth is undermined, and the main truth was being undermined in his congregations. But the methods, including Christ's incarnation, death and resurrection, were the de facto materialization of the truth, as essential to it in their own less dignified way as the formal elements were. Mankind *could* have been saved without Christ's coming into the world, dying and rising, but in God's dispensation *was* not. Still more fundamental is the question of salvation itself. Paul might be seen by Bultmann to have been capable of some kind of salvific attitude that would dispense with notes like God's personality, omniscience, omnipotence; perhaps even certainty about his existence. I would question Bultmann's vision to the extent that he thought this, and would challenge any assumption that Paul could have had any kind of religious attitude significant to *him*, in *his* cultural context, without these and a number of other notes. For Paul it is from Yahweh, and from a Yahweh such as he knew, that salvation comes, or there is no salvation. The question of whether if Paul had lived today he might have thought otherwise is irrelevant to a historical study. I doubt that Paul ever troubled himself with the problems of analogical language about God to anything like the extent that Philo did; but the truth is that even Philo's strong anti-anthropomorphism does not keep him from speaking about God much as Paul himself does. Both would have admitted that certain common ways of speaking about God were what we would call figures of speech; but this is another thing than saying they are no more than human language whose import as to what lies in the "transcendent" must remain undetermined. I think that something like the line of reasoning suggested above—about God's being the prime analogue of language as well as everything else— was implicit in both Paul's and Philo's kind of thinking. I myself think that such reasoning avoids the real philosophical issue; but that is aside from the point.[21] What is to the point is that these men would have felt such confidence in their way of thinking about God as to consider any "anthropological" explanation of notes like those attributed to him above an evisceration of their whole position.

82. To the modern critical mind it is understandably embarrassing to see that Paul accepted precisely the kinds of Divine interventions "between" natural facts that Bultmann says are impossible. Bultmann has to grant this. "To be sure, [Paul] docs not abandon the apocalyptic picture of the future, of the parousia of Christ, of the resurrection of the dead, of the Last Judgement, of glory for those who believe and are justified."[22] But he seems to sweep it all away with the implication that for Paul all this was just inherited dogma to which he had to pay lip service. "The real bliss is righteousness, and with it freedom."[23] The eschatological list above is not directly concerned with the existence or nature of God, but all the same this seems a rather off-hand way of dealing

---

[21] I think that the problem has to be answered theologically in terms of the nature of faith, and philosophically in a more profound study of analogy than has so far been offered us by philosophers. I mean primarily the analogy of being; but the question of Barth's "analogy of faith" would also have to be dealt with. Having resided for many years in India, I have long been impressed with the realization that these problems are anything but new, and in no way limited to Western religious thought. The Hindu philosophers both in Upanishadic and later times were insistent about man's inability to say anything about the Absolute; yet they also asserted that the Absolute was *saccidānanda: sat + cit + ānanda* = existence + consciousness + experience or enjoyment. How could they say so much? My conclusion is that it was either say so much or say nothing at all, and no philosopher likes to be silenced completely! But if they said so much, why not say more? I have treated the matter at some length in "Man's Finality in Shankara's Vedantism," *Divus Thomas* 78 (1975) n. 4, especially pp. 378ff.

[22] Rudolf Bultmann, *History and Eschatology* (New York and Evanston: Harper and Row, 1957), p. 42.

[23] Ibid.

with Paul's appreciation of the parousia, the resurrection of the faithful, and their glory. Paul believed, he hoped; but he certainly knew and felt the difference between believing and hoping and whatever invisible realities go with these exercises in this earthly life, and the experience of meeting Christ face to face, of rising to become a spiritual body, and of receiving "the glory that is to be revealed to us." (Rom. 8:18). "We know that the whole creation has been groaning in travail together until now; and not only the creation but we ourselves, who have the first fruits of the spirit, groan...." (Rom. 8:22-23). This is a peculiar kind of bliss. Suffering is compatible with peace and inner joy, but not with bliss. Now is the time for patience, for peace of soul, for the exercise of freedom, but not yet for bliss. "If we hope for what we do not see, we wait for it with patience." (Rom. 8:25). There is a tension between the already and the not-yet, but that presumes and indeed underscores the realities of both. Whatever "resurrection" and "parousia" and "glory" might mean in the event, Paul was confident that there would *be* an event that those words came closer to describing than others, and he made his confidence a main part of his present attitude at any given time—a motivation that was blended into his experience of any present. "I consider that the sufferings of this present time are not worth comparing with the glory that is to be revealed in us.... In this hope we were saved." (Rom 8:18, 24). This is a way of saying that the event of hoping is far inferior to the event hoped for, and implies that the later is far more event-full. *"Glory" and " resurrection " can never for Paul be demythologized to mean only a now-present event, no matter how much that opens itself to the future.* Because we are "reconciled" (Rom. 5:1) does not mean that reconciliation is glory; because we are a "new creation" (2 Cor. 5:17; Gal. 6:15) does not mean that creation is finished with the start of it. The Genesis view of creation was that it took six days. So it may well be for those who represent this new creation. We have only the "first fruits of the Spirit"—we still wait for the fullness of our "adoption as sons, the redemption of our bodies." (Rom. 8:23).

83. As we suggested earlier, the *prospect* of the future has a place in now-present experience very much like that of memory of the past. The future, after all, is history not yet happened. Paul would say that though not yet happened it is to some extent not unknown. Revelation can and does say something of it to him. And he treats what he knows in much the same way as we saw the history of the past ought to be treated for the fullest use of it. He gathers what facts there are by an induction from what he thinks is revealed. He reconstructs the events, partly in figure and partly prosaically. "We shall not all sleep, but we shall all be changed in a moment.... the trumpet will sound." (1 Cor. 15: 51). He takes the event as a motivation and as an aiming point for the experience of the now-present: "Therefore... be steadfast... knowing that in the Lord your labor is not in vain." (1 Cor. 15:58). In other words, he uses it for what we have called "directionality and dynamism". (69, "b"). And finally, he glories in the assurance itself and in the uniqueness of his present experience among the experiences that men have: "Through him we have obtained access to this grace in which we stand, and we rejoice in our hope." (Rom. 5:2). But it is *hope*—" of sharing the glory of God." "Sharing" presumes the human experience in the future, the future as future, the future-present; as distinct from but parallel to the past-present that is so important for past history and for memorial thinking. And the word also implies the distinction of persons that is so important for past history and memorial.

84. The future is linked to the past; and the flux had, will have, and now has meaning only through this personal factor. If there is to be a parousia, and the Christ who comes is to be known as the same Christ who died for man's salvation, any now-present becomes an event between other events that will have significance as part of the parousial event. It will contribute to the identities of the persons involved because of the lines of "1"-essence leading up to the event—will contribute at least by way of recognition. As God recognizes Christ because he was obedient, so Christ will recognize the Christian because he was obedient; not that the obedience of faith is man's in its primary origin, but because it was man who was obedient, just as it was Christ in his time on earth, just as it is Christ now "who indeed intercedes for us" (Rom. 8:34) at the right hand of God (the same "who died, yes, who was raised from the dead"), and Christ who will "deliver the kingdom to God" (1 Cor. 15:24). Paul will be glorified, like Christ, *because* he suffered (see Phil. 2:9; Rom. 8: 17). God will not only judge adversely on the basis of the past; he will judge favorably—will glorify on that basis. Is there any reason to think that the basis will be forgotten? Quite the contrary: all will be to Paul's glory as the cross is to Christ's. Surely Paul will be known in eternity as on earth as the one through whom "Christ has wrought... to win obedience from the Gentiles." (Rom. 15:18). For God to forget this would be for him to forget his own work; and for men to forget is would be to forget what *God* wrought. Paul may of course sound prosaic when he says "Then every man will receive his commendation from God" (1 Cor. 4:5), or makes other references to judgement and glory. But this is something more than mere promise and reward: it is the victory of truth and justice. The truth is that "He who through faith is righteous shall live" (Rom. 1: 17) and only "wickedness" wants to "supress the truth." (Rom. 1:18).

Other Views Contemporary with Paul

85. Bultmann in his discussions of eschatology is primarily interested in finding an interpretation that will satisfy modern men, and he tries to find it too in the earliest church. I think that rather than looking for it in Paul, so that his subject emerges as a man with a compartmented mind—half of it proto-existentialist and the rest first century apocalypticist, with each compartment inexplicably sealed off from the other—he would have been more at ease concentrating on early Christian groups that show clearer signs of the mind-set he is looking for. The Gnostics naturally come to mind. As we shall see later in this study, they were minimally concerned with history. The Gnostic attitude towards the crucifixion, for example, is well expressed in the famous section of *The Apocalypse of Peter*: "He whom you saw on the tree, glad and laughing, this is the living Jesus." [24] The Gnostic does not always deny the realities of language or the appearances of history: "Jesus said..." is a common formulation with him as with other Christians. But he does deny the salvific significance of history: God does not work through creation and through history, for creation and history are not the work of the real God. Rather, he works in spite of them and on a different plane. There is no salvation history, only fallen history. Even Christ has no salvation history: " He whom you saw on the tree...." is something seen dreamlike, even though it is a truer thing than "this one, into whose hands and feet they drive the nails... his fleshly part." (VII, 3,81,18-21). The latter part, of course—what most people would call the historical part—is not only a lesser reality, but one to be discounted and escaped from.

86. Not so for Paul. Whatever one may think of the future of the flesh in his view, it is clear that he accepted the reality of the flesh as a central arena of salvific acts both for Christ and for the Christian. He may not have been articulate about *how* history really mattered, but *that* it did he saw.

87. Another group, or perhaps another example of a Gnostic group, is suggested by the reference in 2 Timothy to those "who have swerved from the truth by holding that the resurrection is past already." (2:18).[25] James M. Robinson and others have concluded that this was the "Corinthian heresy" that Paul was concerned with in 1 Corinthians.[26] It is a position that telescopes periods and ignores distinctions, and implies that not only God but the one saved is really removed from the toils of history. Paul reacts strongly against this position even though it relates to the

---

[24] Citations from Gnostic works in this study will unless otherwise noted be taken from *The Nag Hammadi Library*, ed. James M. Robinson (New York: Harper and Row, 1977), and located by the name of the treatise and system of notation provided in that volume, with abbreviations suitable to those names. The present reference is thus Apoc. of Peter 3,81,17-18.

[25] Malcolm Peel refers to this in his introduction to *The Treatise on Resurrection* in the *Library*, p. 50.

[26] See James M. Robinson, "The Sacraments in Corinth," *Journal of the Interseminary Movement of the Southwest* (1962), pp. 21-32.

very point that would necessarily be involved in any anti-historical attitude of his own. One can only conclude that he is not historical by mere accident or tradition, but sees his whole theology as essentially linked to history wherever it deals with man, even though at the Divine level it may be above history.

88. Paul did not have to see centuries of Christianity-on-earth stretching out ahead; the point is that he saw any time at all, and that he distinguished within individual Christians like himself discrete historical changes: changes that took place in past-present, now-present, and future-present. (Note that this question does not touch on that of whether an ontological change takes place in these "now-events".) Paul's vocation, his missionary journeys, the Christian's baptism—to take several examples— all have salvational significance of some sort and are patently historical events engaging not only the psychic but the physical powers of the ones involved. There are also the operations of the charisms, the celebrations of the liturgies, etc. Even when the end was expected daily these things went on. Paul speaks of them all in a workaday way, much different from the way the *Nag Hammadi Library* shows as the typically Gnostic one. Paul speaks mystically quite often, but his mysticism is always referable to a genuine historical context. One is not adrift in the tenseless, dreamlike kind of world one so often finds in Gnostic works. God's salvific acts are seen to have their terminations in time and in places. Paul's predestination and his calling through grace are "in order that I might preach... among the Gentiles." (Gal. 1:15). "I went up by revelation; and I laid before them...." (2:2). "I know a man who fourteen years ago... and he heard.... On behalf of this man I will boast...." (2 Cor. 12:2).

89. These recurrent historical references, in memory and in prospect, joined to the evident vitality that Paul puts into doing what he is doing, exemplify the conclusion reached above (83) as to Paul's acceptance of much the same view of history as we arrived at in the previous chapter. There is question of remembered and projected identities: God, Christ, Paul, the Church. Past events like the crucifixion, future ones like Christ's return, have a special dignity in the present experience from their known durational separation from that experience, even while their linkage with that experience by identity or causation enhances meaning for it.

Chapter Summary

90. We may summarize the main argument of this chapter briefly. 1) Paul, like so many of the Old Testament writers in respect of Israel, sees the Church as following a Divine plan for history that will not be denied; yet he feels that he enjoys a personal as well as a theological kind of freedom in doing so. 2) He thinks he can and does know something about the plan from his having been told something about it by God. 3) He gives a central place in his theological thinking to certain perceived Divine historical interventions. 4) He, with many Jews in his time, thinks he knows something even of the future salvation history planned by God. 5) These Pauline attitudes accord closely with the picture sketched in the previous chapter. There we saw a likely Pauline view of the relationship between history and psychology; here we have dealt more with the nature of the theological content of history for Paul. In the following chapter we will try to apprehend the kind of temporal and spacial (cosmological) context in which he viewed this history.

91. If by some subtlety of human psychology Paul did not *really* feel and think in these ways, that fact is certainly not so apparent as to exclude a very good possibility that he really *did*. As we have stated, a good possibility is all we are interested in demonstrating in these matters.

CHAPTER III: **Time, Eternity and Place for
the Biblical Thinker**

Biblical Views of Time and Eternity

92. As was suggested two paragraphs above, something should be
said about the relationship of what we have so far discussed with Paul's
ideas about time and space, for they form the context that qualifies any
historical, memorial, or anticipatory view. We can approach the subject
via the debate stemming from Oscar Cullmann's notion of a "rectilinear
conception of unending time" which he conceives to be the view applicable
to "the New Testament history of Redemption."[1] Putting the discussion
in eschatological terms, he contrasts this view with the "Greek concept
of blessedness [which] is spacial, determined by the contrast between
this world and the timeless beyond."[2] He says that in the Hebrew and
New Testament view the *aiōn* is an "expression of time" that "focuses
upon the extension of time and expresses duration."[3] James Barr has
criticized Cullmann for putting too much weight on the probative force
of the "lexical stock",[4] that is, on the dictionary meanings of words like
kairos rather than on their meaning in context. I think he somewhat
misrepresents Cullmann's intention and actual method, though it must be
admitted that Cullmann occasionally leaves himself open to charges of
exaggeration. Barr seems to underestimate the force of inadequate distinctions—distinctions which allow a statement to be true when read as
given while failing when read in reverse. It is true to say that "*kairos*
can mean the same thing as *chronos* in almost all the latter's meanings,"
but it is not true to say that "*chronos* can mean the same thing as *kairos*
in almost all the latter's meanings." I think the dictionary meanings reflect
this distinction. Barr also criticizes John Marsh and J. A. T. Robinson
for too closely associating *kairos* with "critical time" in New Testament
study, and in this I think he has a point. Non only is *kairos* used for
more ordinary times and seasons,[5] but critical times are expressed in
various ways in the New Testament, and by *chronos* or *aiōn* as well as

---

[1] Oscar Cullmann, *Christ and Time*, rev. ed., trans. Floyd V. Filson (Philadelphia:
Westminster, n. d.), p. 49.
[2] Ibid., p. 52.
[3] Ibid., p. 45.
[4] James Barr, *Biblical Words for Time*, Studies in Biblical Theology no. 33 (Naperville, Ill.: Alec R. Allenson, 1962), p. 14 ct al.
[5] See Barr's discussion of this in *Biblical Words*, pp. 20ff.

by *kairos*. *Kairos* is distinct from *chronos* in that the latter always emphasizes chronology, while the former tends to emphasize content. But the
emphasis on chronology is often merely a way to show anticipation of
content, and can be concerned very much with "critical" events. When
Paul, using *chronos*, says "But when the time had fully come, God sent
forth his Son, born of woman, born under the law..." (Gal. 4:4), there
is a chronological emphasis. But it is at the same time a particularly
effective way of making one reflect on what was going to happen at and
after that moment. Nevertheless, it is true that *kairos* would lead any
investigator doing a word study more directly to content than would
chronos; and very often that would be critical content too. The word-
study can thus serve as a shortcut to a sound view of the biblical notion
of time and to important times.

93. In the sentence from Cullmann cited above, regarding the *aiōn*,
there is a failure to make good use of a distinction he actually explicates,
that between time and duration. If what is extended is "time", there is
of course rationale either for calling the extension itself a "time" distinct
from the earlier "time" or for using some other word for it, like "eternity".
But continuity deserves as much emphasis as discreteness, and while Cullmann sees this, he does not give a clear expression of the synthesis. He
might more discerningly have said, "*Aiōn* is an expression of duration
that focuses on the *extension* of *temporal* duration."

94. His reference to certain *kairoi* as "D-days",[6] meanwhile, underscores the truth that any moment-*kairos* (as distinct from a period-*kairos*)
is an intersection of individuals, or an addition or subtraction thereof.
But his talk of "lines" of time distracts from this fact.

95. In an appendix of his work on time, Marsh says of Cullmann:
"On his own showing the biblical 'line' is not really linear at all," as
"the 'line' of biblical time is not one that is expressed in temporal successiveness, but in the occurrence of *kairoi* 'by the joining of which the
redemptive line arises.'"[7] The truth is that the line of biblical time is
both successiveness and the occurrence of *kairoi*, and I think Cullmann
intuitively sees this. *There is duration of individuals, and there is intersection of durational individuals.* This is a shorthand expression of
the usual biblical way of looking at things, and for that matter, of
Everyman's way.

96. The notion of duration can be expressed in various ways. By
verb-tenses like the continuous and the English perfect; by word-mean-
ings in words like "continue", "persist"; by syntax, as by the juxtaposition

---

6 Cullmann, p. 3 et al.
7 John Marsh, *The Fullness of Time* (New York: Harper and Brothers, 1952), p. 175.

of words implying a present awareness (like "I") with others predicating past or future being or act of them. The Bible, not excepting Paul, is full of such expressions of duration, and others.

97. For events, undifferentiated enduring is not enough. Some change has to occur; at least some new juxtaposition of parts within a being, or of beings relative to one another—"parts" and "beings" here denoting the same idea as "individuals" in para. 94. The first event noted in the biblical record was the differentiation in the formless mass and the darkness—light coming into being. The next was the creation of the firmament: a typical juxtaposition where before (this word is here taken to mean backwards against the durational flow) there had been none.

98. The term "time" may of course refer to moment-events or to durational periods between separate events. A "moment" is really nothing but the durational extent within the limits of some particular change. Thus in a sense it is also a "period", but it is a period of flux as such, whereas the periods *between* events are either relative quiescence or regularly recurrent change seen as regularly recurrent. If a "moment" is not viewed as a period, it is simply marked by some description of the intersection or change involved. We tell time by artificially constructed means of intersection (as of scales and hands) like clocks, or by the entrance of some new item upon our horizon.

99. "Day", like "time", can refer to moments or to periods between moments. The third "day" of creation is the latter; it is made up of elements that act and react in a similar way all through the period.

100. It is apparent that in a view of affairs like that we have been describing, there is no need of a "container" notion of time. The latter is the result of a philosophical abstraction of inter-moment time and of infra-moment time (to provide the two abstract limits of the inter-moment time). Scholars agree that such an idea was not attained by the majority of biblical writers.[8] We today are so familiar with the idea that we often think of events as occurring "in" time just as we are used to seeing beings located in an abstract "space". The physicists seem to have got back to relativity in regard to time; "got back", because the biblical writers saw time not as a kind of space but as an inner-and-inter relationship of extended beings determined on the basis of their durational progression. To put it more concretely—and the view being expressed is really very concrete—there was question of *no other beings* than the ones existing durationally: no container. Cullmann deprecates the "container" view, but seems to have lapsed into a consideration of his time-line as being something of a two-dimensional abstraction of his own. Without ab-

---

[8] See Cullmann, p. 49; Barr, p. 79.

stractions and with a firm appreciation of and grip on material reality
that was very un-gnostic, the typical biblical thinker was able to assign
degrees of reality to the objects of his knowledge that, as our reference
to physicists suggests, is really quite modern. Events did not fill-in a
container, but marked the progression of created realities relative to the
earlier durational stages of those realities and other spatially related ones.
In such a system, memory comes into its own as a recognition of a community of actuality that past events have with the present ones, in distinction from the mere potentiality of future ones; simultaneously with the
recognition that past actuality is backward in the durational flow beyond
the spacial limits of present events. The shared actuality gives not only
the realization of present effects from past events, but that sense of the
"dignity" of the past of which we spoke earlier. (70). Future events even
when anticipated by prophecy lack this effectiveness and this dignity.
Memory and now-experience provided a kind of mental tapestry (we have
used the word already) of intertwined threads of events noted and presumed, unrolled up to the present and unrolling here and now. Cullmann's "line" is a legitimate expression if taken in this sense; but we
shall refer to "tapestry" in order to stress that event and memory of event
are its sole constitutive elements.[9]

101. It is worthwhile emphasizing that the biblical writers evinced
these ideas practically, not philosophically. But they did express them.
They spoke concretely of different aspects and interrelationships of things,
times and periods; in the kinds of words, tenses, and syntax we have noted
in para. 96.

102. The "chronological" notion of time that Marsh, Robinson, and
in his own way Barr [10] take as distinct from a "realistic" or what we might
term an "event" one is at root an "event" notion itself. It simply takes
an accessible source of events like a sundial or clock as a relational criterion
of other events; and another source (like the sun and the earth, signed
by a calendar) as a criterion of the duration of periods. Conversely, the
events thus located always have content that makes the locating worthwhile. Barr says critically: "Marsh's statement that 'it is typical of
Scripture not to locate an event by defining its place on a chronological
scale, but to identify it by its content' is far from doing justice to the
facts. The chronological system is of fundamental importance for the
Old Testament." [11] This is true, if "fundamental" is properly distinguished.

---

[9] Cullmann quotes Karl Heim (*Glauben und Denken*, 1934, pp. 376ff) and Walter
Künneth (*Theologie der Auferstehung*, 1933, p. 170)—the latter to say that time is a
"creation" and "identical in form and content with the existence of man." (Cullmann,
p. 63). This is a valid insight.

[10] See Barr, p, 26.

[11] Ibid., p. 31.

But it is of no particular significance for us since we *have* made the distinction. As for von Rad's idea of a "filled time",[12] it is really not unlike our notion of different threads of event. He might seem to attach too much importance to the modern care for chronology when he says that our way of thinking is unlike that of Israel. Our modern chronology is more unitary in that we refer everything both spatial and durational to it and have an established set of clockings and calendarings. But it is only when we equate the calendar with a "container-time" that we do think differently. Von Rad probably sensed this.

Time as a Term of Creation

103. The fact that finite beings are made of parts, and that there are many such beings, means that there is room in the biblical picture for a thickening of the "tapestry" by the introduction of new threads at some point of the durational flow, presuming some outside source for their being. It is not clear that creation from nothing was a common idea in the first century C.E. in its strict sense of " *a nihilo sui et subjecti* ". Rather, when Paul speaks of a "new creation", he may be able to think only in terms of radical *change*—of rearrangement, separation or joining, or any combination of these. But what is perfectly clear is that such changes were conceived as possible by the direct agency of God, so that they were "creation" in the strict *biblical* sense of a radical rearrangement of the fibers of existence through his agency. Paul sees such a change occurring at the parousia (see 1 Cor. 15 passim). And his frequent references to the workings of the Spirit indicate that he thought of God's creative power working in the world long before the parousia. It could hardly be otherwise for him, since the Spirit had already worked in the Old Testament. The Spirit works within men, mostly: "Now we have received not the spirit of the world, but the Spirit which is from God, that we might understand the gifts bestowed on us by God. And we impart this in words not taught by human wisdom but taught by the Spirit." (1 Cor. 2:12-13). Interestingly, we have here an explicit reference to the power of God manifest in human language.

104. All this for Paul was a matter of fact and is not something that lends itself readily to demythologizing. So we may at this point, as we did earlier in a parallel context, distinguish a statement of Bultmann's. He says that "a miracle in the sense of an action of God cannot be thought of as an event which happens on the level of secular (worldly) events." [13] In its *terminal effect, but still as God's action* in a legitimate sense, it can and must happen on that level; and though one may say in mystical wise

---

[12] See ibid., p. 30. His reference is G. von Rad, *Theologie des alten Testaments* (2 vols., Munich: 1957 and 1960), vol. 2, pp. 112ff.

[13] Bultmann, *Jesus Christ and Mythology*, p. 61.

that when it does happen the secular is elevated and is no longer really "secular", the difference between terminal effect and the Divine Cause has to be admitted if one wishes to preserve transcendence. There is difference; yet the effect somehow deserves the appellation "Divine": *it is not God, but it is God's.* Paul would have thought that God had worked miracles in creating the world and frequently throughout history. Yet God remained transcendent; and indeed, somehow the miracles emphasized rather than detracted from his transcendence, for no other power existed that could counteract his influence—even though Paul seems to have conceived of the possibility of other "spirits" in themselves, to a degree, transcendent.

105. In the light of Paul's belief in lesser spirits, it is perhaps not surprising that Bultmann could speak of "mythological thinking" as seeing "the divine power which effects miracles... as a natural power." [14] But Paul would have repudiated the statement while not repudiating the miracles. He saw no need of justifying the complete, unique transcendence of God. He simply accepted it (see 79) and interpreted it as providing not less but *more* reason for accepting miraculous terminations and interventions. It remained for the development of a theology of creation from nothing to locate the difference between God's direct causation and that of lesser spirits. These were then seen to be created, even though possessed of powers greater than men's. But the theological statement did not explain God; it simply designated him as the locus of the mystery, quite as Paul did before it was made.

106. What of Bultmann's statement that mythological thinking "is understood as an action which intervenes between the... historical... course of events"? [15] And, "The divine causality [in mythological thinking] is inserted as a link in the chain of the events which follow one another according to the causal nexus." [16] A first comment is that for the first-century thinker in the biblical tradition there would be no question of "intervening" or "inserting" in any sense that did not recognize that there are as yet no links beyond the progress of any now-present. A second, that that thinker would never see the Divine *Cause* as inserted, but the Divine *effect*, yet with the mode of termination of that effect ascribed to the *Causal* mystery. For the rest, new effects *were* seen as coming to be that were not explicable by the existing directionalities and dynamisms of natural causality. It appeared that even men could do such things with reference to other created beings (by free will); a fortiori, God could relative to creatures in general and particular. Indeed, even if someone had argued against men's free choice, or against God's (an unlikely eventuality), they

---

[14] Ibid.
[15] Ibid.
[16] Ibid.

would not have argued against God's *power* to intervene. We today might feel burdened with the need to explain how such things could happen, terminally speaking. Hardly so for the first-century thinker, who found his ideas of the divine (including God) ever useful for solving all natural enigmas. We might be concerned as much to save natural causality as to save the Divine transcendence. Paul would see no threat to either. His idea of God explained both, paradoxically, by telling him that God is unexplainable and had explained *that* fact to men through revelation. As for nature, it and the "wonders" men call "miracles" are not essentially different in the Bible. Creation was a miracle operating on pure chaos; the exodus was one superimposed on partial chaos. If miraculous interventions were to be doubted, so would creation.

107. I think that Paul would have felt that Bultmann's idea of God's action taking place "within" as distinct from "between", and his distinction of "miraculous event" from "miracle",[17] removed the possibility that such action have any significance for humans or telling human expression. It might be an event "in" man on some scale not perceptible to the human organism or effective on it, but it could be no new life for man, no "new creation". Unless the Divine action terminates "between" (or more properly, "among"), the world of the spirit is simply a parallel to the world of man, and even the fact of the parallel cannot be known. Indeed, even the existence of the world of the spirit could be known only in hypothesis. Paul certainly did not consider God a hypothesis. A mystery, yes; very much a mystery.

108. What has been said here does not address the problem of whether and to what extent Paul or other biblical writers have to be demythologized in order to make them significant in the modern context. It simply indicates that Paul himself probably did not demythologize at the points indicated because he would have seen no reason to do so. We today may see such reason. But we ought to study carefully the relationships that Paul saw among the various elements that we may wish to demythologize, and admit that when he saw some as essential that we might like to disengage ("dis-relate") from an object of our exercise, the result can only be " Pauline " if we call upon distinctions referent to Paul's thinking like "conscious-subconscious" (or "surface structure-deep structure"). It is scarcely a question of " early Paul-late Paul ", because all his epistles show relationships like this in full vigor and practically across the board. Nor of "explicit-implicit ", because the relationships are often explicit, and the explicit surely prevails over the implicit. The Valentinians made a distinction similar to this last one *within* the explicit: it might be called "coded-uncoded". But it is hard to accept because of the powerful impres-

---

[17] Ibid.

sion Paul would have given by all the supposedly unmeant things he expressed so eloquently in the supposedly uncoded elements. We could, of course, simply say that part of Paul is wrong and part right, but that introduces the question of why we should look to Paul at all rather that some other writer; and more important still, whether what we find "wrong" in him was wrong for his time or just wrong for ours. Deep structure (as a key to distinguishing Paul) is ingenious, but it prompts the same and other questions. It may ultimately be of use as an ancillary means of interpretation, but its value with respect to any given text must depend very largely on factors revealed by the surface structures of the text in one way or another.[18]

109. I would suggest that there is another option, namely to try to demythologize points that up to now have been discarded or downplayed— like law, prayer, merit, and in our own case, memorial. It is not the purpose of this study to do this, but it will hopefully provide a fuller appreciation of the Pauline categories and their interrelationships that will make Paul more amenable to demythologizing attempts. Thus a "Pauline" result may be obtained where all too often it seems that all that is obtained is the de-myth of some element Paul used.

The Gnostic Question

110. As we have already suggested, Paul's mode of thought does not seem to be such as is generally associated with the term "gnostic". (See 85ff). He does occasionally use *categories* that were also used by authors acknowledged to be gnostic. But even when he deals with very gnostic-sounding matters, he shows his own individuality. In a sense, Elaine Pagels is right to say that "To read Paul either... as hypergnostic or hyperorthodox... is to read unhistorically, attempting to interpret the apostle's theology in terms of categories formulated in second century debate." [19] But the very element that makes the statement acceptable, the prefix "hyper", may obscure a necessary truth. Whether the labels "orthodox" or "unorthodox" were ever attached to Paul in his lifetime on the basis of his being gnostic or non-gnostic, or whether he was ever called "gnostic" or "non-gnostic" then, we shall perhaps never really know. But just as it would be unhelpful to say that Paul had made up his mind on every aspect of the material that later gathered at the two poles of the second

---

[18] I think this is adequately shown by a thoughtful reading of an exercise like that of Jean Calloud in his *Structural Analysis of Narrative* (trans. Daniel Patte [Philadelphia: Fortress Press, 1976]). For example, he notes that "Jesus" "designates ... a specific being, its semantic content is a given provided by an 'onomastic code.' .... The name Jesus simply refers to the code and to the situation in which the Gospel has been enunciated." (pp. 89-90). [The word "code" here was not anticipated when the reference in our own text to Valentinus and "coding" was made.]

[19] Elaine Hiesey Pagels, *The Gnostic Paul* (Philadelphia: Fortress Press, 1975), p. 164.

century debate, so it would be to say that Paul had made up his mind about *none* of it. It appears to me that what is commonly called "gnostic" today provides certain concepts that are logically incompatible with other concepts that are often identified as non-gnostic, and that the very identifications have probably been made on the basis of perceptions of such incompatibility. Some scholars have suggested that too much emphasis has been put on concepts for determining what should be called "gnosticism"—that lived actions and attitudes are more important. Be that as it may, it is noticeable that whenever one begins to discuss gnosticism, one deals very largely with conceptual material, not merely because one can only discuss very limitedly in grunts and groans, but because certain concepts press themselves upon one. If one holds that it is somehow unsporting or simplistic to admit that the concepts gathered together into Paul's mind made their way to the light only in the restraining packaging of the principle of contradiction, and that the true genius of man or any man is revealed by the total extent of his linguistic expression without undue attention to the logical consistency or inconsistency within the whole, one might be able to ignore the pressures. But I think most of us, though our logic may sometimes be less than we would like, are constrained —many would prefer to say "guided"— by it to the extent of our individual mental capacities through the channels and breakers of language and culture.

111. If Paul can be thought to have had this common respect for logic, it might be profitable to go beyond merely noting that certain passages of his can be read in both gnostic and non-gnostic ways, and try to discover whether in another place or other places he so firmly determines the meaning of the categories that enter into those passages that it becomes almost inconceivable that he would use the categories *in* them in the sense excluded by the determinations read elsewhere. I think that when this is done it becomes clear that on questions like the pivotal ones of the nature of creation (whether inherently evil or not), the origin of the pneumatic (whether present from the beginning identical with the real human person, or something new), and the mode of achieving salvation (whether by gnosis and Divine revelation alone, or by a more fundamental Divine operation)..... on all these questions Paul is only occasionally ambiguous, and usually leans away from the gnostic view. A text like 2 Cor. 12:1-4 ("I know a man in Christ...."), which has a flavor about it that one finds in many clearly gnostic texts, contains the clause, repeated twice, " whether in the body or out of the body I do not know". As we shall see, Paul takes "body" in the ordinary sense of a sarkic body most of the time. This being so, it is inevitable that a large number of his readers would take it here just that way and conclude that he thought it possible for the sarkic body to enter the third heaven. No true gnostic would think of showing uncertainty on this fundamental point. If doubt should somehow arise, he would clarify by clearly designating any kind of participating "body" by some qualification like "incorporeal", "pneumatic", "fiery", "heavenly"—all these being sharply contrasted with "sarkic". Speaking more positively, Paul in other places gives various indications of allowing some kind of participation in goodness to the sarkic body. Aside from the participation of the body in spiritual gifts like tongues, miracles, teaching, etc., texts like Rom. 6:12-13a, 1 Cor. 6:9ff, Rom. 8:11, 1 Cor. 15: 54, 2 Cor. 4:11, Rom. 8:21-23 show in different ways that the Divine Spirit was thought by Paul to be able to take hold even in the flesh, even on this earth. Undoubtedly he saw the flesh as the location of the main power of evil on earth. He avers, "Our sinful passions were at work in our members" (Rom. 7:5), and speaks of "The law of sin which dwells in my members" (7:23). These texts are ambiguous; others should be used to interpret them. The interpretation does not produce a clear statement of conclusion on Paul's part, but it does seem to show more inclination away from a gnostic dogmatism than from a non-gnostic one. He inclines less to "flesh is intrinsically evil" than to "flesh as such is not only helpless to save but is wide open to evil influences." Thus, when he says "Nothing good dwells... in my flesh" (Rom. 7:18), we must admit the likelihood that he means that flesh as such has no power to save and is the playground of evil forces.

112. This discussion of gnosticism has been introduced here because were Paul to have clearly and consistently adopted a gnostic stance it would be impossible to discuss the text we are concerned with without continual reference to gnosticism insofar as Paul's contributions to and use of the materials were concerned. This in spite of the fact that the text does not easily lend itself to gnostic interpretation—it is not one of the texts that Pagels deals with in her book, and is not likely to have interested Valentinus. As it is, we can study the text from the point of view especially of its own content and immediate context, and feel, when we use analogies from elsewhere in the Pauline corpus, that those do not have to be continually reinterpreted through the glasses of gnosticism.

113. A particular aspect of Paul's general view that is definitely non-gnostic and is of special importance for our text is his notion of God as not only transcendent, but personal, concerned for mankind in an intimate way, and the identical God of the Old Testament. In the "tapestry" view of time, the existence of God seems to constitute a kind of parallel durational entity, this apprehension based on the fact that God is seen as a primal entity separate from his creation, and on the feeling that entity of any kind is duration. (See 100).[20] The transcendence

---

[20] See also our footnote no. 9 for this chapter.

and the Divine unity mean that God is not temporally measurable; at the same time he is frequently spoken of in terms that would imply durationality. The normal tenses are used of his actions in their principiative (causal) aspects. Though no biblical writer ever states in so many words the proposition that God is durational, the placing of God in the same tense schemes as the created objects of his acts leaves the matter obscure. Later Christians saw the need to put God clearly above duration. But not Paul, and not the rest of the biblical writers. Barr says, " There are passages mentioning God himself, the glory due to him, the unseen world, the everlasting fire, and so on, where it is extremely likely, if not certain, that the realities mentioned are taken by the writers to have been existent as such throughout the totality of time." [21] All the same, God was definitely seen as transcendent.

114. Perhaps the nearest approach to a God that is in the space of a heaven but not thought of as enduring is that of the gnostics, as with the " aeon giving Aeon " of the Apocryphon of John (II, 1,4,3). Of him it is said that "time was not apportioned to him" (4,32), but it becomes clear on further reading that this is because "he... exists prior." (4,35). His being is said to be "at rest" (4,12), but he does give forth the first of the lesser aeons and re-absorbs when the resultant activity is over, which implies existence throughout—though hardly intimate concern with— the activity. Even here, then, there is a kind of parallel duration. As for the Old Testament and Pauline God, he transcends created duration by knowledge and power over future events, but is not viewed by the biblical worshippers in general as already having his future being. The psalmist says, "Thou does beset me behind and before...." (Ps. 139:5a), but this is a figure for the effect of God's knowledge and power on all created being. He continues: "...and layest thy hand upon me. Such knowledge is too wonderful for me; it is high, I cannot attain it." (5b-6). The same knowledge and power encompass space and all spaces: "If I ascend to heaven thou art there! If I make my bed in Sheol, thou art there!" (7-8).

The Greek View Cyclic?

115. The picture of the gnostic God given just above bears a noteworthy resemblance to the Stoic primal Fire, and the relationship of creation to God is also similar, though the Stoics are less mythological. The Stoic view is often associated with the so-called "cyclic" concept of time; inasmuch as the world-process is thought to repeat itself. The idea is interesting in relation to history, because it inspires individual action in the hope of a kind of immortality in a sense independent of Divine favor. This interpretation of Stoicism has taken second place to the Stoic

---

[21] Barr, p. 146.

attitude towards misfortune; it could, however, be made to relate to matters like the oft-expressed desire for fame. The subject would wish not only to be remembered but to be reincarnated as worth the memory—repetition of personal experience would be involved—a replay at the same volume. The later Old Testament and Paul see, rather, a persistence and inexpressible increase in the quality and volume of experience, due very emphatically to special Divine favor.

116. Yet there was nothing in the Greek experience that necessitated a reincarnational or cyclic view, even though there was that which made it possible. One of Barr's principal points is that Cullmann and Marsh greatly oversimplify when they say the "Greek" view of time is cyclic and differs from the biblical view. He says, "The following criticisms suggest themselves: (a) 'the Greeks' did not always in fact hold a cyclic view of time; (b) 'the Hebrews' in certain cases and in certain respects did entertain a cyclic view of time; (c) that which 'the Greeks' regarded as cyclic (if they did) was not the same thing as that which 'the Hebrews' regarded as a straight line (if they did)." [22] He proves these points convincingly, and he thereby devalues considerably the common view that the Old Testament and the more Semitic parts of the New stand in "monolithic solidarity against Greek thought." [23] Conversely, his argument also indicates that the Greek elements present in the New Testament by no means force a cyclic scheme on the texts in which they are found. Quite often they are found in non-cyclic contexts in their original Greek habitats, and almost always there is some kind of temporal scheme, even though cyclic in some secondary way. Again, in the Bible they often fit into the heavenly tapestry rather than the earthly, and thus are not incompatible with a strong durational emphasis at the terminal end of the Divine acts.

117. Indeed, there is often no indication at all of cyclic thinking, and the temporal scheme is strongly emphasized. This is manifested clearly in the historical sections of Luke and Acts, which resemble Greek historical writings [24] and remind us that history was one of the strongest areas of Greek literature. The kind of concept of time that grounded Hebrew "tapestry" thinking was quite congenial to the Greek mind once any cyclic elements that might be present due to philosophical or mythical influences were discarded, or others reduced in scale and made subservient to a larger tapestry picture by incorporation within it—as with historical theories of the rise and fall of dynasties and kingdoms. For many Greeks, such elements were probably never present at all.

---

[22] Barr, p. 137.
[23] Ibid., p. 12.
[24] See Richard J. Dillon and Joseph A. Fitzmyer, "Introduction" to "Acts of the Apostles," *JBC*, 45:3.

118. We shall discuss one more temporal concept, Brevard Childs' notion of "redemptive time", in our critique of scholarly positions in Part V. The discussion will not change anything we have seen here, and is more easily handled in the "actualization" setting.

Space and Place

119. We have already made some observations about space relative to the gnostic idea of God. (114). The notion that Greek thought tended to the "spacial" rather than the "temporal" may draw something from such views. To legitimize such a derivation it would have to be shown that these views were representatively Greek, and then that they were exclusively so. The notion itself is common; we have seen Cullmann's application of it in respect of blessedness. (92). But the evidence seems to show that the Hebrews were not all that different from the Greeks in their thinking about God, space and place; no more than the Greeks from *them* in their thinking about time.

120. At first the Hebrews had little to say about the next world and "blessedness" therein. When they did begin to think in these terms the fact of immortality seemed more important than the way of it. Yet, just as it is impossible to think of something spacial without thinking of its enduring, something enduring cannot be conceived without some kind of spatial notion however abstract. The Hebrews always tended to "locate" God in heaven, and heaven was "above". They probably used a rarified notion of extension to ground the thinking. If God is in Sheol as well, it is really by his power. (See 114). Heaven was probably often thought of rather abstractly; though frequently, too, as in the scene of Satan in the heavenly court in Job, more concrete images were used. This kind of thinking moved easily into the stratified-heaven notions common in the first century with all kinds of Jewish and Christian authors. Once again the tension between the transcendence of God and thought and expression about him manifests itself. And once again, I think the Jew and the Christian would have found an answer satisfying to them in the idea of theomorphism. They found expressions like this in their scriptures and traditions, and seeing these as originating with God, were simply willing to presume that *somehow* they expressed the reality—somehow were representative. They found in the same sources conscious objection to representing God in any forms that might come to be taken as *adequate* representations of him. But surely the things he said about himself were true insights into his mode of existence—true, if feeble and sometimes figurative.

121. Simon DeVries, at the end of an exhaustive study of the question of time in the Old Testament, says: "What distinguished biblical religion, even in its primitive forms, from all its ancient rivals, was its emerging awareness of the personalistic basis for the encounter between God and man, and for this, time had more revelational significance than place." [25] Earlier he describes "'that day' future.... Like 'that day' past, it marks a new turning point in man's journey through history in conversation with God." [26] DeVries' reference to "conversation" shows that it was not the notion of person that developed, but the inter-personal relationship that was first established when God was recognized as personal and concerned with man. The "I-thou" between God and man is explictly established as early as Genesis 3. The phrase "emerging awareness of the personalistic basis" might seem to deny this, but what it must mean is that the practical, and one might say "family" implications of the relationship were gradually unfolded, from revelational event to event. DeVries is certainly aware that the Greeks considered the gods to be persons and to have communication with men. The difference was in the nature of their concern, of the powers, and of the use of them for men's welfare.

122. Unfortunately, DeVries fails to exorcize the supposed time-space opposition when he makes statements like "For the man of myth, the supernatural was everywhere in principle but realistically present in the apparatus of the shrines." [27] He says that Yahweh's finding a "resting place" in Jerusalem was "a fateful moment: Israel's unparalleled insight that God was available to man everywhere and always was being threatened by overpowering forces. From this moment, biblical religion was a compromise." [28]

123. Again, one cannot separate duration (or time) and space. When God reveals, he must reveal *somewhere* or there is no contact with man. I think it can be safely said that the place of the revelation was seen to have been just as important for the nomadic Israel as for the settled, and this is very true to the nomadic mind, which puts great store by landmarks. Again, Yahweh was shown by Israel's writing historians to have manifested himself locally even when the Hebrews were on the march, in that he manifested himself to a people who were in any case localized and separated from *other* peoples. Yet there was no notion, at least in later times, that his choice of certain places for revelational events, or his predilection for Israel, limited his powers over the rest of the earth and its peoples, though that idea may originally have been behind the figures of the moving fire and cloud, or the tent of meeting. The developed concept was precisely this: that *Israel* as locally limited had to have a

---

[25] Simon DeVries, *Yesterday, Today and Tomorrow* (Grand Rapids: William B. Eerdmans, 1975), pp. 348-349.

[26] Ibid., p. 331.

[27] Ibid., pp. 348-349.

[28] Ibid., p. 349.

place to meet, hear, and address Yahweh no matter where Israel happened to be. In the view of her formal historians (and that was the view taken by most of those who read them), Israel did not move to Palestine because Yahweh's shrines were there; the shrines moved because Israel did.

124. Men have always felt and will always feel that certain places are more conducive to communion with God than others, whether it be a matter of revelation or of prayer. The desert was supposed in later Israel to be a good place. So were high places and shrines. Samuel hears the Lord and speaks to him in the silence of the night at Shiloh. This was the way the shrine was supposed to be. "My house is a house of prayer" is an ideal of both Old and New Testaments. The modern Muslim has his prayer rug to set him apart from the passing throng, and the throng respects his limited privacy. Even modern Westerners have their chapels in big-city plazas. For Israel, of course, the centralization of the cult had a strong political background; but again, for the historians this was related to worship of Yahweh. And rightly so. The people worshipping in Jerusalem undoubtedly experienced a strong feeling of solidarity around and under Yahweh. They prayed in other places alone and in smaller groups, but this prayer was doubly significant because it was a national prayer. And it was not unnatural that a formal exercise like sacrifice should come more and more to be restricted to the locale where its solemnity could be fully expressed by the magnificent resources of the Temple organization. This change never seriously affected the idea of God or of his availability for revelation and prayer wherever the prophet or petitioner might be.

125. I cannot help feeling that much scholarly nostalgia for Israel's pre-settlement, desert days is based on a lack of sympathy for the ancients' love of ritual and grandeur—a love that is still evident in the East. Particularly targeted, often, are the institutions of Temple and sacrifice. Joseph Hertz counters with perception and eloquence:

> Moderns do not always realize the genuine hold that the sacrificial service had upon the affections of the people in ancient Israel. The Central Sanctuary was the axis round which the national life revolved. The people *loved* the Temple, its pomp and ceremony, the music and song of the Levites and the ministrations of the priests, the High Priest as he stood and blessed the prostrate worshippers amid profound silence on the Atonement Day. And the choicer spirits found expression in words like those of the Psalmist (...43:3,4): —
>
> > "... O send out Thy light and Thy truth; let them lead me;
> > Let them bring me unto Thy holy hill,
> > And to thy tabernacles.
> > Then will I go unto the altar of God,
> > Unto God, my exceeding joy." [29]

---

[29] Joseph H. Hertz, *The Authorised Daily Prayer Book*, rev. ed. (New York: Bloch, 1948), pp. 33-34.

To repeat the main point: this kind of worship in no way saw Yahweh as limited; it simply recognized the limitations of the worshippers. It certainly did not compromise the priestly writer who said,

> The earth is the Lord's and the fulness thereof,
> the world and those who dwell therein; ....
> Who shall ascend the hill of the Lord?
> And who shall stand in his holy place? (Ps. 24:1,3).

126. A small philosophical reflection: There is a danger in associating anything material, whether it be time or place, with human actions directed towards supernatural powers. And I take "actions" here to include speech. But this is merely the danger that accompanies any potentiality for good. The danger of being too spiritual is Satanic pride. That of being too material is magical manipulation. But man is both spiritual and material, which makes him capable of being what the angels cannot be, an artist and a physically demonstrative person. Paul complains about the Galatians' over-concern for times and seasons (4:10). Scrupulosity about chronology was the danger accompanying a legitimate historical interest. It was of course the Jewish times and seasons he was concerned about—these ought to have been of comparatively minor importance for Christians. But the danger was still there for events of Christian history; yet Paul accepts and reemphasizes the event of the Last Supper, and it is hardly likely that he ignored the gatherings on the Sabbath or the Lord's Day.

Cult Versus History?

127. The Hebrews' historical view was not destroyed by their settlement in Palestine or the Temple worship. Probably quite the opposite. When one is engaged in arduous living, one is not likely to give much thought to the significance of what is going on except within narrow limits. The reflections on the greatness of God's acts in Egypt and the desert are largely the result of later reminiscence. The very tradition of remembering was partly a later development. The feasts were ideally suited to focus and generate remembering, for the feasts were etiologically related to the great historical events or the situations connected with such events (harvest naturally fit the settlement in Palestine as distinct from the desert), and were repeated in such wise as to make the remembering itself a pleasant and significant event. DeVries seems to overlook this basic truth when he sharply *distinguishes* cultic from historical event rather than appreciating their conscious relationship. In fact, his problem is not the relationship so much as the *use* made of it. He says, "It is quite true that Israel substituted Heilsgeschichte for myth, but these festivals represent a compromise as much as a triumph." [30] Of the "li-

---

[30] DeVries, p. 347.

turgical command" of Exodus 13:3f he says, "This... displays a... festal repetition of the original event from generation to generation. But the ritual fails to lead to any practical response, ending with no other command than to 'keep this ordinance at its appointed time from year to year.'" [31] Paradoxically, he then goes on to mention sacramentalization. This, in the sense given to the word by many New Testament commentators, is usually part of an attempt precisely to put the liturgical commemoration to use. The manner of the use is not approved by many of these commentators, but it is in fact one that was associated with all the Israelite feasts that we have record of, from the very beginning, in the form of rituals like sacrifice and other oblation. And well before the time of Christ it was certainly accompanied by liturgical prayer that made specific reference to a hope for influence of the original act on the present situation.

128. DeVries, no doubt, would prefer some other kind of system, in which great events were not so much remembered as experienced as ethically fruitful here and now in the lives of individuals. He speaks of Israel's "charismatic tradition", and gives his ideal: "Every day presents a new choice, a new opportunity, a new responsibility." [32] That is certainly true, but it is hardly incompatible with the idea of liturgical commemoration. Although the liturgy has been seen by some as a means of bringing past events into the present in some mystical way (the Caselian school exemplifies this—see 140ff), it is far more regularly seen as a reminder of God's power and concern as exemplified in notable events of the past, this constituting an encouragement to face the everyday challenges and difficulties with the assurance of that same power. Every day is not going to be an Exodus in terms of profundity of unaided present experience; but one can make it more vivid by imbuing it with some of the glory of the past. And particularly, with God's help, little things can be done well or even greatly, so that nobility enters into daily routine. This fits DeVries' demand for paranesis. In fact, paranesis for the Hebrew was ineluctably suggested by the recurrent covenant context of religiously historic events as found in the biblical accounts. DeVries implies as much when he says, "This seems to be the whole impact of Deuteronomy, combining memorialization with urgent paranesis." [33] We shall have reason to return to this question relative to our own text, for Paul very easily brings paranesis into relation with it, since—as is so often the case with liturgical memorial—it calls for it by its very nature.

129. DeVries, in the context of his generalized definition of sacramentalization as a regularization of historically unique events, [34] says that "the

---

[31] Ibid.
[32] Ibid., p. 346.
[33] Ibid., p. 347.
[34] See Ibid., p. 347.

very essence of sacramentalization seems to be the reduction of the *timely* to the *timeless*." [35] As far as the memory of the past event is concerned, we have seen that the more common tendency among viewers of history—and the biblical viewers are surely no exception—is to maintain the autonomy of the past-present while reading from it various kinds of significance for the now-present. In other words, there is a regularization, but not such a reduction as DeVries might seem to suggest. There is, indeed, a paradox. Timefulness *is* made timeless, by being perpetuated, when it is incorporated in the liturgical event; but it remains timeful in its own right because it still retains its dignity as past-present.

130. Together with all this, the Godward reference of Israelite sacramentalizing in every recorded instance is evident, and it is this that really does introduce still another species of valid "timelessness" into the situation. For Yahweh and Paul's God—who is Yahweh—is outside the tapestry of created affairs, even though understandably concerned with them as Creator. And this means outside created time, even if not outside duration as such. Being so, he is, as he was and will be, in control of all that is temporal and aware of it both after and before it happens. This is presumed in normal Hebrew and Pauline prayer, and must be expected to be the normal presumption of any Hebrew and Pauline sacramentalization as well, particularly when that is related to covenant. The "timelessness" at the human level is that of strict memory and anticipation; that at the Divine is that of specific knowledge of past and future, and efficacious power. The "timely" element consists of the past remembered event, the present liturgical event, and a hoped-for and presumably effected third event that in the Pauline scheme at least is somehow linked in both human memory and Divine knowledge to the past remembered event—in several instances by some kind of causal relationship. Thus Paul says that Jesus is put forward "as an expiation" (Rom. 3:25); that he died "to a purpose" (Gal. 2:21); that God glorified him "therefore" (Phil. 2:9). And in our own text, Paul or some earlier contributor specifies that Christ died "for you." (We shall conclude that this is the likely meaning.) The New Testament writers, of course, do not continually explicate their conviction that God is the planner, viewer and guarantor of both Christ's salvific act and whatever benefit it produces for the beneficiaries—it is obvious to them and repetition would be tedious. A natural scientist, studying their writings, would probably insist on bringing such unexpressed considerations into his every calculation along with the expressed ones; this is the way he would do it in his own field, and he could affirm, I think with justice, that without *all* the facts the right answer is unlikely to come out of a calculation in *any* field. But there seems to be a leaning among scholars of other than strictly scientific subjects towards equating "facts" with "ex-

---

[35] Ibid., p. 347. DeVries' italics.

pressed facts" in the supposed interest of more accurate exegesis. It is true that introducing the non-expressed into the picture complicates it; but simplicity is no advantage if it does not happen to coincide with reality. Exegesis may well benefit from more of logical thought and less of systematizing with insufficient facts; more of scientific initiative and less of playing safe by using only the rules that are posted in large letters.

Chapter Summary

131. The main arguments in this chapter have been to the effect that Paul, together with the other biblical writers, had no container view of time, but probably saw beings (concretely, of course, but equivalently) as spacially extended durational progressions, with change the practical proof of the fact of duration. This spatio-temporal view is in fact identical with the "tapestry" scheme we spoke of earlier; for the identities there involved are identically the bearers of the temporal and spacial qualities. These writers seem to have thought of God in much the same way, though in a scheme transcendent to the earthly one. And they definitely saw God's acts as able to terminate within the earthly system and to direct that system through its history of change, both by rearrangement and by the introduction of new efficiencies at the created level. There was nothing in the Greek influences on biblical literature that necessarily modified this mode of thought, nor does Paul seem to have favored gnostic ideas, which might have done so. Geographical locations or separations were associated with certain past salvific acts of God considered in their terminal effects, and could serve as a reminder of the Divine attention for those who were respectfully mindful of such acts, especially when the rememberers were gathered in their own defined ecclesial unity. So for Sinai, the desert, the tabernacle, the land, the Temple. Cult and sacramentalization in no way obliterated the temporal element in religious thought: any "timelessness" they introduced into the earthly scheme was due to the combined transcendence and pertinence to that scheme of the Divine one, in terms of knowledge, direction and power; due too, in a lesser degree, to the perpetuation of the past-present by the liturgical celebration of its dignity.

132. In Chapter I we concluded that Paul would have had a sense of history that by memory attributed to past-present events *as* past-present a continued dignified autonomy in now-present experience, relating them to that and projected future experiences quite as truly as he related the now-present to the future-present. Chapter II saw this scheme as it were supernaturalized by the superimposition on it of views of God as planning and controlling history to make events of all times significant *in* all times for salvation; and of man, in a familial, specifically filial relationship with God, as able willingly to participate in and even to instrument this salvific order, guided by Divine revelation through prophecy. Chapter III explores the cosmological background against which Paul would have viewed such a Divine-human relationship, and finds it quite suitable for its function, with place providing a unique kind of identity and meaning. The whole picture presented by the three chapters adds up to what we have called a "tapestry" view, where God exists and operates in a dimly conjectured transcendent pattern of his own, with man at the durationally forward edge of a growing created tapestry of event and experience whose past constituents are at the natural level kept in meaningful existence by human memory as well as in the form of natural effects; while revelation seems to indicate that some specific past events also retain special salvific effect.

CHAPTER IV: **Truly Human Response to God**

The Implications of Sacrament

133. If God was thought to have communicated with man through prophecy, the question naturally comes to mind whether Paul and his contemporaries saw any possibility of man's response to God in any truly communicative sense, and if so, what significance that might have in the context sketched above. We could approach this question in various ways, but DeVries' introduction (see Chapter III) of the concept of sacramentalization is an especially suitable avenue since its study will show not only that there was traditionally a response but that that involved the use of material objects as well as formulated speech. Let us see how this question of sacramentalization leads into that of communication with God, and what place matter has in the picture.

134. Coming directly from our critique of DeVries' position, a reader might first be impelled to ask, "If the 'very essence of sacramentalization' (130) is not DeVries' species of timelessness, what is it?" It is hardly likely to be any Divine kind of timelessness either; nor in fact the human kind spoken of in 130, for sacramentalization shares that with non-sacramental phenomena such as historical memory, prayer, and (with still less "timely" content) abstract thinking such as that used in mathematics— though in this last the past as such is accorded little honor.

135. A dictionary definition of "sacrament" gives the following:

> A religious act, ceremony, or practice that is considered especially sacred as a sign or a symbol of a deeper reality.... 2: the Christian Eucharist.... 3a: something sacred in character or significance: a spiritual sign, seal or bond (as a covenant held to exist between God and man) b: something that has the significance of a deeply religious act or observance.[1]

What distinguishes the sacramental from the merely sacred, in most cases, is in fact the *sensible* nature of the "something" that *is* sacred. It is an "act, ceremony, practice", such as is exemplified in the Eucharist; which is of course the sacrament we are concerned with principally. There is a "signing". "Sign" itself as commonly understood is defined as

---

[1] *Webster's Third New International Dictionary* (Chicago: G. and C. Merriam Co., 1971), s.v. "sacrament."

> 1a: a motion, gesture, or bodily action by which a thought is expressed....
> b: a unit of language (as a word) that means, stands for, designates or
> denotes something.... 2a: a conventional mark or device. ...[2]

Short of some such sensible phenomenon, and indeed, short of the kind
of "motion, gesture, or bodily action" noted under "1a", there is no real
"sacrament" in the usual sense of the word, even though there may be
something sacred like vocal prayer. In a more liberal sense, such prayer
might be accepted as a sacrament too, for speech is certainly signing.

136. Paul speaks of Abraham's circumcision in terms that closely
accord with the dictionary definition of sacrament cited above. "He received circumcision as a sign or seal of the righteousness which he had
by faith while he was still uncircumcised." (Rom. 4:11). The example
springs to mind; but it may also have significance for our text, which
speaks of "blood of the covenant". The "righteousness" Paul speaks of
is of course that of "the promise... through the righteousness of faith"
(4:13), and this is God's part of the "covenant previously ratified by God"
of which Paul speaks in Gal. 3:17 and again by implication in Rom. 11:
27. The point is that there is a sacramental sign connected with the
Abrahamic covenant in Paul's mind; in fact, there is another "blood sign"
connected with the Sinaitic covenant as well. We shall return to these
points later.

137. It is disturbing to find Ernst Fuchs defining sacrament, before
he ever addresses the problem of the Pauline Eucharist, as "a celebration
that through divine or even supernatural or superhuman means makes
its own a magically effective act."[3] "Celebration" and "divine" certainly
fit the common understanding of "sacrament", but the insertion of the
"magical" suggests a theological interpretation of sacramentalism that goes
beyond the symbolism and the supernatural and sees only one possible
method of working effects. We concluded earlier (130) that for Paul there
is a linking of the "effected third event" with the "past remembered event"
that in several instances involves some kind of causal relationship. Fuchs
goes even beyond this to name the method of linkage—to say *how* the
connection is made. The "how" for him is magic, which he also associates
with the scholastic "*ex opere operato*".[4] His use of the term "magic"
seems to accord with the dictionary definition of that word: "the use
of means (as ceremonies, charms, spells) that are believed to have supernatural power to cause a supernatural being to produce or prevent a
particular result... considered not obtainable by natural means."[5] The

---

[2] *Webster's*, s.v. "sign."
[3] Ernst Fuchs, *Das Urchristliche Sakramentsverständnis* (Bad Cannstatt: R. Müllerschön Verlag, 1958), p. 5. (Trans. by the present writer.)
[4] Ibid.
[5] *Webster's*, s.v. "magic."

question centers around the "supernatural power", which for Fuchs is the "*opus*" that "*operatum*" puts real pressure on the "supernatural being" of our definition—which could be Yahweh in the Hebrew-Pauline scheme. "Could", since it might be thought that the beings in question were in some middle area between God and men, like angels; or even some reservoir of power tappable by magical rites on the analogy of natural reservoirs tappable by physical means operating by visible causalities.[6]

138. If God *was* thought to be involved, is magic—specifically theurgy— necessarily involved too? Knowing what we do today of the nature of many of the sacrificial and other liturgies of antiquity, it can be said without much hesitation that the distant origins of even the Israelite altar ritual must have been in the shadowy past of fetishism, sacred groves, totemism and other primitive practices and beliefs, including magic. But from what we know of that ritual and its surroundings in the times when the Pentateuch was being written down, it must be seriously questioned whether by then the "pressure" that the liturgical celebrations were thought to put on God was anything other than reminders of pressures God was thought to have put on *himself*, as by covenant. The supposition of Divine revelation plus the stress on covenant *in* that revelation, taken in the context of God's transcendence and in particular of his creative activity and foreknowledge, offered Paul referents for any question he or others might have had about God being "bound" by the event in liturgy. He might sense problems, but would simply accept that God worked this way and was not open to questioning about how or why.

139. This is a view compatible with the phrase "*ex opere operato*", for "*opere*" is not an ablative of means but uses the variously interpretable "*ex*". That is, it is not necessarily the work itself that does the pressuring; though it is indeed presumed to be "worked", and may *have* to be worked for God to put the pressure on himself by way of his promises. The work has some kind of relation to the "supernatural being", but that relation is not specified by the phrase itself. The way is open to seeing such "works", whatever else they may be, as liturgical *reminders* to God, "memorials" "before him". (The latter phrase is of course biblical, as is the term "memorial".)

Theories of Memorial

140. Let us at this point do a logical exercise to discover what position such reminders might have in a wider scheme of sacramental

---

[6] See Iamblichus *On the Mysteries*, IV, 2. For Greek text see *Jamblique Les Mystères D'Égypte*, trans. Édouard des Places (Paris: Société D'Edition 'Les Belles Lettres', 1966). English translation in *Hellenistic Religions*, ed. Frederick C. Grant (Indianapolis: Bobbs-Merrill, 1953), p. 176.

possibilities. This will make the estimate of the actual texts easier and more efficient, since we will be less likely after forewarning to overlook such possibilities as may be present there. The theoretical problems were brought to a new level of awareness in many minds a number of years ago by the *"Mysteriengegenwart"* theory of Dom Odo Casel. Concentrating on the Eucharist, which is "the primary and outstanding example of the *Mysteriengegenwart*," [7] Casel holds that "there is neither a real nor a numerical distinction between the Eucharist and the Passion." [8] Denis O'Callaghan, from whose summary of Casel's position the two citations just given were directly taken, goes on to give Casel's essential thinking about memorial: "The Mass as an objective memorial (*Gedächtnis*) reactualizes and projects the sacrifice of Calvary on the altar whenever the words of consecration are pronounced." [9] The Catholic Mass, of course, has traditionally been called a "sacrifice", and Casel appears in part to have been trying to justify the appellation. Further, the "words of consecration" which were seen as representing the sacrificial essence, included and still include an amalgamation of the several formulae of institution found in the evangelists and Paul, along with reference to memorial in the clause *"Hoc facite in meam commemorationem."* Casel thus puts his justification in memorial terms, with the words and ritual actions constituting the memorializing.[10]

141. A verbal key to Casel's viewpoint is his qualifying the term "memorial" with "objective". It appears that for Casel, the function of the memorial rite is not to gain direct access to God, but to gain access to the numerically identical act of Christ that was instituted by God to be uniquely salvific. It may be that Casel looked to the hypostatic union (i.e., the Divinity of Christ) for the efficacy of Christ's act on Calvary. But that is another issue. The Mass as a memorial [for Casel] finds an "object" that reaches God; it does not reach God directly, and so, the reaching of God is not done "subjectively" by those who place the memorial act and the symbolism. Casel uses the figure of the "spring pushed out at the foot of the cross to flow ever since then with the healing power of the cross",[11] and of Christ as the "fountain of youth into which we must step to regain our own youth, to be renewed." [12] For him the Mass is the same spring and water as Calvary, numerically, and the memorial words and actions gain access to it as through a stratum of

---

7 Denis O'Callaghan, "The Theory of the 'Mysteriengegenwart' of Dom Odo Casel, A Controversial Subject in Modern Theology," *Irish Ecclesiastical Review* 90 (1958), 250.
    8 Ibid.
    9 Ibid.
    10 It is probably evident to the reader that the term "memorial" has so far been used in this study in a general sense, to mean "having to do with remembering, reminding, being remembered or reminded, etc."
    11 Donald Bridgehouse, "Dom Odo Casel," *Downside Review* 75 (1957), 145.
    12 Ibid.

concealing ground.   In more metaphysical terms, as O'Callaghan points out:

> The analogy of the presence of Christ *per modum substantiae* in the Eucharist is often employed by Odo Casel to illustrate his doctrine of the presence of the acts of Christ in the *Kultmysterium*.... If the Body of Christ is present *per modum substantiae* in many places without any multiplication of its essence, so, too, is the Passion of Christ evermore re-presented without any repetition and without the historical succession of its component parts.[13]

O'Neill has characterized this kind of theory thus: "Christ's own death must somehow be... suspended in some imaginary yet paradoxically un-imaginable world of shades."[14]   There is no doubt that the Thomistic distinction between substance and accident lends itself to questionable developments like this: if the limitations of space can be so deftly overcome, why not those of time?   It may be noted that this expression in terms of "substance" is even stronger than that of the water-figure, for there is even less suggestion of durational extension.

142. The principal point to be made here is that the Caselian Eucharistic "memorial" is determined by a metaphysical theory in which the function of the memorial is to call into operation—or gain access to the operation of—an ontological reality which, though undoubtedly super-natural in some way in Casel's mind, was all the same created; and although created, seems not merely to open the way to an uncreated Act (as does, for example, Maurice de la Taille's *actuatio creata*)[15] but *by itself* transcends the limitations of space and duration-time.

143. Casel, as Bridgehouse says, argues that "All power proceeds from the mystery.... this is only possible by the power of the mystery itself; it is not independent action, but action *with* God."[16]   What this appears to mean is that while the mystery-act is accessible to the memorial (and so, the memorial is "objective", with this real created act its object), the same act is on the other side accessible to God's infusion of power. But Casel undoubtedly wants to see Calvary as such as the point of real infusion by God of this power, and uses his metaphysical theory to get that power down to the present time.   The theory provides the "objective" access.   He not only wants the power to be present at the created level as in some kind of channel, but wants that channel to transcend the normal limitations of created being.   No doubt he sees this as also due to Divine

---

13 O'Callaghan, 254.

14 Colman E. O'Neill, "The Mysteries of Christ and the Sacraments," *Thomist* 25 (1962), 52.

15 See Maurice de la Taille, *The Mystery of Faith*, 2 vols. (New York: Sheed and Ward, 1940), vol. 2, pp. 32-33 et al.

16 Bridgehouse, 144.

power somehow: what it looks like is a Divine overriding of the ontology of God's own creation.

144. Another basically metaphysical theory is suggested by a reference Neunhauser makes to Johannes Betz, in which he says that the latter wants more value to attach to the symbol than Casel allows for it. Casel, says Betz, has not only a real presence but an absolute one: "...beneath the outer hull of the symbol, the saving act of Christ is given in its absolute self." [17] Neunhauser suggests that Betz has a view of reality-in-symbol that is like the Platonic view: the symbol participates in the reality beyond.[18] This appears to mean that God would create a special order of reality for this particular case; or more likely, for all the sacraments.

145. It seems doubtful whether the ancients were as ready to change the ground-rules for limited being as such theorists are. We have seen already what those ground-rules probably were for most people: a dura-tional-spacial existence that kept the past in the past and the future in the future, even though there could occasionally be miraculous doings in the present. Even the gods were viewed as existing durationally, though more commonly transcending space in various ways. The devotees of the mysteries accepted about the same views. The god could be present in a number of the devotees at the same time, but it does not seem that they ever thought of such a thing as a past event's being present sub-stantially—i.e., in its numerically identical pastness—here and now. In cyclic revitalizations there may have been an exact repetition, but it *was* a repetition. For someone with Platonic views, of course, this concept of a "suspended" state might not be so farfetched. But for the Christian this would raise the question of the relationship with the actual historical act of Calvary. Surely, upleasantness should have no place in a reli-gious world of Platonic Ideas. Yet, how could the eternal Idea of the act of Calvary lack Calvary's gruesome aspects and still really be the Idea of Calvary? The gruesomeness seems as much a part of the essence of the *act* as the nobility does. Assuming that the Eucharist could participate in an Idea; could it participate in the Idea of Calvary? Such considerations may seem somewhat abstruse, but they have a certain relevance in any scheme of transcendence. At any rate, one may ask whether for Betz the Eucharistic "memorial" would be an ἀνάμνησις in the Platonic mode; or more specifically, whether 1 Corinthians 11 might be interpreted in this way on the assumption that such an understanding was behind its for-mulation. Such an understanding would assume a fundamental relation between knowledge in the soul of man and the Idea, and see memorial as the means to follow the channel of this relationship out of the morass

---

[17] Burkhard Neunhauser, "The Mystery Presence," *Downside Review* 76 (1958), 270.
[18] See ibid., 270.

of worldly distraction.[19] Presumably, memory of Calvary, if this is what 1 Corinthians 11 does refer to, would offer a facile access to this channel; memory of Calvary would constitute a beginning of the Platonic remembrance.

146. I do not think most scholars would take seriously the possibility of a Platonic background for the Pauline ἀνάμνησις, the context turning attention towards more obvious possibilities. But the contrast may be helpful for a better appreciation of these latter.

The Power-Effect

147. Central in the Caselian theory as distinct from the Platonic is the concern for power. In an "objective" memorial this power proceeds from an object other than the rememberer, which object is in some way called forth or had access to by the memorializing. We may ask what a "subjective" memorial would be, and the answer seems to be that it would be a memorial that did not find any real object-source of power, but was merely psychological or cognitive. A Platonic memorial would operate this way, so would a Gnostic-type one; both would work through special knowledge to regain a lost status. Similarly with a memorial exercised simply for the experience or effect of the act of remembering itself. In such an exercise the ritual words and acts would be useful for enhancing the experience. I think for our purposes we might avoid possible confusion by dropping the "objective-subjective" terminology—always open to various interpretations—and referring to types like the three just above as "merely psychological" memorials, and to the types looking to power as "power-seeking" memorials. The power in question is not meant to include "memory power" or some other such result that might be got "from within" by psychological exercise, but only power sought from sources outside the seeker himself. By "power" we can understand any termination of creative power that is related to the memorial act: charismatic powers locating in the rememberer himself or someone else; powers terminating in other kinds of things wondrous or no; more subtle helps like mental enlightenment or inspiration to action; miracles, blessings, protection, graces, resurrection, etc. It will be recalled that Fuchs makes "effectiveness" an essential part of sacramentalism. This is what we mean by "power". In truth, the sacramental viewpoint very often does look to power, but as the discussion of merely psychological memorials suggests, there might be other aims to sacramentalizing. Our earlier objection to the Fuchs definition was directed at the presumption that the only way of engaging such power was by magic. Let us now address this point.

---

[19] See Carlo E. Huber, *Anamnesis bei Plato* (München: Pullacher Philosophische Forschungen, 1964), p. 44.

148. Certainly, magic is often thought capable of engaging it. A magical system could be conceived to operate without personal divinities, or on a lower level than such divinities; in the latter case, either as the only source of power directly affecting men, or more likely, as the source of power in certain restricted areas somehow beneath divine concern. There is also the possibility that the divinities be directly pressured by the magical acts, without any intermediary area of power—this being theurgy. If there should be question of memorial, it might be presumed that the power is somehow located in the remembered event, being, or beings; or related to it. If there were a divinity above, it could be that the remembered event or being was engaged ipso facto to intercede for or otherwise try to gain effects peculiar to the divinity. However, such a mediating factor would be redundant if any necessitating pressure were attributed to it; one might as well see the magical act as theurgic— directly pressuring the divinity.

Sacrament without Magic

149. Intercession: this opens up the question of personal relationships and the possibility that the sacramental act has no power to enlist power other than that of moral persuasion or perhaps something even less than that. Whatever it might be, it would be expressed in traditional speech-forms accompanied by formalized gesture or symbol thought suitable to the august occasion. Why, someone may ask, place the addendum "perhaps something even less than" moral persuasion? Because a main problem here, for many moderns, is that God is considered to be above persuasion. Let us study this question relative to the Old Testament and, in particular, to Paul.

150. The argumentation the psalmists use with God is often forceful. "Help me, O Lord my God! Save me according to thy steadfast love! Let them know that this is thy hand; thou, O Lord, hast done it! Let them curse, but do thou bless!" (Ps. 109:26-28). There is something like pressure here, but it is not the pressure of equal on equal. God, with his חֶסֶד relates to the עֶבֶד more like a kindly slave-owner to his servant —the idea being that the Lord should care what happens to his property and the members of his household. God, by reason of his position, should be expected to intervene in the situation. Or again, as we have suggested, he had reason to consider himself pressured by himself by virtue of his previous promises, his covenant.

151. Yet, covenant in the Scriptures is a bilateral thing. Always there was some act of man that was expected as a condition for God's keeping his side of the covenant. "This is my covenant, which you shall keep.... Every male among you shall be circumcised." (Gen. 17:10). "If you will obey my voice and keep my covenant you shall be my own possession...." (Exod. 19:5). This latter is the Sinai covenant, of course. The same picture emerges in the covenant with David, except that in 2 Sam. 7 we find an element that speaks in terms familiar already in the covenant with Abraham and gives Paul a foundation for his interpretation of that in terms of a single offspring (see Gal. 3:16). "When he commits iniquity I will chasten him.... but I will not take my steadfast love from him, as I took it from Saul... and your house... shall be established forever." (2 Sam. 7:14-16). The RSV translation of חֶסֶד as "steadfast love" underscores the importance of the obligations laid on the human members of the agreement:—in spite of God's love being "steadfast", it was removed from Saul. Certain elements of covenant are assured from God's side in perpetuity in every case: his initiative in drawing up the agreement and urging it upon man; his retribution if man does not keep his part of the covenant once that is agreed on; his assurance of blessing if man does. Retribution: even in Paul's mind the necessity of obedience *in act* was not remitted, for it was necessary that there be someone "who knew no sin" (2 Cor. 5:21) to serve as mankind's representative, taking others' sins upon himself; even though this was at God's initiative: "God made him to be sin who knew no sin." At this level, to avoid retribution it is necessary for man to open himself to the blessings that will be forthcoming from God now that Christ has kept man's part of the covenant, or rather, kept the covenant on man's behalf. This is done by "dying with Christ" (Rom. 6:8). It is a mystical death, not only in being effective through a representative, but because it was obvious to Paul that "there is no man who does not sin" (1 Kgs 8:46; Christ being the obvious exception). Put positively, it was the "new covenant" of Jer. 31:33: "I will put my law within them... and they shall all know me." The Christians all know Christ by faith and so know God; for this their representative does not break the covenant as the Hebrews did (see Jer. 31:32), and himself being obedient "unto death" (Phil. 2:8), "knows God."

152. But the problem of retribution remains even after the identification. This is evident from the fact that the flow of blessings from God is often interrupted by all kinds of calamities, and inevitably by physical death. If this is not just retribution it is negligence—or worse, sadism—; for God in Paul's mind was perfectly capable of removing the calamities. Indeed, Paul connects sin with such things in our own text, when he says that it is because they eat and drink "without discerning" that "many of you are weak and ill, and some have died." (1 Cor. 11: 29, 30). This nexus, even after Christ's vicarious death, between sins committed then and suffering and death, is at least part-explanation for Paul's insisting on what is really an Old Testament prophetic ethic, and his praying to God for protection and blessings in terms that are very much like many Old Testament prayers. God still judges. He punishes sins, and in some sense rewards goodness. Man is paradoxically saved and yet not safe, at least not in this life. He has much, but he can have more.

Pauline Prayer—the Texts

153. Recognizing that in terms of human needs there is a legitimate place for prayer in the new-covenant context, we may turn again to the question of how God, in Paul's mind, stands in relation to prayer. The best way to get the Pauline view is to see the Pauline texts. We shall do this in the order Galatians, Romans, Philippians, 1 and 2 Corinthians, to see if there is any development. Our main interest, of course, is in petitionary prayer.

154. *Galatians.* Here, such prayer is restricted to wishes, which in the context of the Spirit's activity within the Christian heart, proclaimed in this epistle (see 4:6; 5:5), may well be a prayer-equivalent. So, "Grace and peace to you from God...." (1:3); "Peace and mercy be upon all who walk by this rule, upon the Israel of God." (6:16); "The grace of our Lord Jesus Christ be with your spirit, brethren." (6:18).

155. *Romans.* There are a number of similar wish-prayers. "Grace and peace to you." (1:7b); "The grace of the Lord... be with your spirit." (4:23). There is a specific linking of wish and prayer: "Brethren, my heart's desire and prayer to God for them is that they may be saved." (10:1). There are references to actual prayers, and indeed, to prayer as a regular practice. "Without ceasing I mention you always in my prayers, asking that somehow by God's will I may now at last succeed in coming to you." (1:9-10). "My heart's desire and prayer...." (as above: 10:1). "I appeal to you... to strive together with me in your prayers to God on my behalf, that I may be delivered from the unbelievers in Judea, and that my service for Jerusalem may be acceptable to the saints, so that by God's will I may come to you with joy...." (15:30-32). There is reference to the Spirit's intercession "according to the will of God" (8:27); and to Christ's, "who indeed intercedes for us" (8:34). There is the urging to "call upon the name of the Lord" (10:13), which is practically defined in 10:9: "If you confess with your lips that Jesus is Lord and believe in your heart that God raised him... you will be saved." Although such confession is not petition, it exemplifies another Divine requirement for human cooperation in the new-covenant arrangement—a requirement involving a physical manifestation. Paul's prayers undoubtedly had such manifestations too. On the other hand, the recurrence in almost all the prayer-texts of references to the will of God, joined to those to the Spirit and Christ as witnesses (see 8:15) and intercessors, show that Paul prayed leaving the outcome of his prayer to God. He has no theory on why God answers prayers, but trusts that he will, somehow.

156. *Philippians.* Wishes for grace and peace in 1:2; 4:6-7; 4:23. Statements about or exhortations to prayer: "It is my prayer that your love may abound more and more, with knowledge and all discernment, so that you may approve what is excellent, and may be pure and blameless for the day of Christ, filled with the fruits of righteousness which come through Jesus Christ...." (1:9-11); "I know that through your prayers and the help of the Spirit of Jesus Christ this will turn out for my deliverance... whether by life or death." (1:19-20); "Have no anxiety about anything, but in everything by prayer and supplication with thanskgiving let your requests be made known to God. And the peace of God... will keep your hearts and your minds in Christ Jesus." (4:6-7). The last citation seems to be almost a definition of Pauline prayer: it is for all occasions, it combines supplication and thanksgiving, it removes anxiety, brings peace. The element of thanksgiving appears prominently in another text, which also introduces memorial terminology: "I thank God in all my remembrance of you [ἐπὶ πάσῃ τῇ μνείᾳ ὑμῶν] always in every prayer of mine for you making my prayer with joy, thankful." (1:3-5). This strengthens the impression which the word δέησις would give in any case, that "prayer" for Paul has entreaty at the very core of its meaning. The epistle also has its reference to confession: "at the name of Jesus every knee should bow... and every tongue confess that Jesus Christ is Lord." (2:10-11). Again there is the reference to external manifestation.

157. *1 Corinthians.* Wishes for grace and peace in 1:3; 16:23. One specific reference to prayer of petition, one prayer to Jesus. "He who speaks in a tongue should pray for the power to interpret." (14:13). "Our Lord, come!" (16:22). Two general references to prayer, in 7:5 ("...that you may devote yourselves to prayer") and 11:4-5 ("Any man who prays or prophesies.... any woman who prays or prophesies...."). An interesting reflection on prayer relative to charisms: "If I pray in a tongue, my spirit prays but my mind is unfruitful.... I will pray with the mind also.... Otherwise, how can any... outsider say the 'Amen' to your thanksgiving...?" (14:14-16). Two things are noteworthy here. First, the prayer is made synonymous with "thanksgiving", showing that this too is a core element of prayer in Paul's mind. Second, the charisms are not the prayer as such, but one of the ways of expressing prayer. It is important to recognize that Paul does not mention prayer in the enumeration of charismatic *gifts* (see Rom. 12:6ff; 1 Cor. 12:4ff; 12:28ff). Prayer is not a special gift for special people or occasions; it is a practice, informed by the Spirit, but engaged in by everyone "without ceasing" (Rom. 1:9). The function of the Spirit is mentioned again in this epistle: "No one can say 'Jesus is Lord' except by the Holy Spirit." (12:3b).

158. *2 Corinthians.* Wishes for grace and peace in epistolary prescript and closing: 1:2 and 13:14. Note that these, though in conventional literary form, are Christian in content, as in all the epistles. References to prayer: "You also must help us by prayer, so that many will give thanks on our behalf for the blessings granted us in answer to many prayers." (1:11). "We pray God that you may not do wrong.... What we pray for is your improvement." (13:7,9). "While they long for you and pray for you...." (9:14). The nexus between thanksgiving and prayer of petition noted earlier is here expanded to show the relationship between the two—they interact and promote each the other. The basic principle is given in 9:8: "God is able to provide you with every blessing in abundance... for every good work." They pray for these blessings, receive them, then pray in thanksgiving and are encouraged to pray for more because of the obviously holy character of the effects. Ultimately the process is referred to God and to Jesus: "That is why we utter the Amen through him, to the glory of God." (4:15).

Reflections on Pauline Prayer

159 The very extent of these references indicates that prayer of petition for Paul and his Christian communities was an accepted fact, a valued part of life. The references come in all kinds of contexts, though they are naturally fewer in very theological sections where Paul is intent on his argumentation. They fall into a wider prayer context that includes doxologies (about six in the epistles studied above), prayers of the Spirit within (four), confessions that Jesus is Lord (five), prayers of thanksgiving (ten). The thanksgivings are for faith (three); for their gifts of knowledge, etc. (one), for comfort (one); general (five). The petitions: for Paul to come to them (one); for the Jews' salvation (one); that they may do no wrong (one); for their improvement (one); for Paul's deliverance from unbelievers (two); for power to interpret tongues (one); general (three). There are four references to prayer in general, one to Jesus as interceding for all. There are also several instances in which Paul speaks of "blessing" people, like "those who persecute you" in Rom 12:14. These may be equivalent to prayers of petition. Again, in Phil. 2:27 there is reference to God's having mercy on an ill man. This suggests prayer by those with the gift of miracles (a gift Paul mentions), examples of which we see in other places in the New Testament.

160. The Spirit praying in the Christian seems to be seen as required by Paul not only for the acknowledgement of Jesus as Lord, but for any effective prayer, since it gives the right to say "Abba". This, with the notion that the Spirit actually directs the pray-er (see Rom. 8:26-27), recalls Paul's idea of the adoption as sons. That is in accord with the "Lord-servant" relationship already discussed (150), since it is another example of personal relationships between persons linked by ties of interest and love, but differently endowed. It recalls the Old Testament analogies of Israel as son and as spouse of Yahweh. All of these are different ways of expressing the link instituted by the covenant, and underline the fact that all Hebrew and Christian prayer is inextricably entwined with covenant, both inspired by it and looking to it as the reason for Divine assistance given or hoped for.

161. The nature of Paul's prayers for the Jewish nation ties in with our discussion of retribution (151-152). He prays that they may be saved —which implies that they be reconciled. As for the Christians, he prays that they may do no wrong. One might ask what happens if they *do* do wrong, but Paul's prayer as such does not indicate a response. He does show elsewhere that they can fail in faith (see Rom. 11:22), and suggests that there might be danger of being lost "in the day of Christ Jesus" (1 Cor. 5:5) due to immorality that is not rectified in time. No doubt one should pray for those in such danger, but Paul does not expressly speak of such prayer.

162. In terms of the discussion about power initiated in 147, what Paul prayed for for the Jews—what he prayed to maintain for the Christians—was the fundamental power of Spirit. And the secondary things were also manifestations of Spirit-power: gifts and blessings of several kinds. We have noted how the Spirit was operative in directing prayer. This is partly a matter of knowing how to pray (see Rom. 8:26-27), but the "Abba" text and that about acknowledging Jesus as Lord imply that the Spirit somehow brings man into relation with the "pressure" that we have spoken of God's putting on himself by virtue of his covenant promises. There is still power involved, and man's mental and vocal activity is related to the Divine giving of it. How? There are, I think, two non-magical logical possibilities for this relationship. 1) The human pray-er is seen as somehow *instrumenting* the Divine saving act in the sense that he is somehow supernaturalized entitatively and incorporates supernatural saving power. 2) The human pray-er is seen as simply *accompanying* the Divine salvific act. Texts like "Unless you confess..." suggest that this accompaniment would all the same be Divinely required. There would be question of man's natural powers (his mind, will, "lips" = physical body) acting as necessary conditions for salvation, even though not being supernaturalized.

163. This again might be seen as occurring in two ways. 1) By God's specially using the human faculties *as natural* instruments so as in fact to impel fulfilment of the condition. 2) By a normal free human compliance. In either case, a human faith would be distinguished from a divine, rather than being itself somehow divine. Note that here we do not distinguish faith and confession: faith "in your heart" involves faith in the human mind, which in turn necessarily involves a material element. Paul was certainly not thinking in terms of some mystical dualism whereby one could believe in his spirit without participating in his conscious human mind.

164. As for the secondary blessings, the same scheme seems to satisfy. For the question is not how great are the blessings, but how God's granting of them is engaged.

A Key Concept—"Referent of Actuality"

165. Whether there is instrumentation, or mere condition, or in some unexplainable manner something still less, the human factor does seem to be a Divine requirement in Paul's view of these things. On reflection, it is apparent that for the "mere condition" position (or the "still less" one, if there can be such—it would be a kind of Divine "un-necessitating" of what for the human level was stipulated), the function of the human act, if it is anything more than a mere psychological experience, is no more than to serve as the *referent of actuality for the Divine knowledge. Put simply: Paul would certainly not have said that God could have foreknowledge of the act if the act never actually occurred.* Much that happened on the Divine side was in its causes and manners ultimately for Paul a mystery; but God did know what went on in the world, and there had to be this relation of fact to knowledge at the very least. Or perhaps better, of knowledge to fact, with "knowledge" first; for I think Paul would have seen some kind of initiative for God even in this area of his knowledge of responsible human actions.

166. The point of the believing or the praying that expresses the belief, therefore, is simply to *do* it, thus providing factual referent for God's knowing that it is done, whether or not that provision strictly contributes to the knowing. In terms of power it might be put thus: God, to act creatively for man's blessing and protection, requires of men, by his own stipulation, that they provide a real created term parallel to his own knowledge, whether that term strictly "ground" the knowledge or not. The mystery for Paul would center in the "created", taken in conjunction with his likely practical assumption of human freedom of choice. But he would see no problem in the requirement as such.

167. Our expression of the situation, like most modern analyses of the kind, is not couched in specifically "Pauline" categories. But I think it does say in terms of explications the things Paul felt to be going on when he spoke in terms like "God", "prayer", "faith", "confession", etc. And in combination with the covenant-promise element, in which power is promised if such a referent is forthcoming, such factors provide a perfect grounding for the use of the figure of "reminding" God, or in sacramental terms, placing "memorials" "before him."

168. For anyone who held an "instrumental" view, this memorial one could simply be considered as a necessary aspect of it—the demonstration of the petitioner's free availability to God for use as instrument in the very act.

Purpose and Modes of Operation of Prayer and Liturgical Celebration

169. We have thus arrived at a number of logical possibilities for sacramental memorials that it will be helpful to list here in a single schema. I add a couple items that fall into place logically once the scheme is set out in outline form; and of course we reserve the right to change the setup as might later be indicated. We shall as we proceed develop further the significance of both the sacramental and the memorial elements; but what we are principally looking at here are the possible ways in which the human act is related to the results that might be forthcoming on its placement, as well as the general nature of those results in each instance.

170. The following schema, then, may be used for reference.

1. Looking to ontological effects directly produced by a supernatural power:
   a. Magical (including theurgy);
   b. Only a condition of the supernatural act:
      y. needed by man but in no sense for the supernatural being;
      z. also needed for the supernatural being's knowledge of its occurrence;
   c. Morally or otherwise *instrumental* of the supernatural effecting;
   d. Not needed by either man or supernatural being: neither instrumental nor conditional, merely conventional;
   e. A moral obligation self-imposed by the power. A "limited theurgy".
2. Looking to effects got by some material means, as in quackery or drug use.
3. Looking to psychic or parapsychic effects; i.e., got by forces natural to man but not at the material level or at least not normally perceived at that level: in the order of ESP or some kinds of mysticism.
4. Looking to effects got by knowing as such, as in Platonism or Gnosticism.
5. Looking to the physical and/or psychological experience of the liturgy as such, without artificial assists like drugs.

Clearly, combinations of some of these are possible. But we shall try to concentrate on the emphases that were probably intended in Paul and the contributors to his text. What were these?

The Probable Pauline Preference

171. As we shall see more in detail, both prayer of petition and sacramental celebrations in hellenistic times, and in Judaism as well as elsewhere, looked to what Fuchs calls "effective acts". (137). Paul is no exception when it comes to prayer, at least. And like the rest of the biblical writers, he looks to God as the power-source of the "effects". How did he see prayer and sacramental act to be related to God's production of the effect? I think that even at this stage of our enterprise it is clear that we ought to focus on at least no. 1.b.z. of our schema.

172. The Jewish tradition of sacramentalism centered about the Temple system of offerings, and the "effective" offerings looked to just the sort of things Paul's prayer looks to: escape from the toils of sin and its effects, protection, gifts and blessings of various sorts. The terminology attached to the different kinds of offerings: "peace", "thanksgiving", "free-will", etc., often obscures the fact that petitionary intentions of suitable kinds were attached to the offering of them. And indeed, many examples of biblical and other religious literature—we shall see some of the more "memorial" ones as we go on—show the close nexus between Temple, offering, and prayer of petition. The prayer was often vocal— Hannah's voiceless vow at Shiloh was seen as exceptional. But voiced or not, prayer was often there, expressing the intentions behind offering or otherwise associated with offering or at least with the sanctity of the shrine. Hannah prayed: "O Lord of hosts, if thou wilt indeed look on the affliction of thy maid-servant, and remember me, and not forget... but wilt give... a son...." (1 Sam. 1:11). Joseph Dan remarks: "Although the Pentateuch does not mention any prayers which accompanied the sacrifices, liturgical additions were made during the second Temple period. These included petitions, blessings, and readings...." [20] Joseph Heinemann says, "We have sources from the days of the Temple itself which clearly indicate that the worshippers were scrupulous to recite their prayers at just those hours when the daily sacrifices were being offered up...." [21] Hertz calls our attention to the fact that "the Temple was conceived as a House of Prayer for all Nations. At the Dedication... Solomon prayed: 'Moreover concerning the stranger... when he shall... pray toward this house; hear Thou in heaven....' (1 Kings 8:41-43)." [22] Matthew 21:13 shows Jesus zealously defending this characteristic of the Temple, and throughout the New Testament there are various examples of the association of prayer with the Temple. Paul adopts the "offering" kind of thinking in connection with works of charity, which he sees as a "fragrant offering, a sacrifice acceptable and pleasing to God," in relation to which "God will supply every need of yours according to his riches in glory in Christ Jesus." (Phil. 4:18, 19). "The point is this: he who sows sparingly will also reap sparingly.... God loves a cheerful giver." (2 Cor. 9:6, 7). The "in Christ Jesus" is put in sacramental terms when Paul speaks of Christ as the sacrificed

---

[20] *Encyclopaedia Judaica*, 16 vols. (New York: Macmillan, 1972), s.v. "Sacrifice", second section, by Joseph Dan, p. 608.

[21] Joseph Heinemann, *Prayer in the Talmud* (New York: Walter de Gruyter, 1977), p. 15.

[22] Hertz, p. 33.

paschal lamb (1 Cor. 5:7). The blood of the lamb brought protection to the sons of Israel. And the Church, of course, is the "Israel of God." (Gal. 6:16). In all this there is no indication of the precise relationship of the effect to the spiritual offering or prayer, except that God knows of the later and is the giver of the former. But this, once more, is something to help us focus our attention, and suggests at least our no. l.b.z. (of the schema in 170).

173. Is there anything further to be said at this stage as to the possibility of Paul's having a magical or theurgical approach to the gaining of protection and blessings? Certainly there is no plain expression of magical terminology, and no expression that cannot be read in terms of condition. (See 170, l.b.). There are several passages in Paul that reveal his belief in a world of created spirits. The pagans for their part effectively offered to demons according to Paul (see 1 Cor. 10:20), but these presumably evil spirits were not at God's level: "The earth is the Lord's, and all it contains." (10:26). Paul will have nothing to do with them; but the truth is we have no indication that he looked for blessings or even for favorable intercession to any *good* spirits he might have presumed to exist, other than "the Spirit". We shall study more at length the questions of Christ's act on Calvary and of his intercessory action after the resurrection. The latter may involve a kind of "parallel" heavenly liturgy—such is pictured by a number of Jewish writings. Additionally, it was probably a main element in a typical Jewish "heavenly judgement scene" such as that so well described by George Nickelsburg.[23] Christ acts the part of advocate, pointing to the efficacy of his death.

Summary of the Main Arguments of Chapter IV

174. The central note of sacramentalism and associated concepts, as shown by general usage of the related terms, seems to be the material signing of some spiritual reality. If "timelessness" is associated with it, that is accidental to this core meaning; so too the idea of magic. The association of magic with sacramentalism is undoubtedly due to the fact that sacramentalism itself has traditionally been related to attempts to enlist supernatural power on behalf of those placing the sacramental signs. In the Bible, the practical way of doing this is by directing the sacramental actions and accompanying prayers towards God, often with the invocation of his promises, with a view to his giving effective, real help, with or without reference to created salvific events previously engineered by God to achieve salvation. In line with the definition above, sacrament can serve here as a material sign accompanying such intent and prayer, as

---

[23] See, for example, George W. E. Nickelsburg, Jr., *Resurrection, Immortality, and Eternal Life in Intertestamental Judaism* (Cambridge, Mass.: Harvard Univ. Press, 1972), pp. 39-42; 114-122.

well as a sign suitable to the reception of the prayed-for effects. Gesture, ritual, and indeed even vocal expression can be understood in this way and very probably were so understood by their more enlightened users throughout later biblical times.

175. The concept of signed prayer suggests that it was God himself who was seen as the link between the created salvific events and any effects they were presumed to have had in later times or other places. That is, such events were supernaturalized by being known by him in some transcendent way and by being related *through* him to the external effects. (An example of this would be the "Therefore God raised him up" of Phil. 2: see 84, 130.) In such a view, all the created acts would be for God "referents of actuality", and the main burden of explaining his relation to the acts itself placed on his transcendence. With God as direct agent there is no need of theories like Casel's "objective memorial", and notions like that of cult as a means of overcoming the temporal gap between past salvific events and the now-present become open to question. Further, theurgy is put out of the question by the reduction of the created acts to the status of Divinely foreknown and required referents, as well as by the recognition that for Paul at least the created acts themselves are empowered by the Spirit and so made suitable for inclusion as such referents in the transcendent causality.

176. The ontology of this relationship was too difficult to be expressed in the everyday approach to God, and more familiar and familial concepts and modes of expression were used, drawn from human situations that were analogous to the relationship with God. So God was asked for things, thanked for things, and the concepts were expressed by word, gesture and ritual. So Paul "prays". He prays for both general and specific blessings of salvation. And he invokes Christ's salvific power as somehow involved in the granting by God of these blessings.

Transition from Part II

177. A brief survey of the material covered in Part II can be made by referring to the summaries at the end of each chapter, namely, in paragraphs 70 and 71, 90 and 91, 131, 174. The relationship of the first three chapters to each other is stated in 132. In 71 the reference in our text to a past salvific event is noted; Chapter IV introduces the idea of such events as instrumental of salvation for later times, while the notion of prayer suggests that God might be reminded not only of the needs of the people but also of that event as a source of blessings operating through God in the manner described. In terms of memorial the first three chapters are mainly concerned with reminding-man. Reminding God of past promises (as of covenant promises) and past salvific events is superimposed upon the reminding-man scheme, and would be very unlikely if not impossible without it.

178. Some aspects of the relationship of the various Parts to one another are noted in 4-7. We should now have some grasp of the problem, the thesis, and the main positions scholars have taken, plus some ideas of various things to look for in the survey of materials available to Paul that will now follow. Was memorial terminology used in them? If so, how frequent, how well distributed was it? Did it include reminding-God? If so, how frequent and well distributed was that? Were the senses of identity, of history, of the importance of past salvific events, of God's promise, well developed? How did these things relate to memorial concept and terminology? At the end of each chapter we shall point out some of the answers that the material surveyed in the chapter seems to provide.

Part III: **THE MATERIAL AVAILABLE TO PAUL**

Chapter I: **The Old Testament Materials**

Introduction to Part III

179. In para. 28 we remarked that familiarity with the materials available to Paul was a prerequisite for making a really well-founded judgement on the meaning for Paul and his readers of the Eucharistic tradition as presented in our text. The fact is that most readers will not be all that familiar with the materials insofar as they bear on our question. Memorial thinking was never a special theological focus of the writers of these works, and even if the reader should be quite familiar with the works as wholes and with certain other aspects of them, the nature and extent of memorial thinking and terminology may never have come to his attention. As for its being *brought* to his attention by modern scholars, Childs and Willy Schottroff have done service here for the Old Testament materials, and Jeremias in a spotty way for some of the inter-testamental ones. But Childs' particular theological interests, which we will discuss in Part V, could distract some readers from the positive findings he makes in regard to reminding-God; further, his work is limited in size so that although he gives appropriate examples, the full scope and force of the memorial content is not brought home to the general reader. Schottroff is more effective in this regard; unfortunately, his work is not available in English. Additionally, both these authors leave out, or on the fringes of their considerations, certain factors, texts or parts of texts that have a bearing on our own. Finally, both Childs and Schottroff use the Hebrew text. We shall take as our text the LXX, which is more likely than the Hebrew to have been influential with the authors of the Greek-language texts of New Testament times. Not that the Hebrew influence would have been much different—in spite of using the Hebrew text Childs' and Schottroff's exegetical findings are in general outline about the same as those we will arrive at using the Greek. But that very fact needs to be shown, and the use of the Greek text will show it.

180. As for the apocryphal and pseudepigraphal materials (in our use of these terms and nomenclature for the materials in question, we will follow R. H. Charles' *The Apocrypha and Pseudepigrapha of the Old Testament in English*), a fuller study is absolutely necessary because of their influence on and chronological proximity to the New Testament scene. Then we must examine the relationship of Greek, gnostic, and other special types of conceptuality (above we were concerned with Greek *language*) to memorial thinking; and although we shall not have space in these areas to show the same proportion of texts as for the other materials, enough will be seen to ground solid judgements on that relationship.

Brevard Childs

181. We may briefly review Childs' and Schottroff's exegetical work. This will be useful for purposes of comparison with our own viewing of the Old Testament materials. Additionally, Childs in particular makes certain interpretative comments on his findings, comments in respect of "spiritualization" of the cult, that bear on his ultimate theological conclusions. For our purposes, something can and should be added to his observations.

182. In 1964 Childs wrote *Memory and Tradition in Israel*, the work that presents his findings on and thought about *zkr*. It was an effort to determine the place of that root in Hebrew religious language and conceptuality, particularly its relationship with cult in the contemporizing or "actualizing" of the ancient texts and traditions.[1] Childs has separate chapters devoted to "Israel Remembers" and "God Remembers".[2]

183. Of the *qal* of *zkr*, Childs says it means simply to remember. The hiphil has two circles of meaning, cultic and juridical. In the cult the form is often related to "name".[3] The verb is used once in the sense of "to make a memorial offering"—a late cultic usage.[4] In the juridical sense "to cause to remember sin" is notable.

184. Of *zkr* with *lĕ* he says it is used only in relation to God's memory.[5] He says of God's remembering that the verb uses two forms: the imperative or jussive in complaint psalms ("Remember us" or "Do not remember our sins"), and the finite form in hymns. He remarks several times that in the complaint psalms the plea is based on the covenant.[6] Of "Israel remembers" he says, "The great acts of the tradition are not removed in past time, but recharged with energy they again become a present event"[7] —a statement that moves towards theological interpretation; we shall discuss the idea again in Chapter V. He provides a basis for locating a legitimate source of that energy, however, when he adds, "Israel encounters

---

[1] See Brevard S. Childs, *Memory and Tradition in Israel* (London: SCM Press, 1962), p. 6.
[2] Childs, *Memory*, pp. 45ff and 31ff respectively.
[3] See ibid., p. 12.
[4] See ibid., p. 14.
[5] See ibid., p. 32.
[6] See ibid., pp. 35, 36.
[7] Ibid., p. 63.

again through memory the God of the past." [8]   In his "study of the nouns"
he distinguishes two meanings: a) the thing itself, "memorandum", passive
use; b) a thing calling something else to remembrance, namely the salvific
acts of the past—the thing being the cultic object or rite.   Such things
shared the purpose of the complaint type of plea for God to remember,
as the hymns of praise praised his remembering.   "His remembering then
issued in his intervention of Israel's behalf based on his previous commitment to Israel." [9]   Of the word *zēkher* he says that it is used in both
late and early writings, sometimes synonymously with *šēm*, but often with
the denotation of the act of uterance as distinct from the result of the
act—the name itself (*šēm*).   In Exod. 3:15 Yahweh "reveals his essence to
Moses in his eternal name (*šĕmî lĕ ʿôlām*), while the cultic pronunciation
of the name throughout the generations is his *zēkher*." [10]   He says elsewhere
that Yahwism tried to stop the "magical use of the name within the
cult." [11]

185. All this material is accurate and useful.   Childs makes other
useful comments too.   He discusses [12] the thesis of Pedersen,[13] who argued
that the Israelites thought in a "primitive" manner that could not
distinguish thought from action, and shows that in fact, though Israel's
use of the word "remember" more often looked specifically to action than
did the hellenic use, there was no basic difference in attitude between
Greek and Hebrew in this regard: a psychological aspect was at least
implicitly distinct from the active response.[14]   The Hebrews did not think
pre-logically, merely concretely.   They saw God's memory concretely too.
"Whatever God remembers always implies his movement towards the
object of his memory." [15]   But also, "the memory is not identical with the
action, but is never divorced from it." [16]   Since Childs notes instances in
which *human* memory *is* divorced from action, this is significant of the
fact that in their prayer and cult the Israelites always looked to an effect
from God.   An effect, since God's interventions were nothing unless they
took effect somehow at the created level.

"Reinterpretation of the Cult"

186. Childs admits that the cult remained important in later Israel,
and cites von Rad to this effect.[17]   He says, however, that the Deuteronomist

---

[8] Ibid., pp. 64-65.
[9] Ibid., p. 74.
[10] Ibid., p. 71.
[11] Ibid., p. 12.
[12] See ibid., pp. 20ff.
[13] See Johs. Pedersen, *Israel*, 2 vols. (London: Oxford, 1926), vol. 1, pp. 99ff.
[14] See Childs, *Memory*, p. 28.
[15] Ibid., p. 33.
[16] Ibid.
[17] See ibid., p. 77.

"radically reinterpreted the cult." [18]   "The emphasis of the liturgy shifts
from concern with ritual minutiae to centre in a joyous expression of
thankfulness for Yahweh's benefits which are attributed solely to his
election love." [19]   If it were a question of a change from nothing but
"minutiae" to pure thanksgiving, or even pure petitionary prayer and
offering, there would indeed be a "radical" reinterpretation.   But none
of these descriptions is nearly adequate for the time it purports to deal
with.   The concern with "minutiae" was certainly present in earlier times,
but it was also undoubtedly present in the actual cult right through to
Christian ones.   On the other hand, there were also present earlier the
elements of praise and thanksgiving.   And later, the element of plea for
Divine assistance—which from its exclusion in Childs' statement might
be thought to be somehow as unworthy of reinterpreted cult as are ritual
minutiae.   We have seen that Paul did not think it unworthy of inclusion
in prayer.

187. We shall discuss others of Childs' views in Part V.   Here let
us reflect further on the suggestion that the early emphasis was on "ritual
minutiae".   Whatever the misty origins of ritual, it is clear that for the
majority of the biblical writers about the early cult, the core of the matter
could be summed up in phrases like "calling on the name of the Lord."
God was looked to and addressed in order to obtain a response, and the
association of such elements with the cultic objects and rituals strongly
suggests that these latter were interpreted as signal of the same sentiments.   The whole process, from this aspect, falls readily under the rubric
"reminding-God".

188. The use of the phrase "calling upon the name of the Lord" is
typical of a type of memorial thinking that was probably "reinterpreted"
from magical or mystical meanings long before the time of the Deuteronomist; it remains in its purified form in the Pauline letters.   In 1 Cor. 1:2
or Rom. 10:13 the phrase means nothing else than to speak to God of
the salvation he has promised through Jesus the Savior—however God
may consider Jesus to have done the saving.   It is a question of blessings:
"The same Lord is Lord of all and bestows his riches upon all who call
upon him." (Rom. 10:12).   The "name" as so often is the sign of the person
and his particular character, and he must be addressed, "named", to
engage his attention and consequently his interest and power.   There is
symbolism here, but nothing necessarily magical—we do this kind of
thing every day at the purely human level.   The analogy of treatment of
humans is carried over to the treatment of God, presumably by his own
wish.   For the first things he creates in Genesis he immediately names,
and he passes on the aptitude for naming to man himself after naming

---

[18] Ibid.
[19] Ibid., p. 78.

him (Gen. 5:2). Subsequently, somehow, he reveals his own name. (Gen. 4:25). Elijah's use of the name Yahweh is a typically prayerful use, engaged in after the priests of Baal had vainly called upon the names of their god all day long. We get a classic picture of the custom of sacrifice and its association with prayer here. "They took the bull and prepared it and called on the name of Baal from morning until noon, saying 'O Baal, answer us!' But there was no voice, and no one answered." (1 Kgs 18:26). Elijah taunts them: "Cry aloud, for he is a god." That is, if he is any kind of god he ought to be able to hear and respond. Then at the time of the "offering of the oblation" (probably a plug for the regular liturgy here by the editor) Elijah prepares the altar of the Lord and calls on *his* name, mentioning also other names for whom God has previously done wonderful things: "O Lord, God of Abraham, Isaac, and Israel, let it be known this day that thou art God in Israel, and that I am thy servant.... Answer me, O Lord, answer me." (18:36-37). The oblation is joined to prayer in the context of covenant memory, and God answers because he does remember and because the caller proclaims himself to be and *is* the servant. The general thinking no doubt was that when a devotee called a god should hear. But *Yahweh* would act not because of some magical force in the oblation or the prayer, but because an occasion was ipso facto presented before him that fit with his covenant promises to his faithful servants. It is not sufficiently emphasized, often, that cult is presented in the Pentateuch as commanded and specified by the Lord. He was seen as having founded the system with its feasts, sabbaths, and oblations, in order to provide himself with occasions for showing his covenant benevolence by granting blessings in response to his people's prayers and offerings. And again (see 165), it was no magical power in these that prompted his action, but his own wish that the people treat him as Lord of all and their own God, providing him with what we have called a "referent of actuality" for his responses.

189. Clearly, an arrangement like this is open to over-emphasis on minutiae, since it can be wrongly seen merely as something commanded, without much attempt to understand *why* it has been commanded; with the result that the best performance might seem to be the one that paid most attention to detail. What we may call "spiritualization" of the cult, as distinct from attempts to abolish or radically reinterpret it, concentrated on increasing the element of understanding of the reasons why God had instituted it. That he *had* instituted it was as time went on taken more and more as a given fact. It was, after all, thus written in the books that themselves came to be more and more accepted, and was an accepted part of the tradition and of daily life. In his day Philo accepted it, Josephus did, Paul did, Matthew did. Such an attitude made the spiritualization of the cult a high priority for sincere Hebrews as well as for the best theologians (sincere too, no doubt). They do not seem to have seriously doubted whether the practice of oblation was a suitable one for spiritualization, for that would have questioned the wisdom of the Divine institutor of it. Probably they felt that the sacrifices were symbolic of the best that men could offer, since blood was a sign of life (see Gen. 9:4) and life was the very summation of all that was good and desirable in man; that oblation of *any* kind was a suitable means of expressing man's acknowledgement of God's lordship. But the main emphasis in spiritualization was not on the suitability of what we have previously termed "sacramentalism", it was on the simple necessity of *relating the externals to real internal religious intentionality in the best sense of the word "religious", so that the externals truly served as symbols of fitting ideas and intentions.* Philo gives us a classic example of the balanced view of the cult, an example particularly valuable because he himself might be thought to be susceptible to the sort of thinking he is criticizing.

> There are some who, regarding laws in their literal sense in the light of symbols of matters belonging to the intellect, are overpunctilious about the latter, while treating the former with easy-going neglect ... as though they had become disembodied souls, and knew neither city nor village nor household nor any company of human beings at all, overlooking all that the mass of men regard. ... These men are taught by the sacred word to ... let go nothing that is part of the customs fixed by divinely empowered men greater than those of our time. (De Mig., 91).[20]

This is reminiscent of our own reflections, in the context of time and history, on the importance of cult to the ancients, and the necessity for man to be "physically demonstrative". (126). Philo, in typical hellenistic style, puts his emphasis on what men think about such behavior—on good repute—but it would be frivolous of us to miss what he accepts as a given fact: that what men think in this matter is based on valid expectations of how *embodied* souls should deport themselves.

190. Philo continues with specific references to the ritual laws:

> It is quite true that the Seventh Day is meant to teach the power of the Unoriginate. ... But let us not for this reason abrogate the laws laid down for its observance. ... It is true also that the Feast is a symbol ... but we should not for this reason turn our backs on the general gatherings of the year's seasons. ... It is true that ... circumcision does indeed portray the excision of pleasure and all passions ... but let us not on this account repeal the law ... for circumcising. Why, we shall be ignoring the sanctity of the Temple and a thousand other things, if we are going to pay heed to nothing except what is shewn us by the inner meanings of things. (De Mig. 91-92).

---

[20] Quotations from Philo are taken from the Loeb Classical Library (London: Wm. Heinemann; Cambridge, Mass.: Harvard Univ. Press), and titled from the Latin.

His conclusion is undoubtedly that of most thoughtful first-century men and women: "If we keep and observe [the letter of the laws]... we shall gain a clearer conception of those things of which these are the symbols." (De Mig. 92).

191. As for the symbolism, he speaks in a not unprophetic mode when he says,

> If the worshipper is without kindly feeling or justice, the sacrifices are no sacrifices, the consecrated oblation is desecrated, the prayers are words of ill omen. ... For, when to outward appearance they are offered, it is not a remission but a reminder of past sins which they effect. But, if he is pure of heart and just, the sacrifice stands firm. ... The thank-offering of such a soul receives immortality. (De Moise II, 107-108).[21]

The Prophets

192. This statement, as the reference to prophets suggests, is one way of interpreting the cultic references made by the prophets. The intent of some prophetic statements about cult is still debated. We make the point here that there has long been a possibility of interpreting even the harsher statements in a sense that still leaves a central place for cult in the religious picture, whether of Judaism or of Christianity. If such interpretations were common in Paul's time, it could mean that whatever the intent of the prophets themselves, a fairly common compromise had been reached between polar positions, by means of a "spiritualized" view of cult such as was described above. Various scholars, especially Jewish and Roman Catholic ones, have argued that the prophets themselves practically meant such a compromise, but that their basic acceptance of cult was lost sight of, due perhaps in part to their hyperbolic manner of speech under the stress of the tense situations in which they spoke. The arguments used by these modern scholars are undoubtedly the same kind that would have been used by first century and earlier "spiritualizers". The view is well summed up in a negative way by the proverb, "The sacrifices of the ungodly are abomination to the Lord, for they offer them wickedly." (Prov. 21:27—LXX). In a word, the remarks about cult would be like the remarks candidates for office in a democratic system make about opponent incumbents. They do not want to get rid of the system, only its corruptions. Hertz states that "it is only against the immoral

---

[21] Notable here, in addition to the point we are making, is the close association of prayer and oblation: the first assumes the second. This same thing appears in Josephus' description of Solomon's installation of the ark in the Temple. Solomon prays: "I have built this temple, and thy name, that from thence, when we sacrifice, and perform sacred operations, we may send our prayers up into the air ... especially thou art present to those that address themselves to thee ..." (Antiq. 8,4-2). Quotations from Josephus are taken from William Whiston, *The Complete Works of Flavius Josephus* (Philadelphia: John E. Potter, n.d.).

conception of sacrifice, and not against sacrifice itself, that [the prophets]... waged... war." [22]   And Anson Rainey:

> It has ... been assumed by many scholars that the prophets condemned all sacrificial rituals. De Vaux has shown the absurdity of such a conclusion since Isaiah 1:15 also condemns prayer. No one holds that the prophets rejected prayer; it was prayer offered without the proper moral commitment that was being denounced; the same holds true for the oracles against formal rituals. Similar allusions in the Psalms which might be taken as a complete rejection of sacrifice ... actually express the same concern for inner attitudes as the prophets.[23]

He also notes that "The wisdom literature sometimes reflects the same concern for moral and ethical values over empty sacerdotal acts. (Prov. 15:8; 31:3,27)." [24]   And, "De Vaux has noted that Jeremiah clearly knew Deut. 12:6-14 and regarded it as the Law of Moses.... The inner attitude was prerequisite to any valid ritual expression. (Isa. 29:13)." [25]

193. Matthew shows Jesus echoing this view when quoting Hosea 6:6 (Matt. 9:13). A brief look at the circumstances and content of Hosea's references to the sacrificial cult may be helpful. He was concerned principally with the northern kingdom and the non-Temple cult. "I will punish her for the feast days of the Ba'als when she burned incense to them... and forgot me, says the Lord." (2:13). "For the children of Israel shall dwell many days without king or prince, without sacrifice or pillar, without ephod or teraphim. Afterward [they]... shall return...." (3:3-5). "They sacrifice on the tops of the mountains, and make offerings upon the hills...." (4:13). "The men... go aside with harlots, and sacrifice with cult prostitutes...." (4:14). "Ephraim is joined to idols... and they shall be ashamed because of their altars." (4:17,19). "Because Ephraim has multiplied altars for sinning, they have become to him altars for sinning.... They love sacrifice but the Lord has no delight in them. Now he will remember their iniquity, and punish their sins; they shall return to Egypt." (8:11,13). From Hosea's wider context it is apparent that Israel's failure to practice God's own cult, and to practice it correctly, are simply one aspect of her failure to heed God's *law*. God's displeasure at this failure will result in her being exiled and placed in a position where none of the accustomed cult practices will be feasible. "They shall not pour libations of wine to the Lord; and they shall not please him with their sacrifices. Their bread shall be like mourners' bread... it shall not come to the house of the Lord. What will you do on the day of appointed festival.... behold, they are going to Assyria; Egypt shall gather them...." (9:4-5). The unlawful altars will be broken down, but there is no mention of breaking down

---

[22] Hertz, pp. 34-35.
[23] *Judaica*, vol. 14, s.v. "Sacrifice," 1st section, by Anson Rainey, p. 604.
[24] Ibid.
[25] Ibid.

the altars of the faithful Judah (cf. 11:12). Objection is made to "hatred in the house of his God" (9:8), not to the house of God itself. The implication is that Judah will continue to "please him with their sacrifices", and that when Israel returns from exile—or hopefully, when she repents and so removes the need for exile—she too will "go to the altar of God."

194. We see the same kind of reaction in Deuteronomy. "Every abominable thing which the Lord hates they have done for their gods; for they even burn their sons and their daughters in the fire to their gods." (Deut. 12:31).

195. Ideas about God, man and the world had to be the basic elements in any Hebraic spiritualization of the cult. Ideas about cult necessarily changed somewhat when Yahweh was recognized as the supreme divinity, as transcendent, as not only personal but as concerned about the world he had made by the exercise of his unique power. They changed, too, when both men and women were seen to be capable of treating with God as persons to a person, with the prospect of dealing with him on familiar terms as did Adam, Abraham, the patriarchs and Moses. And when God was heard to address Israel not only as subject but as servant, as child, as spouse. It is within this context that with the cult "the analogy of treatment of humans is carried over to the treatment of God... by his own wish" (188) and occasions "presented before him that fit with his covenant promises to his faithful servants." (Ibid.). Yahweh did not eat the flesh of the sacrifices, or need them in any way, but he was pleased to accept the gifts that were offered him when they were given with the sentiments that human servants used to their masters, children to their parents, wives to their husbands. To use a homely metaphor, the husband and father may not need the neckties he gets for his birthday, but he would regret not getting them, all the same. The sacramental system not only fit human psychology, it was necessary for it—at least for these relatively simple people. This was Philo's insight. By now it way seem somewhat trite, but trite things were once new and if once true may always remain so. It is, I think, a real danger of scholarly sophistication that in disdaining to mention the obvious it can eventually lose sight of it even when it is a key factor in argument. (Cf. 130 *ad finem*).

Sacramentalism in a Spiritualized Cult

196. The "minutiae" that Childs speaks of were in the event usually concerned with times and places and things—material considerations, all. Is there in his view an implicit derogation of the function of these things in cult? If the answer is "Yes", there are answering arguments. We have already spoken several times of the importance of things and places in Israel's relationships with God—there is a parallel with the emphasis placed on events in past times. The metaphor of a familial interchange of gifts suggests that the cultic association of prayer with material objects and actions is as natural and necessary in dealing with God as that of speech with gift-giving at the merely human level. If this is so, the place of such an association in a spiritualized cult is located in principle. The material things do not *deny* the spiritual: they accompany it, express and manifest it. "Spiritualization" is not a reduction of the worshipper to an angelic, "purely spiritual" state, but is relative. ensuring that matter does not come to *dominate* spirit whether magically or in the psychology of the worshipper. It is to be kept in its place, but it is to be kept, for it is as needful for human worship as man's body is for human being.

197. We have already seen several examples in which the association in question is explicitly mentioned. There are many others, and still more examples in which the prayer is simply stated in conjunction with the statement about the act. "So Jacob... took the stone... and poured oil on the top of it.... Then Jacob made a vow, saying, 'if [you,] God will be with me... then the Lord shall be my God, and this stone... God's house; and of all that thou givest me I will give the tenth to thee.'" (Gen. 28:18-22). The prayer in this case, chosen at random, is a typical mixture of reverence, esteem, flattery, and admission of need. It is not magical but it presumes on privilege freely given by God; in a word, presumes on covenant. (See 28:13ff). It has dignity. The notion of the stone as a house is a very human touch. God, who gives the land, is invited to reside in it something like a generous uncle staying with his beneficiaries. A meaning is attached to the cult object, distinguishing it from a mere fetish. Yet, the stone does not become an idol, as though mystically identified with the divinity. Nor is God thought to be *limited* to some presence in and around the stone, even though his presence *is* assumed. Rather, the stone is significant to the pray-er and gift-giver of dealings with God—it is a "holy" place. The material human situation, which *is* limited, makes such places helpful. God promises to bless their use. R. E. Clements, arguing that "the Divine presence is the basic presupposition of the cult,"[26] cites Exod. 20:14, which shows God establishing the cult and blessing its performance: "An altar... you shall make for me and sacrifice on it... in every place where I cause my name to be remembered I will come to you and bless you." This aspect of Divine presence—God's "being in" or "coming to" a place—was for the Hebrews a kind of "familiarization" of dealings with God, whereby he took into consideration man's limitations; it can be called "spiritual" only in its basic assumptions of God's concern and man's ability to have such dealings at all. But this aspect of the Presence was not *meant* to *be* spiritual, it was

---

[26] R. E. Clements, "The Meaning of Ritual Acts in Israelite Religion," in *Eucharistic Theology Then and Now*, ed. not named (London: S. P. C. K., 1968), p. 5.

meant to *attract* the spiritual. It recognized *signs* (material things) of God. The Temple pointed to God; it had to be assumed that the God it pointed to was some *kind* of being. *What* kind? It was forever necessary to struggle to *remember* what kind. But human nature being what it is, without the pointing the struggle might never have arisen at all—God might not have remained for long within the Israelites' ken. Thus, while it kept the idea of God before the minds of the people, the sacramental system also introduced a tension of paradox. "Spiritualization" was forever needed. In terms of presence, the sacramental view of place had continually to lead into the still more basic view of God as essentially unlimited to particular places. Confusing the issue is the fact that the very expression of this acknowledgement was put in terms that suggested place. While God was seen as present here or there, he was also and simultaneously present in a transcendent kind of place, "heaven". But at least transcendence was admitted. Josephus tries in typically Hebraic manner to express the paradox when he says, in a text we have already referred to in a note, "that from thence, when we sacrifice... we may send our prayers up into the air... especially thou art present to those that address themselves to thee." (Antiq. 8,4,2). The attitudes of the pray-ers, the symbolisms of the ascending smoke and incense, elements of prayer and cult-language, and other factors, indicate that for most Israelite devotees, or at least writers, the Temple and the altar were seen as a kind of focus (and focus within a focus) of the Divine attention; i.e., of God's knowledge and benevolence. Clements notes that the expression "see the face" of God [27] was spiritualized to expressions like "appear before", which emphasized God's seeing man but man's inability to see God, except by faith. Samuel Terrien says, "Israel knew that her God was both present and elusive whenever she performed her ceremonial of adoration." [28] This knowledge was "multi-dimensional", [29] and this was particularly true of the Christian view of Divine presence. But it by no means excluded at the human end the function of things and places. As Terrien says of Amos, in a context of spiritualization, "Nevertheless, Zion remained important, for it was the place—the geographical location—in which God would raise the new community of the faithful." [30]

198. We said that prayer was as naturally associated with cultic acts as human speech is with gift-giving. Conversely, cultic acts were to prayer as formal gesture is to speech. Prayer was of course offered independently of oblation as well as with it, and it was even then normally accompanied by gesture. This fit with the thinking that the relationship with God

---

[27] See Clements, note 9, p. 6.
[28] Samuel Terrien, *The Elusive Presence* (San Francisco: Harper and Row, 1978), p. 4.
[29] Terrien, p. 466.
[30] Ibid., p. 204

should be expressed in a fully human way. But the unique position of Yahweh made the conventional forms of dealing with the gods not less but more obligatory in dealing with him. Oblation was universally accepted as a mode of encounter used in treating with the gods. It was not always possible on the grand scale that befitted divine dignity, but when possible it was used. One raised one's eyes and hands to heaven whenever one prayed, but one also raised the savor of incense, the smoke of sacrifice, the blast of trumpet, when one could afford them. (The trumpet was the magnified and formalized version of the "voice raised loud in prayer".) As for God's attitude towards oblation and other cultic acts, his stipulations that they be performed suggest that they were for him, like prayer, "referents of actuality".

The Oblation as a Manifest of Intentionality and of Prayer

199. The very names given to the types of oblation indicate the inevitability of associating prayer with oblation. Prayer was offered in praise and thanksgiving, for forgiveness, for blessings. There were "peace" offerings and "sin" offerings and "thank" offerings—the latter, as Rainey remarks, being "the most frequently mentioned type of peace offering." [31] Hertz describes some of the symbolism involved.

> The *burnt-offering* expressed the individual's homage to God and entire self-surrender to His will; the *peace-offering*, gratitude to God for his bounties and mercies; the *sin-offering*, sorrow at having erred from the way of God and the firm resolve to be reconciled with Him. The *congregational sacrifices*, furthermore, taught the vital lesson of the interdependence of all members of the congregation as a sacred Brotherhood. [32]

Perhaps the most clearly religious meanings attach to the sacrifices offered for the public good. Sin offerings often had a social aspect, and so did the peace offering, which Rainey, using the term "communal" in a somewhat restricted way, says "is the basic sacrifice of all communal offerings; the others [this does not include sin offerings] are simply different types of peace offerings." [33] He presently adds,

> The peace offering was only specified [there is an emphasis on the latter word in Rainey's mind, as the following will show] in three instances; i.e., in the celebration of Shavuot ... in the ritual for completion of a Nazirite vow ... and at the installation of the priesthood. ... Other public ... National events that called forth the peace offering were: successful conclusion of a military campaign ... cessation of famine or pestilence ... acclamation of a candidate for kingship ... or a time of national spiritual renewal. ... At the local level they were sacrificed for the annual family

---

[31] Rainey, p. 604.
[32] Hertz, p. 33. See also *Judaica*, vol. 10, s.v. "Kipper," by Jacob Milgrom.
[33] Rainey, p. 604.

reunion ... and other festive events such as the harvestry of the first fruits.[34]

(The relation between *spiritual* renewal and sacrifice is of course noteworthy.) Obviously it is eminently rational and religious to distinguish the nature and circumstances of the offerings in accord with the purposes for which they were offered, and as noted, inevitable that once the distinctions had been made, prayer for the same intentions would be offered as a matter of course. Such an association was expressed in the confession that Adolph Büchler demonstrates to have accompanied the placing of hands on the victim for the sin offering: [35] "The undisputed main part of the definite statement of R. Yosé the Galilean not only describes the procedure at the first and personal part of the sacrifice, but also shows that the offerer of it had to confess his sin over the animal dedicated for the special purpose named." [36] He adds that certain circumstances suggest "the offerer was already at this stage asked about, and had to inform the priest, of the object and the general character of his intended sacrifice, whether it was to be a peace- or a thanksgiving- or a freewill-offering or an atoning sacrifice." [37]

200. We have already noted how Paul associates prayer of petition with that of thanksgiving, and how such prayers were explicit at second Temple services and earlier. (159, 172). An early reference to such an association is Genesis 8:28, where Pharaoh tells Moses, "I will let you go, to sacrifice... in the wilderness.... Make entreaty for me." A late one, 2 Maccabees 1:23ff: "And while the sacrifice was being consumed, the priests offered prayer.... O Lord... accept this sacrifice on behalf of all thy people Israel and preserve thy portion and make it holy." Petitionary intent is often obvious from the circumstances of the offering or the statement of the consequences if it be not offered. "Let us go, we pray... into the wilderness, and sacrifice to the Lord our God, lest he fall upon us...." (Gen. 5:3). Petitionary intent was undoubtedly present in many of the psalms of praise and thanksgiving that were used on cultic occasions, by way of flattery and anticipation of further blessings. It is important to stress this association because descriptions like those of Hertz (199), while useful for showing the generosity that could be brought to the cult, might give the impression that the Hebrews thought there was something wrong about looking to God for, and asking for, blessings. This was the last

---

[34] Ibid.

[35] See ibid., p. 600: "The offerer executed the symbolic act of laying his hand on the offering (Lev. 4:4 and passim), thus identifying it with himself." This has particular reference to sin-offerings. But he says presently of peace-offerings, "The presentation and laying on of the hand were the same as for other offerings ... " (p. 604).

[36] Adolph Büchler, *Studies in Sin and Atonement* (New York: Ktav Pub. House, 1967), p. 417.

[37] Ibid.

thing an Israelite would have thought of. And in this at least, Paul was a true Israelite (as well as a typical representative of his age). In the context of covenant it could hardly be otherwise. By covenant man was granted dignity and the privilege of access to forgiveness and blessing. But it was a *grant*, to one with desperate needs and in the expectation that those needs be acknowledged in the interests of truth and justice and sound filial love.

201. The process of spiritualization is no less notable in the area of sin offering than in those of burnt or peace offering. Johannes Hermann makes the statement that "Sins committed with deliberately evil intent... cannot be expiated by sin offerings...." [38] From such a statement it might be thought that sin offerings were only concerned with various unconsciously contracted impurities—a mere carryover into later times of primitive kinds of purifications practised by guilt and taboo-ridden pre-logical thinkers. But there are plenty of indications that guilt offerings [which Rainey defines as "a special kind of sin offering (cf. Lev. 5:7), required when someone has been denied his rightful due...."] [39] were often related consciously to real moral lapses. Things like robbery, fraud, and cheating, like those mentioned in Lev. 6:1-6 or 5:16-24—things for which the text requires not only the offering but restitution to the harmed neighbor— were surely not thought to be done without some element of evil intent towards the neighbor. Hermann's statement is based on an interpretation of Numbers 15:30 and context that does not allow for the presence of the kind of intent just spoken of, evidenced by Lev. 5 and 6. The immediate context of Num. 15:30 makes frequent reference to sins that can be expiated, and all of them are referred to as being committed "בשגגה", "through inadvertence" (RSV "unwittingly"). The text itself is probably meant—at least by the latest editor—to contrast with this. "But the person who does anything with a high hand... reviles the Lord... has despised the word of the Lord...." (Num. 15:30-31). This seems clearly to refer to an evil intent directed consciously towards God. But it is not proved that the "unwittingly" would always indicate a lack of malice. The Hebrew text of v. 28 reads: "And the priest shall make atonement for the person who has erred in sinning through inadvertence before the Lord....", and the placing of the last phrase may hold the key to the meaning. In comparison with actions that are consciously against the Divine mandate, the "inadvertent" sins may be actions done with a lack of knowledge of or insufficient reflection on the Divine prohibition, but not necessarily without malice towards the neighbor. It is difficult for us today

---

[38] *Theological Dictionary of the New Testament*, ed. Gerhard Kittel, trans. and ed. Geoffrey Bromiley, ten volumes (Grand Rapids: Wm. B. Eerdmans, 1964), s.v. ἱλάσκομαι, by Johannes Hermann, p. 309.

[39] Rainey, p. 601.

to make a distinction between sinning against God and sinning against the neighbor: the combination of the two is so common that we take the second as of equal import with the first.   But it would hardly be so for an early Israelite, who with his strong sense of awe towards the invisible powers might consider it quite proper that a sin known at the time of commission to be against God's law be left to the direct judgement of God, while one commited with malice towards a neighbor but not so known be left to a judgement mediated by men through sacrifice.   It is possible, of course, that the Numbers text does mean to show any intentional sin to be unforgivable, and represents a very early situation that as time went on ceded to one governed by milder laws like those of Leviticus.   I doubt, however, that the Numbers text means this, or that the editors of the book were convinced it did, for otherwise they could probably have expurgated or edited it.   Not two chapers further on Moses asks Aaron to make atonement for Israel for murmuring against him (17:11 in Hebrew text).   Clearly this was a conscious opposition not only against an equal but against Moses as leader of the people.   But it is directed against him as an individual, much like 16:13, and far from being meant against God may have been meant in his favor, for the people tell Moses "It is you who have caused the people of the Lord to die" (17:6, Hebrew text).   They do not see Moses as a divinely instituted leader here, but as a self-instituted one.   And so their sin is forgivable, even though it is punished in part. And indeed, when Aaron "stood between the dead and the living... the plague was stopped." (17:13, Hebrew).

202. This interpretation would show a rather early stage in the development of the idea of the Divine mercy, but a stage further advanced than one in which no real ill will could be forgiven.   The final stage is suggested by Milgrom.   "This... does not mean, as many critics aver, that sacrificial atonement is only possible for involuntary wrongdoers.... A more correct assertion... would be that the priestly system prohibits sacrificial atonement to the unrepentant sinner." [40]   This is not just the statement of an ideal.   Repentance of a very practical sort was required of the one guilty of sins against the neighbor in the text of Leviticus discussed above. The offering was no "easy way out" that dispensed with any real attempt at reconciliation with the neighbor who had been harmed.   Once the fact that a sin against God *had* been committed was recognized, his mercy allowed forgiveness to be obtained, at least in part, by a way that *was* easy compared with suffering.[41]   But Yahweh was not a god who could overlook injustice.   He also demanded restitution.

---

[40] Milgrom, p. 1041.

[41] Among others, the following citation from Lev. 26 shows that in effect suffering was a requirement for gaining absolution.   "If they confess their iniquity and the iniquity of their fathers ... if then their uncircumcised heart is humbled and they make amends ... then I will remember my covenant with Jacob, and I will remember my

> If any one sins and commits a breach of faith [וּמָעֲלָה מַעַל] against the
> Lord by deceiving his neighbor in a matter of deposit or security, or
> through robbery ... in any of all the things which men do and sin therein,
> when one has sinned and become guilty, he shall restore what he took ...
> he shall restore it in full, and shall add a fifth to it, and give it to him
> to whom it belongs, on the day of his guilt offering; and the priest shall
> make atonement for him before the Lord, and he shall be forgiven. ...
> [Lev. 6:1-6; see also Lev. 5:16-24].

The prophetic calls to true repentance could scarcely do better than to
point to this principle with insistence on its being observed. "Repentance from the heart" could only be real where wrongs were practically
righted. The prophetic tirades against empty cult practices were undoubtedly directed against those who took advantage of situations in which
wrongdoing and harm to neighbor could be blurred over or excused on
the pretext of ignorance or legitimate (by the laws of man) business practice
or politics, and admission of guilt limited to peccadillos. Perhaps, too,
against a priesthood that performed atoning acts in such cases—when
restitution was really due—without demanding restitution. But the argument could not justly have been with the system as such, which combined
God's mercy and justice in a unique way, insisting on both for the good
of all. The "breach of faith" idea underscores the fact that sin against a
neighbor is God's business, and that his laws have in fact made clear
what such sins are. If the sinner had been more careful in reading his
Scriptures or searching the traditions he would have discovered this. When
he does discover it be recognizes that he has de facto failed in his covenant
commitment and has sinned against the Lord.

    203. These reflections are to my mind reminiscent of the develop-
ment of the "first antithesis" in Matt. 5:21ff. A short survey of 5:23-24
shows what great religious potentialities there are in the Leviticus texts
and the close relationship that exists between a sincere concern for justice
towards one's neighbor and the admission before God in the cultic act
of guilt in this regard. The individual whom Christ addresses remembers
that his brother has something against him. In other words, he remembers that he has sinned against his brother. In the context of judgement, there is question of something for which judgement would be
exacted in favor of the brother; and in the religious context of gift-offering,

---

covenant with Isaac and my covenant with Abraham, and I will remember the land.
But the land shall be left by them ... Yet for all that, when they are in the land of
their enemies, I will not spurn them ... so as to destroy them utterly and break my
covenant with them ... but I will for their sake remember the covenant with their
forefathers, whom I brought forth out of the land of Egypt ... I am the Lord." (Lev.
26:40-46. Our italics). For a modern Jewish survey of various means of atonement,
see *Judaica*, s.v. "Atonement," author given as "editor". The means include mere
repentance for certain kinds of sins; for others, variously: punishment, celebration
of the Day of Atonement, fasting, prayer, death.

this becomes a matter for the eschatological judgement. What is required before favorable judgement is reconciliation with the one sinned against. The word διαλλάσσω, which occurs only here in the New Testament, has the basic meaning of "change", and there can be no doubt that what is required of the offerer here is a practical change of the unfavorable judgemental situation he finds himself in with regard to his brother. A reestablishment of damaged personal relationships is required, but as various examples of the use of compounds of ἀλλάσσω show, this is always a practical kind of thing. (See 2 Mac. 1:2-5; 7:33; 8:28). It does not necessarily require a deep emotional attachment; rather, a straightening out of practical problems and of difficulties that would obstruct a working family relationship. Matthew's text is very like Leviticus. Both equivalently affirm that love of God cannot really be manifested in cult unless there be love of neighbor.

Summary of the Foregoing Sections

204. We have undertaken this discussion of cult in commentary on statements by Childs about "ritual minutiae" in the context of "reinterpretation of the cult." (186). Paragraph 192 states the principal point that point to this principle with insistence on its being observed. "Repentance from the heart" could only be real where wrongs were practically that Paul and his contemporaries could have a "prophetic" bias in their religious thinking without having a bias against the general ideas of prayer, of oblation, of sacramentalism in the commonest sense of that word. There were cogent arguments in circulation that presented the relationship of the spiritual and the sacramental more as a partnership than as an opposition. The only way to judge which way our primary materials point is to study them with minds open on this subject. We are all aware of the danger of magic or theurgy in sacramentalism, and those who deal with it from day to day may be quite as concerned about the danger as those who view from a distance. But an a priori definition like that of Fuchs seems simply to ignore the arguments for a genuine "partnership". It does not seem to me that that is because they lack cogency; perhaps the cause is unfamiliarity with sympathetic conceptual and/or practical treatment and practice. At least, after meeting in the previous pages with some statements by rabbinic and other authors who have background and interests that qualify them for presenting the partnership position, we cannot plead a conceptual unfamiliarity with the main "anti-magical" arguments. As we have said, all that we need to demonstrate about Paul's attitude is a real possibility that he accepted the partnership position. As we meet more facts, of course, our minds may swing from mere possibility to good probability one way or the other. The facts we have already met do seem to point more in one direction than another. There is Paul's use of and encouragement to prayer, his lack of sympathy for the gnostic antipathy towards matter, his passing on of cultic traditions and his use of them as part of his teaching, as in our text.   We must stress that "in one direction" does not mean an exclusiveness in Paul's mind: this direction is precisely towards a kind of pluralism, a practical rejection by him of exclusivism in this area of his thinking.   Such an attitude accords with the situation in respect of other areas where commentators have long tended to force his mind into exclusivism.

205. Particular attention to oblation and sacrifice has seemed advisable partly because this sphere has long been one of exclusivist positions, and partly because oblation is inevitably drawn into any discussion of Eucharist whether by way of identification or by relating the Eucharist to Calvary considered as an oblation, or by opposing such positions.   Here too we have made use not only of primary texts but of modern authors who have taken an interest in the question as qualified and articulate exponents of the positive view.   Many of their arguments are of course dependent on older views, as the several references to rabbinical literature suggest.   To add an example, E. P. Sanders is reflecting directly on the rabbinical sources when he shows that the process of atonement was not conceived by the rabbis to be automatic on the performance of certain words and acts.   His argument is especially significant for us in view of what we said above (130,195) about the danger of failing to take the unspecified or the trite into consideration in our argumentation.

> The Rabbis did not go to the trouble of saying that man, by confessing, fasting and praying on the Day of Atonement, makes atonement *and* God forgives him.   They simply said, "The Day of Atonement atones." ... their way of phrasing the sentences about atonement may mislead readers into thinking that they conceived the process of atonement to be automatic.   The Rabbis ... did not suppose that atonement would be effective apart from the reconciling forgiveness of God.   They pictured God as always ready to forgive, and so had no need of saying "repentance atones if God chooses to forgive." [42]

He suggests that this was part of a general rabbinical theological attitude.   "As is usual, the Rabbis did not dwell on God's side, and forgiveness was not singled out for special attention as part of the overall reconciling process.   They could use simply 'atonement', which properly should refer only to man's action, to indicate the entire reconciliation." [43]

Schottroff and Others on Memorial

206. Willy Schottroff arrived at about the same exegetical conclusions as Childs at about the same time, without concluding to a "radical reinter-

---

[42] E. P. Sanders, p. 16.
[43] Ibid.

pretation" of cult. We may list some of his findings as summarized in his book.[44] The word is used of men and of God. It is associated with a movement towards act. This is already true where there is question of men's recall of past events, in particular, those of salvific import, and in this area is linked with men's faith and obedience to God. This human recall as such, if associated with cult, does not entail any strict actualization of the earlier salvific acts. Applied to present matters, the word expresses concentrated awareness. It looks to effect when expressing community relationship or prayer or covenantal protection related to God's *ḥesed*. This is true of God's remembering as of man's. God also remembers man's good and evil deeds, with resultant salvation and blessing or wrath and death. This meaning is not forensic in origin but cultic. The hiphil has a relationship with the Akkadian *zakāru*, with a meaning of "speak", "name"—as in the naming of the god in cult. Other meanings of the word related to the persistence or oblivion of the names of the dead. (Schottroff also remarks on the frequent use of the root in the Bible as a constituent of given names like Iozachar and Zachary.) *Zikkārôn* is used in the context of cult, whether for God's remembering or man's. *ᵓAzkārāh* has the meaning of a "calling of the name" of the god over the offering.

207. P. A. H. de Boer wrote a small book on memory at about the same time Childs and Schottroff were writing.[45] He puts much emphasis on the "knowing" and "naming" notions, almost to the extent of seeming to ignore the clear specialization of the meaning as time went on in the direction of "remembering" a past event. His insight remains useful for us, however, in that it underlines the fact that remembering is basically a kind of knowledge. Further, what we have already said about "calling on the name of the Lord" (188) shows the close relationship between naming God and reminding him.

208. J. Behm's TDNT article "ἀνάμνησις-ὑπόμνησις" is meagre. But O. Michel's article on μιμνήσκομαι and related words is clear and to a degree penetrating. He says,

> In the LXX this concept became central to the biblical view of God. It corresponds almost exclusively to the Mas. זָכַר. God remembers certain persons and turns to them in grace and mercy. ... The fact that He does so means that a new situation is created and effective help is extended to man in his need. God's remembering is thus an efficacious and creative event.[46]

---

[44] See Willy Schottroff, *'Gedenken' im alten Orient und im alten Testament*, rev. ed. (Neukirchen-Vluyn: Neukirchener Verlag, 1967), pp. 339-341.

[45] See P. A. H. de Boer, *Gedenken und Gedächtnis in der Welt des alten Testaments* (Stuttgart: Franz Delitzsch-Vorlesungen, 1960).

[46] *TDNT*, s.v. μιμνήσκομαι by O. Michel, p. 675.

The fact is that the same emphases are easily discernible in the Hebrew text, but there is a unifying and firmer statement of the theology in the LXX. The translators interpreted—and occasionally misinterpreted—some key texts, but generally the interpretation is quite in accord with at least the implications of the Hebrew text. We shall deal with one special example of misinterpretation as we proceed. Michel goes on:

> Above all, God remembers His covenant which He made with the fathers Noah, Abraham, Isaac and Jacob, and He binds Himself afresh to the grace promised therein. ... Conversely, a basic element in OT piety is that man remembers the past acts of God, His commandments and His unexhausted possibilities. ... Dt. especially develops a theology of remembering.[47]

Finally: "Because God's remembering, though ineffable, is concrete and actual event, faith can turn to Him with the request μνήσθητι ...."[48] In truth, this is not an answer to the problem of how man can address God this way, it simply suggests the area of response. The real answers, for the Israelite, lay, as we have seen, in the practical order. God had not only sanctioned, but had ordered a memorial approach to him. God knows best. And it was only common sense that in order for God to have knowledge as to whether his order was fulfilled, it had to be fulfilled by the performance of the memorial acts.

209. Michel points out that

> God's remembering does not always bring grace and mercy; God can also remember the wicked acts of the enemies of Israel, and take vengeance on them. ... Thus in the Nehemiah tradition it is possible to find together in the prayer μνήσθητι, a sense of one's own guilt, hope in God's mercy, expectation of an acknowledgement of one's own righteousness, and also expectation that the adversaries of God will be punished. ...[49]

He makes the judgement that "The limitation of OT μνήσθητι may be seen in this unexplained juxtaposition."[50] In fact, if the possibilities for spiritualization of the various concepts involved are seriously considered, it is difficult to see how such a juxtaposition offers much of a problem. With regard to prayers for punishment, it is evident that the stage of prayer for forgiveness of enemies has not been attained, but leaving vengeance in God's hands is certainly an advance over taking it into one's own, just as at an earlier stage the lex talionis was an advance—an "eye for an eye" being considerably better than "a life for an eye." The fact of limitation at this stage may be admitted, but it must also in fairness be admitted that the ideal of forgiveness of enemies was still probably something of an ideal among the early Christians. "Beloved, never avenge your-

---

[47] Ibid.
[48] Ibid.
[49] Michel, pp. 675-676. God also notes and punishes *Israel's* wicked acts!
[50] Ibid., p. 676.

selves, but leave it to the wrath of God...." (Rom. 12:19), says Paul. The need for and fact of spiritualization was real, but its practice was uneven and will ever remain so. But the principles of memorial as distinct from the particular aims of its practitioners are not affected. As for those aims, early on they show the main areas of expected Divine response: forgiveness, protection, blessings; these for oneself and others, and, increasingly, with some kind of eschatological as well as this-world application. These, we recall, are exactly the things Paul busied himself (and God) with in his eucharistic and petitionary prayer.

Key Memorial Texts in the LXX

210. The Greek word group we are especially interested in consists of μιμνήσκω, μνάομαι, μνεία, μνήμη, μνῆμα, μνημεῖον, μνημονεύω, with compounds especially of ἀνα- and ὑπο-, as ἀναμιμνήσκω and ἀνάμνησις. Let us view each of these in turn, citing the more important religious uses and noting the number of occurrences of the "secular" ones. The English citations are from Brenton's translation of the LXX.[51]

A. Μιμνήσκω [μνάομαι]

211. Some 150 occurrences—too many for full citation. We shall take a sampling of representative texts. *Genesis*: 1) "God remembered Abraham, and sent Lot out...." (19:29). 2) "And God remembered Rachel, and God hearkened to her, and he opened her womb." (30:22). 3) "When the bow is in the clouds, I will look upon it and remember the everlasting covenant...." (9:16). 4) Add four seculars. *Leviticus*: 1) "And I will remember the covenant of Jacob... the covenant of Isaac... the covenant of Abraam will I remember. And I will remember the land...." (26:42-43). 2) No seculars. *Deuteronomy*: 1) "Thou shalt remember that thou wast a slave in the land of Egypt and the Lord thy God brought thee out... therefore the Lord appointed thee to keep the sabbath day and to sanctify it." (5:15). 2) "Thou shalt surely remember all that the Lord thy God did to Pharao...." (7:18; 8:2 is similar, referring to the wilderness). 3) "But thou shalt remember the Lord thy God, that he gives thee strength... even that he may establish his covenant, which the Lord sware to thy fathers, as at this day." (8:18). 4) "Remember, forget not, how much thou provokedst the Lord...." (9:7). 5) "Remember Abraam, and Isaac, and Jacob thy servants, to whom thou swarest by thyself: look not upon the hardness of heart of this people...

---

51 See *The Septuagint Version of the Old Testament, with an English Translation,* translation by Sir Lancelot C. L. Brenton (New York: Harper and Bros.; London: Samuel Bagster and Sons; 1851). These two volumes have recently been combined and reprinted (Grand Rapids: Sondervan Publishing House, eighth printing, 1980). I have compared the Greek text used by Brenton with *Septuaginta*, ed. Alfred Rahlfs, editio minor (Stuttgart: Deutsche Bibelstiftung, 1935), introducing the few changes that might be significant into the Brenton English text.

and their sins." (9: 27). 6) "And thou shalt remember that thou wast a servant in the land of Egypt, and the Lord thy God redeemed thee...." (15:15). 7) "And thou shalt sacrifice the passover.... Seven days shalt thou eat unleavened bread with it... that ye may remember the day of your coming forth out of the land of Egypt all the days of your life." (16:2-3), 8) 16:2 is like 5:15; so, 24:11; 24:20; 24:22,24; 25:17; 32:7. 9) No secular uses. *Joshua*: 1) "Remember the word which Moses the servant of the Lord...." (1:13). 2) No secular uses. *Judges*: 1) "Israel turned... and made for themselves a covenant with Baal.... and... remembered not the Lord their God who had delivered them out of the hand of all their enemies round about." (8:33-34). 2) "And Sampson... said, 'O Lord, my Lord, remember me, I pray thee, and strengthen me...." (16:28). 3) One secular use. *1 Samuel*: 1) "And she vowed a vow to the Lord, saying, 'O Lord ... if thou wilt... remember me, and give to thine handmaid a man-child, then will I indeed dedicate him to thee...." (1:11). 2) "And the Lord remembered her, and she conceived." (1:19). 3) Also two less pertinent religious uses, one in the sense of "mention" (4:18). *2 Kings*: 1) "Lord, remember, I pray thee, how I have walked before thee in truth..." (20:3. The Lord responds: "I have heard thy prayer... behold, I will heal thee."— 20:5). 2) No seculars. *Amos*: "I will not turn away from [Tyre]... because they shut up the prisoners of Solomon.... and remembered not the covenant of brethren." (1:9. This is not a covenant with God, but shows God's concern for human covenants). *Jonah*: 1) "I remembered the Lord; and may my prayer come to thee into thy holy temple.... I will sacrifice to thee with the voice of praise and thanksgiving." (2:8,10). 2) No secular. *Habacuc*: 1) "O Lord... thou wilt in wrath remember mercy." (3:2). 2) No secular. *Malachi*: 1) " Remember the law of my servant Moses.... for all Israel, even the commandments and the ordinances." (4:4 [in Rahlfs, 3:24]). 2) No secular. *Isaiah*: 1) "Sing to the Lord, call aloud upon his name, proclaim his glorious deeds... make mention that his name is exalted." (12:4—so also 48:1; 62:6). 2) "Lord, in affliction I remembered thee...." (26:16. Similarly 17:10, 44:21; 46:8-10; 47:7; 57:11). 3) "Remember, Lord, how I have walked before thee in truth...." (38:3. This text is a parallel of 2 Kgs. 20:3, and the Divine response is noted here too). 4) "I, even I, am he that blots out thy transgressions for mine own sake, and thy sins; and I will not remember them. But do you remember, and let us plead together; do thou first confess thy transgressions that thou mayest be justified." (43:25-26). 5) Also nine or ten other secular and religious uses. *Jeremiah*: 1: "Ye that are far off, remember the Lord, let Jerusalem come into your mind." (28:50). 2) "Thus saith the Lord, I remember the kindness of thy youth, and the love of thine espousals...." (2:2). 3) "God was not pleased with them. Now will he remember their iniquities." (14:10). 4) "Refrain for thy name's sake, destroy not... remember, break not thy covenant with us." (14:21). 5) "O Lord, remember me and visit me...."

(15:15). 6) "Remember [O Lord] that I stood before thy face to speak good for them, to turn away thy wrath from them" (18:20). 7) "Ephraim is a beloved son, a pleasing child to me: for because my words are in him I will surely remember him... therefore I will have mercy upon him, saith the Lord." (38:20. This in the context of the new covenant). 8) "Behold, the days come, saith the Lord, when I will make a new covenant with the house of Israel... and Juda: not according to the covenant which I made with their fathers... for they abode not in my covenant, and I disregarded them, saith the Lord. For this is my covenant.... I will surely put my laws into their mind.... And they shall not at all teach every one his fellow... saying, Know the Lord: for all shall know me... for I will be merciful... and their sins I will remember no more." (38:31-34. This of course is *the* new covenant text). 9) "I will turn the captivity of Juda and... Israel, and will build them... cleanse them from their iniquities... and will not remember their sins...." (40:7-8). 10) "Did not the Lord remember the incense which ye burned [to foreign gods] in the cities of Juda... ye and your fathers and your kings, and came it not into your heart?" (51:21). 11) One secular use (11:19). *Ezechiel*: 1) "And I will remember my covenant made with thee in the days of thine infancy, and I will establish to thee an everlasting covenant. Then thou shalt remember thy way, and shalt be... dishonoured.... And I will establish my covenant with thee; and thou shalt know that I am the Lord: that thou mayest remember, and be ashamed... when I am reconciled to thee...." (16:60-63. Another equivalently "new covenant" text). 2) "And when the righteous turns away... his righeousness shall not be remembered...." (3:20. Note the "Divine passive". Similarly in 18:22; 21:23; 33:16). 3) "They of you that escape.... shall remember me [God]." (6:9. Other "man remembers" in 16:22,43; 23:27; 36:31). *Hosea*: 1) "The names of Baalim... shall be remembered no more at all. And I will make for them in that day a covenant with the wild beasts... and I will break the bow... and will cause thee to dwell safely. And I will betroth thee to myself for ever... and thou shalt know the Lord." (2:17-20 [in Rahlfs, 2:19-20]). 2) "I remember all their wickedness...." (7:2). 3) "For if they should offer a sacrifice, and eat flesh [in communion], the Lord will not accept them; now will he remember their iniquities." (8:13). 4) "He will remember their iniquities, he will take vengeance on their sins." (9:9). 5) No seculars. (Nor for Ezechiel). *Psalms*: Approximately forty-five incidences. 1) "The Lord... send thee help from the sanctuary, and aid thee out of Sion. Remember all thy sacrifice.... fulfil all thy petitions." (19:1-3,5). 2) "Remember thy compassions, O Lord, and thy mercies.... Remember not the sins of my youth... remember me according to thy mercy, for thy goodness' sake, O Lord.... All the ways of the Lord are mercy... to them that seek his covenant...." (24:6-7,10). 3) "O my God, my soul has been troubled within me; therefore will I remember thee.... I will say to God, Thou art my helper; why hast thou forgotten me?" (41:6,9 [in Rahlfs, 41:7,10]. "Why hast thou forgotten me" is " διὰ τί μου ἐπελάθου '). 4) "Remember [O God] thy congregation which thou hast purchased from the beginning: thou didst ransom the rod of thine inheritance...." (73:2). 5) "And they remembered that God was their helper, and... redeemer... neither were they steadfast in his covenant." (77: 35,37). 6) "And he remembered that they are flesh...." (77:39). 7) "Remember not our old transgressions.... Help us, O God our Saviour." (78:8-9). 8) "I became... as the slain ones cast out, who sleep in the tomb; whom thou rememberest no more...." (87:4-5 [in Rahlfs 87:5-6]). 9) "For he knows our frame; remember that we are dust.... But the mercy of the Lord is... upon them that... keep his covenant and remember his command-ments to do them." (102:14,17-18). 10) "He has remembered his covenant for ever... and he remembered his oath to Isaac.... to Israel for an everlasting covenant." (104:8-10). 11) "For he remembered his covenant...." (105:45). 12) "He has caused his wonderful works to be remembered.... He has given food to them that fear him: he will remember his covenant for ever." (110:4-5). 13) "Lord, remember David, and all his meekness: how he sware to the Lord, and vowed...." (131:1-2). 14) In addition to these there are at least eleven other instances of God's remembering (usually the people, Sion, the pray-er, etc.), an equal number of men's remembering God, his works, power, mercy, judgements, name. There are four uses of the word in the sense of "mention", and only three or so that might be called "secular". *Job*: Eight occurrences: one God's active remember-ing, one probably the same, one divine passive, one men's remembering God's works, four secular. *Ecclesiastes*: "Remember thy Creator...." (12:1). Three secular.

212. There are similar occurrences in the other books. We may note some salient points from the above. 1) An almost universal heavily re-ligious use of the word: God is practically always either speaking, spoken to or spoken about. 2) The spread of usage is very even throughout the whole Old Testament: it is found in early and late; law, prophet and wisdom. 3) God's remembering and the people's are often associated. 4) God's re-membering is several times associated with prayer and oblation. 5) And often with covenant. In particular, three "new covenant" texts involve memorial terminology, two of them God's remembering. 6) Several times there is question of God's or man's remembering the salvific actions of a man of God: Abraham, Jeremiah, David, Isaac, etc. 7) Man's remembering is focussed on God, his works, power, mercy, judgements, as well as man's own failures or successes in relation to the covenant. 8) Roughly doubling the frequency of the concepts are "forgetting" texts, often used as parallels. The main verb used here is ἐπιλήθω-ἐπιλανθάνομαι. 9) Other parallelisms show what "remembering" really means when applied to God: "Look upon", "hearken to", "consider", "regard", "be mindful of" are common English translations where no past event is involved: there is clearly question of knowledge and concern. Where past events are in question, "remember" is usually used, extending the present knowledge and concern to the relationship of past events and attitudes to the present. 10) The idea of "mentioning" (= making to be remembered) is usually used with the name of God as object. 11) The "divine passive" is used several times, equivalent to "God remembers". 12) The incidence of God-remembers texts is roughly equal to that of man-remembers ones. And of the former, many convey the idea of "reminding-God".

B. ἀναμιμνήσκω

213. Twenty occurrences. The chief religious ones: 1) "God remembered Noah... and God made a wind blow...." (Gen. 8:1). 2) "And ye shall be had in remembrance before the Lord." (Num. 10:9. So Ezek. 33:13: "His righteousness shall not be remembered.") 3) "It is a sacrifice recalling sin to remembrance." Num. 5:15. So 1 Kgs. 17:18; Job 24:20; Ps. 108:14; Ezek. 21:23 [in Rahlfs, 21:29]; 29:16). 4) "You shall make no mention of the names of other gods" (Exod. 23:13). 5) Secular uses are more common than with the unprefixed verb. A typical one: "He had no son to keep his name in remembrance." (2 Sam. 18:18). Another: "Josaphat was recorder" (2 Sam. 20:24; 1 Kgs. 4:3; 2 Kgs. 18:18).

214. Instances of man's remembering here are limited to secular matters—the religious usages are all related to God's remembering, chiefly the divine passive. A notable point is the use of this form to refer *both* to sins and to righteousness or the individual himself. Covenant and sacrificial connections are again present.

C. μνημονεύω

215. Only ten occurrences. No instances of God remembering. Most of the references are religious: remembering God, his works, "this day" (Exod. 13:3). Only one is cultic: "this day" refers to the passover. There is one instance of God's reminding: "Remember ye not the former things...." (Isa. 43:18).

D. μνησικακέω

216. "Remembering injuries" is represented as wrong and is several times condemned: see Prov. 21:24; Ezek. 25:12; Zech. 7:10. The word is never used of God. The fact corroborates what might be called the basic principle of the hoped-for Divine attitude towards sin, well expressed by texts like Hab. 3:2: "Thou wilt in wrath remember mercy." In the light of this principle, the links with covenant—in which God promises to forgive—and oblation—whereby the hope and prayer for forgiveness are manifested—are not only understandable, they must be expected.

E. μνημόσυνον

217. This is usually translated "memorial". We may classify texts by the various things that are called "memorials".

218. *God's name*: "This is my name for ever, and a memorial to generations...." (Exod. 3:15. So Pss. 101:12 [in Rahlfs, 101:13] and 134:13).

219. *God himself*: "[Jacob]... had power with God.... the Lord God Almighty shall be his memorial." (Hos. 12:5 [in Rahlfs, 12:6]).

220. *Feasts*: 1) "And this day [the pasch] shall be to you a memorial, and ye shall keep it a feast to the Lord through all your generations... for a perpetual ordinance. Seven days ye shall eat unleavened bread...." (Exod. 12:14-15). 2) "And thou shalt tell thy son in that day, saying, Therefore the Lord dealt thus with me, as I was going out of Egypt. And it shall be to thee a sign upon thy hand and a memorial before thine eyes, that the law of the Lord may be in thy mouth.... And preserve ye this law according to the times of the seasons...." (Exod. 13:8-10). 3) "And Mardochaeus wrote these things in a book... to establish these as joyful days, and to keep the fourteenth and fifteenth of Adar.... these days were to be a memorial kept in every generation.... for ever...." (Est. 9:20-21,27). 4) "In the seventh month, on the first day of the month, ye shall have a rest; a memorial of trumpets: it shall be to you a holy convocation." (Lev. 23:24).

221. *Part of an oblation—"its memorial"*: 1) "And if a soul bring a gift, a sacrifice [προσφέρῃ δῶρον θυσίαν] to the Lord, his gift shall be fine flour; and he shall pour oil upon it, and shall put frankincense on it; it is a sacrifice. And he shall bring it to the priests... and having taken from it a handful of the fine flour with the oil, and all its frankincense, then the priest shall put the memorial of it on the altar: it is a sacrifice [ἐπι τὸ θυσιαστήριον· θυσία], an odour of sweet savour to the Lord." (Lev. 2:1-2). 2) "And if he cannot afford a pair of turtle-doves...; then shall he bring as his gift for his sin... flour; he shall not pour oil upon it, nor... frankincense... because it is a sin-offering. And the priest having taken a handful of it, shall lay the memorial of it on the altar of whole-burnt offerings to the Lord; it is a sin offering.... and that which is left shall be the priest's." (Lev. 5:11-13. So in Lev. 2:9-10 and 2:16, where the memorial is called a "burnt offering". Also Lev. 6:16-18 [in Rahlfs, 6:8-10]; Isa. 57: 8; 66:3). 3) "...his gift for her... barley meal: he shall not pour oil upon it, neither... frankincense... for it is a sacrifice of jealousy, a sacrifice of memorial, recalling sin to remembrance." (Num. 5:15. The use of this is explained in 5:18ff. The woman holds it, and God is called on as a witness to leave or curse her).

222. *Other cultic objects*: 1) "And Eleazar... took the brazen censers, which the men who had been burnt brought near, and they put them as a covering on the altar: a memorial to the children of Israel that no stranger might draw nigh... to offer incense before the Lord." (Num. 16: 39-40 [in Rahlfs, 17:4-5]). 2) "And Moses and Eleazar... took the gold from the captains... and brought the vessels into the tabernacle of witness, a memorial of the children of Israel before the Lord." (Num. 31:54). 3) "Thou shalt engrave the two stones with the names of the children of Israel.... put the two stones on the shoulders of the shoulder piece: they are memorial stones for the children of Israel: and Aaron shall bear the names of the children of Israel before the Lord on his two shoulders, a memorial for them" (Exod. 28:11-12; also 36:14; 28:23 [in Rahlfs, 28:29]). 4 ("And thou shalt take the money of the offering from the children of Israel, and shalt give it for the service of the tabernacle of testimony; and it shall be to the children of Israel a memorial before the Lord, to make atonement for your souls." (Exod. 30:16. [In 30:12 this is called "a ransom for his soul to the Lord, then there shall not be among them a destruction in the visiting of them."]). 5) "And the Lord... wrote a book of remembrance before him for them that feared the Lord...." (Mal. 3:16. This seems to be an element of the "parallel liturgy" we spoke of in 173).

223. *The just man*: "The righteous shall be in everlasting remembrance." (Ps. 111:6. [εἰς μνημόσυνον αἰώνιον ἔσται δίκαιος]).

224. *Progeny, name, or both*: 1) "Thy memorial is abolished from the earth, even thy sons and daughters." (Job 2:9). 2) Let his memorial perish... and his name... publicly cast out." (Job 18:17). See also Deut. 32:26; Neh. 2:20 (in Rahlfs, 12:20); Ps. 108:15.

225. *A written formal record*: "Write this for a memorial in a book..." (Exod. 17:14).

226. *Miscellaneous*: 1) Stones from the Jordan to be carried by the twelve tribes to symbolize the passage into Palestine: "These stones shall be for a memorial for you for the children of Israel forever." (Josh. 4:7). 2) "Her [Tyre's] trade and her gain shall be holiness to the Lord; it shall not be gathered for them, but for those that dwell before the Lord.... for a covenant and a memorial before the Lord." (Isa. 23:18).

F. ἀνάμνησις

227. Four occurrences: 1) "And ye shall... make... twelve loaves.... And ye shall put them in two rows... on the pure table before the Lord. And ye shall put on each row pure frankincense and salt; and these things shall be for loaves for a memorial, set forth before the Lord.... for an everlasting covenant." (Lev. 24:6-8. [in Rahlfs, 24:5-7. The Greek is καὶ ἔσονται εἰς ἄρτους εἰς ἀνάμνησιν προκείμενα τῷ Κυρίῳ.]). 2) "And the priests the sons of Aaron shall sound with the trumpets.... And in the days of your gladness, and in your feasts... ye shall sound with the trumpets at your whole burnt offerings and... peace offerings; and there shall be a memorial for you before your God." (Num. 10:8,10). 3) A psalm-title: "A Psalm of David for remembrance concerning the Sabbath day" (37:1). 4) Sic. "For the end, by David, for a remembrance, that the Lord may save me" (69:1).

G. μνεία

228. 1) "Because my words are in him, I will surely remember him [Ephraim]". (Jer. 38:20. [μνεία μνησθήσομαι αὐτοῦ]). 2) "O that... thou shouldst set me a time in which thou wouldst remember me!" (Job 14:13 [μνείαν μου ποιήσῃ]). 3) "Sing many songs, that thou mayest be remembered." Is. 23:16. [ἵνα σου μνεία γένηται]). (So Ezek. 21:32 [in Rahlfs, 21:37]; 25:10; Zech. 13:2). 4) "He has caused his wonderful works to be remembered." (Ps. 110:4). 5) "We have hoped in thy name, and on the remembrance of thee." (Isa. 26:8. [ἐπι τῇ μνεία ᾗ ἐπιθυμεῖ ἡ ψυχὴ ἡμῶν = "on the remembering which our soul longs for"]). 6) One other instance of remembering God's works (Deut. 7:18). 7) One secular use.

H. μνήμη

229. 1) "Sing to the Lord... and give thanks for the remembrance of his holiness." (Ps. 29:4 [in Rahlfs, 29:5]; also 96:12; 144:7). 2) "Let us swallow him alive... remove the memorial of him from the earth." (Prov. 1:12). 3) "There is no remembrance of these men...." (Eccl. 2:16). 4) "Their memory is lost." (Eccl. 9:5).

I. μνημεῖον *and* μνῆμα

230. These are always found in the meaning of "tomb".

Notable Points about the Nouns

231. A regular difference between μνημόσυνον and ἀνάσνησις on the one hand and μνεία and μνήμη on the other is that between "reminder" and "remembering". This is a very important distinction and one that has not been clearly enough noted either in translations or in discussions. For example, in Ps. 69:1 the first words of the psalm are "Draw nigh, O God, to my help." The meaning is "as a reminder [to the Lord] to save me." In Ps. 37:1 it is not clear who is being reminded, though as Douglas Jones notes, Darwell Stone long ago "with exemplary caution" stated that "'the probability is very strong that a memorial before God is denoted.'" [52] In any case, the meaning "reminder" always construes into sense, and is usually limpid. The meaning may have been originally causative: "to make to remember"; but that is no longer obvious.

---

[52] Jones: 183.

232. The idea of "reminding God" is evident from the context in the instances of the "memorial portion" in the Leviticus texts. God is reminded of the whole of the offering and of course through that of the offerer and his intentionality. Similarly with the "sacrifice of jealousy" (Num. 5:15), the gold (Num. 31:54), the memorial stones (Exod. 28:11 etc.), the money for ransom (Exod. 30:16), the book of remembrance (Mal. 3:16), Tyre's trade (Isa. 23:18); and for ἀνάμνησις the loaves of proposition and the trumpets. (We shall discuss both later.)

233. The point made in 232 about context would not be so evident if it were not clear that the nominal memorial terminology is simply part of the same memorial thinking that our survey of the verbs has shown to have been so common. Nominal and verbal terminology are often combined in the texts—or immediate context of the texts—we have cited above or (especially) similar ones in the later literature to which we shall presently turn our attention. V.g., in Num. 5:15 we find "θυσία μνημοσύνου, ἀναμιμνήσκουσα ἁμαρτίαν"; in Num. 10:9 the purpose of the trumpets is expressed thus: " ἀναμνησθήσεσθε ἔναντι Κυρίου" (this with ἀνάμνησις). And of course there is the common usage "μνεία μνησθῆναι". In a climate of thought where "God remembering" was so common, it was inevitable that usages like those noted in 232 should be interpreted to mean that, just as usages tending towards or clearly indicating human remembering or calling-to-remember would be easily read in those senses due to the prevalence of *those* ideas.

234. The uses of both the "reminding" words are heavily religious, and within the religious area, heavily cultic. There seems to be little difference between the two words in this cultic area. *The idea is that of a symbol—a word or thing or act—that is so said or placed or done as to attract the attention of the one who is meant to read it and thus turn his attention to the matter symbolized.* Phrases like "before him", "to him", "for him" are often indicators of the one to be reminded. So, again, is the location of the memorial, which in the case of memorials "before God" is usually at the kind of "focus" of attention we spoke of in 197: the tabernacle, the altar; or within the tabernacle, the "hilasterion"— "mercy seat" or "propitiatory".

235. Memorials that have to do with sin are specially treated (see Lev. 5:11-13 and Num. 5:15). Oil and frankincense were not associated with them, very likely a carryover into the cult of the attitude John McKenzie notes when he says of oil: "The use of the unguent was a sign of joy... and was omitted during fasts and mourning." [53] *At the same time, there is a distinction of basic import between a memorial that is to remind*

---

[53] *Dictionary of the Bible*, by John L. McKenzie (Milwaukee: Bruce, 1965), s.v. "Oil."

*of the presence of sin that is not openly acknowledged, as in the case
of the "sacrifice of jealousy" in Numbers; and one that is to remind of
sin acknowledged, as in the "sin offering".* The former is meant to "bring
sin to [primarily God's] remembrance" (Num. 5:15) if sin should exist,
and its effect in that case is to bring punishment upon the sinner (see
Num. 5:27ff). The latter, the sin offering, is not meant to bring sin to
remembrance except as the cause of the situation; rather, it is meant to
bring *repentance* for sin to remembrance, and to achieve the *forgiveness*
of sin. "When a man is guilty... he shall confess the sin... and he shall
bring his guilt offering to the Lord.... and the priest shall make atonement
for him for the sin... and he shall be forgiven." (Lev. 5:5-6,10). Of course,
the sin has to be recalled in order to permit its forgiveness (and confession), and this explains the omission of the oil and frankincense in the
case of the sin offering. But it is *sin as acknowledged and repented that is
recalled,* not, as in the case of the "sacrifice of jealousy", sin that is present
but *not acknowledged.*

236. The fact that the memorial in Lev. 5:11-13 substitutes for a
sheep prompts the question whether the use of the blood and fat of these
animals in the sacrifice are "memorial" uses too. For the blood and fat
for communion sacrifices was a portion similar in significance to that
of the memorial portion for meal offerings. The fat was burned (see
Lev. 3:9, etc.) as a sign that "All the fat belongs to the Lord.... ye shall
eat no fat and no blood." (Lev. 3:16-17). The blood was not burned but
was sprinkled or smeared on or at the altar (see Lev. 1:5,15; etc.). In
fact, the author of Hebrews suggests that the blood was looked on as
being used "memorially" when, using the term ἀνάμνησις, he says, "In these
sacrifices there is a reminder of sin year after year. For it is impossible
that the blood of bulls and goats should take away sins." (Heb. 10:3-4).
He is saying that the old sin offerings had no more ability to take away
sins than did, for example, the "sacrifice of jealousy": they only called
God's attention to the sins that were present, acknowledged or not. This
outright denial of the traditional belief—made, of course, because the
author had in his mind reduced the issue to "either Christ or the old
offerings"—must have aroused considerable outrage among some of his
Jewish readers. But the point for us is that he was making use of a
view evidently current in his milieu that sacrificial blood was a memorial.
Clearly it was used in such a manner as to have memorial value, being
placed at the focus of Divine attention (the altar; or even more a focus,
the *hilasterion*) and displayed by spreading about in one way or another—
these dispositions adding to its fundamental quality of high visibility due
to its color and liquidity. The burning fat of the sacrifices is frequently
spoken of as providing a "sweet odor to the Lord" (v.g., Lev. 1:9; Ezek.
20:41)—terminology expressive of the kind of Divine mindfulness of the

offerers present that is in question here; i.e., expressive of "memorial" in that sense though not in the sense of memory of past events.

237. It should not surprise us that these cult materials should by New Testament times be called "memorials" when the word had been so variously applied already in the Pentateuch. Our question above as to blood and fat was prompted by their being analogous as portions to the memorial portions of meal offerings. But an extension of memorial terminology to other cult objects than those specifically mentioned in the Old Testament texts was probably inevitable. Even in the Pentateuch "memorial" is applied not just to portions of different offerings, but to undivided collections like the money offerings, the memorial stones worn by Aaron. The extension to Tyre's trade in Isaiah shows how far this could go. The LXX gives a notable example of the process. The Masoretic text for Lev. 24:7 has, "And you shall put pure frankincense with each row, that it may go with the bread as a memorial portion to be offered by fire to the Lord." (RSV). The Greek reads, "And ye shall put on each row pure frankincense and salt; and these things shall be for loaves for a memorial...." The term "memorial" is now applied not to the frankincense (which may have been meant to go with a portion of the flour from which the loaves were made), but to the loaves themselves. The LXX translators may have had a Hebrew text that did this already; but there is also a possibility that they did it because this understanding had somehow come to be established in the hellenized Jewish milieu. The original idea of "memorial" when used of memorial portions may have been that God's attention would be drawn to the whole of the offering and that the nexus with the offerer would then be evident from the situation; or it may have been that the portion was intended to call attention directly to the offerer. The existence of whole memorials like those mentioned above probably shows a tendency to see the whole as a memorial in all cases, and to predicate "memorial" more nearly to the offerer. Another example of this: in the text of Ezekiel referred to in 236, though the material cultic offerings are referred to ("On my holy mountain... I will require your contributions and the choicest of your gifts, with all your sacred offerings" [Ezek. 20:40]), the equivalently memorial terminology is in terms of the offerers themselves: "As a pleasing odor I will accept you." The spiritualization of the cult contributed pressure for such extension of terminology. So did the fact that *all* the portions of the offering (where they had "portions") were treated in some way that in fact cultically "reminded" God: the loaves of proposition were "set forth before the Lord", the parts for communion were "waved" (see Lev. 7:30, etc.) or at least "brought to the Lord." (Lev. 7:29). If such treatment could make some things "memorial", it was hard to see why it would not make others similarly treated the same. Super-special treatment (like burning of fat or sprinkling of blood) for certain objects or parts retained its relative significance, but the whole offering was in truth treated memorially and may well have been *called* "memorial" too, and quite early.

238. A similar terminological question arises with regard to cultic sacrifice. The term "sacrifice" in English seems for most people to denote animal sacrifice, and frequently almost to denote rather than merely connote killing. In Hebrew the word was קָרְבָּן or מִנְחָה, and was used of other offerings than animal offerings as well as of those. (Special words were also used for special kinds of offerings; v.g., עֹלָה for a whole burnt offering: = "that which rises" [to God]). The LXX usually translates the former δῶρον, the latter θυσία. This word usually comes into English as "sacrifice". Certainly the LXX did not visualize animal slaughter as necessary for a θυσία, we have seen at least three examples where the word was used of meal offerings. L. & S. says of θυσία, "prop. burnt-offering....", and of θύω, "I. Act., offer by burning...." [54] It is obvious that the term came very early to be used of the whole of offerings, not just of parts that were burned—an extension parallel to that spoken of above with regard to memorial or equivalently memorial terminology. But in English, as was already remarked, the process seems to have been the opposite: the term has for many come to mean animal offerings. McKenzie, for example, says that "the manipulation of the blood... very probably symbolizes the essential note of the sacrificial symbolism." [55] In fact, the manipulation of the blood is merely a specific instance of the kind of memorial treatment that for the Hebrews made the offering a thing holy to God—that "*sacrum fecit*" ("*sacri-ficium*")—so that the essence of sacrifice should rather be identified with such generic action.

239. As with the verbs, there is a strong association of covenant with the "memorial" nouns, and in particular with those that have to do with reminding God. Of course, as we have noted already, the cult as such was ordered by God as part of the Mosaic covenant agreement, and the same is implied for the new covenant by the text from Ezek. (20:24) cited above (237). But two of our texts make explicit mention of covenant, and another covenant connection relates to all the sacrificial offerings. This is the "covenant of salt". "And every gift of your sacrifice shall be seasoned with salt; omit not the salt of the covenant of the Lord from your sacrifices: on every gift of yours ye shall offer salt to the Lord your God." (Lev. 2:13. The nearest nominal memorial terminology is in 2:16. The "covenant of salt" is also spoken of in Num. 18:19). The salt was actually offered, and apparently by burning: the perfumed incense used

---

[54] *A Greek-English Lexicon*, comps. Henry George Liddell and Robert Scott (Oxford: Clarendon Press, 1968), s.v. θυσία and θύω.

[55] McKenzie, s.v. " Sacrifice."

in the tabernacle is "seasoned with salt" in Exod. 30:35 of the Hebrew text. In other words, it was used in the most "reminding God" way possible. It seems to have symbolized covenant itself. McKenzie notes that "A covenant of salt is a covenant of friendship (Nm 18:19; 2 Ch. 13:5); the eating of the salt of another is a symbol of friendship in many languages." [56]   But the covenants made by Yahweh are themselves expressions of friendship, and the salt becomes a kind of seal of the covenant. As for the two texts spoken of just above: a) In Isa. 23:18 the terms "covenant" and "memorial" are paired in Brenton's translation; in the Greek the reading is " εἰς συμβολὴν μνημόσυνον [ἔναντι Κυρίου]": the idea in the context seems to be that the good things provided by Tyre will serve as a sign to all concerned (so, as a memorial) of God's friendship with those who dwell before him. A hyphenated "covenant-memorial" might be better than "covenant and memorial", but that is adequate. b) In Lev. 24 we have the twelve loaves "for a memorial, set forth before the Lord.... for an everlasting covenant." (vv. 7-8). The salt is an element here too (in the LXX only), for the loaves are laced with salt (v. 7); but either that has imparted its covenant significance to the loaves themselves, or they are seen to have such significance of themselves, especially as representative of the twelve tribes.

Jones and " ἀνάμνησις "

240. Douglas Jones, in the article already cited, tries to make the point that "ἀνάμνησις" in the LXX is not a technical word. He first shows the discrepancy we have remarked on above (237) between the Hebrew and Greek texts of Lev. 24:7 and says of the loaves as a memorial, "No such ᵓazkārah was ever heard of!" [57] He holds that there is question of nothing else than mistranslation from the Hebrew, and says, "When a translator finds such difficulty with an extremely common Hebrew idiom, no weighty argument can be based on his choice of words." [58]

241. Even granting that there was a mistranslation, it is necessary to recognize that just such an ᵓazkārah was not only heard of but inevitably became a common notion once the LXX translations came to be read and propagated. Whatever its mistakes, additions or omissions, it must be acknowledged by any student of the New Testament that "the LXX is of enormous significance in that it furnished the cultural milieu and the literary vehicle for the preaching of earliest Christianity to the Gentile world.... The LXX is the form in which the OT was most widely used in apostolic times...." [59]

---

[56] McKenzie, s.v. "Salt."
[57] Jones: 184.
[58] Ibid.: 184-185.
[59] Patrick W. Skehan, George W. MacRae, Raymond E. Brown, "Texts and Versions," *JBC*, 69:54.

242. But it is not all that sure that there *was* a mistranslation. As the *JBC* article says, "In general, the Pentateuch translation is faithful, competent, and idiomatic...." [60]   Of course, as the sentence goes on to note, there were different translators, but one must presume some kind of competence and, additionally, some kind of editing of the translations.   The fact is that we do not know what Hebrew text this translator used; or whether he consciously incorporated into his translation data from some additional text, some tradition, or some going cult practices.

243. Jones uses another argument, namely that the use of μνημόσυνον instead of ἀνάμνησις to render אַזְכָּרָה in texts like Sir. 38:11 and 45:16— where there are offerings roughly similar to those in the Lev. 24 text— shows that ἀνάμνησις was not a *"terminus technicus."* [61]   The texts read, respectively: "In thy sickness.... leave off from sin.... Give a sweet savour, and a memorial of fine flour.... Then give place to the physician, for the Lord hath created him."   And "He chose [Aaron]... out of all men living to offer sacrifices to the Lord, incense, and a sweet savour, for a memorial, to make reconciliation for his people."   These texts, as he properly notes, are like many memorial texts in the Pentateuch and elsewhere.   But all they show is that *two* words, not just one, were used as technical terms when there was question of *cultic* memorial.   We underscore "cultic" because it is clear that these words, like many others used in certain contexts in technical senses, were non-tecnical in some contexts.   A word like "line" (taken at random) has a technical sense in fishing but would hardly be called technical in the phrase "waiting in line".   Once we convey the impression that the context in which the word is used is specialized somehow, the word can become "technical".   On the other hand, several words may be used to give the same technical sense.   For example, in fishing, "pole" and "rod".[62]   From the data we have seen, I would suspect that μνημόσυλον and ἀνάμνησις were used interchangeably in the Hebrew cultic milieu, though when there was question of reference to some specific LXX text, the word used or thought of would more likely be the one used in that text.   The "memorial" idea, however, underlay all the cultic uses of both words, so that such an adherence would hardly be an unbreakable rule.

244. Actually, what troubles Jones is the notion that ἀνάμνησις might have a necessarily Godward reference in 1 Cor. 11:25.   This, he thinks, would be "perilous in the extreme," [63] since he sees the text as concerned with sin, and he holds without any distinctions that when God

---

[60] *JBC*, "Texts and Versions," 69:54.

[61] Jones: 185, note 1.

[62] For some fishermen these terms might seem exact synonyms.   The elite would make distinctions.   But they *are* synonyms, and "technical" within the realm of fishing as a whole.   In other instances, the exactness of synonyms would be less in dispute; v.g., "bucket" and "pail", or in the cult, "offering" and "oblation".

[63] Jones: 186.

remembers sin he punishes it. It is salubrious for *man* to remember sin, but not God. "Human remembrance or, better, the human act of recalling, revivifies, so to speak, the sin, in order that God, in the divine ordinance, may obliterate it or wipe it out.... If this is not done, then God's remembrance will revivify it in the act of divine punishment." [64] Now from what we have seen, ἀνάμνησις is not technical in that it necessarily reminds *God* in every case, but in that it involves a cultic statement, object or act that reminds *someone* (or some parties) concerned with the cultic event. Whom it reminds depends upon the context: it will always be either God or man or both, of course. Our position will be that in 1 Cor. 11:25 there is a very high probability that it does remind both God and man. We clearly could not hold this if Jones' position on God's remembering were true simply as stated. We have already seen why it is not. Jones fails to distinguish between God's remembering sin offerings like that in Lev. 5:11-13 and his remembering offerings like the "sacrifice of jealousy" of Num. 5:15. (See 235). Both types are "memorials", but in the first case the remembering brings forgiveness because the sin, though present, is acknowledged; in the second, it brings punishment if the sin is present and the sin is *not* acknowledged. In the first case God remembers the sin only in remembering that it is acknowledged in the cultic act—he remembers it only to forget it. In the second case he remembers it to punish. The question of whether the punishment here might be forthcoming even if the sin *were* acknowledged is aside from the point: there is a clear distinction of Divine attitudes towards the two kinds of memorial. Our point with respect to 1 Cor. 11 will not be that the Supper is a sin-offering, but that it is a memorial of an event that is at least closely analogous to one, namely Jesus' death on Calvary. As for the term ἀνάμνησις in particular, none of the four Old Testament uses we have studied involves reminding God of sin in the manner of a "sacrifice of jealousy", and the Hebrews text only does so paradoxically, in that the sin offerings in question fail of the effects the old Israel commonly ascribed to them—they do not gain the forgiveness of sins because only Christ's does that.

Contents of Chapter I

245. In this chapter, in addition to surveying the exegetical work of several authors (Childs, 183-185; Schottroff, de Boer, Michel, 206-209), we have discussed the question, introduced by Childs, of "reinterpretation of the cult" and gone on to study the subject of spiritualization of the cult in terms of sacramentalism, prayer, sacrifice. Paragraph 204 gives a summary of this discussion. Subsequently we viewed a considerable number of memorial texts from the LXX, pointing out salient results (and commenting) in 212, 214, 215, 216, 231ff. A critique of some of Douglas Jones' principal positions is given in 240-244.

---

[64] Ibid.

The Texts

246. Using Charles' *Apocrypha*[1] as the source of our English text and the criterion of nomenclature for the material dealt with in the chapter, let us now survey the memorial usages in the Apocrypha of the Old Testament. After the name of the book, we shall insert an estimate of its dating based generally on the introductions given in Charles.

247. *1 Esdras* (c. 300 B.C.?): Nothing at all, religious or secular.

248. *1 Maccabees* (c. 125 B.C.): 1) "[Judas']... memorial is blessed forever." (3:7—τὸ μνημόσυνον αὐτοῦ). 2) "Remember how our fathers were saved.... And now let us cry unto heaven, if he will have mercy on us and will remember the covenant of the fathers and destroy this army... who redeemeth Israel." (4:9-11). 3) "And this is a copy of the writing which they... sent to Jerusalem... that it might be with them there for a memorial of peace and confederacy." (8:22—μνημόσυνον. See also 14:23). 4) "We therefore at all times... do remember you in the sacrifices which we offer, and in our prayers, as it is right and meet to be mindful of brethren." (12:11).

249. *2 Maccabees* (c. 125 B.C.): 1) "May God do good unto you and remember his covenant with... his faithful servants; may he give you all a heart to worship him and do his pleasure.... and hearken to your supplications; may he be reconciled to you.... Such are our prayers for you in this place." (1:2-6). 2) "These things were narrated also in the memoirs of Nehemiah...." (2:13—ὑπομνηματισμοῖς). 3) "[Eleazar]... died, leaving his death as... a memorial of virtue to the nation." (6:31—μνημόσυνον). 4) "But the mother was... worthy of honorable memory...." (7:20—μνήμη).

250. *3 Maccabees* (c. 100 B.C.): "But as thou hast said, Not even when they were in the land of their enemies have I forgotten them...." (6: 15—Οὐδὲ ὑπερεῖδον αὐτούς [from ὑπεροράω = overlook. The translation "forgotten" shows the close relationship between memorial and what we have called "equivalently memorial" terminology and thinking.]).

251. *Tobit* (c. 230 B.C.): 1) "When I remembered my God with all my soul, the Most High gave me grace and favour." (1:11). 2) "Bring in

---

[1] See *The Apocrypha and Pseudepigrapha of the Old Testament in English*, ed. R. H. Charles, 2 vols. (Oxford: Clarendon Press, 1913).

whosoever of our brethren is mindful of the Lord." (2:2). 3) "And now, O Lord, remember thou me, and look upon me, not my sins." (3:3). 4) "Remember [your mother]..., son... be mindful of the Lord all thy days, and let not thy will be set to sin... do acts of righteousness." (4:4-5). 5) "And Tobias remembered the words of Raphael, and took.... And... the demon... ran away...." (8:2-3). 6) "And now, when thou didst pray and Sarah, I did bring the memorial of your prayer before the glory of the Lord: and when thou didst bury the dead, likewise." (12:12—μνημόσυνον).

252. *Judith* (c. 100 B.C.?): "Remember all the things which [God]... did to Abraham...." (8:26). No other memorial terminology.

253. *Sirach* (300-200 B.C.): 1) "He that honors his father maketh atonement for sins.... and what time he prayeth he shall be heard.... as a substitute for sins it shall be firmly planted. In the day of affliction it shall be remembered to thy credit. It shall obliterate thine iniquities...." (3:3-5, 14-15). 2) "In all thy doings remember thy last end...." (7:36; see also 8:5,7). 3) "Say not: 'I am hidden from God, And in the height who will remember me?'" (16:17). 4) "He remembereth not the Most High." (23:18. I.e., he forgets that God sees him). 5) "My memorial is sweeter than honey, and the possession of me than the honey-comb." (24:20; Wisdom is speaking. The Greek is μνημόσυνον). 6) "His sins (God) will surely keep (in memory).... Remember thy last end, and cease from enmity.... Remember the commandments.... and (remember) the covenant of the Most High." (28:1,6-7). 7) "Appear not with empty hands in the presence of the Lord, for all this (shall be done) because it is commanded. The offering of the righteous maketh the altar fat, and its sweet savour (cometh) before the Most High. The meal-offering of a righteous man is acceptable, and its memorial shall not be forgotten." (35:4-7. Gk. μνημόσυνον). 8) "Dismiss the remembrance of [a deceased friend or relative, after a day or two of mourning]... and remember [his and your own]... end." (38:20). 9) "I would fain remember God's works...." (42:15). 10) "Beloved of God and men was Moses of happy memory." (45:1—οὗ τὸ μνημόσυνον ἐν εὐλογίαις). 11) "And he [God] clothed him... and encompassed him... with resounding bells round about, so as to cause the sound of him to be audible in the inmost shrine, for a memorial for the children of his people." (45:8-9— εἰς μνημόσυνον υἱοῖς). [Box and Oesterley, the translators in Charles, add the note: "i.e., 'they were to call God's attention to Aaron as the representative of his people' (McNeile on Exod. xxviii. 33); cp. Exod. xxviii. 35 ('And the sound thereof shall be heard when he goeth in unto the holy place before the Lord, and when he cometh out, that he die not'). It has also been thought that their purpose was to apprise the people when Aaron had reached the Holy Place."] 11) "For a memorial in graven writing, according to the number of the tribes of Israel." (45:11—these are the twelve stones of Exod. 28:21,29). 12) "He chose him out of all living, to bring near the burnt-offering and fat pieces, and to burn a sweet savour and a memorial, and make atonement for the children of Israel." (45:16. Note that the sin offering is a "sweet savour" to God). 13) "Then the sons of Aaron sounded with the trumpets... for a remembrance before the Most High." (50:16. Gk. εἰς μνημόσυνον. This is of course a reference to Num. 10:2ff, as Box and Oesterley note. There ἀνάμνησις is used, showing the interchangeability of the two words. Douglas Jones admits the reminding-God force in the Numbers text: "No one would seek to maintain that ἀνάμνησις is incapable of bearing this godward reference.")[2] 14) "Then did I remember the loving-kindnesses of Jahveh.... And I lifted up my voice... cried: 'O Jahveh... forsake me not....' Then did Jahveh hear my voice, ...and delivered me...." (51:8,10-12).

254. *Wisdom of Solomon* (Probably after 50 B.C.): 1) "Better than [being evil and having children who die young]... is childlessness with virtue; for in the memory of virtue is immortality." (4:1—ἐν μνήμῃ. So in 5:13). 2) "Thou dost chastise... them that fall... and, putting them in remembrance by the very things wherein they sin, dost thou admonish them... that they may believe on thee, O Lord." (12:2—ὑπομιμνήσκων). 3) "They were troubled for a short space, having a token of salvation, to put them in remembrance of the... command... for he that turned toward it was not saved by that which he saw, but by thee, the Saviour of all." (16:6-7—εἰς ἀνάμνησιν ἐντολῆς νόμου σου. More simply, "as a reminder of the command of your law.") 4) "For a blameless man hasted to be their champion: bringing the weapons of his ministry, even prayer and the propitiation of incense...; by word did he subdue the minister of punishment, by bringing to remembrance oaths and covenants made with the fathers.... the destroyer gave way... these he feared." (18:21-22,25—ὑπομνήσας. The one reminded here is "Thine all powerful word" of v. 15; i.e., the angel of God). 5) "And they skipped about like lambs, praising thee, O Lord, who delivered them. For they still remembered what came to pass in the time of their sojourn." (19:9-10).

255. *1 Baruch* (Whitehouse [in Charles] says c. C.E. 78. The *Jerusalem Bible* says of much of the book, "[it]... may be as late as the 2nd or 1st century B.C.")[3]: 1) "I will give them a heart... and they shall... think upon my name... for they shall remember the way of their fathers, which sinned.... And I will make an everlasting covenant with them...." (2:31b-33,35). 2) "O Lord... hear now the prayer of the dead Israelites, and of the children of them.... Remember not the iniquities of our fathers: but remember thy power and thy name.... for we have called to mind all the iniquity of our

---

[2] Jones: 185.
[3] The "Introduction to the Prophets," *The Jerusalem Bible* (Garden City, New York: Doubleday, 1966), p. 1128.

fathers...." (3:4-5,7). 3) "Be of good cheer, my people, the memorial of Israel." (4:5. Gk. μνημόσυνον 'Ισραήλ. The meaning of the noun here may be explained by 4:27: "Be of good cheer, O my children, and cry unto God: for ye shall be remembered of him that hath brought these things upon you." Or it may simply mean the present Israel). 4) "Arise, O Jerusalem... and behold thy children gathered... rejoicing that God hath remembered them." (5:5).

256. *Bel and the Dragon* (c. 100 B.C.): "Then said Daniel, (Yea), for the Lord who forsakes not those who love Him has remembered me." (v. 38).

257. *Additions to Esther* (B.C. 125 to C.E. 90): 1) "And Mardocheus besought the Lord, calling to remembrance all the works of the Lord..." (13:8). 2) "Remember (us), O Lord...." (14:12). 3) "Do you also among your commemorative festivals keep it a notable day... a day of salvation to us... but a memorial of destruction to those who conspire against us." (16:22). 4) "For I remember concerning the dream which I saw... So God remembered his people...." (10:5,12).

258. The short works *Epistle of Jeremy, Susanna,* and *Prayer of Azariah* have no memorial terminology.

Significance of the Apocrypha

259. As in the regular Old Testament texts the religious memorial usages in the apocryphal books are widely diffused, existing also in the wisdom materials, and making up the large majority of memorial references. God's remembering occurs in the verbal form about ten times, several of them "reminding-God". There are about five "reminding-God" nouns. God remembers his own mercy, covenant, or past works; the people's persons, penitence, faithfulness (this including that of the fathers or special individuals), prayer and cultic acts. The people remember in about the same number of cases: God, his works or law, his covenant. There are half a dozen explicit covenant references in the texts themselves, spread through five different books; and numerous additional references to covenant contexts or material. Additionally, the contexts of the texts cited frequently contain explicit references to covenant. 1 Baruch provides a "new covenant" text as well as "God remembering" terminology. Μνημόσυνον is the favorite "reminding" noun, with ἀνάμνησις used only once (in Wis. 12:2), where it refers to God's chastisement serving as a reminder to men of their having sinned against God's law. On the other hand, μνημόσυνον substitutes for the ἀνάμνησις of the "reminding-God" text of Num. 10:10. The two words are interchangeable for this writer—probably for many at this time.

260. Without exception, these books show a strong support for the traditional cult, for Temple, sacrifice and prayer. The many references to these institutions are interwoven with the memorial terminology and its equivalents. Frequently the references are indirect but all the more meaningful for that. "But Judith fell upon her face, and put ashes upon her head... and the incense of that evening was now being offered at Jerusalem in the house of God, and Judith cried unto the Lord with a loud voice, and said...." (Jud. 9:1). Again, "Neither is there at this time prince, or prophet, or leader, or burnt-offering, or sacrifice, or oblation, or incense, or place to offer before thee and to find mercy. But in a contrite heart and a humble spirit let us be accepted, like as in the burnt offerings of rams and bullocks...." (Pr. Azar. 1:15-16). The cult must ever be guarded against contamination, "detestable works of enchantments and unholy rites, merciless slaughterers of children, and sacrificial banqueters on men's flesh and blood...." (Wisd. 12:4-5). That this is no condemnation of cult as such, but directed against alien cultic practices and corruptions of God's cult is clearly show by the same book, which eulogizes Aaron and the "weapons of his ministry, even prayer and the propitiation of incense.... bringing to remembrance oaths and covenants made with the fathers...." (18:21-22).

261. Memorial thinking in the Old Testament and the Apocrypha is thus not a subject of particular reflection by this or that theologian, but a widely and indeed generally accepted fact that founds an equally general manner of expression. *Memorial thinking and terminology is likely to occur where there is a cluster of ideas like God, Israel, cult, covenant, promise, law, sin, petition, thanksgiving, sacrifice or other oblation, faithful servants of God.* In such cases "reminding-God" or "God-remembering" terminology is as likely to appear as is "reminding-Israel" or "Israel-remembering" terminology. But whichever appears, the other is always possible in the context; if Israel is reminded, it is usually God who directly or indirectly reminds her—which of course presumes that God himself "remembers". And it is always Israel or some member of it that reminds God, or takes note of his remembering. *In other words, whichever terminology appears, the thinking related to the other terminology is implicit. This is especially evident in cultic contexts.*

262. Some of the above-discussed texts may have been written originally in Greek, in whole or in part. Yet that, or their translation into Greek, does not seem to have affected the use of memorial ideas and terms to any significant extent. But the situation is different with respect to some of the pseudepigrapha and writers like Philo and Josephus. In order to appreciate why this is so, it seems best at this point to discuss the classical Greek attitude towards these ideas and terms.

CHAPTER III: **The Typical Greek View**

263. There is no question but that the Greeks had a strong sense of history—of "man's remembering man". They were also very "mindful of the gods". We are principally interested here in discovering their views on the god's remembering, and on whether their gods were reminded, in prayer and cult, in the manner we have seen to have been so common with the Hebrews.

The Rational Quality

264. E. R. Dodds refers to an episode in which a young man he met at the British Museum remarked to him about the evident rationality of Grek art. Dodds goes on to ask himself, "Were the Greeks in fact quite so blind to the importance of non-rational factors in man's experience and behaviour as in commonly assumed both by their apologists and by their critics?"[1] He then details and comments on a large number of phenomena that have to do with the unknown and the felt: that is, on the one hand with unknown objects of the experiencer's rational consciousness; and on the other, with non-rational but sentient reactions (or elements in a mixed rational-non-rational reaction) on his part, whether towards the known or the unknown. An example of the first class would be to placate unknown forces by means that might rationally be thought suitable for placating; another, to gain knowledge from unidentified sources, as in shamanism; a third, the attribution of events to Fate rather than to some identified specific source. The second class would include a wide range of non-rational experiences such as dreams, visions, ecstasies and exaltations.

265. Reading Dodds and other relatively modern authors who deal with these subjects, one might almost come to forget about the rational factor (the originally evident one!) in Greek religion, or at least to conclude that it was, after all, the irrational that made that religion truly religious. The impression deserves to be consciously counter-weighted. Guthrie, like Dodds, speaks of the "non-rational element of religion, without which it would not be religion,"[2] and argues that "The word religion could go out of use if it stood for something that could be entirely accounted

---

[1] E. R. Dodds, *The Greeks and the Irrational* (Berkeley: University of California Press, 1951), p. 1.

[2] W. K. C. Guthrie, *The Greeks and Their Gods* (Boston: Beacon, 1960), p. 205.

for by rational and consistent thought, since all that it represents could
be expressed by other terms—philosophy, ethics or metaphysics." [3]   The
accent in this citation from Guthrie is again on the irrational, but it is
part of a balanced presentation which sees both the rational and the non-
rational as legitimately religious, and necessary for religion.   For the Greeks,
in particular, explanation was always desirable.   The frequently recurring
notion of Fate paradoxically demonstrates this.   Whatever its origins, it
came to be used as *an explanation for what was inexplicable by inherited
mythical structures*.   Again, rationally satisfying causes consistent with
those structures, like gods, demons and shades, repeatedly enter into what
seem at first sight to be purely irrational areas.

266. Reitzenstein makes the distinction between public cults and
secret ones,[4] a distinction which is indirectly related to that of rational
vs. non-rational in that it was the secret cults, the mysteries, that contained
the largest element of the irrational.   This distinction too might give rise
to a misapprehension were it to be assumed that the "public" cults were
empty of religious significance for the individuals who witnessed them,
or that there was no individualist practice related to the cults' mythical
background.   I think it perfectly true to say that there is no true religion
without the individualistic element—mere pomp is not religion.   This
accords with the most common kind of definition of religion in English
usage,[5] and I think the Greeks would have agreed with the evaluation.
This personal element was, however, associated with the public cults in
innumerable ways and instances.   "Public" must therefore be read with
reservations.   The "public" cults were traditional in the political entities
in which they were mainly found, were publicly as well as privately
practised, were usually open to participation or at least viewing by the
public, and were publicly authorized or approved—largely because they
were not generally considered to pose a threat to the state; quite the opposite.[6]   But they were also "private" in various ways.

267. Another distinction that might cause a somewhat similar difficulty is that which modern commentators so frequently make between
elitist and popular beliefs, putting the accent on the rational in the former
case and the non-rational in the latter.   It is in one sense true that professional philosophers are more rational than professional fishermen; but
fishermen can be eminently rational about catching fish, buying and mend-

---

   [3] Guthrie, p. 307.
   [4] See, for example, Richard Reitzenstein, *Hellenistic Mystery-Religions*, trans. John
E. Steely (Pittsburgh: Pickwick, 1978), p. 116.
   [5] See *Webster's* s.v. "religion."   The first meaning given is "The personal commitment to and serving of God or a god with worshipful devotion."
   [6] See Reitzenstein, p. 132.
   [7] The relative national wealth of India must have increased a third during the
past ten years due to the large amounts of gold in jewelry held by ordinary people.

ing boats, and buying security by buying gold jewelry.[7] They can also be quite rational about many aspects of religion, even though they may accept into their religious outlook more elements of the irrational than the philosopher would. I do not speak merely of religious practices, but of beliefs as well. The Greek man in the street probably knew, or thought he knew, that most of the banes and benefits of his life ultimately came from the gods, and knew or thought he knew the sensible means to avert the banes and obtain the benefits. He may not have seen *every* eventuality as necessarily resolvable within this context: there may have been certain things about which, in his view, neither he nor the dead nor the daemons nor the gods could do anything; other things due to influences for which his inherited mythology was inadequate; and others which he lacked the means to accomplish because of some accident of personal means or geography. But the very recognition of such a situation, and the casting about for ways to meet it, was a rational reaction in the true Greek style remarked on above, and it may well have been a truly "popular" ore. The rationality went further. As was noted above, the concept of Fate may have been a part-solution to such problems. And if "Fate" was acknowledged as this kind of ultra-ultimate cause, perhaps one could discover how Fate had determined affairs and see whether one might not escape evil by reading good for oneself—for by reading good one would ipso facto prove that good was fated! Thus the recourse to divination, to astrology, to visions of the future. Undoubtedly there were those who felt that an evil fate would result no matter what one did, but it was not really Greek to stay indefinitely in this depressing bind. Fate came to be seen more as a general than a personal law, and ways and means were sought to evade evil. Knowledge was the best means, and here again the gods entered the picture, for they were ideal sources of knowledge. If one's own gods could not provide the needful, one could seek other gods and better one's prospects—a recourse very popular in the hellenistic age. But first, one tried to improve prospects by appealing to the known gods in ways determined by their known qualities. This is rational, and memorial thinking fits into this rational scheme.

The Importance and Functions of the Gods

268. Memorial thinking when fully developed requires personal divinities seen as capable of influencing human affairs—gods. As was intimated above, the gods in historical times always had a central place in the Greek world-view. Equally ancient, perhaps, was the concept of those gods as part of a cosmic system. It was precisely this cosmic context that made the concept of Fate a possibility and a necessity. We have noted that the gods were given a place in the drama of Fate through their knowledge of the future; but this was not the only way that they and Fate were merged into a working synthesis. The movement towards a truly

supreme deity was a gradual development; but from very early the gods
were felt to have some real say in the progress of events. "Pray to the
gods, for theirs is the power." [8] Lucian has Cyniscus ask Zeus why men
should sacrifice to the gods when the gods can only do what the fates
ordain.[9] The question had arisen centuries earlier. Thucydides' Athenians
implicitly give a part-answer to it with a developed theology when they
say, "For of the gods we hold this belief, and of men we know, that
by a necessity of their nature wherever they have power they always
rule." [10] As in the case of divination, we have here a generalizing of the
influence of Fate that liberalizes an earlier, more pointedly deterministic
approach. In the generalized view Fate does not ordain that the god must
do this or that here and now, but that the god act in a manner that is
predictable in an overall way: that he be pleased by offerings and able
to respond to them; angered by arrogance; even, occasionally, arbitrary
in action. If a man knows the manner, and acts accordingly, he will have
a minimum of clashes with Fate. The sure way to know that Fate has
ordained one's downfall is to challenge the gods! Lucian's Zeus suggests
as much when he tells Cyniscus, "Fate does it all through us." [11] Later,
Lucian has Zeus say that the gods "are soothsayers and foretell all that
the Fates have established," [12] but this interpretative role for the gods if
held exclusively would in effect contradict the instrumental view previously
put forward by this Zeus, and the instrumental view carries within it
the possibilities of the more general approach expressed by Thucydides.
Indeed, the interpretative view has wider possibilities too, for as we have
seen, it was incorporated into the scheme whereby Fate is neutralized
by divination. Lucian's treatment fails to take into account the development of theology within the traditional system. Indeed, he is not ultimately
concerned with possibilities within the system, but with the system as
such. He resents the lack of a scientific or experiential demonstration of
the validity of the basic mystical presuppositions—resents the claims for
the existence of more-than-human beings. It is the acceptance of whatever
cannot be demonstrated that he directly objects to; he has no feel for
consistency within a system if it violates his own prescriptions. He is
against dogmatic theology qua dogmatic; what he probably yearns for,
really, is a "natural" theology, one demonstrable by experience alone or
by logic based on experience. This is significant in the light of Guthrie's
remark about the word "religion" going out of use "if it stood for something that could be entirely accounted for by rational and consistent
thought." [13] The ordinary Greek accepted the superhuman as data of

---

[8] Theognis, *Elegies* 171, quoted in F. M. Cornford, *Greek Religious Thought* (New
York: J. M. Dent and Sons, 1923), p. 38.
[9] See Lucian, *Zeus Catechized* 4ff, in LCL, *Lucian II*, trans. A. M. Harmon.
[10] Thucydides 5,105,2 in LCL, *Thucydides III*, trans. Charles F. Smith.
[11] Lucian, *Zeus Catechized* 11.
[12] Ibid., 12.

faith; that is, because he was told that it was so; and much of what he was told had not been checked out in any objectively experiential way by those who inaugurated or passed on the material. Thus, the ordinary Greeks' concepts and practices could *not* be *entirely* accounted for by rational and consistent thought, and could be religious (by Guthrie's definition) even though rational in their developments in the manner described earlier. (264ff).

269. The religious philosopher and the religious mystic each in his own way tries to solve Lucian's problem without contradicting religious beliefs. The mystic would like to say, and often says, "I have experienced God"; the philosopher, "I have proved that the incomprehensible exists concretely." But both these attitudes, even when presumed unsuccessful, allow for the use of myth: the incomprehensible almost demands it by definition; the experiential seeks it because experience is necessarily ultimately related to something outside oneself. Thus, Greek philosophers could sincerely participate in the traditional cult, and the devotees of the mysteries could see these against the traditional mythical background. Both groups, too, could share in dogmatic developments such as eschatological judgement, or immortality by some kind of apotheosis. There is no doubt that philosophers tend more easily than ordinary citizens to let received dogmas and cult suffer because of mental abstractions; similarly the mystery devotees, because of mental absorption. But the fact that both groups could omit the same things shows that there was a middle ground of mixed reason and emotion that was legitimately "religious". It may even suggest that the true genius of religion is more readily found there than elsewhere.

270. Writing in the first century B.C. Diodorus of Sicily notes that "the great generality of men are restrained from evil doings by two things—judicial penalties and the visitations of the gods." [14] Sextus Empiricus, using an argument probably derived from Posidonius (who was about contemporary with Diodorus), says that "Practically all men, Greeks and barbarians alike, believe that such a thing as a Divine being exists, and for this reason agree in offering sacrifice and prayer... to the gods.... The idea of the gods... has been there from the beginning of time and lasts till the end of time." [15] Maximus of Tyre in the second century C.E. says practically the same thing, but even more forcefully. [16] Frederick Grant gives many examples of the vitality of institutional and traditional

---

[13] See our note 2. It should be remarked that by the dictionary definition given in our note 5, a God found by a "natural" theology could still be the object of true religion.

[14] Diodorus 34,2,47; quoted in Edwyn Bevan, *Later Greek Religion* (London: Dent, 1927), p. 78.

[15] Sextus Empiricus, *Adversus Mathematicos* 9,60-61, in Bevan, pp. 79-80.

[16] See Maximus of Tyre, *Orations* 11,10-12, in Bevan, pp. 142ff.

[17] See Grant, pp. 3-69.

religion in Hellenistic times,[1] and prefaces them with the remark that "It is a great mistake to assume that the old, traditional religion was dead, and that only the secret mystery cults were alive." [18]

271. Several Christian testimonies to the persistence of traditional forms of pagan practice and belief are given in *Acts*, and there is no reason to think that they are not accurate representations. There is the episode in ch. 14 in which "the priest of Zeus, whose temple was in front of the city, brought oxen and garlands to the gates and wanted to offer sacrifice with the people." (v. 13). There is Paul's reference to the religiousness of the Athenians: "For as I passed along, and observed the objects of your worship...." (17:23). There are the references to Artemis' temple and the little silver shrines, in ch. 19. Syncretistic as this Artemis cult may have been, it still made use of traditional concepts, cult acts and objects. As Grant suggests, one could get the notion from some present-day commentators that in Hellenistic times there was nothing but scepticism on the one hand and ecstasy—or the search for it—on the other. Certainly, archaic reactions were often smiled at by the sophisticated, or looked on as political devices to pacify the populace. Polybius says condescendingly of the Romans, "To such an extraordinary height is [scrupulous fear of the gods]... carried on among them, both in private and public business, that nothing could exceed it." [19] But as the excerpt itself reveals, the fact that some of the intelligentsia saw little of worth in the old ways does not mean that these ways had no appeal. Indeed, they were probably the normal ways of the vast majority, including not a few intellectuals. Diodorus, Sextus and Posidonius were not country bumpkins.

272. Many sincerely religious thinkers strove to justify the mythical as such, and to present the cruder myths in a more favorable light. The spiritualization we have seen to be operative among the Hebrews had its parallel here. Pausanias in the second century C.E. still believed in the old gods and some of the lesser myths, and provides many examples of others who felt likewise. Plutarch argues that many of the unpleasant things in religion were done by or related to demons: v.g., "rites of soothing and propitiation designed to turn away the malice of bad daemons." [20] Magical practices could be and no doubt were excused as connected with these sub-divinities, thus not compromising the more elevated forms of worship. The use of images was defended by Dio Chrysostom: "Unable to show the unimaginable and the unrepresentable by an example of it, we try to do so by means of the visible and the representable. We so use this that it has the virtue of a symbol." [21] So too Maximus of Tyre.

---

[18] Ibid., p. 3.
[19] Polybius 6,56, in Bevan, p. 77.
[20] Plutarch, *On the Cessation of Oracles* 12, in Bevan, p. 125.
[21] Dio Chrysostom *Orations* 12,59, in Bevan, p. 114. ("συμβόλου δυνάμει.")

"It is not that the Divine Being stands in any need of images or statues. It is poor humanity, because of its weakness... which has contrived these things as symbols." [22]   We have seen how divination might be justified rationally. Its methods, or some of them, are repellent to the modern mind, but once one accepts the gods and their concern for men, it can make sense. The gods know future events, and place signs revelatory of those events where they might very properly be expected—in nature or in the materials used for divine worship. Or at least, the gods know where such signs are located. Even astrology could be associated with the gods in one way or another.

273. Guthrie describes the Indo-European or Olympian tradition as centering around the father-god—a powerful person able to harm or aid, to be contracted with somewhat as an employer might be by an employee; non-mystical, daylight and basically rational. The Asian mother-goddess tradition was more open to non-rational elements, especially at the level of practice. But here too the basis of the cult was recognition of a personal relationship, and not all cult practices were non-rational. Guthrie emphasizes the "adoption possibilities" in the Asian cults,[23] but such possibilities in that context should not be taken to mean that mysticism is the only means to adoption. Indeed, today the word "adoption" has many cold, legal connotations, and no doubt it always did. The later Greeks saw the possibility of apotheosis even in the old Olympian tradition. Pausanias says, "Indeed, men were raised to the rank of gods in those days.... Aristaeus... Britomartis... Herakles... Amphiaraus... Pollux and Castor." [24]   The way was open for a development of theology in this line even in the Olympian tradition. Guthrie, after giving some examples of the "continuing influence of the dead," [25] remarks that "We may well suppose that the Homeric conception of the 'strengthless dead' was a somewhat artificial construction only lightly imposed on the very different groundwork of popular religion." [26]   But the relative scarcity of clearcut apotheoses among the early Greeks seems to suggest either that the strength of the dead was after all not so great, or that of the gods was indeed *very* great. Suppositions and suggestions aside, the evidence definitely indicates a notable inherent superiority of the gods over men living *or* dead, and the difficulty of breaking the barrier.[27]

274. At the same time, both gods and men recognized one another as persons. Guthrie defines δίκη as "the right, great or limited, of a certain

---

[22] Maximus of Tyre, *Orations* 2,2, in Bevan, p. 147.
[23] See Guthrie, p. 34 et al.
[24] Pausanias 8,2; 8,3-7. In Bevan, pp. 154-155.
[25] Guthrie, p. 235.
[26] Ibid.
[27] It might be helpful to note that traditional Christianity accepts an adoption possibility while at the same time insisting on the continued essential distinction between the Divine Persons and the human adoptees.

station in life." [28] The gods, like the aristocrats among men, had a code for dealing with feudal inferiors such as men. But just as the Homeric aristocrats recognized their feudal inferiors as men, so the gods recognized theirs as persons—in *this* like the gods themselves.

275. As for the code, it protected men as long as they kept the proper observances towards the gods. It was within this framework that contracts were made. The balance of privilege and power within the cosmic society of course lay with the divine nobility, and as we have already remarked, a certain arbitrariness was expected of them. It was paradoxically part of their δίκη. However, they did have definite responsibilities, and to balance the arbitrariness there was a kind of *noblesse oblige*. Further, there were always certain fundamental liberties available to men, as for the ordinary Greek even in the Homeric picture. Certain adjustments in allegiance were possible, and laxness as well. For that matter, so were impiety and scepticism, if one was willing to face the consequences.

276. This acknowledgement of power supremacy and of some arbitrariness in its use effectively helped to protect the pantheon against excessive demands of theurgy almost universally until the religious uncertainties of the late fifth and fourth centuries; indeed, among large numbers of conservatives right down through Hellenistic times.

277. Theurgy is probably associated in our minds more often with beliefs and practices that are shared by Olympian and chthonic types of religion, like sacrifice, than with those that are thought of as typical of the mysterics; but it can as justly be associated with the latter. In either case, there is a kind of theurgy that is open to a more favorable interpretation, what we might call theurgy in a loose sense of the word. (See 170, no. 1,e). It is seen as an arrangement stipulated by the god himself, or by Zeus or a council of the gods. If the gods are free to make contracts, they are free to establish means whereby they will invariably be placated when the means are used. This kind of contracting could be seen as something done in the long distant past; indeed, in legendary times. More objectionable would be a type of theurgy in which the god was seen as simply fated to respond favorably to certain practices and unfavorably to others—a view that could in practice work out very like pure magic. This kind of approach can be seen to accord closely with the determinist view of the relationship between Fate and the gods proposed by Lucian.

278. From the devotees' point of view such a position had as much against it as in its favor; in fact, it tended to lead to gloom and despair. A theological development in the direction of greater liberty for the gods

---

[28] Guthrie, p. 124.

with concomitant generosity towards men could therefore be expected. This paralleled a development of doctrines of immortality. At the same time, until such doctrines were developed, it was inevitable that some men, especially sensitive and artistic types, should succumb to a kind of death wish involving both themselves and the gods. This is one of the paradoxes of Greek religious history: that there were forces working, and working effectively, for the liberation of the gods at the same time as other forces worked for their enslavement and extinction. It was a tug of war present in a primitive form already in Homer and Hesiod; what happened was that with the passage of time it ceased to exist *in toto* within the individual minds of all believers, but was in large part resolved in one way or another in the minds of individuals and groups, so that by Hellenistic times there were high-minded monotheists, crude theurgists, utter sceptics, and a sizeable group whose theology was conservative and traditional, whether in the Eastern or the Western traditions, or a mixture of both. Plutarch has Cleombrotus say, "Some men deny that God is the cause of anything at all, and other men make him the cause of absolutely everything. Both these views miss the line of reason and discretion." [29]

279. Developments like the belief in personal immortality by no means excluded the element of personal relationship with the god, any more than did the trend towards private rather than public cult. Nor was mystic union the only way that one might share in the gods' immortality. For many believers the concept of the immortality of the soul had come to be an accepted doctrine—a strengthening of or substitution for the ancient notion of the shade, with the transfer of the place of beatitude from the half-light of Hades to the brightness of the far western isles, or even to Olympus. Cyniscus is asked by Zeus, "Don't you know... what punishments await the wicked when life is over, and in what happiness the good abide?" [30] Even Cyniscus does not categorically deny the possibility of such blessedness; he simply says, "When I die I shall find out whether there is really any such thing...." [31] When in the early days the gods were thought of as having their own bodies—but bodies that had ichor for blood, that breathed aether instead of air, and were nourished by heavenly foods—this kind of sharing in their lives would have been thought presumptuous; but with the spiritualizing of the concept of the gods and especially with the evolution of a notion of a spiritual soul, it became thinkable. There were the apotheoses already mentioned to show the way. This being the case, it was conceivable that the gods had a say in the matter of who should be their companions for eternity, whether by way of initial admission to heaven, or readmission. As usual there

---

[29] Plutarch, *Cess. of Orac.* 10, in Bevan, p. 122.
[30] Lucian, *Zeus Catechized* 17.
[31] Ibid.

were philosophers who saw no such possibility: for example, the Epicureans, for whom the gods were beyond caring about men; and the Stoics, for whom they were still the only true immortals, their personalities the only ones to survive the conflagrations that terminate the cosmic cycles.[32] But one did not have to take Stoicism pure; the powers and ways of the gods were after all not easy to define.

280. And, of course, believing in immortality did not lessen the usefulness of the gods in many men's minds for dealing with the things of this world. This, after all, was their traditional function. It was a function that is seen as operative even today, when there are so many "natural" ways of dealing with our earthly problems, and the hope of so many more; in Hellenistic times when scientific knowledge was so rudimentary, it was a function that forced itself upon the mind as one of the high probabilities.

Communication with the Gods, and Memorial

281. It is into the man-to-god relationship in the non-mystery tradition that the concept of memorial such as it developed among the Hebrews would most naturally fit. And it would also fit naturally with the practice of personal prayer, which is the most spontaneous natural expression of man's recognition of that relationship, presuming the believer recognizes some means of communication with these persons he believes in. Cleombrotus deprecates "those who... do away with the possibility of intercourse and communication between gods and men." [33] Most Greeks undoubtedly felt with him. They thought that the gods could perceive the spoken word and the cultic act. Often they used both together and spoke of both together, like Sextus Empiricus. (270). This association was in the earliest tradition in Greece as in Israel, and carried through to the end. "The Son of Abas did set up an altar that was the place of many prayers." [34] "Now first must merry men hymn the God in holy story and pure word, then when they have made libation and prayed for power to do what is right.... there's no wrong in drinking just so much...." [35] "The priests of Apollo shall make the prayers customary for the feast of Eumeneia." [36] The prayers usually included requests for the acceptance of the sacrifice, libation, or other ritual offering. "Hera... accept... this birthday sacrifice, these heifer victims.... Thus Maximus prayed as he

---

[32] See Bevan, pp. 29-30; 33. Diogenes Laërtius notes: "Cleanthus says that all souls remain in being till the next Conflagration, but Chrysippus says the souls of the wise only." (Quoted in Bevan, p. 33).

[33] Plutarch, *Cess. of Orac.* 10, in Bevan, p. 124.

[34] Bacchylides, *For Alexadamus* 40, in LCL, *Lyra Graeca III*, ed. and trans. J. M. Edmonds, no. 38.

[35] Xenophanes, elegiac poem, in LCL, *Elegy and Iambus I*, trans. J. M. Edmonds, elegy no. 1.

[36] Anonymous inscription, in LCL, *Lyra Graeca II*, ed. and trans. J. M. Edmonds.

poured the libation, and she granted his prayer without fail...." [37]   All this parallels the usage in Israel. Similar too was the use of gesture with simple private prayer: "Men put up their hands and besought the immortal gods...." [38]

282. The gods knew the nature and significance of the ritual actions and prayers. In the early days what Guthrie says may be true: "The only means of access to men is ⌊the gods'⌋ physical presence, so they could stride or fly." [39] At a slightly later stage the god stayed in heaven and sent messengers to pick up data about men. So, Hesiod speaks of "thrice ten thousand ministers of Zeus, immortal watchers of mortal men." [40] Lucian caricatures what in fact was a further stage of development when he pictures Zeus at prayer-time: "He let the just prayers come up through the orifice [in the floor of heaven] and then took them and filed them away at his right; but he sent the impious ones back ungranted..." [41] There is specific mention of sacrificial smoke: "The smoke came up and told Zeus the name of each man who was sacrificing." [42] In spite of himself Lucian here reveals a function for the cult object that goes beyond the original crude idea that the Gods "are especially fond of dining on the smoke from the sacrifices, which comes up to them all savoury, and on the blood of the victims that is shed about the altars when people sacrifice." [43] Duller spirits right through the ages undoubtedly thought that the gods did actually eat or drink the offerings somehow, but the persistence of sacrifice and other offering in ages when large numbers definitely did *not* think this indicates that these people, many of whom were quite sincere about sacrificing, must have had some alternative belief. The symbolic, "attention-catching" one was certainly widespread.

283. This view of cult objects and acts contains several elements that are exactly parallel to elements central in the view that the Hebrews expressed in specifically memorial language. Did the Greeks associate it with such language too? In particular, did they speak of "reminding" the god of the offerer by means of a cult act or object?

284. Memory was associated in the Greek mind with the gods in various ways. The Titaness Mnemosune bore the Muses to Zeus. [44] Or, as Michel says, "Μνήμη is the mother of the muses (acc. to Plat. Euthyd.,

---

[37] One Diodorus, a dedicatory epigram, in LCL, *The Greek Anthology I*, trans. W. R. Paton, bk, 6, no. 243.

[38] Bacchylides, *For Alexadamus* 40, no. 10.

[39] Guthrie, p. 208.

[40] Hesiod, *Works and Days* 225, in Cornford, p. 28.

[41] Lucian, *Icaromenippus* 25, in LCL, *Lucian II*.

[42] Lucian, *Icaromenippus* 26.

[43] Lucian, *Icaromenippus* 27.

[44] See Mark Morford and Robert Lenardon, *Classical Mythology*, 2nd ed. (New York: David McKay Co., 1977), p. 61.

275d), or the muse itself, to which there were sacrifices in Boeotia (Paus. 9,29,2). Μνήμη, μνεία and μνημοσύνη were cultically venerated." [45]   The waters of the lake of memory were recommended to the departing soul as a means to blessedness,[46] and according to Pausanias were made available in an earthly form to the suppliant to the oracle of Herkyna [47] in order that he might remember what he saw when he descended to the abode of Trophonios.   In the Stoic doctrine of the persistence of the gods through the cyclic conflagrations, the gods retained the memory of the past periods into the succeeding ones, a kind of primal example of the sort of recollection supposedly had by select individuals (such as Pythagoras) in transmigration.   The Platonist thought that knowledge itself was a recollection from the pre-existence in the world of ideas.

285. In fact, memory is seen by the Greeks as a special quality of divine life: its sources are in the other world whether the Olympian or the chthonic. The gods live at these sources, they do not forget; and they have the power to share remembrance with others. We saw Lucian portraying Zeus as having a kind of filing system for the deeds of men—a notion that can be taken as a figure of memory. Euripides suggests the currency of this idea when he asks, "Do you think that deeds of wrong fly up on wings to heaven, and then someone writes them on the tablets of Zeus, who looks upon the record and gives judgement upon men?" [48] Zeus deals mostly with man's day-to-day existence. But all men, and particularly those whose prayers are such as to be rejected by Zeus, ought themselves to remember that their deeds are recorded by another divine memory. Aeschylus says, "For Hades, 'neath the earth waits every soul, / A mighty judge who watcheth to enscroll / All sins on his eternal memory's roll." [49]

286. Occasionally, one finds even in earlier times references to the gods' attitudes towards prayer in terms of memory. With regard to Zeus, Aeschylus has the chorus in *The Suppliants* pray, "Be a rememberer of many things...." [50]   (Gk. πολυμνάστωρ), and the purpose of this remembering is that Zeus may "renew" ancient things—i.e., remember memorable and presumably sacred events of the past and on present analogous occasions provide a response similar to the previous benign ones. This viewpoint and prayer is anticipated in Lysias by the Greek participants in the battle of Salamis: "What supplications, what reminders of sacrifices, were

---

[45] *TDNT*, s.v. "μνήμη," by O. Michel.
[46] See Guthrie, p. 230.
[47] Pausanias 9,39; in Guthrie, p. 225.
[48] Euripides, *Melanippe*, fragment cited in Cornford, p. 154.
[49] Aeschylus, *Eumenides* 273-275, in Clifford H. Moore, *The Religious Thought of the Greeks* (Cambridge, Mass.: Harvard, 1925), p. 91.
[50] Aeschylus, *The Suppliant Maidens* 535, in LCL, *Aeschylus* I, trans. H. W. Smyth.

not sent up to Heaven!" [51] (ποῖαι δ'οὐχ ἱκετεῖαι θεῶν ἐγένοντο ἢ θυσιῶν
ἀναμνήσεις). What is noteworthy for our purposes here is that it is almost
certainly not the sacrifices that are spoken of as reminders; the sacrifices
are some of the "sacred things" Aeschylus' chorus prays about: the *prayers*
are the "reminders". Here in Lysias the sacred past occasions were sacrifices, and whether or not they were answered previously benignly, the
suppliants hope they will be answered now. All the same, there *is* a divine
memory of past sacred events, and a human reminding of the god.

287. We may conclude that on occasion prayer and such things as
the smoke of sacrifice might in the stress of the suppliants' personal
emotion (or in the poet's figured speech) be spoken of as "reminders"
to the gods, and this even in early times. Yet this mode of speech does
not seem to have been common, as it was among the Hebrews. One
place where we might expect to find it in abundance, if anywhere, is in
the votive offerings. These, by their very nature, by the location in which
they were placed, by accompanying inscriptions, indicate symbolic meaning
in the minds of their offerers, along with the hope that this symbolism
will be read and responded to by the god. W. H. D. Rouse says of votive
offerings (within which category he includes sacrifices) that "When complete, the offering stands as a memorial forever: it may be to remind man
of God's providence, or to remind the god of his worshipper's gratitude,
or both." [52] Speaking of "objects dedicated for what they imply," [53] he
says,

> The whole of this class may be called ideal, as meaning more than appears
> on the surface; and memorial, as intended to keep the god's beneficence
> before the mind of man, and no less the man's piety or gratitude before
> the mind of the god. This persistent idea is illustrated on the one side
> by the silver sow of Epidaurus,[54] on the other by the recurrence of the
> word 'memorial' on so many early inscriptions. In the later age, when
> thoughts were no longer understood only, but exprest, the idea is distinctly
> stated: as when Akeson, in offering a relief to Asclepius, says, "you know
> why; if not, this table will remind you." [55]

Here we have the Hebrew memorial exactly. *But as regards reminding
the god*, it strikes the reader that *the use of the terminology is not
traditional, it is occasional*. The "you know why" seems much more in
the Greek tradition than the "this tablet will remind you." I do not
think that the example's coming from a "later age" shows a true develop-

---

[51] Lysias, *Funeral Oration* 39, in LCL, *Lysias*, trans. W. R. Lamb.
[52] W. H. D. Rouse, *Greek Votive Offerings* (Cambridge: University Press, 1902; reprinted 1976), p. 351.
[53] Rouse, p. 356.
[54] Reference is to an example Rouse gives earlier (p. 226) of a case in which the
god tells the dedicant to remember something foolish she has done.
[55] Rouse, pp. 356-357.

ment of a usage. There is a notable scarcity of "god-reminding" terminology among the many examples of religious memorial terminology available to us, in spite of the fact that much of the contextual material intends and often expresses a godward reference. "May the city now have this memorial of the flourishing citizens Smikros and his sons, O city-protecting mistress Athene." [56] "This memorial of his prowess was set up unto Lord Poseidon by Pausanias the ruler of spacious Greece." [57] It was not for lack of familiarity with memorial terminology that the Greeks generally abstained from "reminding" the gods. Why was it then?

The Greek Differences

288. We have made the point that the gods in later times were not seen by many worshippers as requiring sustenance from men. In truth, they were scarcely needful of reminding either, at least as far as enlightenment was concerned. The Greeks like the Hebrews placed great emphasis on the divine omniscience, at least in the case of Zeus. Even the literary horseplay of Lucian reveals this. Morford and Lenardon remark that "Omniscience is most often reserved as a special prerogative of Zeus and Apollo, who communicate their knowledge of the future to men." [58] The statement is applicable to the whole course of the traditional stream. Zeus knows the future; a fortiori he knows past and present. [59] Presumably he always will know. What of the more philosophical believers? Epictetus, "when someone asked him how a man may be convinced that every one of his acts is seen by God.... said.... does not God perceive... every movement [of our minds] as closely akin to Him?" [60] Again, "God is within, and your daemon. What need have they of light to see what you are doing?" [61] These are Stoic expressions, but the Platonists might have said much the same.

289. Zeus like Yahweh knew everything. Yet—again like Yahweh—he expected prayer and cult. It was part of his δίκη. Prayer to him did not effect a transfer of knowledge about the pray-er's intentions, any more than with Yahweh. Yet it behoves man to take note of and make requests of the gods. And the Greek would have said that even a god cannot *answer* a request unless one is made—the idea of "referent of actuality" again. Similarly with offerings. The offering was an ἀνάθημα, from ἀνατίθημι: it was a material object or act "set up" before the god as well

---

[56] Inscription given in Rouse, p. 259. Translation by this writer.
[57] Anonymous inscription cited by Nymphis of Heraclea, in LCL, *Elegy and Iambus II*, insc. no. 17.
[58] Morford, p. 74.
[59] One way in which he was conceived to know the future was from his knowledge of the cyclic past, which was thought by some to repeat exactly in later cosmic cycles.
[60] Epictetus, *Discourses* 1,14; in Bevan, p. 107.
[61] Ibid., p. 108.

as before men—an idea having a parallel in the Latin *of-ferre* (with the participle *ob-latum*) = "to bring over against". Yet, prayer was seldom phrased in memorial terms, and though the term "memorial" is often used of votive offerings, it seems clear that the ones reminded were primarily the human beings who might pass by subsequently and see the offerings. For this reason, the "memorial" had to be a permanent thing— animal sacrifices and other transient offerings do not seem to have been called "memorials".

290. I think the difference between the Greek and the Hebrew usage was due to the closer, more familial attitude that the Israelites had towards their God. For the Greeks, it was enough for the offerer to express himself clearly and carry out the symbolic rites that gave communicative quality to the offerings. Man's approach to the gods was ideally personal, but not *highly* personal. Zeus was a "father", but he was more a father of the gods than a father of men: he was far distant, Olympian. Yahweh was the father of Israel, a man and a nation. He went with him in the way. "What great nation is there that has a god so near to it as the Lord our God is to us, whenever we call upon him?" (Deut. 4:7). For the Greek, warmth of devotion, coaxing or childlike affection would be familiar; so would reminding. To remind the gods would be something of an insult; not so much to them, perhaps, as to the cosmic system. Not so for the Hebrews. Israel was the child, the companion, the spouse. What wife does not remind her husband? Yahweh was of course omniscient, omnipotent, transcendent in a truer sense than Zeus ever was for the Greeks. And yet he was all these other things too. On Yahweh lay the burden of the speech he uses of himself and the speech it prompted in his chosen ones. He could bear the burden!

291. And that, perhaps, touches on the root difference. *Yahweh was great enough to be able to risk unbending.* The God of Israel, unlike Zeus, is not one star, however great, in a firmament of stars; he is beyond the firmament, and thus, paradoxically, can go beneath it. He is not the first regulation in a cosmic law, but is above the cosmos and is the maker of laws. Prayer and cult are not cosmic expressions, but are mandated by Yahweh's law. They fit human inclinations because God has made man to incline as God chooses. Yet he has made him also after his own image. Hebrew prayer and cult, by memorial terminology, recognized the filiation even while it recognized the transcendence. The Greek traditionally maintained a cool distance in their rational exchanges with God. Or rather, as the Hebrew would have said, with their god.

292. We have been speaking of "reminding God" primarily with reference to the now-state of the one reminding. But Yahweh was reminded equally of past salvific events. This aspect reveals a further difference between the Greek and the Hebrew view, and further exemplifies the same two qualities of transcendence and condescension (this in no pejorative sense, obviously) that Yahweh's nearness in every "here and now" reveals. Yahweh was seen as having done things that merited remembering in later times, and as having joined to them promises to repeat similar and greater things in the future when those things and those promises should be remembered by the descendents of the favored ones to whom they had been made—remembered by them, and he himself reminded by them in their childlike manner. Greek gods and goddesses were often credited with doing marvelous things for favorite individuals and groups among the sons and daughters of men, but these deeds were seldom seen as linked to promises for an everlasting future, nor were promises seen to apply to the whole Greek people—which in some measure explains why that people never became a nation. No covenant was concluded with any Greek Abraham, Moses or David. And it is the covenant that gives historical depth to the memorial scheme in Israel.

The Cult of Heroes

293. Otto Piper notes that "The School of Comparative Religion held that the term *anamnesis* pointed to a memorial celebration, and in particular to a memorial meal, as was customary in ancient Greece and Rome." [62] He does not favor the view, calling attention to the fact that these meals were not regularly repeated as was the Eucharist. Eduard Schweizer is stronger, saying "it is out of the question to think that the Lord's Supper was ever thought of as such a commemorative meal for the dead." [63] His argument is that "The death of Jesus is *proclaimed*—in all four accounts, in fact—as a death which took place *for* the participants." [64] He concludes, "The attempts to trace back this participation... to Hellenistic conceptions can be regarded, in the main, as having failed." [65]

294. This argument seems to assume that the dead had to be helped and could not help. Indeed, Karl Prümm says of the memorial rites: "It is clear that the so called offerings to the dead derive from another purpose entirely than other offerings. Basically, these 'offerings' to the dead from the very beginning were thought of as contributions supplying sustenance for the support of the shade." [66] He points to a difference in

---

[62] Otto A. Piper, "The Lord's Supper in New Testament Perspective," *Journal of the Interseminary Movement of the Southwest* (1962), p. 13.
[63] Eduard Schweizer, *The Lord's Supper*, trans. James M. Davis (Philadelphia: Fortress Press, 1967), p. 1.
[64] Ibid.
[65] Ibid., p. 2. He refers to G. Wagner, *Das religionsgeschichtliche Problem von Römer 6, 1-11* (Zürich: Zwingli Verlag, 1962), pp. 13-88; 271-306.
[66] Karl Prümm, *Religionsgeschichtliches Handbuch* (Rome: Päpstliches Bibelinstitut, 1954), p. 494.

type of offering to the dead and to the chthonic deities.[67] If this were the whole statement of the case, both Piper's and Schweizer's objections would be themselves unobjectionable. It is difficult to imagine a group of Greeks gathering for typical funeral feasts on the third, ninth, and thirtieth days, and somewhere then or in the cycle of "years' minds" deciding to reverse the process and have the celebrations more often rather than less, without some strong incentive for the reversal. Yet such an incentive seems to have been offered by notions of special power to be exercised on behalf of the living by *certain* deceased individuals who were "heroized". If this influence could be envisioned as beneficial on anything like the scale the individuals enjoyed when alive, or could be envisioned as permanent, then their deaths might well be "proclaimed". The notion of the dead influencing the living was of course an ancient one. Rouse says of the Scythians, "Partly for fear of what harm the ghosts could do, and partly from hope of their help, the survivors were scrupulous in doing what might please them." [68] It is not clear whether it was this idea that developed into the "hero feasts", and Rouse might seem to imply the opposite when he says that "a distinction soon grew up between burial rites and divine ritual." [69] But this "divine ritual" was not "hero" ritual except in a few clearcut cases of apotheosis. Harrison shows this when she says, "The banqueter [i.e., the dead man in the heroic reliefs of which she is speaking] is in some sense divine.... yet he is no real god... rather he is a man masked to his descendents as a daimon, as *the* Agathos Daimon. The dead individual grasps a perennial function and thereby wins immortality, he is heroized." [70] She describes a still further stage, which all the same falls short of full equality with the gods: "A daimon-hero receives *the* daimon, the god Dionysos—ὁ δαίμων ὁ Διὸς παῖς .... One daimon receives another and a greater than himself." [71] Rouse certainly suggests a development when he proposes that in course of time all the dead became heroes.[72] But the important points are that there were dead men and women who were heroized, given a cult, and to whom powers were ascribed that might help or hinder living men. Both Rouse and Harrison note the widespread nature of hero worship, and Rouse says, "The worship continues throughout Greek history.... lingering longest in rural places or country villages, and in cities supported rather by the poor than by the rich and great. It lingered too... because so little was needed in the way of [cultic] apparatus." [73] As to the powers and the cult: Harrison quotes Aristophanes: "Yes, and with holy offerings we sacrifice/To them as to

---

[67] Ibid.
[68] Rouse, p. 4.
[69] Ibid., p. 5.
[70] Jane Ellen Harrison, *Themis* (Cambridge: University Press, 1927), p. 308.
[71] Ibid., p. 315. The Greek quotation is from Euripides, *Bacchae* 416.
[72] See Rouse, p. 9.
[73] Rouse, p. 12.

the gods—and pour libations,/ Bidding them send good things up from below." [74]   Rouse gives many examples of hero-helpers of mankind, and says, "The idea of power in general is never lost sight of, and it is ascribed to the mighty dead throughout Greek history." [75]   Again, "The heroes do more than protect mankind; they also punish them for wrongdoing, or at least for an ofference against themselves." [76]   And he says, "In their honour recurrent feasts were to be kept up, with sacrifice and libation...." [77]

295. Much of this is compatible with the ideas of Jesus had by the early Christians, and with Eucharistic practice in Paul's times and communities.   Jesus was certainly thought of as heroic.   He was in some way divinized so as to achieve a unique position in the hierarchy of the dead.   He had power.   There was a meal cult that commemorated him, and there was a sacrificial nexus.   Differences exist, of course, between the hero feast and Paul's Eucharist, and they are significant.   The hero feast seems to have been only incidentally related to the hero's death; the sacrifice was not that *of* the hero, but that *to* him.   Most important, however, was the absence of a covenant nexus with a supreme God and with the past.   Whoever put together Paul's Eucharistic scenario saw it as making sense in a "new covenant" context.   The "new" suggests that there may have been elements present that were lacking in the old covenants. The covenant aspect is present in the Marcan account too, and its location at the center of a cluster of ideas and terminology whose larger portion, whatever the hellenic analogies, is quite at home in the Hebrew milieu, makes it likely that that milieu rather than those analogies was the chief determining factor in the selection of the various elements, whether in Mark or in Paul.

Concluding Thoughts on the Hebrew Preponderance

296. There is a more general reason, it seems to me, for understanding a basically Hebrew character for the Eucharistic meal.   I find it nearly inconceivable, after spending many years in India and observing Hindu culture and religion in a country strongly influenced by Western ideas and language, that a group of Palestinian Jews, even from the villages of Galilee, would have been following Greek funeral customs or practising Greek hero worship unalloyed, so that the Eucharist as Paul presents it would have developed from such a beginning.   Jewish fellowship meals may have been prompted by deaths as by other events, but meals would more likely have followed Jewish patterns than pagan, whatever the occasion.   There was undoubtedly a widespread Greek influence in Palestine,

---

[74] Harrison, p. 316.   Quotation from Aristophanes, *Tagenistae* frag. 1.
[75] Rouse, p. 8.
[76] Ibid., p. 9.
[77] Ibid.

and some influence on Jewish religion. But there is little real evidence to support the view that it was all that different from the kind of influence the British had on Hinduism. That, religiously speaking, was practically nil, *especially* in the area of cult. This was partially due to the mobility of the Indian peasant, who even today thinks nothing of walking a hundred miles to a fair or on pilgrimage, and doing it several times a year. The point is that the Hindus knew not only something of the religious customs of the foreigners, but a good deal about those of other Hindus around the country. It is very much like the picture we get in the Gospels, in Josephus, and elsewhere. Trips to Jerusalem for the feasts were more a picnic than a chore. But really, walking to Jerusalem was not all that necessary to learn about Judaism. Archaeology demonstrates that the Gospel picture of synagogue practice in Galilee is factual. The Jewish establishment there may not have been perfectly "Jerusalem orthodox", but it was there and it was probably Hebrew in most of its content and practice just as it was in Alexandria to the west.

297. What does seem to me quite credible is that early-on some Jewish Christians (and they all seem to have been Jewish early-on) were doing something acceptably Hebrew into which they introduced something Greek that—although not acceptable to the majority of their coreligionists because it *was* a change and was *too* clearly Greek—was actually ideologically and even liturgically compatible with the Hebrew framework. The idea of a hero cult would have been something Greek. However, it is hard to show that it fits any better with the picture of the Eucharist that Paul gives us than would a Hebrew communion meal (related as these were to festal and other "memorials") presented as mandated by a legitimate Hebrew hero. We shall later discuss a Greek thing that I think *was* definitely introduced this way. As for the hero cult, I suspect that what actually happened was that a Hebrew-type cult grew up that was easily recognizable by Greeks as being similar to their own kind of cult. If in fact it happened the other was round, it is still necessary to recognize that Paul and others before and after him found it essential to make the majority of the elements in the Eucharist idea-cluster (and term-cluster) Hebraic. For some reason, it had to make sense to Jews. In this study we are less interested in the reason than in the fact. *It is our thesis here that whichever way the development went, the tradition as presented by Paul was so heavily Hebraic in idea and terminology that it was inevitable for the "memorial" aspect to be interpreted, by those who grasped those ideas and terms, in a manner that would include both reminding-God and reminding-man.* They might find the memorial usage ambiguous, but for them this would simply mean they would have to allow for *both* meanings.

298. We have seen that the idea of reminding-God was very weak in the traditional Greek cult. The introduction of the hero would make the notion easier to accept as far as prayer and cult directed to the hero himself was concerned. He was acknowledged to have been a man and still to be something less than Olympian. However, most Christian prayer sems to have been directed towards God rather than Jesus (another sign, probably, of the Hebrew background), so that generally speaking, the increasing influence of Greek thinking and practice on the Eucharist would naturally tend to reduce the Christians' appreciation of the reminding-God aspect of their cult, presuming that to have been present originally. Indeed, the Greek distaste for reminding-God terminology probably had its effect on Paul's own tastes and in a special way on his writings when they were directed, as they usually were, to largely Greek communities. And in fact, except when passing on the tradition of the Eucharist *as* a tradition, he prefers equivalently memorial to explicitly memorial terminology. He could not easily have foreseen that such a policy might eventually lead to a widespread inability to appreciate important aspects of the cult he defends in *1 Corinthians*—aspects he himself was perfectly able to comprehend as "an Israelite, a descendant of Abraham." (Rom. 11:1).

299. The LXX has shown us that the use of the Greek *language* did not of itself dissuade people from using reminding-God language in abundance. There is a good-sized body of religious literature that brings the proof of this right up to Paul's time and shows us how prevalent the memorial ideas of the Old Testament were in his thought-world. Let us now study these works—again, as for the Old Testament apocrypha, using Charles' English version and nomenclature. (See 246).

CHAPTER IV: **Old Testament Pseudepigrapha**

The Texts

300. *Jubilees* (or Apocalypse of Moses. Date, c. 110 B.C.): 1) "I [Moses] explained to thee its [the feast of weeks] sacrifices that the children of Israel should remember.... And on the new moon[s]... are the days of remembrance.... And Noah ordained them for himself as feasts for the generations for ever, so that they have become thereby a memorial unto him." (6:22-23). 2) "And they placed them on the heavenly tablets... from one to another (passed) their memorial...." (6:29). 3) "But Lot we saved; for God remembered Abraham...." (16:7). 4) And [Abraham]... remembered the words which He had spoken to him...." (17:3). 5) "And my [Abraham's] name and thy [Isaac's] name shall not be forgotten under heaven forever." (21:24). 6) "And do thou, my son Jacob, remember my words, and observe the commandments of Abraham, thy father." (22:16). 7) "And so they inscribe as a testimony in his [Levi's] favour on the heavenly tablets blessing and righteousness before the God of all: And we remember the rightousness... until a thousand generations they will record it... and he has been recorded on the heavenly tablets as a friend and a righteous man." (30:19-20). 8) "All this account I have written for thee [i.e., God has written for Moses] to say to the children of Israel, that they should not... break the covenant... (but)... should fulfil it and be recorded [on the heavenly tablets] as friends." (30:21). 9) "Behold, an angel descended [to Jacob, in a vision] from heaven with seven tablets in his hands.... And Jacob said: 'Lord, how can I remember all that I have read and seen?' And he said unto him: 'I will bring all things to thy remembrance'... And he celebrated there yet another day, and he sacrificed... and the... days he called 'the Feast.'" (32:21,25-27). 10) "Remember the commandment which the Lord commanded thee concerning the passover." (49:1). 11) "And do thou command the children of Israel to observe the passover throughout their days, every year... and it shall come for a memorial well pleasing before the Lord, and no plague shall come...." (49:15). 12) "This work alone shall be done on the Sabbath-days in the sanctuary of the Lord your God; that they may atone for Israel with sacrifice continually from day to day for a memorial well-pleasing before the Lord, and that He may receive them always... as thou hast been commanded." (50:11).

301. *Letter of Aristeas* (date disputed: 200 B.C. to after 33 C.E.):
1) "[The king] ordered Demetrius to draw up a memorial.... The following
is a copy of the memorial. The *Memorial* of Demetrius to the great king....
When this memorial had been presented, the king ordered...." (vv. 28-29,
33). 2) "For he [Moses] has marked out every time and place that we may
continually remember the God who rules and preserves (us). For in the
matter of meats and drinks he bids us first of all offer part as a sacrifice
and then forthwith enjoy our meal. Moreover, upon our garments he has
given us a symbol of remembrance... and... upon our gates and doors...
upon our hands, too.... (vv. 157-159).

302. *Book of Enoch* (various parts from before 110 B.C. to 80 B.C.):
1) "'Observe, Enoch, these heavenly tablets....' And I... read the book of
all the deeds of mankind...." (81:1-2) 2) "Hide not thy face from the
prayer of thy servant, O Lord." (84:6). 3) "And this one who wrote the
book carried it up, and showed it and read it before the Lord of the sheep,
and implored him on their account...." (89:76). 4) "Be it known unto
you (ye sinners) that the Most High is mindful of your destruction." (97:2).
5) "In those days make ready, ye righteous, to raise your prayers as a
memorial [εἰς μνημόσυνον]¹ and place them as a testimony before the
angels, that they may place the sin of the sinners for a memorial [εἰς
μνημόσυνον] before the Most High." (99:3). 6) "I swear unto you, that in
heaven the angels remember you for good [ἀναμιμνήσκουσιν εἰς ἀγαθὸν]
before the glory of the Great One." (104:1).

303. *Testament of the Twelve Patriarchs* (c. 108 B.C.): 1) "And Isaac
colled me [Levi] continually to put me in remembrance of the law of the
Lord...." (T. Levi 9:6). 2) "By thy [Levi's] seed shall be blessed in the
earth, and thy seed shall be enrolled in the book of the memorial of life
[ἐν βιβλίῳ μνημοσύνου ζωῆς]² unto all ages." (v. 59 of a Gk. fragment of an
original source of the T. Levi and Jub.)³

304. *Sibylline Oracles* (dates uncertain, some may be B.C.). Nothing.

305. *The Assumption of Moses* (7-29 C.E.): 1) "And all the tribes [all
are in exile] shall mourn... saying: 'God of Abraham... Isaac... Jacob, remember Thy covenant....' Then they shall remember me [Moses], saying...
'Is not this... Moses... who... called heaven and earth to witness against us,
that we should not transgress His commandments, in the which he was a
mediator unto us?'" (3:8-13). 2) "Then there shall enter one who is over
them, and he shall spread forth his hands, and kneel upon his knees and

---

¹ Greek from *Apocalypsis Henochi Graece, Fragmenta*, ed. M. Black (Leiden: E. J.
Brill, 1970), p. 39.
² Greek from *The Greek Versions of the Testaments of the Twelve Patriarchs*, ed.
R. H. Charles, 3rd ed. (Oxford: University Press, 1966), p. 252.
³ See Charles, *Apocrypha*, vol. 2, p. 366.

pray on their behalf, saying: '...Regard and have compassion on them, O Lord of heaven.' Then God will remember them on account of the covenant which He made with their fathers, and He will manifest His compassion in those times also." (4:1-5). 3) "[The Amorites say] If the enemy [the Hebrews] have but once wrought impiously against their Lord, they have no advocate to offer prayers on their behalf to the Lord, like Moses... reminding Him of the covenant of the fathers and propitiating the Lord with the Oath." (11:16-18).

306. *Book of the Secrets of Enoch* (*2 Enoch*: c. 1 C.E.). Nothing.

307. *Syriac Apocalypse of Baruch* (*II Baruch*: last half of 1st cent. C.E.): 1) "'How shall the name of Israel again be remembered? Or how shall one speak of Thy praises?'.... And the Lord said unto me: 'This city... will not be given over to oblivion.'" (3:5-6; 4:1. See also 44:9). 2) "[Baruch says] 'Hear, O Israel.... Forget not Zion, but hold in remembrance the anguish of Jerusalem.'" (31:3-4). 3) "[Baruch prays] 'Thou carest for the number which pass away that they may be preserved, and thou preparest an abode for those that are to be. Thou rememberest the beginning which Thou hast made, and the destruction that is to be Thou forgettest not.... Hear Thy servant and give ear to my petition.'" (48:6-7,11). 4) "And walked every man in his own works, and remembered not the law of the Mighty One." (48:38. See also 75:7). 5) "'Let this epistle be for a testimony between me [Baruch] and you, that ye may remember the commandments of the Mighty One, and that also there may be to me a defence in the presence of Him who sent me. And remember ye the law and Zion... land... brethren, and the covenant of your fathers, and forget not the festivals and the sabbaths. And deliver ye this epistle and the traditions... to your sons after you, as also your fathers delivered to you. And... pray diligently... that the Mighty One may be reconciled to you, and that He may not reckon the multitude of your sins, but remember the rectitude of your fathers.... according to... His mercies....'" (84:7-11).

308. *IV Ezra* (*2 Esdras*: 100-135 C.E.): 1) "[Ezra prays] Regard not the deeds of the godless, but (rather) them that have kept thy covenants in tortures; think not upon those that have walked in devious ways before thee, but remember them that have willingly recognized thy fear... love them...." (8:27-28,30). 2) "And I answered... take courage, O Israel.... For you are remembered before the Most High, the Mighty One hath not forgotten you for ever. But as for me, I have not forsaken you... I have come to this place to... supplicate mercy...." (12:46-48).

309. *Psalms of Solomon* (perhaps middle of 1st cent. C.E.): "Thou hast wiped out their memorial [το μνημόσυνον αὐτῶν] from the earth."

(2:19).[4] "The righteous remember the Lord at all times, with thanks-giving.... And the Lord counteth guiltless every pious man and his house.... The destruction of the sinner is for ever, and he shall not be remembered, when the righteous is visited." (3:3,10,13-14. See also 4:24; 6:2 [the name of the Lord]). 3) "Happy is he whom God remembereth in a due suf-ficiency...." (5:18). 4) "Happy is the man whom the Lord remembereth with reproving.... And the Lord remembereth His servants in mercy. For the testimony (is) in the law of the eternal covenant.... on the ways of men in (His) visitation." (10:1,4-5). 5) "Remove not Thy mercy from me, O God, Nor Thy memorial [τὴν μνήμην] from my heart until I die.... Preserve my goings in remembrance of Thee [ἐν τῇ μνήμη σου]." (16:6,9).

310. *IV Maccabees* (at least before 70 C.E.): 1) "Remember of what stock ye are, and at whose fatherly hand Isaac for righteousness' sake yielded himself to be a sacrifice." (13:12). "And... for a memorial to future generations of our people: 'Here lies....'" (17:8-9—εἰς μνείαν).

311. *Story of Ahikar* 100 B.C.?): 1) "Look towards God, and remem-ber the love that there was between us, brother... and remember that thee also... I slew... not...." (3:9). 2) "And when Nadan my son came, no funeral feast did he make for me, nor any remembrance at all, but gathered him the vain and lewd folk, and set them down at my table... with great joy...." (4:15). 3) "Remember me before God, and say, O God... hear the voice of Thy servant Aḥikar, and remember that he sacrificed to Thee fatted oxen...." (4:18). 4) "Swear to me, my lord the king, that... this sin shall not be remembered against me." (5:10).

312. *Pirke Aboth*:[5] 1) "Comely is study of Torah with worldly oc-cupation, for toil in both makes sin forgotten." (2:2). 2) "When two sit and there are between them words of Torah, the Shechinah rests between them, as it is said: 'Then they that feared the Lord spake one with another, [and the Lord hearkened and heard, and a book of remembrance was written before him....].'" (3:3. Herford[6] comments: "The quotation from Mal. III. 16 is also probably original, at all events the first clause.")

Summary and Reflections

313. A review of the above material shows much the same picture as the apocrypha. Memorial material of whatever kind is thin on the ground but present in almost all the books, with religious uses strongly predominant. The verbs are used with God remembering in eighteen cases in seven books, with man remembering in eighteen cases in eight books.

---

[4] Greek from *Les Psaumes de Salomon*, trans. [into French] J. Viteau (Paris: Letou-zey et Ané, 1911), p. 260.

[5] Included among the pseudepigrapha by Charles.

[6] In *The Ethics of the Talmud: Sayings of the Fathers*, ed., trans., comm. R. Travers Herford (New York: Schocken Books, 1962), p. 67.

God remembers covenant specifically in five of the cases in three different books; man remembers covenant once. Nouns occur at least fourteen times, as memorials before God six times, for men nine, for both several. The idea of heavenly tablets or records occurs in two books, four times for God's perusal or as a testimony before him; twice for men. Covenant is explicit in one of the God-related instances. Besides covenant, God remembers his faithful servants, the suppliants (presumed servants), their sins and their penitence, the sins and non-penitence of sinners, cultic acts, etc. The nouns are used as reminders to God of both good and evil. The difference between the "reminding" and the "remembering" nouns continues; the term ἀνάμνησις does not occur, however.

314. Two areas of developing theology are very evident: that of the interceding angels, and that of the heavenly records, which are occasionally called "memorials". Similar to the angels are the interceding humans of special stature, like Moses and Baruch. Attempts are made to spiritualize this idea of human mediation. The Divine initiative is stressed. "The Lord hath on their behalf appointed me [Moses] to pray for their sins and make intercession for them.... not for any virtue or strength of mine, but of His good pleasure.... For I say unto you.... it is not on account of the godliness of this people that thou shalt root out the nations." (As. Mos. 12:6-8). The writer links this scheme to God's foreknowledge and the covenant: "For God will go forth who has foreseen all things forever, and His covenant has been established and by the oath which.... [sic: this is the end of the text]" (12:13). Incidentally, "oath" is one of the ways in which covenant is indirectly indicated. The covenant is several times presented as a mutual oath. As in the LXX and the apocrypha, it is suggested in other terminology as well: that of command, obedience, fidelity. These materials are extremely abundant in the pseudepigrapha, often too in the larger context of memorial texts.

315. As with the apocrypha, there is strong support for cult, Temple, sacrifice and prayer. It is found even in places like the *Sibylline Oracles* (see 3:570,573,624,702; 5:267). In *2 Enoch* there is what Charles calls "the same spiritual appreciation of sacrifices"[7] as in *Sirach*. He tends to see this as anti-Temple, but as with Sirach it is rather evident that it is really anti-wrong intention. "Whoever hastens to make offerings before the Lord's face, the Lord for his part will hasten that offering by granting of his work. But whoever increases his lamp before the Lord's face [a reference to liturgical lights] and make not true judgement, the Lord will not increase his treasure in the realm of the highest." (45:1-2). The purpose of liturgy is put thus: "All that only tests the heart of man." (45:3). Again, "For man brings clean animals to make sacrifice for sin, that he may have

---

[7] Charles, *Apocrypha*, vol. 2, p. 458, XLV note 3.

cure of his soul. And if they bring for sacrifice clean animals... man has cure, he cures his soul." (59:2). The reference here is to improper modes of preparing animals for sacrifice, but more spiritual aims appear in 66:2. "Bow down to the true God, not to dumb idols, and bring all just offerings before the Lord's face. The Lord hates what is unjust." A similar acceptance of cult with exhortation to purify it is found in *The Assumption of Moses*. (See 4:4; 5:3; 8:5). There is more emphasis on intercessory prayer in situations where formal cult is for some reason impossible, but this is not seen as denigration of that cult: "And the two tribes shall continue in their prescribed faith, sad and lamenting because they will not be able to offer sacrifices." (As. Mos. 4:8. This is prefaced by a reference to Daniel as intercessor).

316. The "memorial of Demetrius to the great king" in the *Letter of Aristeas* is significant. It was an official reminder to the king for the approval of the executive details of an ordinance previously given by him, and for the funding of the execution. This is a close secular analogy to the institution of the "mandated memorial" in Israel, where God is the Great King. God gives the order for moral, cultic and other acts, and expects to be reminded of the specifications for and requirements needed for the execution. It is impossible to say just what interaction there may have been between this specifically religious concept and the more general one, but it is not impossible that the latter was a very ancient idea that the Israelites adopted and canonized by a process of "*a minore ad maius*", replacing the worldly kings by the Great One. The notion fits well with the idea of the heavenly tablets and angelic intercession; and with the two-stage memorial process shown in 1 Enoch 99:3, where the prayers are placed before the angels as a memorial, and they place their content (pleas for punishment of sinners or for blessings on the pleader, as the case may be) as a memorial "before the glory of the Great One." (104:1). This process is meaningful because of Paul's notion of Christ's present heavenly intercession. The terminology is so because of the clear possessive sense: it is *Demetrius'* memorial, though he is only the mediator of the materials it contains. This possessive *idea* is of course present frequently. To "raise your prayers as a memorial" (1 Enoch 99:3) means that the memorial is "yours".

317. Other cultic ideas that occur in these books: 1) Prayer is often related to oblation; wine is used as an offering (e.g. Jub. 6:3), as is bread (2 Enoch 45:3). 2) Sacrifice is seen as memorial (Jub. 50:11). 3) The pasch is seen as sacrifice and the salvific use of paschal blood noted—the pasch itself being a "memorial" (Jub. 49:15ff). 4) The "salt of covenant" is associated with oblation (Jub. 21:11). 5) The altar is seen as "God's table" (Sib. Or. 5:266; Aboth 3:5. This latter text is interesting for its comparison of God's table with that of the pagans: "Three who have eaten at one table and have not said over it words of Torah, lo, they are as if they had eaten sacrifices of the dead.... But three who have eaten... [with] Torah are as if they had eaten from the table of God... as it is said: '...This is the table that is before the Lord.'" Reference is to the horned altar of Ezek. 41:22: "αὕτη ἡ τράπεζα, ἡ πρὸ προσώπου Κυρίου"). 6) The sacrifice of Isaac is recalled in terms that go beyond mere simile: "...of Isaac, who was offered as a burnt offering...." (4 Mac. 18:11. Gk. τὸν ὁλοκαρπούμενον Ἰσαὰκ). 7) The ark and mercy seat are shown to be current concerns: 2 Bar. 6:7; 35:4; 2 Esdr. 10:22.

318. There is a good deal of apocalyptic and visionary material in the pseudepigrapha, and it seems rather clear that there is something of a clash between vision and memorial. When the devotee is in the heavens himself, it is redundant to send up pleas to be "remembered". It may be that the notion of the heavenly ministers was developed partly to harmonize these views. Additionally, emphasis on prophecy of the future (as in T. 12 Patr.) tends to eliminate references to God's memory of past covenant. In general, however, the ideas and terminology of memorial are as widely current in this period as in the past, finding new modes of expression to accommodate to other theological and terminological changes, when those are at all amenable to accommodation. We shall now see two final areas in which this currency is demonstrated, Qumran and the New Testament.

CHAPTER V: **Qumran and the New Testament**

Qumran, the Texts

319. *The Zadokite Documents* [1] [Numeration refers to page and verse as marked in Rabin]: 1) "But when 'He remembered the covenant of the forefathers', 'He caused a remnant to remain....'" (1:4). 2) "Abraham... was recorded as a friend, through keeping the commandments of God.... Isaac and... Jacob kept [God's commandment]... and were written down as friends of God and His covenanters for eternity." (3:2-4. "Written down" is ויכתבו from כתב, of which Rabin notes, "The term used for recording in the sect's registers, xiv. 4&c; also used Jub. 2.20; 30.20.") [2] 3) "But God remembered the covenant...." (8:3). "But... the keepers of the covenant of God... God shall hearken to their words, 'and He will hear, and a book of remembrance [ספר זכרון] shall be written before Him for them that fear God....'" (20:19).

320. *War of the Sons of Light* [3] [Numeration by column and verse as in Yadin]: 1) 3:2ff is a section on what in 7:12 are called the "trumpets of remembrance." So in 16:3; 18:4. Yadin summarizes. "While with [other nations]... [trumpets]... were mainly for tactical purposes, to encourage the warriors and frighten the enemy... their principal function in Israel was to stress the religious character of the war—to be remembered before the Lord—and only secondarily for signalling." [4] He says the scroll shows this by "allotting the task of blowing them to the priests... also by the inscriptions engraved on the trumpets", and cites a Midrash (Lev. Rabba xxix, 4), "They [Israel] know how to win the favour of their Creator with the fanfare!" [5] So also in 10:7-10. "If there cometh a war... we shall blow an alarm with the trumpets, and ye shall be remembered before your God, and... saved.... a people of men holy through the covenant...." 2) "The elect... the names of all their host is with Thee in Thy holy abode.... Mercy of blessing and the covenant of peace Thou hast engraved for them with a stylus of life...." (12:1-3). 3) "O God... Thou

---

[1] The translation used is that of Chaim Rabin: *The Zadokite Documents* (Oxford: Clarendon Press, 1954).

[2] Rabin, *Zadokite*, p. 11, note 4 to v. 3.

[3] The translation used is that of Batya and Chaim Rabin, *The Scroll of the War of the Sons of Light against the Sons of Darkness*, ed. and comm. Yigael Yadin (Oxford: University Press, 1954).

[4] Yadin, p. 113.

[5] Ibid.

madest a covenant with our forefathers.... there has been remembrance of Thy [being] in our midst for the assistance of the remnant...." (13:7-8). 4) "Remember ye the judgement [of Nadab and Abi]hu, the sons of Aaron... [but Eleazar] and Ithamar He preserved for Himself for a covenant...." (17:2-3).

321. *The Thanksgiving Hymns*: [6] 1) "What can I speak that is not foreknown; and utter that is not foretold? Everything is inscribed before Thee in a memorial inscription, unto all eternal times...." (1:23-24. Mansoor in a note says "Dupont-Sommer believes that this is an allusion to the celestial tablets upon which the destinies of the world are engraved...." [7] I myself think this is probably, for our writer, a memorial of his sin. He is "an edifice of sin" (v. 22) and in v. 25 asks, "What can a mortal say about his sin, and that can he answer to all the just judgement?" It is not despair, however: v. 32 has, "[And thou didst] clean[se him] from the multitude of his iniquity.") 2) "Then I said in my transgression: I have been abandoned by Thy covenant. But whenever I remember the might of Thy hand with... compassion, I am fortified...." (4:35. Again, God perceives the sin of the penitent only to forgive and purify).

322. *Other texts* [From Gaster]: [8] 1) "When... the months begin; on their feasts and on holy days... each as a memorial in its season...." (1 QS 10:5). 2) "O Lord.... Remember me; do not forget me, neither involve me in things too hard for me.... let not my transgressions be remembered against me." ("Poems" 3:10-13).[9] 3) "In calling to mind thy power my heart finds strength." ("Poems" 4:12). 4) "I will call down a blessing, O Zion, on the memory of thee." ("Poems" 5:1). 5) "Lord... besides their sins, remind Thyself also of Thy peculiar favors...." ("Prayer for Intercession" II).[10] 6) "Therefore, remembering the Covenant... Thou didst not then abandon us...." (Sic V). 7) "In the time of Thy good pleasure, Thou wilt (again) choose unto Thyself a people, for Thou hast remembered Thy covenant... and Thou wilt renew Thy covenant unto them... and Thou wilt appoint for them a faithful shepherd...." ("The New Covenant" Col. 2).[11]

The New Testament, the Texts

323. A) Μιμνήκω: 1) "If you are offering your gift... and there remember...." (Matt. 5:23). 2) Peter remembers Jesus' saying. (Matt. 26:75). 3) "We remember how that imposter said...." (Matt. 27:63). 4) "He has

---

[6] The Translation used is that of Menahem Mansoor: *The Thanksgiving Hymns* (Leiden: E. J. Brill, 1961).

[7] Mansoor, p. 101, note 11.

[8] *The Dead Sea Scriptures*, trans. with notes, Theodor H. Gaster, 3rd ed. rev. (Garden City, New York: Anchor Press/Doubleday, 1956).

[9] Gaster, pp. 221f.

[10] Ibid., p. 273.

[11] Ibid., p. 438.

helped his servant Israel, in remembrance of his mercy...." (Luke 1:54).
5) "Blessed be the Lord... as he spoke by... the prophets... that we should
be saved... to perform the mercy promised to our fathers, and to remember his holy covenant, the oath which he swore...." (Luke 1:68-73). 6) "Remember me when you come into your kingdom." (Luke 23:42). 7) "Remember how he told you... that the Son of man must be delivered.... And
they remembered his words." (Luke 24:7-8). 8) "His disciples remembered
that it is written...." (John 2:17. See also John 2:22; 12:16; Acts 11:16).
9) "Cornelius, your prayer has been heard and your alms have been remembered before God." (Acts 10:31). 10) "What is man, that thou art
mindful of him... carest for him.'" (Heb. 2:6). B) Μνημονεύω: 1) Only one
"God remembering" text: "God has remembered her iniquities." (Rev. 18:
5). 2) Among the things men remember are the five loaves, Lot's wife,
the word of Jesus about persecution, other words of Jesus (twice), a
woman's anguish in child-bearing, Paul, his fetters, Abraham's home, the
exodus, the Christian leaders, God's gifts, "Jesus Christ... as preached in
my gospel." (2 Tim. 2:8). The Gentiles are to remember their past
alienation from the covenants of promise. (Eph 2:11). C) Ὑπομιμνήσκω:
Six "reminding" texts in which various humans are reminded—once by
the Holy Spirit (John 14:26)—of various religious matters and words. Once
"Peter remembered the word of the Lord." (Luke 22: 61). D) Ἐπιλανθάνομαι
1) "God is not so unjust as to forget your work and the love you showed
for his sake." (Heb. 6:10). 2) "Not one of them [sparrows] is forgotten
before God. Even the hairs of your head are numbered." (Luke 12:6).
3) Men forget to do good, to show hospitality. E) Μνῆμα and μνημεῖον:
always "tomb" or "monument". F) Μνήμη: only once: "And I will see to
it that after my departure you may be able to remember all these things."
(2 Pet. 1:15. [τὴν τούτων μνήμην ποιεῖσθαι]). G) Μνημόσυνον: 1) "Truly I say
to you, wherever this gospel is preached in the whole world, what she
has done will be told in memory of her." (Mark 14:9; parallel slightly
expanded in Matt. 26:13. Marcan Greek: "ὅπου ἐὰν κηρυχθῇ τὸ εὐαγγέλιον
εἰς ὅλον τὸν κόσμον, καὶ ὃ ἐποίησεν αὕτη λαληθήσεται εἰς μνημόσυνον αὐτῆς.")
2) "Your prayers and alms have ascended as a memorial [εἰς μνημόσυνον]
before God." (Acts 10:4). H) Ἀνάμνησις: 1) "In these sacrifices there is
a reminder of sin year after year." (Heb. 10:13). 2) " 'Τοῦτο ποιεῖτε εἰς τὴν
ἐμὴν ἀνάμνησιν' " (1 Cor. 11:24,25; Luke 22:19).

Summary and Reflections

324. The Qumran materials continue the "memorial" tradition as
we have seen it in the LXX, the apocrypha and pseudepigrapha. Memorial
usages are well diffused, not a theological subject but a theological mode
of expression. There is a heavy emphasis on God's remembering and
reminding-God, on covenant, and on the idea of heavenly records parallel

to the lists of the covenanters on earth. Secular uses are very few. In the religious ones, for the verb, we find God remembering nine times, the people four. For the noun, God is reminded four times, the people three; with *both* God and people reminded, quite evidently, in two of these instances. The covenant is explicit in the verbal texts six times for God, twice for the people; in the nominal texts twice for God, once for the people. The heavenly memorial idea appears at least four times. A point clearly made is that memorials involving sin need not mean punishment; that only ensues if the Divine decision is "against" the sinner. The accompanying reminder of the covenant and God's mercy can be the occasion of God's memory of these, and of forgiveness. In one instance (see 322, no. 7) God's remembering the covenant in this way is linked to "new covenant" terminology and accompanied by a reference to a messianic leader.

325. The New Testament references given include all but a very few secular uses. For the verbs there are seven God-remembering or reminding-God instances, twenty-four man-remembering or reminding-man, one instance of the earthly Jesus being asked to remember when he has reached his heavenly estate. God remembers or is reminded of man; man's prayer, alms, work and love; man's iniquity (once); God's own mercy (once), his covenant and oath (once). Jesus is reminded to save. Men remember or are reminded of God's gifts, Scripture (four times), Jesus, Jesus' words (seven times), sins (twice—once with a covenant nexus), their own good works, their leaders, the exodus, Paul, and several domestic things like home, a wife, childbearing, loaves.

326. The nouns, excluding our own text and the parallel in Luke, show one reminding-God use of μνημόσυνον and one of ἀνάμνησις: the things recalled being respectively prayer (and alms) and sin. There is one typical "remembering" use of μνήμη and a use of μνημόσυνον (that concerned with the Bethany woman's deed) that on the analogies we have seen ought almost certainly to be translated "as a reminder of her" rather than the "in memory of her" cited above, or the "in remembrance of her" of the *Jerusalem Bible*. It is the human hearers of the gospel who are reminded, of course, so that the imprecision causes no particular trouble in respect of this text. But the more widespread the feeling of accommodation to imprecision, and the more likelihood of trouble in *other* texts.

Relevance of Lexical Materials

327. It is true that the Lexicon gives "remembrance" as one of the acceptable meanings of μνημόσυνον.[12] But the examples given show that

---

[12] L. & S., s.v. "μνημόσυνον."

what is meant is a reminder: the word is used with verbs like λείπω to mean something left behind as a memorial to posterity: this is certainly not capable of being construed as a "memory", as the above-mentioned translation would allow. The other meanings given in the lexicon are all clearly reminders: "memorial", "memorandum", "mark", "scar", and "reminder" itself. The Gospel word in Mark 14:9 obviously fits the "reminder" idea. It is not a memory itself, for it is not human; but the subtle switch from the non-human to the human point of view in the translation "in remembrance" is screened by the flexibility of word-meaning permitted by English phraseology. Even if μνημόσυνον should occasionally carry the meaning of human remembering, it would be unacceptable to translate it thus without strong indications from the context. There are none in the Marcan text, and I think the same can be said for every other text we have seen that uses the word.

328. What of ἀνάμνησις? This word has a more complex history. It, too, however, is basically a "reminding" word. Its ultimate source is μιμνήσκω, of which the lexicon says, "causal Verb... *remind, put in mind...*" [13] The meaning "remember" results in the middle and passive, to "remind oneself" or "be reminded of" something. This is the sense that grounds the use of the noun by Plato, Aristotle, Philo, etc. in the meaning of "recollection", in which sense these authors distinguish it from "memory". (See Plato *Phileb.* 34b; Aristotle *On Memory* 451a).[14] Memory is the actual possession of the knowledge—this is μνήμη. Ἀνάμνησις is the recapturing of the knowledge when one has temporarily lost it. Aristotle describes this: "This is why we follow the trail in order, starting in thought from the present, or some other concept, and from something similar or contrary to, or closely connected with, what we seek. This is how recollection takes place [διὰ τοῦτο γίνεται ἡ ἀνάμνησις]." (*De Mem.* 451b, 20). Such a meaning is plainly quite consistent with the mode of operation of a liturgical act, if the act is taken as part of the "trail" (ἐφεξῆς = "one after another") that leads to recollection. "Εἰς ἀνάμνησιν" can thus mean "towards recollection"; but it might also mean "as a reminder". Both operations are intended when " ἀνάμνησις " is used: if one is mainly intended the other is always implied. But a problem arises when, as in the 1 Corinthians text, an imperative is addressed to the human reader and a translation "towards recollection" is used. *Ipsis verbis*, the possibility of God's being reminded is excluded. On the other hand, a translation "as a reminder" allows other parties than the one addressed to recollect. We must thus ask what justification there is for a restrictive translation in 1 Corinthians.

---

[13] L. & S., s.v. "μιμνήσκω."
[14] Plato, *Philebus*, trans. Harold N. Fowler, in LCL, *Plato III;* and Aristotle, *On the Soul*, trans. W. S. Hett, in LCL *Aristotle, On the Soul, Parva Naturalia, On Breath*.

329. The lexicon, of course, also gives the sense "reminder" quite simply, as well as that of "memorial sacrifice".

Modern Jewish Liturgical Remnants

330. Before turning to first-century materials in which the typical Greek avoidance of "reminding-God" is apparent, let us remark some possibly ancient memorial remnants in the modern Jewish liturgy. A first is the *Zikhronot* verses from the *Musaf* prayer of Rosh Ha-Shanah. This is described in the *Encyclopaedia Judaica* article.

> This ... contains ten biblical verses (four from the Pentateuch, three from Psalms, and three from the Prophets) praising God who remembered, among other things, Noah during the flood, the Israelites in Egyptian slavery, and His covenant with Abraham, Isaac, and Jacob. The prayer closes with a plea that God remember the binding of Isaac (see *Akedah*), and, through Abraham's merit, bestow mercy upon his descendents. These *Zikhronot* verses express the most characteristic significance of Rosh Ha-Shanah, the Jewish New Year, as a "Day of Remembrance" (*Yom ha-Zikkaron*). At the end of their recital (as with the *Malkhuyyot* and *Shofarot* verses) the *shofar* [ram's horn—the "trumpets" of our 232, 320] is sounded.[15]

The author of the article notes that "The reciting of the *Zikhronot* on Rosh Ha-Shanah is mentioned already in the Mishnah (RH 4:5-6) and is believed to have been part of the Rosh Ha-Shanah liturgy in the Temple." [16]

331. There is the *Amidah* ["standing"] prayer, frequently occurring in the liturgy. The memorial portion: "Thou rememberest the noble deeds of our ancestors and, because Thou art a God of love, Thou wilt bring a redeemer to their children's children after them." [17] Bokser has the note: "The final edition of the *Amidah* occurred under the supervision of Rabban Gamaliel II, after the destruction of the second Temple. But some elements of it have been ascribed to the Men of the Great Assembly, about the fourth century B.C.E." [18]

332. Ascribed to Rabbi Akiba is the use of the prayer *Avinu Malkenu* ("Our Father, our King"), which today contains the following words: "Cancel the records of our transgressions.... remember us favorably.... inscribe us in the book of a happy life.... of redemption and deliverance.... of sustenance and abundance." [19]

---

[15] *Judaica*, s.v. "Zikhronot," by "Ed.".
[16] Ibid.
[17] *The Prayer Book*, trans. and ed. Ben Zion Bokser (New York: Hebrew Publishing Co., 1957), p. 51.
[18] Ibid.
[19] Ibid., p. 61. A note states: "The Talmud cites Rabbi Akiba as praying in the words of this prayer." (p. 60).

333. Notable memorial terminology is also found in the meditation before putting on the *Tephillin*, in the continuation of the *Amidah* on the Ten Days of Penitence, in the "Hymn on Sabbath" ("Keep and Remember were fused as one word... at Sinai"), in the "Prayer for Rain" on the feast of *Shemini Atzeret*, in the "new moon" prayer, etc.[20] The latter contains the statement: "The atonement offerings which they brought unto Thee were to them all as a memorial before God, and a help against the adversary within us."

334. The larger number of these instances are "reminding-God", but the nouns in particular allow for remembering by both God and the devotee. This applies also to the use of the *shofar*, which, incidentally, is also used at the close of the *Yom Kippur* celebration.

The Didache

335. In the *Didache* there is one man-remembering instance: "My child, thou shalt remember, day and night, him who speaks the word of God to thee." (4:1). But especially interesting is the Eucharistic prayer addressed to God the Father: " Μνήσθητι, κύριε, τῆς ἐκκλησίας σου, τοῦ ῥύσασθαι αὐτὴν ἀπὸ παντὸς πονηροῦ καὶ τελειῶσαι αὐτὴν ἐν τῇ ἀνάπῃ σου." (10:5). Since this is the only memorial terminology in the section on the Eucharist, it may represent a traditional interpretation of memorial material related to that which appears in Paul in the nominal form. Be that as it may, it shows the strength of reminding-God thinking even in the face of notable Hellenic influence.

---

[20] Ibid., pp. 3, 51, 106, 179ff, 193 respectively. To the last passage in question, Bokser attaches a long note on the significance of the Temple sacrifices.

CHAPTER VI: Literature Downplaying Memorial

336. Let us now take note of some examples of that influence in Jewish and Christian religious literature. We may discuss in order Philo, Josephus, and the gnostic and magical literature.

Philo

337. Generally, Philo avoids reminding-God terminology, but he does repeat some Old Testament usages in which God is reminded, without change. So in De Moise I, 317: "...laid them up in the consecrated tabernacle as a memorial of their thankfulness." [τῆς εὐχαριστίας ὑπόμνημα]. Again, "Observe also the loaves set forth upon the holy table... in sets of six each, as memorials of the twelve tribes [μνημεῖα]...." (De Herede 175). This, incidentally, shows the persistence of the LXX version of this incident. In De Moise II, 107 he speaks of a "reminder of past sins" (ὑπόμνησις); and a few sections further on in the same work he presents the notion of *amnesty*: " πρός τε ἀμνηστίαν ἁμαρτημάτων "—II, 134). His contexts sometimes put ambiguity where it was lacking in the original, but he never *denies* God's remembering.

338. Philo has explicated his views on reminding, and his doctrine explains why, left to himself, he avoided "reminding-God". Like Plato he distinguishes memory (μνήμη) from recollection (ἀνάμνησις), which implies forgetting. So, "Reminding takes second place to remembering, and so too the one reminded to the one remembering." (De Cong. 39). "The man who is reminded must have forgotten what he remembered before." (Ibid.). With this teaching explicit, and with a similarly explicit doctrine of God's omniscience ("In his prescience he had comprehended all things not only after but before they came to pass" [De Conf. Ling. 140]), he is not likely to push the notion of reminding-God. At the same time, he defends cult (see 189ff) and prayer. "It is wont for God to bestow these gifts in answer to the word of supplication, from which he does not turn his ear away.... both on those who are to become wise, and for their sake on others." (De Mig. 120). The tension appears in the following: "The Hearer asks—asks we may call it, though He does not really ask, since all things are known to God—'What is it that thou criest so loud to me?' Is it in supplication for ills to be averted, or is it in thanksgiving for blessings imparted, or in both?" (De Herede 15). He has the wherewithal to argue for reminding-God just as we have done (see 290ff), for he shows that Moses and Abraham cry to God out of friendship rather than presumption. (See De Herede 21). But his Greek intellectualism seems to restrain him from making the most of the classical Hebrew position. Or perhaps he is restrained more by the fear that if he should make the most of it, his Greek readers will be repelled by his presentation.

339. Philo uses at least one memorial term when referring to a Scriptural text in which there is no explicit memorial terminology. "The memorial of the divine and heaven-sent food was enshrined in a golden jar...." (De Cong. 100—μνημεῖον), a reference to Exod. 16:36, where the manna is to be "laid up for your generations; that they may see the bread which ye ate in the wilderness." It is to be "laid up" "before God", "before the testimony"; which normally implies reminding-God. The example has the special value of showing that these "before God" memorials could be seen as reminding *both* God and men. Like the "testimony" (the ark and contents) they were *between* God and men and placed so as to be visible to *both*.

Josephus

340. Josephus provides us with a most obvious example of conscious exclusion of memorial terminology. He does use the term "memorial", but in the most accepted Greek manner: "Every one of them that perished were worthy of a memorial." (Wars 6,3,2—μνήμης ἀξίων). Hebraic technical usages, except for those that involve reminding the people in the original, are either "dememorialized" completely or turned into generalities of remembering. The frankincense and the loaves of Presence are mentioned without use of the term "memorial" which is prominent in the LXX. (Ant. 3,10,7; compare with the unabashed use of ὑπόμνησις for the brazen censers "as a reminder to posterity" in Ant. 4,3,4). Josephus also avoids covenant terminology almost completely, presenting the Israelite covenant as a horizontal national union. This underscores our point that memorial and covenant are inextricably intertwined in Hebrew thinking. If you accept one, you accept the other; if you omit one, you might as well omit the other.

Gnostic Usages

341. The picture presented by gnostic literature can be seen rather clearly from a statistical review of memorial occurrences in the Nag Hammadi texts. The figures given represent the number of times verbal God-reminded, verbal man-reminded, and nominal memorial terminology (respectively) occur in the books mentioned. The names and order of the books, numerology and translation are those of *The Nag Hammadi Library*.[1] *The Apocryphon of James*: 1-3-0. *The Gospel of Truth*: 0-0-0.

---

[1] See our note 24 in Part II, Chapter II.

The Treatise on Resurrection: 0-0-0. *The Tripartite Tractate*: 4-2-3. *The Apocryphon of John*: 0-1-1. *The Gospel of Thomas*: 0-0-0. *The Gospel of Philip*: 0-0-0: *The Hypostasis of the Archons*: 0-0-0. *On the Origin of the World*: 0-0-0. *The Exegesis on the Soul*: 0-2-2. *The Book of Thomas the Contender*: 0-0-0. *The Gospel of the Egyptians*: 0-0-0. *Eugnostos the Blessed*: 0-0-0. *The Sophia of Jesus Christ*: 0-0-0. *The Dialogue of the Savior*: 1-0-1. *The Apocalypse of Paul*: 0-0-0. *The First Apocalypse of James*: 0-1-0. *The Second Apocalypse of James*: 0-0-0. *The Apocalypse of Adam*: 0-0-0. *The Acts of Peter and the Twelve Apostles*: 0-0-0. *The Thunder, Perfect Mind*: 0-0-1. *Authoritative Teaching*: 0-1-0. *The Concept of Our Great Power*: 0-0-0. *The Discourse on the Eighth and Ninth*: 0-0-0. *The Prayer of Thanksgiving*: 0-0-0. *Asclepius*: 0-0-0. *The Paraphrase of Shem*: 0-1-4. *The Second Treatise of the Great Seth*: 0-1-0. *The Apocalypse of Peter*: 0-0-0. *The Teachings of Silvanus*: 0-0-0. *The Three Steles of Seth*: 0-2-0. *Zostrianos*: 0-0-0. *The Letter of Peter to Philip*: 0-0-0. *Melchizedek*: 0-0-0. *The Testimony of Truth*: 0-0-0. *The Interpretation of Knowledge*: 0-0-0. *A Valentinian Exposition*: 0-0-0. *Allogenes*: 0-0-0. *The Sentences of Sextus*: 0-1-0. *Trimorphic Protennoia*: 0-0-0. *The Gospel of Mary*: 0-0-0. *The Act of Peter*: 1-0-0.

342. These do not include a dozen or so references to the Gnostic type "oblivion" or "forgetfulness" (v.g., in the Gosp. of Truth 17,15; 18, 18; etc.; the Trip. Tract. 77,20; Apoc. of John 13,14; 21,9; etc. ["bond of forgetfulness", "chain of forgetfulness", "water of forgetfulness"]; First Apoc. of James 28,7; Par. of Shem 1,28; Teach. of Silv. 89,12) and a very few completely secular references to remembering something or other. We are left with figures for the whole body of literature of 6-15-10. And in fact, the first figure is inaccurate, in that for purposes of simplification I have included in it one example of Jesus remembering (Apoc. of James 10,7), one of the Logos (Trip. Tract. 82,1ff), and three of the Totalities. The one left is in *The Sentences of Sextus*, a treatise that Wisse says "cannot really be considered a Gnostic treatise."[2] If we compare the figures with the straightforward ones for the apocrypha (12-20-16 for eleven books), the pseudepigrapha (13-8-12 for thirteen books), Qumran (8-3-4), the New Testament (8-24-7) and the Didache (1-1-0), the difference in the reminding-God category of the verbs is especially apparent. As for the nouns, a glance at the things that constitute the gnostic "remembrances" will show the same difference. They are the Logos' being in the Pleroma (1), the Logos' memory of existing things (1), the Pronoia (1), the Father (1), an "idea" (1), remembering of revelation and cosmic powers (1 and 3), a book of remembrance that is one with God (1). The last-mentioned item is the

---

[2] *The Sentences of Sextus*, trans. with introd. by Frederik Wisse, *Nag Hammadi Library*, p. 454.

only one that accords in phraseology and idea with the cultic materials we have seen to be so common in the other literature, and the difference between it and them is immediately apparent: it is not "put before" God but *is* God. The memories of the Cross and death of Jesus and of Jesus himself occur in a text that according to the editor "may be Gnostic." [3]

Magical Texts

343. In the Greek magical papyri as found in Preisendanz,[4] about the only mention of memory or remembering is in attempts to obtain good memory as a gift. Perhaps the clearest example of this is in III, 424. "Transcription from a holy book. Foreknowledge and recollection [πρόγνωσις καὶ μνημονική]." The idea was to gain knowledge of past and of future. "Memory assistance... say three times to Helios in praise: 'Enter my heart, sending memory to my soul, to my eyes... so that what I once hear I will remember my life through.'" (III, 469).

344. The magical texts are especially interesting because they contain a large amount of prayer material and show clear Jewish influences of different kinds. However, there is very little sense of history, though the names of past religious figures are frequently mentioned—many of them Hebrew. The names are mixed with purely mythical figures indiscriminately. The god under various names—the more the better—is addressed in prayer and enticed or impressed to come and do what is required. A good deal of history or myth is simply assumed: Moses, for example, is presumed to have been a great magician. But he is not explicitly "remembered", nor is God asked to "remember". The whole area of historical and covenant memory is really left untouched, as is covenant itself. And the Greek aversion to God's remembering seems to carry over into his remembering the now-present (as well as the past-present).

Conclusions and Reflections in Respect of Chapter VI

345. Gnosticism shares with magic insensitivity to history, and reinforces the coldness with a disdain for material creation and its God. This makes it insensitive to this world's future as well as to its past, and results in a two dimensional kind of thinking, with time left out. We might say that magical thinking is two-and-a-half dimensional, with interest in the future but none in the past for its own sake—only for the sake of a marvelous power of memory to be put to practical use. Of course, as was remarked above, some history is presumed in magical ritual, and this holds for gnosticism too. It is a minimal concession to the way things really are.

---

[3] *The Apocryphon of James*, trans. with Introd. by Francis E. Williams, *Nag Hammadi Library*, p. 29.
[4] *Papyri Graecae Magicae*, ed. and trans. [into German] Karl Preisendanz, 2 vols. (Leipzig, Berlin: B. G. Teubner, 1928-31).

346. A further discouragement to memorial thinking in gnosticism is the distance the "Father" is from the worshipper. The "fatherhood" is one of mystic and remote generations that leave a flock of mediators of various kinds; the close, familial relationship that bases Hebrew memorial is missing. In magical thinking and prayer the gods are close enough but are treated almost impersonally. All they need know is what is here being said and done; all the devotee need know is what need be said and done. The word "gods" is significant: it is generally a question of powers less than Supreme, as though the Supreme God leaves this kind of thing to lower beings.

347. Patently, Josephus is anti-memorial for other reasons than are the magical thinkers and the gnostics. He is very much interested in history, and no doubt felt as close to God as most Jews. His aim is simply to appeal as strongly as possible to a hellenized readership, and the sophisticated hellenist was averse to reminding-God. Philo undoubtedly felt much the same, but as an exegete rather than a historian he respected the presence of memorial in the texts he was exegeting. If the wise man Moses put it into the text, Philo was not the one to take it out.

348. The magical papyri present us with yet another example of cultic prayer. It is frequently sacrifice-related prayer, but is often meal-related as well; which would be expected, too, if the sacrifice were a communion one. Ordinary Jewish meals were, of course, accompanied by prayer, and we have heard Xenophanes in his elegy tell of the prayer and libation accompanying Greek meals. (281). The present Jewish grace after meals involves praise, petition, a covenant reference, thanks. "Praised be Thou.... Because of Thy goodness unto us we have never been in want of food. O may we never be in want of it.... We thank Thee for the covenant sealed in our flesh, for the Torah...." [5] Bokser gives a note:

> The duty to praise God after taking food is expressed in *Deuteronomy* 8:10: And you shall eat and be satisfied and praise the Lord your God. The Midrash, *Bereshit Rabbah* 54, ascribes the institution of Grace after meals to Abraham.... The original Grace consisted of the benediction for food, ending with הזן את הכל; ... for the land ... for Jerusalem.... The various additions to the above three benedictions are of later origin.[6]

The four elements we have noted above belong to the "original" grace. They are all elements that are typically found in reminding-God prayer; so indeed would Xenophanes' elements have been had the Greeks been given to such prayer. *The point is that where we find a "memorial" meal cult that bears indication of Jewish influence it is highly likely to involve reminding-God even while it is at least de facto reminding men of God's*

---

past and present beneficence. The Eucharist as Paul presents it certainly shows such indication. One thing that could eliminate reminding-God would be now-present magical intention. But such "here and now" intention is not only not manifested, it is practically excluded by the framework into which the Pauline Eucharistic words are cast, as well as by the likelihood of Paul and his communities' having alternate intentionalities (like the "referent of actuality" one) in their performance of the Eucharist. Part of the "framework" mentioned is the twice-occurring "memorial" word itself. It is out of keeping with magical practice and nomenclature.

Transition from Part III

349. An overview of the materials covered in this Part can be got by rereading the following paragraphs: 245, 259-261, 296-299, 313-318, 324-329, 330-340, 345-348. The place of the Part relative to those which precede and follow it has already been stated in paragraphs 4-7, 177, 179-180.

350. Several times in Part II and elsewhere we have noted (e.g., in 204) that Paul shows not a few indications of being amenable to memorial thinking and to modes of thought and practice that—as we just saw in specific ways in Part III—were frequently associated with it in his time. Most of the material surveyed in Part III was available to Paul in one way or another; not always in the form of written scrolls or entire works, but at least in that of currents of ideas and terminology. We shall now attack the Pauline question frontally, trying to place him on a scale that might use as reference points, from right to left, the following in order: the Old Testament and OT apocrypha and pseudepigrapha; the New Testament in general, the Didache, Philo (these last three across the middle); and towards the left, the traditional Greek view, with, finally, such strange partners as Josephus, the gnostics, the users of magic.

PART IV: **THE PAULINE CONTEXT, AND OUR TEXT**

CHAPTER I: **Paul on Memorial—an Overall View**

351. As to Paul, there are really two factors to be considered. His use of the term "ἀνάμνησις" in 1 Corinthians is by his own admission an element in his transmission of a tradition. "For I received from the Lord what I also delivered to you, that...." (11:23). How far does what he transmits in respect of memorial conform with his own views on the subject? Something can be argued, of course, from the very fact that he *did* transmit it, and not only transmitted it but returned to the subject later on (in our epistle) to defend his doing so. Paul seems to have founded the Corinthian church. What freedom did he have to select what would be taught his new flock and what would be omitted? It seems likely that the Eucharist was so firmly established in the other churches by the time Paul first went to Corinth that he felt that a church without it would not be a truly Christian group, or at least would not be recognized as such. Perhaps he was completely in favor of the ἀνάμνησις usage, whatever that was; did he perhaps emphasize the traditional nature as a means of shifting responsibility for something he felt uneasy with? His reference to "the Lord" as the source of the tradition would seem to discredit this idea, since a shifting of responsibility to the Lord betokens an assurance of the rightness of the view.

352. What of memorial usages elsewhere in Paul—are there any? Indeed, there are several—about the number one might expect of someone near the middle of our scale. Aside from the *Corinthians* use of ἀνάμνησις, Pauls uses ἀναμιμνήσκω twice, μνημονεύω three times (if I Thess. be accepted as Pauline), μνεία four times (sic). Timothy reminds the people of Paul's ways in Christ (1 Cor. 4:17); Titus remembers their obedience (2 Cor. 7:15); Paul remembers the poor (Gal. 2:10). The people remember Paul's labor and toil (1 Thess. 2:9). Then there are the typical "eucharistic" prayer texts. "We give thanks to God always for you all, constantly mentioning you in our prayers [μνείαν ποιούμενοι ἐπὶ τῶν προσευχῶν ἡμῶν], remembering before our God and Father [μνημονεύοντες ὑμῶν τοῦ ἔργου ... ἔμπροσθεν τοῦ θεοῦ καὶ πατρὸς ἡμῶν] your work of faith." (1 Thess. 1:2-3). This text is certainly representative of Paul, for it echoes the other two eucharistic texts. "I thank my God through Jesus Christ for all of you.... For God is my witness... that without ceasing I mention you always [μνείαν ὑμῶν ποιοῦμαι πάντοτε] in my prayers, asking that somehow by God's will I may now at last succeed in coming to you." (Rom. 1:8-10). And, "I thank my God in all my remembrance of you[εὐχαριστῶ τῷ Θεῷ μου ἐπὶ πάσῃ τῇ μνείᾳ ὑμῶν], always in every prayer of mine for you all making my prayer with joy, thankful for your partnership...." (Phil. 1:3-5).

353. What does it mean to "mention you in my prayers"? The 1 Thess. text seems to define the idea in the parallel "remembering you before God". No doubt it is possible to "mention someone in prayer" simply by saying "Lord, help N." But we have seen two ways in which the notion of remembering enters more reflectively into the picture. One is where the prayer is seen as a memorial placed before God. The second is where the prayer-form is "Lord, remember N." The prevalence of the μνήσθητι in the materials we have seen directly suggests the second;[1] but it would also be an indicator of the simultaneous likelihood of the first, especially where there was a theology of mediation which involved the mediation of all prayers, including those directly addressed to God. The idea of praying with God as witness, or praying "before God", is obviously compatible with both prayer-memorial and μνήσθητι.

354. It is interesting that in Paul's writings there is no instance of direct address to God, and only one to Jesus: "Our Lord, come!" of 1 Cor. 16:21. This may be the result of the letter form, which after all already has a specific human addressee. It is also just possible that Paul shuns such formulations because he does not wish to reveal so bluntly his views on whether or not to pray in explicitly reminding-God terms. But what he does do by the way he speaks *about* prayer is leave the matter open to speculation, and further, to leave it open while not only not excluding, but in truth definitely *suggesting the possibility that he himself prays in such terms.*

355. This bears on the Corinthians 11 text. It becomes impossible to argue from these prayer references that Paul excluded reminding-God from his general thinking and terminology—that he could not, therefore, have favored it in the particular case. More, *we must ask whether the positive suggestion of possibility* (that Paul prayed in reminding-God categories) *is also present in this text.* Let us now close in on the text in order to see if anything excludes this possibility.

---

[1] Ahikar 4:18 equivalently defines "Remember me before God" as praying with the explicit use of "μνήσθητι". "Remember me before God, and say, O God ... hear the voice of Thy servant Ahikar, and remember that he sacrificed to Thee ... " The reference to past sacrifice is notable.

CHAPTER II: 1 Corinthians: The First Ten and a Half Chapters

356. Since our text is located in the middle of a lengthy letter, it seems absolutely necessary to see whether the material that precedes it throws any light on its meaning. Let us therefore follow the development of 1 Corinthians up to our text. The exercise may or may not be productive of something of positive use to us, but it ought to be done in any case. Our interest, of course, is in content.

357. Paul presents himself as the elect apostle of Christ Jesus. He addresses the Corinthian church as one of his own founding, but one in which others have subsequently worked or had influence: e.g., Apollos or Cephas. In 1:10 the theme of dissension arises, and since it does so immediately after the conventional introductions, it may well be Paul's main reason for writing the letter—though it presently becomes clear that they have communicated with him about several things. A main cause of dissension seems to have been factionalism focussing on the question of baptism. Paul tries to undercut this by putting baptism in proper perspective relative to the gospel and life through Christ. (1:17; 1:30). Power and life come through the crucifixion (1:17,22; 2:2,8), and externals should express unity of source and effect.

358. This is true wisdom. He declaims against [humanly] "eloquent wisdom" (1:17) as distracting from the power of the cross. God has used what the world calls folly to show the superiority of his wisdom over that of the Greeks, at the same time refusing to submit to the demands of the Jews for *ad hoc* wonders. (1:22—this is not the way the cross's power is to be used). And not only did he choose an improbable manner of redemption "to shame the wise" (1:27); he chose those the world actually *calls* "fools" and otherwise despises as the first recipients of his own wise salvific power, "so that no human being might boast in the presence of God." (1:29).

359. Paul presents himself as a specially chosen minister of this dispensation (thereby putting himself in a very favorable light!). On the other hand, if the "rulers of this age" had understood it, they would not have crucified Jesus. (2:8). There are four references to the crucifixion in the first thirty-three verses of the epistle: it is clearly fundamental in Paul's view of the *modus operandi* of salvation, as the single source of a single life.

360. He claims that all this has been "revealed" (2:10), and forestalls objections by saying that although human faculties like eye and ear cannot understand the effect any more than the cause, the Spirit can, because the Spirit is a divine faculty. This Spirit has been given to Christians (2:12). And it has been given to Paul to enable him to teach them, with the assurance that they will grasp the mystery since they have the same Spirit. (2:13).

361. Having shown them their own potentialities as Christians and God's expectation of them, he again speaks explicitly of factions. He sees their cliquishness as a worldly and fleshly affiliation that is diametrically opposed to affiliation with Christ through Spirit, and warns that if they persist in it they will be rejecting Spirit and living by the spirit of the world. And that is destruction. (3:17). "Let no one boast of men." (3:21).

362. Perhaps aware that all this is paradoxical, and that he himself in urging his own view must also appear a paradox, he uses irony to paint glowingly the fleshly wisdom they hanker after, comparing it with his own apparent foolishness as an apostle of Christ. (4:8-13). He disparages his outward appearance. And how else should they expect a servant of Christ to appear? As for his motivations, he leaves that for God to judge. To soften the effect of his words he makes an appeal in the light of his particular interest in them as the one who fathered them by the gospel (again paradoxically strengthening his own position); he recalls his sending Timothy, who has the proper view towards both Christ and Paul. Finally, as a father he claims the power to chastize those who are "arrogant" (4:18), which in the light of the previous material can only mean those who continue to be partisan (and so anti-Christ, and in a true sense, anti-Paul!) even though warned not to be. Their fleshly power will be shown to be nothing.

363. Paul's references to sexual immorality in 5:1ff should very likely be seen as a kind of proof of the arrogance he speaks of: this is what it results in. They have become worse than those who do not even know Christ. Such behavior obviously requires correction, so that the individual's *pneuma* (5:5) may be saved "in the day". Again he speaks of their "boasting", and warns of its effects on their whole way of life. It leads to "malice", not Christ's "sincerity and truth". The problem is not cured by living in a ghetto but by countering the influence of the "leaven" that spoils the paschal "unleavened bread" associated with Christ's paschal sacrifice. (5:6-8). He and they must exercise a juridical function towards their own members, as ministers of God, leaving non-Christians to God alone (5:13)—though at the end they will judge those too (6:2). So little have they understood their privileged position that they have actually looked to outsiders for judgement, and this on matters that should never arise among Christians (6:8).

364. Though concerned about all kinds of sins among them, he circles back to his special case, sexual immorality. In the context of his condemnation of unrighteous acts in 6:9ff, it is clear that "all things are lawful" (6:12) is not meant to reclassify or legitimize immoral behavior, but to found the judgement of what is immoral and moral on a firmer basis than formerly, when for the (formerly) chosen people, and for Greeks as well, this was all a matter of legal codes and conventions. The criterion is union with Christ, becoming one spirit with him (6:17). Immorality shatters this union and so must be shunned (6:18). As for sexual immorality, it is the very symbol of severance from Christ, manifesting the sin, as it does, by physical union (6:16). The body should rather manifest the life of the Spirit dwelling within (6:19).

365. Having dealt with the things he himself considers most important for the Corinthians to know, he turns to things they have written him about. One of these is marriage. He relates his answer to the previous section on immorality (7:2), and in fact adopts the same criterion, salvation (7:14,16). This should be the criterion whether in regard to remaining single (7:9) or marrying (7:12) or separating (7:15). After a slight digression he expands his views on marriage in 7:25ff, the aim again being as far as possible "to secure your undivided devotion to the Lord" (7:35—this recalls the "devote yourselves to prayer" of 7:5). The digression may have been prompted by questions from them on circumcision and slavery. An insight on his statement that "all things are lawful" is given in 7:19. What counts is "keeping the commandments of God." Union with Christ and salvation, manifested by moral behavior, give the true freedom and liberate the Christian from legal and civil restraints like circumcision and bondage—or rather, from concern about such things. (7:18a,21).

366. There is an obscure reference to "knowledge" (γνῶσις) in 8:1bf, related to cultic offerings. This might refer to mystery cults; more likely, I think, is a reference to attempts to gain knowledge by magical rites. (See 343). In the light of the "puffs up" of 4:6 and the "he does not yet know as he ought to know" here (8:2—this is "imagined" knowledge), it seems probable that Paul is trying to draw out the thread of his "wisdom-folly" theme. The reference to love would confirm this, in view of previous references in 2:9 and 4:21. Again, the love of God is parallel to the keeping of the commandments in 7:19. Here his point is that what counts is the true knowledge found not in mystic rites before idols but by seeking wisdom in God and Christ, and loving them. [We now have quite a list of things that "count": wisdom, union with Christ, salvation, keeping the commandments of God, moral behavior, love].

367. 8:6 echoes 6:14: "The body for the Lord and the Lord for the body." The RSV "an idol has no real existence" seems to be misleading.

A literal "an idol is nothing in the cosmos" is much more likely. Paul undoubtedly believed in the existence of angels and "powers", like most of his contemporaries. And it is probable that he thought that within certain Divinely-set limits they did have power. After all, the law showed the Egyptian magicians turning rods into serpents (see Exod. 7:12). Further, the "gods of Egypt" (Exod. 12:12) certainly manifested interest in the idols dedicated to them. The issue is not one of existence, therefore, but of relative power. Aaron's rod devours the rods of the magicians; the gods implied by Paul are "divine" only in a secondary sense, exercising power only when God permits it. They are "nothing" relative to God. In this context, the statement about Christ, "through whom are all things and through whom we exist" denotes an unparalleled sharing by him of the Divine power.

368. The concept of sacrifice to angels and powers would for Paul as a Jew have been completely unacceptable. On the principle "There is no God but one" (8:4), actual sacrifice to the "gods" is no threat to God; it could only have effect through these lesser powers by his permission. But sacrifice for the Jew included an acknowledgement, at least implicit, of Divine uniqueness—it was for God alone. So, Paul would have presumed that God would deny such permission to a Christian. The Christian could thus sacrifice to the gods only through ignorance or disobedience. Eating the food of idol-sacrifices at formal communion services would of course suggest that the ones eating shared the sacrificial intent—this would be "partaking of the table" in the sense of 10:22. But eating such food independently of the ritual need involve no erring intent and could look merely to the Divine sway over all things. On the other hand, there might be Christians who at one time had made such offerings and eaten at pagan communion-tables, and now found it hard to shake off the feeling that even ritually unrelated eating had attached to it agreement with erring intent. Paul evidently recognizes as a moral principle that a man will be judged (8:11) not only by the objective rightness or wrongness of his acts, but additionally by his subjective view of right and wrong; and he does not want to scandalize these "weak" ones. And since it is not objectively wrong *not* to eat such food, he is willing to permit such abstinence until they should come to a more mature understanding.

369. Probably prompted by another query from Corinth (see 9:3), Paul presents an apologia for his personal interpretation of freedom. They of all people should know that he speaks at one with Christ and has the freedom, wisdom and power he has been talking about. He claims such freedom in the areas he has been talking about, too: marriage and food (9:4-5). He himself has opted for uncommon abstinence in these areas, but he might have chosen otherwise had it been more useful for himself and for them (9:19). In 9:13 he introduces a comparison he uses elsewhere, of his apostolate with a priestly service and some kind of offering. Like the body (6:13) and existence itself (8:6), his apostolic activity is for God. As the sacrifice is important for the meaning behind it and not for any material sharing in it judged apart from that meaning, so with him it is not the preaching as such, or any rewards from that, but the meaning and content of the preaching: Christ's gospel (see also 3:11). Paul is driven not by human compulsions or interest in inferior rewards, but by the Spirit, by Divine necessity (9:16). It is a deeper compulsion and promises a higher reward, implied by the content of "gospel" itself (9:23).

370. In 9:24 he exhorts them to be as serious as he is about their Christianity, and he implies that what they need is something of the same spirit of restraint in material things that he himself has. This interpretation is strengthened by his referring to immorality again in 10:1ff. He compares the Corinthians with the chosen ones of the Old Testament (whom he links mysteriously with Christ in a manner reminiscent of Rom. 11), who sinned and were destroyed—the sins being actual idolatry, impatience and grumbling, and probably sexual immorality as well, the "rising up to dance" (10:7; see Exod. 32:6). The reference to temptation in 10:13 suggests that the Corinthians, like their spiritual ancestors ("our fathers"— 10:1) may themselves have been impatient at God's failure to provide immediate solutions to their pressing problems, and been tempted to revert to mystical or magical practices in order to gain or force such solutions, whether from God himself by theurgy, or from lesser divinities. The mysteries and magical rites were widespread in the Greek world, and many of the new Christians had undoubtedly participated in them in their past lives. The suggestion of religious orgies in connection with such rites provides Paul with just one more reason for threatening them should they so revert—but a reason with independent importance in view of the behavior of some of them (see ch. 5) and of Corinth's unsavory reputation. Incidentally, the association of immorality of various kinds with idol-worship no doubt inclined Paul to the opinion that gods who responded to such rites were in fact evil. God could, after all, give anything that his inferiors might give. Good spirits would have enough to do implementing worship of him and his own response, should he use them as instruments.

371. The framework of the argumentation in 10:14ff seems to be as follows: "Shun the worship of idols.... What pagans sacrifice they offer to demons and not to God.... You cannot drink the cup of the Lord and the cup of demons... partake of the table of the Lord and the table of demons. Shall we provoke the Lord to jealousy? Are we stronger than he?.... Do all to the glory of God." (10:14,20,21,22,31). The key idea seems to be that of provoking the Lord to jealousy by sacrificing to demons. This "jealousy", of course, is simply God's insisting on the truth that he alone deserves such worship, for "idols are nothing." (10:19). Admitting this is one way of "giving glory to God", since glory in Scripture is generally the manifestation of power and wisdom—showing where they lie.

The Reference to Calvary

372. Paul's reason for repeating these ideas again here is probably that he sees a real danger for them of a reversion such as was suggested above. (370). The question of eating the food of pagan sacrifices in 8:1ff was apparently one that *they* had asked *him*. Now he says that some of them may be in danger of eating such food in an *unacceptable* way—by actually joining in pagan rites. He reasons that to do this would make their eating the sacrificial food symbolic of an affiliation with the god that eating independently of sacrifice would not do. They must shun the *worship* of idols. Offering is central to worship. Their own worship must be specifically *Christian*—a participation in the body and blood of Christ that makes them a new body, analogous to the old Israel κατὰ σάρκα that was constituted around the old altar. There is a clear suggestion here that the body and blood of Christ are themselves analogous to the old sacrifices, at the "altar" stage of the process of worship leading up to the communion. But Paul has made it clear in ch. 8, and here in 10:25ff does so again, *that the eating must be cultically related to the sacrifice. This is the "participation"* (κοινωνία) *repeated in v. 16. Presumably it takes place by virtue of an intentional reference symbolized cultically: anything less would be either empty of meaning or uncultic. But when it takes place, it makes them the Christian "body" that they would not be even if they ate in fellowship together without this cultic reference.*

373. Paul's advocacy of the eating of pagan sacrificial food in ch. 8 and here in vv. 25ff thus becomes a key factor in the interpretation of his attitude towards the Christian Eucharist. *It provides the wherewithal to locate the difference between the Christian cultic meal and just any communal meal. There must be an intentional and cultic reference. In the Eucharist, that reference is expressed by the phrases "body of Christ" and "blood of Christ".* (10:16). Interestingly, Paul separates these two references here and inverts them, which shows that he is not making use of some cryptic formula "body and blood", but is referring to something concrete. *On the basis of the analogy with the Hebrew "altar", this is almost certainly a separate historical incident in which Jesus' body and blood figure in some way analogous to sacrifice.* From the references to the "cross of Christ" in 1:17, "the cross" in 1:18, the crucifixion in 1:23 and 2:8, we can deduce from 1 Corinthians alone—and without looking further in it—that *this incident is Christ's death by crucifixion.* Evidently, this was in some way associated in the manner of its happening with the shedding of blood. Further, the offhand reference to Christ as "our paschal lamb [that] has been sacrificed", in 5:7, shows that there was in fact either an already established tradition of referring to Christ's death as a sacrifice, or at least that the analogy was so evident to Paul that he thought nothing of using it as a passing metaphor, with no need of explanation.

374. Because of the not uncommon tendency to "spiritualize" Paul, it is useful to underscore the fact that it is "*Because* there is one bread [that] we who are many are one body." (10:17a). Paul repeats the point himself: "*For* we all partake of the one bread." (17b). These forceful expressions seem to show that Paul saw the Eucharist as an essential element of Christian living. His attitude towards baptism in ch. 1 suggests to me that he looked on the Eucharist as a kind of projection of baptism (i.e., of the *initial* Christian cultic act) into the day-to-day Christian life with which he as a pastor was principally concerned.

375. Having made his own point again, he returns to their lesser one about eating (as distinct from offering) sacrificial food. In 10:30 he makes use of a eucharistic pun. If he directs proper thanks to God as he eats the food offered to idols, he is certainly not joining in intentionality with those who, while worshipping the idols, gave thanks to them. In putting the issue in relation to freedom (vv. 23,29), he reminds them that cult is nothing else than the outer expression of their reaction to the Christian situation before God and Christ; a point he makes still more clearly in v. 31: "Whatever you do, do all to the glory of God." This phrase "glory of God" recognizes again the basic fact of Divine power, the power that has raised Christ and will raise them (6:14) if they remain united as "one spirit" (6:17) to him, since it is unique (8:6; 10:26) and is uniquely shared with Christ.

376. In 11:2 Paul commends them for "remembering"him, and specifically his having originally preached the gospel to them. He refers to "the traditions" that he gave them, which in the context of 11:23 ("I received....") undoubtedly refers not merely to the central gospel message but to other ancillary teachings and practices as well. But he then recalls —or notes, as he follows their letter—another matter concerned with the relationship between men and women, but this one specifically liturgical. He solves this in terms of a conventional symbolism, and then turns to a more important liturgical matter in which "I do not commend you"—one of which he has apparently been informed by some third party. ("I hear:" 11:18. "Οὐκ ἐπαινῶ" in 11:17). This is their manner of celebrating the Eucharist, to which we shall turn in a moment.

Unity and the Memorial Connection

377. By his references to traditions, and to specific past historical events like the crucifixion, the occasion of his first preaching to them, their baptism; and by a clear distinction of their present state from that of "the day" (1:7—a distinction maintained in texts like 4:5; 5:5; 7:31; 9:24), Paul shows us his position in regard to the importance of salvation history, his practical view of time and eternity and interpretation—the matters we treated in Part II. His view of the Eucharist reveals his judgement of the necessity of sacramentalism, and his demand for reference to the crucifixion (to the Lord's "blood" and "body") links that sacramentalism in both intentionality and symbolism to his view of history; or rather, locates it in his historical framework. *This is another way of saying that it demands memorial thinking in the Christian cult. The communion only forms a true Christian community if it is memorially joined to the [analogue of] sacrifice.* But it implies the reminding-God aspect, for the community only takes on reality and strength through the Divine power operating in God's loving awareness of the crucifixion and the individuals' uniting themselves with it and the Power behind it and in it by thought and cultic act.

378. In Part II (87) we spoke of James Robinson's identification of the "Corinthian heresy" with the notion of a resurrection already achieved. He links this with their view of baptism: "For the view of the heretics that 'there is no resurrection of the dead' (I, 15,12) has in recent research come to be seen to involve not so much a rationalistic Greek denial of resurrection as a fanatical elevation of baptismal regeneration to the rank of the definitive resurrection making any future resurrection irrelevant." [1] Though I accept that dogmatic problems related to the resurrection among the Corinthian Christians might have included a "resurrected already" one as well as a "no resurrection" one; and that the former may have been seen by the "heretics" in terms of results of baptism; I doubt very much if Paul took the dim view of baptismal and Eucharistic effects that Robinson seems to take. It was not a question of *whether* effects could be had through cult—this Paul would not only have allowed, but expected—but of what the effects of Christian cult actually *were*. He was a realist: the resurrection was not yet. As a main dogmatic problem, the "resurrection already" view might merit the name "the Corinthian heresy". But I think that it represents only one aspect of the greater problem with which Paul is concerned in the epistle—*the problem of heresy* [sectarianism] *itself*. It is only "some of you" (15:12) who hold this errant dogma; but *all* the Corinthians are threatened by this faction in the sense that it destroys Christian unity. So do the other divisive influences Paul deals with throughout the epistle: cliquish loyalties, court battles, sexual aberrations, marriage disputes, liturgical differences, reversion to idol worship, selfishness about food. Paul's continual concern, once he has founded a church, is to maintain and strengthen that church's bond of unity "in Christ". Any practice or doctrine that disrupts unity is fit subject

---

[1] Robinson, p. 23, his note 5.

for his strictures; anything that maintains and strengthens, worthy of use. Thus he now returns to the Eucharist, which is the very symbol and part-source of Christian unity, and rails not against some abstruse dogma but against divisive practice. If they are one "because there is one bread" (10:17), it is only so insofar as they have not contradicted the oneness in thought and action and so separated themselves from the sacramental unifying effect. The effects of the sacrament are not given by God without reference to intentionality (any more than they are given without reference to the sacramental forms instituted by Christ, forms that are meant precisely to symbolize the intentionality), and unity is one main effect of the sacrament. *They must strive for unity in order to be* enabled *by God's power—the only supreme divine power—through Christ, to achieve it.* And since unfavorable judgement is always the alternative, if God is not shown the wherewithal to make favorable, "anyone who eats and drinks without discerning the body eats and drinks judgement upon himself. That is why many of you are weak and ill, and some have died." (11:29).

CHAPTER III: **The Immediate Context**

379. The factions in this second Eucharistic passage are the unfeeling well-to-do and the poor; Paul wryly comments that the forming of divisions during the meetings by the former, at least has the advantage of determining which of those present are *not* unfeeling. (11:19). It is wry, but it is ominous too, in the light of 11:29-30. God is given material wherewith to judge. For the selfish, the judgement will at least result in "chastening" (11:23a), so that they may repent and avoid condemnation (11:32b). This echoes a more general statement earlier in the epistle: "If the work which any man has built on the foundation [Christ] survives, he will receive a reward. If any man's work is burned up, he will suffer loss, though he himself will be saved, but only as through fire." (3:14-16). This latter text is also in the context of Christ crucified. This for the Christian is the only foundation, as Käsemann has insisted. Indeed, in Paul's mind it was the foundation for Christ himself, in that the resurrection sprang from it. "...γενόμενος ὑπήκοος μέχρι θανάτου, θανάτου δὲ σταυροῦ. διὸ καὶ ὁ Θεὸς αὐτὸν ὑπερύψωσεν καὶ ἐχαρίσατο αὐτῷ...." (Phil. 2:8-9). The cross is as it were the contact-point of Christ the foundation with God the Rock. And this is reflected in the realities of Christian life: the resurrection is awaited, not now had. As Robinson puts it: "...Paul cites the tradition identifying Jesus' death and resurrection as *the* saving event (15:35ff), and just as in 4:8ff Christian existence in this life is a sharing of Jesus' death and only paradoxically (as the power to hold out) a sharing in his resurrection...." [1] I think that this difference between already and not-yet is paralleled in Paul's mind by a difference in salvific method in the two phases of Christ's durational existence: the cross and the resurrection. Christ died and now lives to be our advocate before God. "Who shall bring any charge against God's elect? It is God who justifies; who is to condemn? Is it Christ Jesus, who died, yes, who was raised from the dead, who is at the right hand of God, who indeed intercedes for us?" (Rom. 8:33-34). In God's plan, the intercession is as necessary for our justification (which comes from the One who is implored) as was the dying. It is a continuation of the prayer and intentionality that went with the sacrificial offering, but exercised now from the privileged position granted by God in view of that offering. There is a paradoxical recognition by all concerned of the difference in method and of the unity in it, a paradox reflected in the two

---

[1] Robinson, p. 24.

clauses of the text of Rom. 4:25, "ὃς παρεδόθη διὰ τὰ παραπτώματα ἡμῶν καὶ ἠγέρθη διὰ τὴν δικαίωσιν ἡμῶν". The picture, clarified by the Philippians text, seems to be that *Jesus by his death gained the gift* (ἐχαρίσατο αὐτῷ ὁ Θεός) *to be an undefeatable advocate, able in his new and lordly vitality to point back to that same death as the source also of justification for any follower whom the powers of evil might claim as their own* ("accuse"), *and who with sincere faith calls upon Christ once crucified to save him.* This process will continue until the follower's own death—"The last enemy to be destroyed is death" (1 Cor. 15:26), when its efficacy will be proved by his resurrection. It is in this sense that Käsemann's statement, "Christian faith... gains access to the cross in no other wise than by the resurrection of Jesus"[2] would, I think, have been accepted by Paul.

380. From our special point of view, this scheme is significant in that it adds a further perspective to the picture of memorial. Just as the reference to the cross is necessary for the follower of Christ in this life (377), so it is necessary for Christ himself at the stage of existence he enjoys in this interim period before the "final enemy" is destroyed, before "the day". As advocate in the position of influence at God's right hand, Christ reminds the Father—who only waits to be reminded—that he, Christ crucified, was as "first fruits" (1 Cor. 15:20) empowered by God at his exaltation to defend the believer against any adversary until "by him should also come the resurrection of the dead" (15:21). This is part of the heavenly "tapestry" of which we spoke several times in Part II (v.g., 116, 173), parallel to the earthly one, and like it seen by the pious first-century Christian (unless of gnostic or similar persuasion) as retaining its wholeness and meaning through the power of memory. In the end, the tapestries will be joined; already Christ figures in both, dying in the lower at a point in human history, exalted to the upper where he now lives gloriously, able to intercede. The situation is suggested by the prayer of the thief: "Jesus, remember me when you come into your kingdom." (Luke 23:42).

381. The contrast of the good with the unrepentant thief prompts the question whether Paul's references to judgement would mean, in memorial terms, that a sinning and accused Christian would not be remembered (acknowledged) by Christ his counsel until such time as he might of his own accord rejoin himself to the power of the crucified by intentionality, obedience, and we may suppose, prayer. Certainly, this counsel tries to avoid at all costs remembering sin against the Christian in the sense of taking the stand as a witness for the prosecution and working for a definitive judgement of "guilty". Rather, he has the prerogative of exercising a temporal judgeship himself, as in the "chastening" function

---

[2] Ernst Käsemann, *An die Römer*, 2nd rev. ed. (Tübingen: J. C. Mohr [Paul Siebeck], 1974), p. 121.

in 11:32. In this text it is almost certainly Christ who judges: the appellation used of the chastener here, "the Lord", is used unmistakably of Christ four times in the preceding verses (11:23-30). It is this same "chastening" judgeship of Christ that Paul himself claims to share when he judges the sinner "that his spirit may be saved in the day of the Lord" (1 Cor. 5:5). He says, "I have already pronounced judgement in the name of the Lord Jesus." (5:3-4). And in 2 Cor. 13: 2-3: "I warned those who sinned... and I warn them now... that if I come again I will not spare them—since you desire proof that Christ is speaking in me. He is not weak in dealing with you, but is powerful in you." Thus, as long as life lasts, Christ does not forget, but inasmuch as in these cases he cannot point to a proper state of reference to the crucifixion on the part of the defendant, he gives a temporary sentence of chastisement as a reminder to provide that referent. The initiative remains with heaven, as always. Christ remembers the sinner as well as his own salvific death, and continues to remember and to remind.[3]

382. From what we saw in Part III, the Pauline picture just described is much the same as the Pentateuchal one. The sin must be acknowledged in order to be forgiven. (244, etc.). There will be chastisement to prompt repentance; perhaps also as punishment. But the punishment for Israel will only be a temporary affair, not a total catastrophe as might occur with the nations. The Levitical text expresses all these elements (see 202-203, with reference to Lev. 26:2-6), but we see the same system in operation throughout the Pentateuch. Typical: Israel sins, Moses prays to avert Divine wrath, a penalty is exacted, the nation goes on. Sometimes the penalty has to be paid partly by Moses himself. "The Lord was angry with me on your account, and he swore that I should not cross the Jordan." (Deut. 4:21). The immediate context of the latter text, incidentally, shows how closely the system was integrated into the whole covenant scheme. 4:23-24 read: "Take heed to yourselves, lest you forget the covenant.... For the Lord... is a devouring fire, a jealous God." (Note too the "forget": the covenant scheme is of necessity linked to memorial). All this is the practical working of the "blessing-curse" of Deut. 11:26ff; 30:1ff. We have seen how it was related to the cult. The sin offering was the cultic expression of admission of guilt and plea for Divine mercy. (232, 236; 244).

---

[3] This kind of heavenly courtroom scene has been well described by Nickelsburg (see our note 23 of Part II, Ch. IV). Speaking of Enoch 94-104, he says, "In heaven the angels 'remind' God about the righteous. They call his attention to the unjust oppression of the righteous and plead for judgement in their behalf. Like the Spirit of Truth in Testament of Judah 20, they are advocates for the righteous and accusers of the wicked. Different from Michael (Dan. 12:1) and the great angel (As. Mos. 10:2), and like the Spirit of Truth (Test. Jud. 20:5), they are functioning right now and not simply in the eschatological future." (pp. 120-121).

383. But the other side of this coin was the "blessing" aspect. We have seen Paul combining the two aspects in 1 Cor. 3:14, speaking of "reward" and "loss". (...μισθὸν λήμψεται ... ζημιωθήσεται). We may judge that he is not thinking here solely in terms of some rigorous quid pro quo, but of the Divine Goodness which "loves a cheerful giver" (2 Cor. 9:7), even when the giving is not to Him directly. The 2 Corinthians text is bracketed by, "He who sows sparingly will also reap sparingly, and he who sows bountifully will also reap bountifully.... God is able to provide you with every blessing in abundance." (9:6,8). Undoubtedly, the offering of gifts to God himself in cult would provide occasions for a similar if not greater beneficence, were the Christian to possess an "offering" kind of cult. We have seen that Paul almost certainly inherited, and accepted, a tradition of Jesus as an analogue of Old Testament sacrifice. (373). And without any doubt, he sees all blessings to come through Christ and through the cross-resurrection. In the Old Testament, sacrifice was offering *par excellence*. It all fits rather well.

384. When, therefore, we see Paul ascribing loss to those who celebrate the Eucharist selfishly, we may expect—since there is an expressly covenant context—that there is blessing forthcoming for those who celebrate it discerningly. Indeed, if the Eucharist be viewed as a communion service temporally delayed but essentially related to a historical offering-event, it becomes the very symbol of the forgiveness and/or blessings to be associated with such an offering. We look with new interest at a statement like, "The cup of blessing which we bless, is it not a participation in the blood of Christ?" (10:16). This "bless" is almost certainly the thanksgiving of 11:24, from which the Eucharist probably gets its name. But the "blessing" is far more likely to express the *reason* for this thanksgiving than the thanksgiving itself. One blesses God because God first blesses. The cup represents the acknowledged source of Christian blessings, the crucifixion-death; this is what "Eucharist" is all about. Barrett[4] cites the Jewish blessing over food to which we earlier referred (348), and this clearly shows the emphasis on the Divine giving. Lietzmann makes use of even more descriptive terms when in speaking of the Corinthians' Eucharist in connection with the liturgical "*Sursum corda*" he says, "'Lift up your hearts' may have summoned them from talk of earthly things to the prayer over the cup of blessing and to a remembrance of the Lord's blood of the covenant."[5] We must of course ask whether, when the term "ἀνάμνησις" was made part of the narration, this prayer and others, and indeed the whole of the ritual, was not meant in the traditional manner of so many "memorials" to remind God as well as men of his covenant blessings.

---

[4] See Barrett, p. 266.
[5] Hans Lietzmann, *Mass and Lord's Supper*, trans. Dorothea H. G. Reeve (Leiden: E. J. Brill, 1964), p. 187.

385. 11:20. "When you assemble as a church...." (ἐπὶ τὸ αὐτὸ). The Vulgate has here *"in unum"*, which I think expresses the idea somewhat more clearly: in English, something like "as a unity". The contrast with the rest of the verse, "...I hear there are divisions among you", is more apparent with such a translation.

386. 11:20b. "...it is not the Lord's supper that you eat." (For 11:19 see 379). Here is the origin of another name for the Eucharist. There is an intended contrast between "κυριακὸν δεῖπνον" and "ἴδιον δεῖπνον" in the next verse. "...each one goes ahead with his own meal." The significance of such behavior is suggested by 10:16-17. The Eucharist is actually constituted by participation in the blood and body of Christ; the participants are one body *because* of *this* κοινωνία. If they do not celebrate the *Lord's* supper, therefore, they are not *really* one. They do not even posit the symbolic, outward part of the Eucharistic essence properly, and certainly their intentionality is vitiated by their selfishness. (On this essence, see 372; another clear statement is given in 378 just before the italicized section). How can they be one with Christ when they are at odds with those he loves? As for the *name* "Lord's supper", I doubt if it derives historically from the essential Christ-reference; after all, this is Paul's explanation of the meaning—shared, no doubt, with others, but hardly the sort of thing on which to found nomenclature. The tradition as Paul gives it shows "the Lord Jesus" (11:23) at a meal performing actions and saying things that would have made that meal unique. This is un-doubtedly the origin of the phrase—factual-historical (at least purportedly so), not theological-historical.

387. 11:21b. "One is hungry, another is drunk." Extremes, emphasiz-ing the division. There may also be an implied criticism of drunkenness on such an occasion, in the light of 10:7ff. "The people sat down to eat and drink, and rose up to dance." 11:22 ("Do you not have houses to eat and drink in?") I think justifies the view common among scholars that Paul wanted to separate the Eucharist and ordinary meals. This does not mean that he thought the original Supper was not part of a genuine meal; his view was probably that the Lord had prestige enough to keep that one event under control, but the Lord was not a visible presence at subsequent Eucharists!

CHAPTER IV: **The Tradition**

388. Our chapter title simply refers to the fact that Paul has called what follows a "tradition". Since we are mainly concerned with the tradition at the Pauline stage, we shall not spend time debating whether he might or might not have made subtle additions to what "I received from the Lord." As for his introduction, we might also wonder just what he means by "from the Lord", but the important thing for our purposes is that he founds his version of the tradition on Christ's authority. I do not think the contrast between "Lord" and "Lord Jesus" indicates that the former here refers to God rather than Christ. The "Lord Jesus" is used to give an authentic ring to the tradition as such. "Lord" is perhaps "Jesus Christ" of Gal. 1:12. "God" is used of God from 11:1 (and before) to 11:22, and "Lord" clearly refers to Jesus in the next three occurrences of the word. "What I also delivered to you...." is some justification for thinking Paul has not changed the tradition recently.

389. "On the night when he was betrayed." (11:23b). This Paul includes in the tradition. Mark combines the note of betrayal (14:10-11) with a chronological one: "On the first day of Unleavened Bread, when they sacrificed the passover lamb...." (14:12). It requires some credulity to think that Paul's reference to "Christ our paschal lamb" is unrelated to this association of the betrayal and the pasch; further, it is unlikely that the Marcan tradition of association was unknown at the Pauline date. The association would explain why Paul refers to Christ as having been "sacrificed". The paschal lamb was a sacrificial offering and the use of the blood on the lintels a simple extension of the manner of its disposition at the altar—something probably less regulated in earlier times than in later, in any case. On the pasch as sacrifice see Exod. 12:27, Deut. 16:5, Jub. 49:9,19, etc. The Jubilees texts read: "And the man who is free from uncleanness, and does not come to observe it on occasion of its day, so as to bring an acceptable offering before the Lord, and to eat and drink before the Lord on the day of its festival...." (49:9). "And they shall offer its blood on the threshold of the altar... and they shall eat its flesh..." (49:19). These texts bracket "it shall come for a memorial well pleasing before the Lord...." (49:15), and the "before the Lord" in the first one indicates that the memorial nature pertains to the offering and eating equally. These considerations are important because Paul must have realized that by putting the Supper in a paschal setting, calling Christ "our paschal lamb", and speaking of "memorial" all within the confines of the same letter (and with the "memorial" linked to the paschal setting), his readers would almost inevitably be led to think of the Supper as a new-covenant paschal meal. The fact that the Marcan account explicitly speaks of sacrificing the lamb and eating it (14:12) certifies the conclusion that the association was deemed quite believable by the early Christians. The Mishnah's description of the passover service provides a separate tradition to justify such a belief. In view of the Pauline setting, a review of this description (in *Pesaḥim*) seems advisable here.

Pesaḥim [1]

390. "A man must eat naught until nightfall.... they must not give them less than four cups of wine to drink." (10:1). The order describes a) a first cup with blessings over the day and then over the wine (10:2) with food "until he is come to the breaking of bread; they bring before him unleavened bread.... And in the Holy City they used to bring before him the body of the Passover-offering." (10:3). b) The second cup, and the passover haggadah. (10:4). The first psalm or two (pss. 113, 114) of the *Hallel*, devoted especially to praise. R. Akiba is said to have added a short prayer including a petition for the opportunity to celebrate further passovers: "May we eat there of the sacrifices and of the Passover-offerings whose blood has reached with acceptance the wall of thy Altar." (10:6). c) A third cup, at which time "he says the Benediction over his meal." (10:7a). d) "[Over] a fourth [cup] he completes the *Hallel* and says after it the Benediction over song." (10:7b). This is apparently an especially solemn part of the meal, and is accompanied by the rubric: "If he is minded to drink [more] between these cups he may drink; only between the third and fourth cups he may not drink." (Ibid.). The last part of the *Hallel* (Pss. 114 or 115 to 118) seems to carry the burden of the prayer-element of the celebration, containing praise, thanks, and petition, in solemn juxtaposition. It includes assurances of the Lord's future blessings (115:12-15) followed by the statement "we will bless the Lord"— demonstrating the "blessings-blessing" relationship we spoke of earlier (384). There is also the wish-prayer: "May you be blessed by the Lord" (115:15); a definition of "calling on the name of the Lord" ("O Lord, I beseech thee, save my life!"—116:4); more petition and thanksgiving. Finally (116:12-19), there is embedded in the middle of the song a powerful expression of determination to go on celebrating the liturgy that might easily have served as a part-pattern for the Eucharist. "I will lift up the cup of salvation and call on the name of the Lord... in the presence of all his people. Precious in the sight of the Lord is the death of his saints."

---

[1] Quotations from the *Mishnah* are taken from *The Mishnah*, trans. Herbert Danby (Oxford: University Press, 1933).

Verse 17 refers to sacrifices of thanksgiving, which in the Temple context would be the best expression of eucharist for a Jew. Used at the pasch, they were probably taken to refer to the paschal sacrifice itself. It is notable that there is no reference to Israel's sin in these psalms. The "cup of salvation" was very likely interpreted to mean cups like those being drunk at the passover celebration, with perhaps a special emphasis on the fourth cup, with which (in the Mishnah tradition at least) this part of the *Hallel* was associated. This "cup" is only incidentally related to the thanksgiving sacrifices.

391. I have used the RSV version for the psalms cited above, since there seems a good chance that the passover was celebrated with Hebrew prayers. However, the LXX has all the same elements. And significant for our thesis is the presence in both versions of explicit covenant-related memorial terminology, including both God-remembering and man-remembering, in the very first psalm of the *Hallel*.

> He has caused his wonderful works to be remembered;
>   the Lord is gracious and merciful.
> He provides food for those who fear him;
>   he is ever mindful of his covenant. ...
> He sent redemption to his people;
>   he has commanded his covenant for ever.
>   (Ps. 111:4-5,9—RSV)

This should of course be linked with the reflections made above (378), prompted by the memorial terminology from *Jubilees*.

The Variety of Analogues of Christ's Death

392. The notion that a paschal meal was the historical origin of the Eucharist does not mean that the Eucharist had *only* paschal significance. The need to see a wider meaning in it may well explain why Paul uses the "paschal sacrifice" analogue only in passing. Paul's fundamental theological point was Christ's saving from the power of sin, and the Eucharist's setting and content as he shows them to us both point to the death on the cross that he repeatedly identifies as the event that grounded that salvation. That death was also associated with the pasch, and Paul knew that the pasch was a thank offering meant in part to gain for the Hebrews not only salvation from external oppression but additional blessings of various kinds. He was very much interested indeed in the Christian analogues of such protection and blessings—the latter, after all, included the resurrection of every believer. But more fundamental by two degrees than milk and honey, and by one than salvation from external human oppressors, was the salvation from sin that involved only oneself and God. This kind of redemption was associated in Hebrew thinking with sin offering. Paul would not have wanted to risk the loss of such associations for his Christians by overdoing the paschal analogy. On the other hand, he would not have wanted to exclude the paschal meaning either, and in the context of his own emphasis on man's bondage to sin, *that* meaning needed even more protection that did that of liberation from sin. He could very easily have used the analogy of "sin offering" for Christ. In fact, though he introduces ideas that point strongly to it (e.g., the "for sin" of Rom. 8:3, with his clear portrayal of Christ as personally sinless and obedient), it remained for the author of Hebrews (in 10:12) to introduce the terminology itself.

393. In analytical terms: Paul was willing to use metaphor, a strong form of analogy, in calling Christ a "paschal sacrifice". But he was aware of the tendency for such metaphors, in human minds, to harden into the form of species. A logical species is the result of an evolution in thought, working through a narrowing process of specific differences from higher strata (genera) that may themselves be sub-species. There is a definite assumption that once the difference is admitted there is no way for the individual to belong to other species at the same evolutionary level. Paul, if queried explicitly on the subject, might perhaps have allowed Christ to be placed strictly in the species "mediator"—which is well above its sub-species "sacrifice" in the logical gradation. But even here, in the context of pre-existence indicated by a text like Phil. 2:6ff, he might have felt that the use of the *term* "mediator" might encourage a restriction on the functions of his Lord. What he preferred to do and constantly did was limit himself to general and various ways of describing Christ's functions, only occasionally, as with "paschal sacrifice", using nominal labels. He may have felt on these occasions that in his wider context no reader would ever take them exclusively (but if he did so he badly mistook reader-tendencies!); perhaps it was just that the currency of the expressions lulled his apprehensions.

Williams' Positions

394. One inherited "mediatory" idea that Paul expressly associates with Christ is " ἱλαστήριον" in Rom. 3:25. This text has rather recently been studied at some length by Sam Williams, and this seems a proper stage of our own study to discuss some of his arguments and conclusions.

395. Williams translates his text *per partes;* the total result is something like this: "God set forth (before or to *himself* [his italics]) Christ, (as) ἱλαστήριον,[2] as a means of expiation [3] through the faith of which Jesus

---

[2] Sam K. Williams, *Jesus' Death as Saving Event, the Background and Origin of a Concept,* Harvard Dissertations in Religion 2 (Missoula, Montana: Scholars Press, 1975), p. 37.

[3] Ibid., p. 52.

is the source." [4]   He paraphrases this, or a slightly corrected version of
it, thus: "God has 'regarded' Christ crucified as a means of expiation in
order to manifest his righteousness by making righteous the man who has
that faith whose source is Jesus (or: the man who shares Jesus' faith)," [5]
adding, "This act of justification is understood in terms of forgiveness of
sins." The change from "set forth" to "regarded" is explained by the statement that

> If one assumes that the formulation does not wish to suggest that God
> was responsible for the execution of Jesus, προέθετο must point to a
> divine act or decision subsequent to, in light of, the crucifixion; that is,
> the verb refers to God's response to man's evil act of killing Jesus the
> Christ. ... God is not responsible for the death of Jesus; He *is* responsible,
> according to Rom 3:25, for enfolding that death within his own purpose
> by regarding it in a certain way, namely as ἱλαστήριον.[6]

I would agree that even a first-century Christian would not have seen God
as directly responsible for Jesus' death when human agency had undoubtedly been involved. But Paul's undoubted conviction about God's
complete control of events, plus a number of references to obedience on
Jesus' part and to planning on God's in direct connection with the death
(v.g., Rom 4:25; 5:6ff; 8:3ff), make it clear that for Paul too God was at
least seen as letting Christ move into the situation that resulted in his
death. As Luke puts it, "...this Jesus, delivered up according to the definite
plan and foreknowledge of God...." (Acts 2:23). God is therefore responsible
for the situation in which men were faced with (and made) the decision
of life or death for Jesus. He planned the situation and foreknew the
decisions. This means that although God did indeed "regard" both
situation and decisions, a translation of προέθετο as "regard" would be
insufficient, as Williams undoubtedly realized when faced with the actual
task of translating the Greek word itself. His paraphrase unjustifiably
weakens the meaning. That meaning is almost certainly that God did
"set" Jesus in the situation, with the knowledge—mysteriously had by reference to the human decisions involved—that it was as *hilasterion* that
Christ was there. Indeed, not only knowledge but will, once given the
knowledge.

   396. This picture is of moment for us because it describes a typical
God-remembering situation. There is Divine initiative, the known human
response cultically expressed, and—if the Divine planning should be associated with Divine promises made in the past (as through the prophets)
—a covenant aspect as well. Even Williams' paraphrase allows for a
certain amount of memorial content, but it excludes the element of Divine

---

   [4] Ibid., p. 54.
   [5] Ibid.
   [6] Ibid., pp. 37-38.

initiative that was of supreme importance to Paul himself in this area of God's dealing with sin.

Hilasterion

397. I would further differ from Williams in his estimate that "ἱλαστήριον", which he describes as "means of expiation", would not for Paul have been related to the Old Testament "mercy seat". He cites Sanday and Headlam's view that ἱλαστήριον for Paul probably would not mean "mercy seat" "*because* the sprinkling of the mercy seat was the one rite which was withdrawn from the sight of the people,"[7] doing so relative to their preference for translating "προέθετο" set forth publicly". We may note that the emphasis of the "public" elements is questionable as far as translation is concerned; but it is made irrelevant by the fact that the public aspect is in any case a question more of knowledge than of ocular vision. No Christian *sees* Christ's solitary prayers on mountain or in desert; yet these have in a true sense become public events. As for the crucifixion, it is "public" for the vast majority of Christians far more because of its being preached than because it once lay open to public gaze. Sanday and Headlam's suggestion to read Gal. 3:1[8] actually emphasizes this. "O foolish Galatians! Who has bewitched you, before whose eyes Jesus Christ was publicly portrayed as crucified?" What was public was Paul's *preaching* of Christ as crucified, even though the event itself was hidden from their mortal eyes by gaps of time and space. Or, if we may apply a figure based on the context of "mercy seat", the "curtain" of time and space. The things in the holy of holies were paradoxically the more public because they were more private. They were not only publicly effective, they were publicly known, and the *hilasterion* in particular, with the ark of the covenant of which it was the cover (Hebrew כַּפֹּרֶת; its function of covering the ark is clear from Exod. 25:21), is commonly mentioned in all eras of Hebrew literature—the epistle to the Hebrews is only one example of it. (Other examples: As. Mos. 2:4; 8:5; 2 Bar. 6:7; 2 Mac. 2:1; Philo, De Moise II, 95).

398. Williams seeks the historical origin of the idea of *hilasterion* in the Romans tradition, and thinks he finds it in the expiatory death of Hebrew martyrs in *4 Maccabees;* which deaths in turn he sees as finding their origins in Greek notions of heroic death. I think Williams provides us here with another example of the tendency to make what really cannot be proved to be more than historical *analogues* into definite historical *origins.* I do not feel that he has proved the "origin" theory for the Romans text; though in drawing attention to de facto analogues of Christ's

---

[7] Ibid., note 73, p. 34. (Williams' italics.)
[8] See ibid., note 73, p. 34.

death he has done a useful service. Unfortunately, his pressing of the
"origin" idea encourages "specific hardening" of the type we spoke of
earlier (393). Even if he had been able to prove that the martyr-deaths
and picture of expiation in *4 Maccabees* were in fact the historical sources
of the Romans text, it would still be desirable to prove that Paul was
aware of the fact; otherwise, there would be no impediment to his thinking
and composing in terms of any other meanings of "*hilasterion*" that might
occur to him. The similarities between Paul and *4 Maccabees* that Williams
points out hardly prove such awareness. And with Paul's manifest familiarity with the Pentateuch, the idea of "mercy seat" would almost surely
have occurred to him.

399. Influencing him in his thinking would have been the nominal
form of the term he uses. Williams says of the Romans usage: "The word
should probably be taken as a neuter substantive (τὸ ἱλαστήριον) rather
than as the accusative of the adjective ἱλαστήριος." [9] It is the latter that
we find in 4 Mac. 17:22: "And the Divine Providence saved Israel, aforetime
afflicted, by the blood of those pious ones, and their propitiatory death
(ἱλαστηρίου θανάτου)." The expiatory idea here is linked grammatically
with "death"; it does not identify the person as such, as it does in Romans.
Williams argues quite rightly that ἱλάσκεσθαι implies the averting of Divine
wrath, this in turn demanding purification and the forgiveness of sin. [10]
"Thus it is precisely the expiation of sin which effects propitiation.... The
term... does not confront the exegete with a choice between two mutually
exclusive concepts, expiation *or* propitiation." [11] But the question is, just
how is Christ viewed in Paul's tradition as *hilasterion*? Undoubtedly, his
death is viewed by Paul as propitiatory, and in particular, his blood and
the body from which that came would be so viewed. This would fit both
the *4 Maccabees* and the Levitical view. But why call *Christ* the *hilasterion*
rather than calling the death, blood or body "propitiatory", as in *4 Maccabees*? Were it not for the "mercy seat" analogy's being so common, we
could think it a case of a new-formed metonymy. At any rate, I would
suggest that the tradition wishes by the usage to stress the *location* of
the expiatory event, leaving the method to be expressed by the reference
to blood. The point of the " ἱλαστήριον " is that *God sets Christ forth before
himself* (as Williams puts it), in the same manner that the cover of the
ark was prescribed by God to be set before the Divine Presence in the
holy of holies. Because it was the blood displayed upon the cover that
effected the propitiation, the use of the term for the cover itself was in
fact metonymical. But this metonymy was long since established when
the Christian text was formulated, and was well known. It is unlikely
that the text "re-metonymizes".

---

[9] See Williams, p. 38.
[10] Ibid., p. 39.
[11] Ibid.

400. The emphasis on location was in Paul's own mind as he approached his citing of the tradition. In 3:20 he says, "No human being will be justified in his sight [literally, 'before him'] by works of the law." What " ἱλαστήριον " functions as here, therefore, is a symbol of *mediation*, of *location* between God and man. This fits ideally with Paul's "in Christ" theology, and may partly explain why he felt such terminology to be acceptable. The suitability of the *hilasterion* as a symbol of mediation is evident both from the idea itself and from the history of the nomenclature associated with it. The Divine Presence was supposed to be located immediately above or on it; the propitiating blood of the most solemn of sin offerings was placed there too. On the one side was the Lawgiver, on the other the law. On the one side God, on the other, man. As for the name, the Greek, while emphasizing the human element, strongly connotes the Divine. The Vulgate Latin is *"propitiatorium"*, but Luther, as Fitzmyer notes,[12] preferred to stress the Divine aspect and spoke of *"Gnadenstuhl"*, whence the English "mercy seat" = "seat [place] of mercy".[13] It is, in fact, in the Hebrew view, the "place of mercy and propitiation". Of it, Philo says, "It appears to be a symbol in a theological sense [i.e., as it relates to God] of the gracious power of God; in the human sense, of a mind which is gracious to itself and feels the duty of repressing and destroying with the aid of knowledge... conceit... pride." (De Moise II, 96). He sees the need of a *double* symbolism: from *both* sides. His description of the human side in terms of knowledge of course reflects his personal theories of propitiation.

Sin Offering and Scapegoat

401. If this is a correct interpretation, Williams' one-sided preference for hellenistic hero deaths rather than sacrifice as the analogues behind the Romans 3 text is of course put in question, since the "mercy seat" was closely associated with sacrifice. Since he rightly sees both the Romans and the Maccabees texts as presenting examples of "vicarious expiatory suffering",[14] he attacks the idea that sacrifice is vicarious expiation, holding that "Isaiah 53 is the single OT text in which the idea of vicarious expiatory suffering is to be found (if, indeed, it is present there)." [15] Citing R. B. Townshend on the one side of the "Is sacrifice vicarious expiation?" debate, and R. de Vaux and Eichrodt on the other, he summarizes three of Eichrodt's arguments, which we may review here because they have been influential. 1) If the sacrifice were a vicarious satisfaction, it could not be replaced by a non-sacrificial offering as in Lev. 5:11ff. 2) The victim is in fact

---

12 See Joseph A. Fitzmyer, "Pauline Theology," *JBC* 79: 86.
13 See Colson's note b to De Moise II, 95, in LCL, *Philo VI*.
14 Williams, p. 229.
15 Ibid.

considered holy, whereas if it were thought to be laden with sin and guilt it would be unclean. 3) In P non of the sins expiated by the sacrifice are transgressions worthy of death.[16]

402. The understanding represented here gratuitously saddles the whole of the opposition with the unsupportable thesis that sacrificial substitution would mean substitution for the *sin* of the offerer. The argument: "Sacrificial substitution would mean this. But the victim is pleasing to God. Therefore, the victim is not substitutionary." Good logic, but a questionable premise. Whatever the remote historical origins, *developed Hebrew theology saw the sin offering as representative directly of the confession rather than of the sin itself.* It is something that was truly "holy" in the Hebrew sense of the word קדשׁ—"set aside for God". What the sacrifice represents is clear even from the case of the "sacrifice of jealousy" that we discussed earlier (232, 235). Here, the "water of bitterness", after the curses are symbolically dissolved in it, is given to the woman and purportedly, if she is guilty, turns into evil for her. But the offering itself is given to God, and logically represents her willingness to submit herself to judgement—*a quite legitimate intentionality even should she in fact be guilty.*

403. Another case where a multiplicity of ritual shows the true nature of the sin offering is that of the scapegoat. R. Faley says, "The idea of sin transference to animals is found among the primitive customs of various people...."[17] Unfortunately, he fails to take note of the spiritualizing possibilities of the combination of this rite with that of the second goat's being offered as a sin offering. The LXX reads: "And [Aaron]... shall make atonement... for their trespasses in the matter of all their sins...." (Lev. 16:16). (He has already done the same with a calf for his own sins). The atonement is particularly intended, on this occasion, to "hallow" the holy places "from the uncleanness of the children of Israel" (16:19,33), and is recommended for repetition, "a perpetual statute." (16:29). There is no indication in the text that the scapegoat was to be used in subsequent rites of atonement, so that its importance may well have been seen by the writer as secondary to that of the sacrificial goat and calf. The scapegoat is eminently suitable to serve as a strong *symbol* of the removal of the sins both from the people and from the holy places *as a result of* the atoning sacrifice—which, for the Hebrew writer, undoubtedly meant as a result of God's forgiveness. This interpretation is suggested in the text by the temporal subsequence of the scapegoat ritual to the sacrificial one, by the fact that the scapegoat is driven far from the holy places and the people, and by its being left alive to continue the

---

[16] See ibid., p. 104.
[17] Roland J. Faley, "Leviticus," *JBC* 4:34.

symbolism into an indefinite future. It may be, of course, that the editor
of the Levitical passage still thought there was some sort of actual
transferral of sins to the scapegoat, occasioned at the instant of Aaron's
laying on of hands. The Hebrews' idea of sin as some kind of almost
tangible reality was shared with most early peoples. On the other hand,
the clause "and the goat shall bear their unrighteousness" can be interpreted in terms of pure metaphorical symbolism. One thing the *Mishnah*
makes clear is that *its* writers considered God to be the agent of removal
of sin. According to *Yoma* 6:2, the high priest [the Mishnah sees the scapegoat rite as part of the later Temple ritual] "used... to say: 'O God...
forgive, I pray, the iniquities and transgressions and sins which thy
people... have committed.... For on this day shall atonement be made for
you to cleanse you: from all your sins shall ye be clean before the Lord.'"
"Atonement" here refers to the sin offering, even though the prayer
described is part of the scapegoat ritual: the words "For on... Lord" are
a citation from Lev. 16:30. As for earlier interpretations, the possibility
of actual transference of sin to the live goat in response to the atonement
effected relative to the sacrificial one depends on the viewers' notions
of what might happen to sin when God "wipes it away" from the sinner.
A transference would see it as a kind of dust, to be dispersed in the deserts
outside the city. There may in fact be something of this same idea in
the disposal of the remains of the actual sacrificial animals after their
blood has been used in the atonement. The man that burns them outside
the camp has to bathe just as does the one who drives out the scapegoat.
(See Lev. 16:28).

404. The scapegoat incident underlines the special nature of the sin
offering as few other Old Testament incidents do. Commentators have
not always read the distinction, however. One reason may be that the
Scriptural writers themselves, in later times, sometimes seem to have
combined the notions. This is quite possible, logically, if one is willing
to forego some elements of ordinary sin offering on the one hand, and
scapegoat on the other, and add some elements as well. A main addition
is the humanization of the [now] single victim. He is thus enabled to
be a sin offering in his internal intentionality while looking externally
more like something laden with sin than something dedicated to God.
It would be possible, certainly to understand references to the Suffering
Servant's "bearing sins" in terms of sin offering alone (to which reference
is made in Isa. 53:10). The sin offering in every case has to bear the
results of sin, the main result being death. Again, it would be a simply
metonymy. Indeed, since there is no specific reference to scapegoat in
the Servant text as there is to sin offering, this is probably the preferable
interpretation. It depends partly on whether one would be willing to
accept an actual transferral of sin to the scapegoat. This would obviously

have to be the main element in the analogy, and since no good Hebrew would see the sin offering as *being* sin, it would *destroy* the analogy, really. But if the scapegoat is merely a *symbol* of transferral, the Servant could *appear* to be sin while really being sinless, and both the analogies could be understood. Note, again, that we do not speak of "partial" analogies. Every analogy is partial; it is simply a question of more or less of sameness and difference.

405. If the sin offering did not substitute for sin, what did it substitute for? It "represents" repentance and confession of sin, but how is representation related to substitution? The point, of course, is whether Christ *as* a sin offering could be said to substitute. The Suffering Servant substitutes in the sense that he achieves a vicarious expiation. Does he do this as a sin offering? The mention of the phrase in the text suggests that the author thought he did. In fact, incidents like that of Isaac's sacrifice also suggest that the animal victim was meant as a substitute for its owner. Not that the offerer always intended to offer his whole life; but life was the best summation of what he had to offer. And we must recognize that all the intentionalities that constituted the form and dynamism of his offering act also constituted the best of his life's ontology. Life was a kind of summation of all that was most worthwhile in human activity—thinking, loving, praying, praising, thanking. "What profit is there in my death, if I go down to the Pit? Will the dust praise thee?" (Ps. 30:9). The psalmist's question provides a theological justification for the law's prohibition of human sacrifice—men are better praisers of God alive than dead. But the appeal of the idea of offering a life remained, and the notion of substituting another life that *could* legitimately be given, to indicate what one would be willing to give if one were permitted, must have occurred to someone in very early times. The fact that honesty probably forced most offerers to admit that they might not be willing to go as far as giving their lives if they were permitted to do so would not detract from the dramatic appeal of the substitutionary idea. What it would do would be to make the substitution not so much that of life for life as of life for *part* of life—the intentionalities already mentioned. And this in turn would suggest the use at the substitutionary end not only of animal sacrifices but of things that were not complete lives but were closely related to life: grain, cakes, fruit and drink. It was inevitable that what was offered would come to be judged by its value to the offerer. In a pastoral society where animals were in large part the very currency of wealth, the animal sacrifice had a double appeal: it was most directly related to life, and it was most valuable in itself. The tie of ownership was evidently deemed necessary, but a closer kind of tie is suggested by a story like that Nathan tells to David in 2 Sam. 10.

406. The sin offering, therefore, can be explained in terms of substitution as well as of symbolism; in fact, the two are merely different emphases describing the same process. As a symbol, the offering points to the offerer in a signing function; as a substitute, it materializes and localizes for liturgical handling what at the same time must remain part of the offerer. Turning, now, to Eichrodt's arguments. (401). His first one seems to involve the presupposition that to found an effective substitution the substitute would have to be actually equivalent to the sinner. But this was surely not the Hebrew's idea. It was evident that the animal was of less worth than the human; thus, taking something of still less absolute value as a substitute did not invalidate the idea of substitution, providing that that something was of genuine value to the offerer. "Life for life" is most suitable, but other things can substitute too. The argument may also intend to impose an unlikely concept of "satisfaction" on the substituting offerer. The Hebrew offerer would hardly have seen the animal as a satisfaction in the strict sense of the word (Latin, "making sufficient"). He would look to God's forgiveness, as with his peace offerings he would look to God's blessings past and future. He would hold that *no* offering can "satisfy" unilaterally; and this might even lead him to reflect that if under certain circumstances God were to be satisfied (in the general sense of the word) with nothing more than his sincere repentance, no further expiation at all would be needed. The thinking about the exile came close to this.

407. Eichrodt's second argument, that the victim was thought to be holy, only takes effect on the presumption that the substitution is for sin. We have seen that it was not. As for his third argument, it presumes he same kind of parity between offering and offerer of which we spoke relative to his first one. As less than an animal life could in certain circumstances substitute for a human life, so an animal life could substitute for less than a human life.

Ransom

408. Another concept that I think Paul would have accepted as a basis for analogy with Christ in his saving function is that of ransom. Büchsel is of the opinion that Paul does not favor the idea, pointing out that he does not use the substantive (λύτρον). But his statement that "The more concretely we take the idea of ransom, the less it is in place alongside that of ἱλαστήριον," [18] suggests that he too is thinking "specifically" and not allowing sufficiently for the potentialities of the very "more and less" that he admits to be conceptually possible. In fact, his distinction between *lutron* and *hilasterion* seems to be seen as that between a specific

---

[18] *TDNT*, s.v. "λύω," by F. Büchsel, p. 355.

and un-Pauline means of redemption (this is *lutron*) and a general one (*hilasterion*) which he considers Pauline, and which he associates with the term "ἀπολύτρωσις", used by Paul in the Romans text. Indeed, he goes further and seems to hold that in Rom. 3:24 Paul is thinking in terms of effect but not of act. "Even the other Pauline verses (R. 3:24; 1C. 1:30...) do not have in view an act in virtue of which liberation comes. They think only of the act of emancipation itself...." [19] Yet he presently notes that "To show *how* redemption is brought to pass, Paul uses the concept of ἱλαστήριον...." [20] [My italics]. Such a distinction between act and effect is surely too strong. Earlier in his article he says that "For the Jew... the ref. to a ransom can easily carry with it the thought of expiation by the vicarious sufferings of the righteous...." [21] Would this association be hidden from the Jew Paul? Indeed, Büchsel does not hold to the distinction when speaking of *apolutrōsis*. "It is an outworking of His [Christ's] love and self-offering for us, Gl. 2:20." [22] [παραδόντος ἑαυτὸν ὑπὲρ ἐμοῦ]. He relaxes here, I suspect, because for him "self-offering" is a general concept, which must not be pressed into strict specific molds. Is this not our own argument against "specific thinking"? Not at all: we argued against *excluding* any technical terms simply because Paul clearly fixes on one or another special one. But we were talking precisely about technical terms. Nor is it merely a question of terms. By arguing against ransom because Paul does not use the substantive, Büchsel passes over other indications that the *idea* might have appealed to Paul. He admits that Paul "has in view a payment in Gl. 3:13; 4:5, but this does not mean that this is also implied in R. 3:24." [23] The term in Galatians in both cases is of course ἐξαγοράζω. 3:13 reads, "Christ redeemed us from the curse of the law, having become a curse for us...." The idea in the context is very close to ransom, and very Pauline; further, the citation Paul adds, "Cursed be every one who hangs on a tree", shows that he was thinking of the crucifixion. I would certainly agree that "ransom" thinking is not the only type of thinking involved in Rom. 3; but I would not exclude its presence there either, along with other kinds of thinking that Paul manifests elsewhere. As for Paul's avoiding the *term* "ransom", it is once again explicable on the basis of a fear on his part that the public's tendency to think in strict specifics might inhibit his message should he give them occasions to follow the tendency. After all, he uses "*hilasterion*" and "*pasch*" only once each of Christ, and these, probably, in inherited formulas. They were terms that, though legitimately applicable to Christ, have certainly proved to be foci of dissension.

---

[19] Büchsel, pp. 354-355.
[20] Ibid., p. 355.
[21] Ibid., p. 341.
[22] Ibid., p. 354.
[23] Ibid., p. 355.

409. Ransom does indeed offer several important points of sameness with Christ. The ransom is a good thing substituted for someone under duress or threat. In the Old Testament ransom was to be paid to God to free the firstborn son from the fate of being sacrificed to God. As Huesman remarks, "The practice is explained by reference to... the tenth plague." [24] It is also reminiscent of the sacrifice of Isaac, and like it is a commentary on the Hebrew theology of God's rights and his mercy. In Numbers God asks for the Levites as the ransom for the first-born of Israel (3:41,45): the Levites will live on as special servants of the Lord. Since they substitute for sacrificial victims, it would be logical if they themselves were considered offerings, and in fact their function is so described: "You shall cause the Levites to attend Aaron and his sons, and shall offer them as a wave offering to the Lord." (Num. 8:13). The lamb that was ransom for the firstborn of an ass (Exod. 13:13) was undoubtedly sacrificed. The "atonement money" (Exod. 30:14) that was a ransom for the people was called a "tax" (εἰσφορά—RSV "offering", since it was given to God); as we have seen, it was appointed "for the service of the tent of meeting; that it may bring the people of Israel to remembrance before the Lord, so as to make atonement for yourselves." (30:16). There is an interesting etymological link in Hebrew between "mercy seat", "ransom", and "atonement". These are, respectively, כְּפָרִים ,כֹּפֶר ,כַּפֹּרֶת·

One might perhaps speculate on the possibilities for substitutional errors should some misapprehension have taken place during translation into Greek. According to the lexical etymologies, the similarities seem to be fortuitous. However, the texts we have seen show definite associations of the *idea* of atonement with both mercy seat and ransom. And with memorial. As for ransom, it is especially closely linked to offering. On the other hand, the notion of Christ as curse is close to the scapegoat idea, and the same points about his *being* sin and his merely *appearing* to be so as were made above (404) of scapegoat may be made here. If the latter position is taken, both curse and offering could simultaneously be seen as analogues of Christ. Ransom is related to curse too, of course. We may note that an idea closely related to the "appearance of sin" one would be that of a victim being held in duress by the power of sin not in obedience to sin (as were the Romans before their conversion: Rom. 6:17) but in obedience to God. This was Paul's view of the sinless Christ: see Rom. 5:19; Phil. 2:8. A sinless individual, incidentally, would not fall under the Sinaitic covenant curse. He would not be delivered into the power of sin by the law; it would have to be by a *special* Divine decree. This too fits Pauline thinking.

410. We have seen Williams conclude that the concept of effective or vicarious expiatory suffering/death occurs in typical Hebrew literature

---

[24] John E. Huesman, "Exodus," *JBC* 3:32.

only in Isa. 53, if at all. He comes to this view partly on the basis of a denial that sacrifice is substitutionary, and since we have seen good reason to doubt this position of his, it seems necessary to rethink the implications of related ones. One point about the Hebrew theology of sacrifice we may not like to accept, but it was apparently true: that God was granted the right in theory to demand human sacrifice. Another that seems quite acceptable: he admitted the vicarious function of the greatest of the atonement sacrifices, that on the Day of Atonement itself. (Of others too, of course.) All that remained for a Hebrew to think in terms of a human expiatory sacrifice was an incident, whether fictional or factual. The Suffering Servant text is a prophetic literary expression of just such an incident. The fact that a Greek poet like Euripides expressed the same thing in formal drama is merely corroboration of the ubiquity of potentiality for such an association of ideas in an age when sacrifice was itself universal. Williams takes *IV Maccabees* as an example of (and perhaps direct influence on) the thinking behind Romans 3:24-25.[25] It is scarcely accidental that the writer of *IV Maccabees* himself turns to the sacrificial analogue in a noteworthy way when summarizing what had happened to Eleazar and the rest. He has one of the brothers say: "Remember of what stock ye are: and by the hand of what father Isaac endured to be slain for the sake of piety." (13:12). The response is, "Let us sacrifice with all our hearts our souls to God who gave them, and employ our bodies for the keeping of the law." (13:13). It is a parallelism expressing the giving of life in two different ways, and even if it should intend a dichotomy between soul and body and a "spiritualization" of the notion of sacrifice, sacrifice is still the analogue—not that there is any indication that this particular kind of spiritualization would be present in the Romans 3 tradition. Someone might argue that the Greek translated above (in the Brenton translation) as "sacrifice" is ἀφιερόω a word that might or might not mean sacrifice. The obvious answer to this is to look to the context, and that is the Isaac incident. This is mentioned again in 18:11, in close proximity to the text that speaks of the expiatory death (17:22), and there is no ambiguity here: it is τὸν ὁλοκαρπούμενον Ἰσαάκ".

A Look Back at our Discussion of Analogues

411. It should be clear by now that to insist on sacrifice as the *only* analogue of Christ's death as Paul represents it would be as far from our point as to exclude it. *Ransom, martyrdom, akedah, mercy seat, scapegoat were other almost inevitable terms of comparison.* Whatever the historical origins of the traditions in Romans 3 or 1 Corinthians 11, when Paul ran them through his mind preparatory to setting them down in writing, he must have thought of such things. Indeed, he explicitly

---

25 See Williams, pp. 233ff.

mentions several of them. In turn, the only way he could have kept a high percentage of his readers from thinking of them and dwelling on the similarities would have been explicitly to deny them. He does not do that, any more than he makes them "types" by focussing on their individual similarities with Christ's death and calling special attention to them in one-to-one terms—as with Adam in Rom. 5:14. Rather, his method is much like that of the author of *IV Maccabees* himself, who at the end of his work offers what amounts to a rubric as to how to think about what he has said. The whole of the text in which the Akedah is mentioned reads thus: "He used to read to you the slaying of Abel by Cain, and the offering up of Isaac, and the imprisonment of Joseph. And he used to tell you of the zealous Phinehas; and informed you of Ananias and Azarias, and Misael in the fire. And he used to glorify Daniel, who was in the den of lions...." (18:11-13). This was not meant to be an exclusive list: the writer would scarcely object if we added Isaiah and Jeremiah to it, for example. Paul never gets around to making such a list, but his incidental references to *hilasterion*, paschal lamb, "buying", etc., have a similar if less concentrated effect. Nils Dahl provides us with one example of the workings of such a policy on Paul's part:

> Early Christian use of Scriptures was not differentiated from contemporary Jewish Midrash by some new hermeneutic. ... For Judaism, the story of the binding of Isaac provided help in understanding that the God of the fathers allowed the sufferings and death of faithful Jews in the days of Antiochus Epiphanes and later. The same story helped followers of Jesus to overcome the scandal of the cross and to understand what had happened as an act of God's love and a manifestation of his righteousness. ... Not any competition, but the close correspondence between the Akedah and the atonement was stressed. ...[26]

Paul is very sparing with typology, and almost as sparing with metaphor and open simile. But, taking advantage of the wide diffusion of Jews in his various congregations, with the knowledge of Old Testament matters that this made available to his readers; taking advantage, too, of their familiarity with the Greek world...... he makes large use of what we may call "implied simile", whether by design or simply by half-conscious allowance. The approach assures him a wide appeal without the constricting disadvantages of the use of more pointed figures.

412. The above dozen or so pages were prompted by the phrase "on the night he was betrayed" in 1 Cor. 11:23b (389). They provide a useful

---

[26] Nils Alstrup Dahl, "The Atonement—an Adequate Reward for the Akedah?", in *The Crucified Messiah and Other Essays* (Minneapolis: Augsburg, 1974), p. 160. (Reprinted from *Neotestamentica et Semitica, Studies in Honor of Matthew Black*, ed. by Ellis and Wilcox [Edinburgh: T. & T. Clark Ltd., 1969]). I would hesitate to agree with his further venture, represented by the four dots in our citation, that " ... quite possibly [the close correspondence was stressed] to the extent that the redemption by Christ was seen as an adequate reward for the binding of Isaac." On the relationship of Akedah and the Christian atonement, see our discussion of Geza Vermes in 485ff.

background for the following verses. Indeed, more than useful, near-necessary. For I do not think any satisfactory appreciation of what Paul tells us can ever be reached without a grasp of what we have been discussing. It is true of the memorial element and of all the rest as well. Almost every word Paul uses is to some extent a term of analogy for one or several analogues; the same for word-combinations. This does not mean, however, that we can make what we want of the text. The cultically significant analogues, for example, are definitely limited by the material Paul gives us, while differences between the Christian terms and the Hebrew or Greek ones narrow down the number of notes of similarity in each analogue. The multiplicity of analogues, obviously, suits the richness—indeed, it is in large part the way we *learn* of the richness— of the Christian event. It opens up avenues of meaning where otherwise there would often be only a dull reporting of incident with or without somewhat pedestrian explanation, often, again, directed at particular groups with particular problems. We may note that the question of whether it is actually possible to locate Christ's death and other aspects of Christianity in *species* like "sacrifice" or "sacrament" or "martyrdom" is really a separate question that depends on definitions both ancient and modern. Most word meanings have a certain amount of latitude in usage. At any rate, this is not our concern here.

413. The passover setting presented the formulator of the Pauline tradition with a wealth of possibilities. There was a historic cultic occasion closely related spacially and temporally with the crucifixion and resurrection. There was the Temple context and an actual Temple sacrificial victim. There were bread, wine, eating, drinking; prayers of praise, thanksgiving and petition. On such a physical basis, and with all these elements to furnish denotation and connotation, the Eucharistic tradition is set by both the synoptists and Paul. One of the strongest connotations immediately apparent to anyone familiar with the materials is the memorial one. The pasch was the classic festal memorial, and sacrifice as such was a memorial. Here, then, is the significance, at least in part, of the simple "On the night when he was betrayed....", taken in the light of Paul's reference to "our paschal lamb" and the synoptic paschal tradition. But Paul, typically, does not introduce any special reference to "pasch" just here. That would limit his options in reading off meaning from the text. The text is capable of paschal meaning, but of more.

Our Text Continued—the Core Verses

414. In the following it is presumed that the reader has at hand the compartmented text of our para. no. 1.

11:23b

415. The paschal setting provided bread, wine, a roasted lamb. It is noteworthy that there is no specific direction as to the frequency of repetition of the rite. The "it" in the RSV of 25h is not in the Greek, so that in theory they might celebrate as often as they drink wine. (An "it" in the paschal context might be thought to signify a particular paschal cup). Wine, as Yeivin says, "was considered the choicest of drinks" [27] in biblical times. All the same, it seems to have been quite common, and was probably available even to the poor for use at the more important meals—at least in the meaner qualities and lesser quantities. The same was not true of meat. "Meat meals were not usual: the *kerah* or *zevah...* was part of some festive occasion." [28] There was no refrigeration, and animals were relatively expensive, partly because they were useful for other purposes than for their flesh. Bread, however, was a staple, so much so that the word itself stood for "food". Thus, the use of bread rather than flesh as the analogue of "body" may very well have been a practical one looking to the frequent repetition of the rite. There might have been other reasons too, of course; for example, the avoidance of any suspicion of cannibalism. Bread is almost as suitable an analogue of body as wine is of blood—not perfect, but close enough to be easily associated with its term of comparison. Yet it is clearly not "meat".

11:24 (less 24e,f)

416. *11:24a.* "...and when he had given thanks...." Possibly a prayer of some length, including praise, thanks, and petitions for blessings related to "the body of Christ which was sacrificed on the cross for the community.... the blessing which issues therefrom to liberate the community and to unite it with Christ...." [29]

417. *11:24b.* "...he broke it...." Paul's explanation in vv. 26 and 27 ("as often as you eat," "whoever eats") indicates that the "for you" of 24d was symbolized by a distribution, almost certainly following on this breaking. Mark makes this clear by adding "gave it to them," (14:22). Mark also reflects prevailing custom by referring to "dipping bread into the dish with me" (14:20). The bread was probably a large, flat, pan bread of the type still common in Eastern countries. The distribution at this stage of a festal meal may have been ceremonial; however, *Acts* (which of course may be reflecting prevailing *Eucharistic* custom here) speaks of the same thing happening at an inn (24:30). The distribution by the head of the family may have been a regular thing, like carving the meat in modern Western custom.

---

[27] *Judaica,* s.v. "Food," by Ze'ev Yeivin, column 1418.
[28] Yeivin, col. 1415.
[29] *TDNT,* s.v. "σῶμα" by E. Schweizer, p. 1068.

418. Paul makes no mention of the number of people present; Mark mentions "the twelve". (14:17). The breaking legitimizes the question of numbers, especially since Paul speaks of "the twelve" in this same epistle and relates the group to the period of the crucifixion and resurrection. The wording of the passage is remarkably like that of 11:23, and suggests that it may be part of one tradition which Paul breaks up for his own purposes. "For I delivered to you... what I also received, that Christ died for our sins... was buried... raised... and that he appeared to Cephas, then to the twelve." (15:3-5). The "for our sins" could be a parallel to "which is for you" of 11:24d, expressing at least part of the significance of the crucifixion. This single and passing Pauline use of the phrase "the twelve" shows that the tradition was firmly established when Paul wrote, something that needed no explanation. Its association with the last supper may have been quite as well attested in his tradition as in Mark's, and we must ask whether the notion of distribution of bread to "the twelve" might not have been a reading that Paul knew would be made. The likelihood seems very good, and its memorial implications are considerable. The notion of the "loaves of proposition" would almost surely come to the mind of anyone familiar with Jewish writings, in a "bread" and "twelve" context. That notion was current in the literature; we have seen that Philo (337) and Josephus (340) use it; other examples at random are 1 Mac. 1: 20; 4:49; Sir. 45:20; 2 Chron. 2:4. The idea would be especially attracted to a context of memorial and covenant. We heard Philo speaking of "loaves set forth upon the holy table as memorials of the twelve tribes" (337), and *Leviticus* specifies that they are "for an everlasting covenant" (Lev. 24:8). If we further recall that the "memorial" text is one of the few "ἀνάμνησις" ones, the likelihood that the loaves of proposition would have occurred to Paul and his readers as analogues of the bread distributed by Christ would be high even *without* a specific reference to "the twelve". The cluster "bread, distribution, covenant, memorial, ἀνάμνησις" would provide the connotative terms. And there may have been still other pressures in this direction. From Mark 2:26 we know that there was what Bultmann calls a "debating saying" [30] about the loaves of proposition in which Jesus likened his own attitude towards eating (in the Marcan text, grain off the stalk) on the Sabbath to that of David towards the loaves: "and [David] ate the bread of the Presence... and also gave it to those who were with him." [31] Mark has other "bread" material that shows there was a tendency towards mystical thinking in relation to bread and eating, and that one aspect of that thinking was an association with numbers. "'Why do you discuss the fact that you have no bread?.... do you

---

[30] Rudolf Bultmann, *History of the Synoptic Tradition*, rev. ed., trans. John Marsh (New York: Harper and Row, 1963), p. 146.
[31] One can see how such a text might be used to further a change of liturgical celebration from Sabbath to "Lord's Day."

not remember? When I broke the five loaves for the five thousand, how many baskets...?' They said to him, 'Twelve.' 'And the seven for the four thousand...?' And they said to him, 'Seven.' " (8:17b-20). People were looking for "twelves" and "sevens" relative to bread. Given the above texts an Alexandrian would no doubt fasten on the fact that five loaves plus seven loaves make twelve. Most of us smile at such thinking, but it was a very popular sort of thinking in the hellenistic age, and indeed, even today numerology finds plenty of adherents.

419. The loaves of proposition were primarily a reminding-God type of memorial. But the Marcan text shows that people too were supposed to recall the incident that involved them. "Have you never read what David did...?" (2:25). The "five-seven" text puts this directly in terms of remembering, since there were as yet no Christian Scriptures to read. "Do you not remember?" (8:18b). For Luke, the breaking of bread becomes a criterion for the recognition of Christ: "He was known to them in the breaking of bread." (24:35). Undoubtedly the broken bread at the Last Supper was a prime object of Christian recollection. Indeed, Mark shows us what it means for the faithful *not* to remember. "Do you not yet perceive or understand? Are your hearts hardened? Having eyes do you not see, and having ears do you not hear? And to you not remember?" (8:17b-18).

420. *11:24c.* "This is my body...." τοῦτο—a neuter. Following the action of the taking and breaking of bread, it seems most natural to read this as referring to the bread, but as interpreted by the equated σῶμα. "Σῶμα is what the bread now is." There is a parallel to this construction in Philemon v. 12. "['Ονήσιμον]...ἀνέπεμψά σοι...αὐτόν—τοῦτν' ἔστιν τὰ ἐμὰ σπλάγχνα ." The Vulgate translation of the latter clause is interesting: *"Tu autem illum ut mea viscera suscipe."* If this thinking were applied to our own text it would read about thus: *"Vos autem hunc panem ut meum corpus accipite."* There is of course no simile-word (*"ut"*) in the Greek; what we have is either a metaphor or some stronger kind of identification. As for the shift in gender from masculine to neuter (τοῦτο, not οὖτος), it is simply explained by the elision of the αὐτον that appears so awkwardly in the Philemon text, with a sole focus on the significant predicate nominative. The latter not only attracts the gender of the demonstrative but its number as well: the bread is now one even though broken.

421. It is clear how this notion parallels the Pauline idea of the church as a mystic body that is one though made up of many members. But it *is* a *parallel* for Paul. 10:17 has shown us that it is "Because there is one bread [that] we who are many are one body." (See 372ff; also E. Schweizer as cited in 416). This is also one of the implications of the "which is for you" in our text—the κοινωνία is primarily the *effect* of the reference to Christ's crucified body as source of blessings. A distinction between the "body" and "you" is clearly evident. Willi Marxsen would have the sharing in the meal, as distinct from the distribution or the bread itself, as "what is being interpreted" [32] in the pre-Pauline formula. "It is not the food that is interpreted; rather it is clear that the fellowship is constituted at the meal. It is this fellowship which is described as... 'the body,' namely, the body of Christ." [33] For Marxsen, therefore, the τοῦτο points to the community, and there is no special reference in the bread formula to Christ's death. He does admit such a reference for the blood formula,[34] but he argues that at the pre-Pauline stage a parallelism between the two formulas should not be seen. Be that as it may, a parallel is clearly present at the Pauline stage itself, and it is permissible to expect that for Paul, as the "cup" refers to Christ's death, so does the "bread-body". This would conform to the reference to altar in ch. 10, where the "bread" in question is clearly what is eaten, whose analogue-referent, "the body of Christ", is seen as the *cause* of the group. We can certainly admit that it is not directly the "food" that is being interpreted, and that the fellowship is constituted at the meal. But the fellowship is being constituted by the crucified body of Christ in some way, and since it is the bread that is seen as referring to that, the bread is somehow being interpreted. Further, since the action looks to Divine blessings as a fruit of the crucifixion-resurrection event, the bread has a valid "food" symbolism: its eating is an essential element in the external part of the cultic act that unites with Christ and under God produces the blessings. The "under God" aspect is of course fundamental. *It is only God who can "actualize" in the sense of producing really saving and life-giving blessing.* Marxsen's view of actualization is that "the group which is celebrating, praying, and giving thanks is the 'body of Christ'; as such it is actualizing 'the new covenant.'" [35] The group certainly does "actualize" in a psychological and dramatic way. But this degree of actualization alone would scarcely have satisfied a first-century devotee, whether Jewish or Greek. We shall devote a special chapter to the notions and terminology of actualization in our final Part. For us, here, cult is related to the kind of actualization expressed in the italics above, related precisely by reminding-God. As we shall see in the Part referred to, there is a definite place for this in the logical pattern of actualization.

422. Conzelmann summarizes the word of interpretation over the bread thus: "The bread is the body in the sense of sacramental identity.... in the sacramental food the executed body of the—now—exalted Lord is

---

[32] Marxsen, p. 11.
[33] Ibid., p. 12.
[34] See ibid., pp. 9-10.
[35] Ibid., p. 13.

presented. By this means the participant obtains a part in him, in the sacramental communion." [36] The identification of the personal body of Christ is clear here, as is the importance of the cultic act of eating. Thus, as far as it goes, it is a valid expression of the far more common opinion on the significance of the bread as between "church body" and "Christ's personal body". Conzelmann further speaks of "the remembrance of the death of Christ" as a part criterion "against the sacramental enthusiasm which takes its stand upon an exaltation Christology." [37] He seems to link this factor to what he calls "a further interpretative element in wholly different terminology: the death of Christ was (!) a sacrifice 'for you.'" [38] One wonders why this should be seen as a "wholly different" terminology, in view of the traditional relationship between sacrifice and communion. This relationship in the present case—if the Eucharist were seen as an analogue of communion with the crucifixion as the sacrificial term—would depend even more than usually on memory as the link joining the elements of the total cultic event, this because of the greater temporal lapse. But as in the more usual cases it would depend for its fruitfulness for men ("for you") on its acceptability to a similarly (though transcendently) "remembering" God. This element of remembering Conzelmann is unwilling to allow as within the signifying capabilities of the term "ἀνάμνησις" as found in our text. He speaks of Jeremias' interpretation as being "in contradiction to the plain wording. The meaning is: 'in remembrance of me.'" [39] Since he makes no further statement on the *anamnesis* question, we may reserve full comment on this statement until we have discussed the question of the cup. If that too seems to point to the possibility of a reminding-God signification, an even firmer objection to the limitation will have to be made than seems already indicated. What does seem clear is that neither Marxsen nor Conzelmann sees his way clear to integrating the meal organically with the crucifixion event. The "for you" is for Conzelmann really restricted to the sacrifice; it is only *commemorated* in the later cult. "The death of Christ was (!) a sacrifice 'for you.'" But the Pauline text says, "τὸ ὑπὲρ ὑμῶν", and I think the RSV is quite justified in giving the translation "which is for you", with the indeterminate "is". This seems to accord with the common first-century view of communion as a genuine means to gain the Divine blessings— especially those flowing from the sacrifice. It is precisely the reminding-God element that would make this organic unity of sacrifice and communion possible for the Christian cult without any recourse to magic or theurgy. *The crucified body both on the cross and in the role of present advocate would be seen as a blessing-source through God's viewing it as*

---

[36] Conzelmann, pp. 197-198.
[37] Ibid., p. 202.
[38] Ibid., p. 198.
[39] Ibid., p. 202.

a reminding-God memorial "set forth" by him as his referent of actuality.
The communion part of the cult would serve as a similar memorial and
referent, with the difference that it also refers backward in time, like any
communion, to the sacrificial event (as well as "upward" to Christ risen).
This in the spirit of Divine "new covenant" promise associated with that
event and the communion commemoration.

423. The discussion here has been set in terms of sacrifice and communion because these are the categories Conzelmann introduces. But
the picture just given ("The crucified body.... commemoration") would fit
other kinds of analogues such as those listed in 411. The Eucharistic
cult in Paul represents some minimal kind of dramatic presentation; and
as long as the basic referent was the crucifixion event, reminding-God
would be in place for a commemoration of that event as of an act of
martyrdom, Akedah-type offering, *hilasterion*, ransom or scapegoat. All
of these as well as sacrifice of several types seem to be connoted as possibilities with the reading of the text in its Pauline context. There is
here a legitimate pluralism that finds a common key in the full notion
of cultic memorial. In passover terms—to take one of the types of sacrifice
connoted—the importance of a eucharistic-type cult is beautifully expressed
by the saying attributed to Rabban Gamaliel: "In every generation a man
must so regard himself as if he came out of Egypt.... Therefore are we
bound to give thanks... and to bless him who wrought all these wonders
for our fathers and for us.... so let us say before him the *Hallelujah*." (Pes.
10:5). This thanks was undoubtedly in part anticipatory of future blessings,
and was as we have seen accompanied by (or perhaps, in a Hebrew sense,
more accurately "partly constituted by") positive petition.

424. We have tried to demonstrate that Paul would have been open
to the idea of "blessings from cult" as long as it was carefully guarded
against magic or theurgy. (See 150ff, 137ff, 152ff). But he was undoubtedly
wary of expressing himself too forcibly on this issue precisely because of
the possibility of being misunderstood in a magical or theurgic sense.
This was especially important in writing to the Corinthians if, as we have
conjectured, there was real danger of their relapsing into idolatry. (See
366-368; 370). Morton Smith has recently underlined the strong propensity
of first-century men and women to seek more-than-natural blessings from
cult, by his thesis that the Christian Eucharist was

> an unmistakably magical rite, ... In all the sources we see it variously
> interpreted, moralized, and adjusted to Old Testament legend, by additions
> to the wording, by commentary, or by location in a secondary, theologically
> motivated framework. When such window dressing is stripped away,
> what remains is an absolutely primitive figure: a magician-god who unites
> his followers to himself by giving them his body and blood to eat and
> drink.[40]

---

[40] Morton Smith, *Jesus the Magician* (San Francisco: Harper & Row, 1978), p. 146.

Smith could not have made his statement plausible were it not a fact that there was in hellenistic times, among all kinds of people, including Jews and Christians, a natural and passionate interest in "what's in it for us?" and the uses of cult in getting it. The "theological window dressing" was quite likely partly meant to provide a set of orthodox correctives to the suggestions of magical practice that the "eating", "drinking", "body" and "blood" aspects of the Eucharist do manifest. I think Smith's work should be welcomed for its strong statement of the then situation. What is less commendable is the same tendency towards "specific" thinking we spoke of earlier, with insistence on origins where on the evidence it seems equally likely that there was, rather, an influence of historical analogues. Further, Smith passes by in silence the significance for Christian belief of the Pauline point in Christian history, and the suitability of some of the "window dressing" to save the cult-blessing relationship while excluding strictly magical and theurgic elements. The Pauline statement of the Eucharist has been incorporated into numerous Christian liturgies, prayers, and presentations of the Word from the earliest days of Christianity, and continues in use today. Even from a purely historical point of view, the theological elements surely deserve better than the "window dressing" treatment Smith accords them. As for his central emphasis, we shall return to it after discussing the "cup" word.

425. Barrett, in speaking of "body", calls attention to Jeremias' contention that what Jesus originally said was "my flesh". After noting like ourselves that he (Barrett) is concerned less with origins than with the use Paul makes of the report, he concludes that "body" "should probably be understood in the light of the reference, in Pesahim x.4 [see our 390, a], to the 'body of the Passover (lamb)'." [41] He is probably close to the mark here. The Hebrew of Pesaḥim reads גופו של פסח"; for גוף Koehler gives "mhb. ja., ...body, person." [42] It should not be thought that because Christ's body was left intact he would necessarily—if the crucifixion were considered a sacrificial analogue—be as victim analogous only to the "whole" offering. He might be that too, like Isaac in 4 Mac. 18:11. For in practice, in the traditional text, the whole offering was itself cut up into pieces: see Exod. 29:18; Lev. 1:9,13; etc.; also the presence of the knife in the Genesis story of the Akedah. The whole offering was of course meant exclusively for God; there was no communion. Why then this cutting? It was probably a carry-over from a primitive notion that the god ate the food and ought to have it carved for him. Obviously, a Christian adaptation of any kind of sacrifice would have to dispense with the idea of carving. The use of the term "body" rather than "flesh"

---

[41] Barrett, p. 266.
[42] *Lexicon in Veteris Testamenti Libros*, ed. Ludwig Koehler (Leiden: E. J. Brill, 1958), s.v. "* גוף".

would underline this point. Of course, "flesh" can refer to the material aspect of body even when the flesh remains an integral part of the body, but it is "flesh" that is eaten when the parts of the body are separated from one another by carving.

426. On the other hand, in the traditional account blood *was* separated from the body of Christ at the crucifixion, and reference to the event could not disguise this fact by any change of terminology. What Paul does, I suspect, is to soften the "blood" word by referring to "blood" obliquely rather than directly, this suiting his desire to emphasize the covenant angle in any case. In the event, his wording results in a combination of a clear reference to the death, the retention of the sacrificial analogue, and an incorporation of the reference into an "eating-drinking" rite. The Marcan tradition is less subtle. But in any case, it was clear that what was eaten in the Eucharist retained every quality of bread, and what was drunk every quality of wine, so that the mystical intent of the predication of "body" and "blood" was evident. This being so, there could be little repugnance even for someone of Hebrew antecedents in this eating and drinking, even if he should see the predication in terms of some kind of identification.

427. Paul would hardly have wished to exclude the application to Christ of the basic notion of complete dedication that was associated with whole offerings; on the other hand, the fact that these were not communion sacrifices would have deterred him once again from making specific identifications, especially in a communion context like 1 Cor. 11. In other words, here again he would avoid speaking "specifically", but would prefer analogy and connotation.

11:25 (less 25i)

428. *11:25b.* "Also the cup...." In the paschal setting this would be one of the cups of wine over which blessing was said (see 384, 390). The contents would in any case be wine. Since "contents for container" is one of the commonest forms of metonymy, and is used often where the contents are known from the context ("He had a glass with his friends after work"), there can be no force to any argument that sees an exclusion of the denotation of wine here. This is especially true in view of the reference to blood in 25f: "This cup... is in my blood." The best sense is something like "in terms of my blood", which would presume an understanding very close to that of 24c ("This [bread] is my body"); that is, "This [wine] is my blood." We are not concerned here to enter into the debate as to which way the tradition was moving: whether Paul compressed two parallel statements for theological emphasis, especially that on new covenant; or whether the exact parallel was worked out from his formula.[43]   If the latter, it was a logical development; if the former, a logical compression.   This is the more evident because of the traditional association between wine and blood in both Hebrew and Greek literature. "The dark immortal dewdrops... the blood of Bacchus...." (Timotheus, Cyclops).[44]   "[God] made him [eat] ...the finest of the wheat—and of the blood of the grape you drank wine." (Deut. 32:14).   It was impossible to mention "cup" in conjunction with "blood" without the attention being drawn in some measure to the wine in the cup as a fitting symbol of the blood.

429. At the same time, "cup" was a well known Hebraic figure for the Divine wrath,[45] probably because of an association of its effects with a bitter drink.   This seems to be the basis of the idea of the cup of suffering in the synoptics.[46]   Since, as Goppelt notes, this is an aspect of Divine judgement, what he calls "the Rabb. harmonising of the cup-images of the OT"[47] to include cups for good as well as those for evil was a legitimate expansion of the image.   But Paul, when speaking of the results of "eating the bread or drinking the cup of the Lord" in 11:27 and 28, keeps the emphasis on the bitterness of the judgement, undoubtedly because his reason for introducing the whole tradition here in the epistle is non-commendatory. (See 11:22).   The obvious implication, however, is that when the cup is drunk worthily it will be sweet rather than biter; will result in blessing rather than curse.

430. *11:25c.* "μετὰ τὸ δειπνῆσαι...." The reading could be "the after-supper cup".   In the paschal meal, this would probably be the fourth cup, associated with the recitation of the last part of the *Hallel*, with all the implications of that for the meaning of the rite. (See 390ff).   Mark of course ends his meal episode with "when they had sung a hymn...." (14: 26).   Perhaps this was not meant to be the *Hallel*, but as Gnilka notes, "wie sollte ein griechisch schreibender Autor das Hallel Bezeichnen?"[48]

431. *11:25d,e.* "This cup is the new covenant...."   Paul refers to both the old and the new covenants and recognizes both.   "The law... does not annul a covenant previously ratified by God, so as to make the promise void." (Gal. 3:17; see also 4:24).   Paul is "minister... of a new covenant, not in a written code but in the Spirit...." (2 Cor. 3:6).   It is a covenant giving freedom from sin.   "These women are two covenants... Sinai is in slavery with her children.   But... Jerusalem... is free, and she is our mother."

---

[43] See Barrett, p. 268.
[44] Timotheus 12, in LCL, *Lyra Graeca III*, trans. J. M. Edmonds.
[45] See *TDNT* s.v. "ποτήριον," by Leonhard Goppelt, p. 152.
[46] See Goppelt, p. 152.
[47] Ibid., note 39, p. 152.
[48] Joachim Gnilka, *Das Evangelium nach Markus*, 2 vols. (Neukirchen-Vluyn: Benziger Verlag and Neukirchener Verlag, 1978), vol. 2, p. 247, note 46.

(Gal. 4:24-26). This passage, in explicit covenant terms, is parallel to the core of Romans. The law ensured transgressions for all, because in the event "all men sinned." (Rom. 5:12). But it also promised blessings for obedience, and since Christ the Son was the sinless exception to the rule, God, in conformity with promise, enabled him to extend his mede of blessing to sinners and redeem them from the curse of Divine wrath. This is in a true sense a fulfilment of the old covenants: of the Sinaitic one because the blessings promised to obedience are the saving factor in the new arrangement; of the Abrahamic one because that contained the promise. But it was "new"—a rearrangement of the Sinaitic covenant scheme—because it cancelled the sinning individuals' being answerable independently of the mediating sinless Christ.

432. This picture is the Pauline Christian expression of the "new covenant" statements by Jeremiah and Ezechiel. The law is now to be written "upon their hearts" and "they shall all know me." (Jer. 31:33,34). That is, inspired by the recognizing Spirit, they will know God in knowing by faith Christ, the means of salvation he has put among them, the "law of [that is] Christ". (Gal. 6:2; 1 Cor. 9:21). This is really the "wisdom" message of the first part of 1 Corinthians: see 359, 360, 366, etc.) The knowledge in question is put by Jeremiah in terms of forgiveness of sins. There is no longer to be a desperate searching about for means to remedy the universal failure to keep the covenant. "No longer shall each man teach his neighbor and each his brother, saying, 'Know the Lord [this way or that way],' for they shall all know me... for I will forgive their iniquity, and I will remember their sin no more." (Jer. 31:34). It is not that there will be no more sinning, but that the means to forgiveness will be evident; occurring not in a written form that points to sin as a sure occasion for Divine wrath, but in the living "law of Christ" which emphasizes that it is an occasion for forgiveness. God's not remembering sin is a cipher for the whole of this scheme. In Jer. 50:5 it is put in terms that include the human remembering element as well: "Come, let us join ourselves to the Lord in an everlasting covenant that will never be forgotten." Neither God nor man will forget. (See Ezek. 16:60-63).

433. Paul evidently saw the Mosaic covenant as subsumed under the Abrahamic one in this picture. It was meant not only to provide a God-fearing way of life for Israel, but paradoxically to point up the need of the new law by underlining the problem of sin. It was an intermediary stage. The real issue between Paul and the Jews was and remains just this: whether Christ was needed to solve the problem of sin, or whether the Mosaic law had sufficient means within it to do that without him. As E. P. Sanders says, "*this is what Paul finds wrong in Judaism: it is not*

Christianity." [49]   Paul's response is clear, and it calls on Abraham and the "new covenant" prophecies for support.

434. *11:25f.* "...in my blood". For Paul, the new arrangement was ushered in by Christ's death and sealed by his resurrection. "While we were yet sinners Christ died for us. Since, therefore, we are now justified by his blood, much more shall we be saved by him from the wrath of God." (Rom. 5:9). The "much more..." seems to refer to Christ's continuing advocacy in respect of personal sins committed by the Christian after his initial sharing in Christ's saving act: see 379. As for the death, the author of *Hebrews* sees it as a necessity. "Where a will is involved, the death of the one who made it must be established." (Heb. 9:16). Paul at least takes Christ's death as the de facto manner of salvation. Using the analogy of the wife freed from the law by the death of the husband, he says, "Likewise, my brethren, you have died to the law through the body of Christ." (Rom. 7:4). The death invokes the "will", which in the parallel is the contextual Abrahamic promise of the new covenant arrangement to come into effect at the death.

435. The reference to "body" in the text just quoted is significant for us, of course. It establishes a link between the "blood" word and the "body" one. As for the latter, Paul's view of the relation of blood to covenant seems to be similar to that of the relation between death and covenant. For the author of Hebrews, it was a principle. "Without the shedding of blood there is no forgiveness of sins." (Heb. 8:22). Paul, if he did not see it as a principle, at least saw it as the de facto manner in which Christ's saving mission had been implemented. "We are now justified by his blood...." (Rom. 5:9); we have "expiation by his blood." (Rom. 3:25).

436. The author of Hebrews was thinking "specifically" in terms of sacrifice. He relates his discussion of Christ's saving acts first to the Mosaic covenant sacrifice, which he describes (see 9:19ff), and then to the sin offering for the people on the Day of Atonement (9:24ff). This pluralism would have been acceptable to Paul, who was undoubtedly aware that with the juxtaposition of the terms "blood" and "covenant" at least the first analogy would be assumed by the reader. For while he might refer specifically to "new covenant", the interpretation of that could only be made by comparison with "old" covenants in the same Hebraic tradition from which, in his wider context, his phrase would inevitably be thought to derive. And in fact covenant and sacrificial death and blood were closely related in that tradition. The covenant of Noah was prompted by God's "smelling the pleasing odor" of sacrifice (Gen. 8:21); sacrifice was the Divinely prescribed preliminary to the covenant with Abraham in Gen. 15;

---

[49] E. P. Sanders, p. 552; his italics.

the blood of circumcision is presumed in the account of the covenant in Gen. 17; the sacrifice of Isaac occasions a reiteration of the covenant promises in 22:15; Isaac himself builds an altar at the similar occasion in 26: 25; and Jacob, on the occasion of making the covenant with Laban, with God as witness, "offered a sacrifice on the moutain and called his kinsmen to eat bread." (31:54). Sacrificial or ritual blood is thus almost invariably involved with covenant institution or renewal, and the same is manifestly true of the Sinai covenant, which offers the classic analogue for any later covenant incident. This covenant, in the first place, was clearly related to the earlier ones by the pentateuchal editors. "God remembered his covenant with Abraham, Isaac and Jacob, and... saw the people of Israel, and... knew their condition." (Exod. 2:22-25). Here God remembers now the promise made then. So in 6:4, where he promises to reaffirm it. In 19:7, before giving the material for Moses' "book of the covenant", (24:7), he anticipates the content and result of the reaffirmed pact: "If you will obey my voice and keep my covenant... you shall be to me a kingdom of priests and a holy nation." Finally, after an enumeration of the contents of the book, the pact is sealed (24:4ff). Sacrifice of peace offerings is made, half the blood is poured on the altar, half on the people; they say, "All that the Lord has spoken we will do, and we will be obedient." "And Moses took the blood and threw it on the people and said, 'Behold the blood of the covenant.'" The sprinkling of the people here is reminiscent of the special use of blood on the doorposts at the pasch in Egypt; it is in addition to the usual sacrificial use of blood, as the earlier (paschal) use undoubtedly was too. A similar use of sacrificial blood occurs in Exod. 29:19ff in the ordination of Aaron, and there the significance of it is thus expressed: "he and his garments shall be holy, and his sons and his sons' garments with him." It is a sanctification—a setting aside for God. This incident too includes a covenant, with Aaron. (See Num. 18:22; 25: 12). The nexus of sacrifice and covenant is expressed in a general form in Ps. 50:5. "Gather to me my faithful ones, who made a covenant with me by sacrifice!" (RSV). The LXX has "τοὺς διατιθεμένους τὴν διαθήκην αὐτοῦ ἐπὶ θυσίαις".

437. Blood, of course, could not be drunk by a Hebrew. As the symbol of life it was suitably offered completely to God. But in these incidents uses of some of the offering are authorized that bear a likeness to sacramental communion. The drinking of something (wine) that symbolizes covenantal blood is a way in which such blood can actually be tied in with the communion itself.

438. The "my" used with "blood" in our text in the Greek is the pronominal adjective, whereas that used with "body" is the pronominal genitive of possession. The "new" with "covenant" constitutes a mild emphasis that is more easily read because "covenant" parallels a previous

statement about "body". With this preparation, the second "my" can bear
an emphasis. The result can be something like "There is covenant here
and it is not the old, deficient kind of covenant; there is blood of covenant
here, and it is mine, not that of some animal". An emphasis of a similar
kind on the first "my" would be awkward, coming out of nowhere.

The Eucharist and Magic

439. We have referred to Smith's contention that the historical origin
of the Eucharist was the service of a "magician-god who unites his followers
to himself by giving them his body and blood to eat and drink." (424).
Except for the "magician" and the small "g", this is as close as one could
get to the traditional Roman Catholic interpretation of the rite. The history of exegesis seems to show that the texts offer some basis for an
alternative to the "eating body" and "drinking blood" interpretation. As
was implied by the reference in 420 to "metaphor or some stronger interpretation", I would admit that the core of the text—what is left after
"stripping off O.T. window dressing"—is open to more than one reading.
But let us see how the two core elements, the "body" word and the "blood"
word, compare with the magical analogues, in order to judge whether this
question might have some bearing on our thesis.

440. We have already noted that the magical papyri are lacking a
sense of history and are almost devoid of memorial thinking in the traditional Hebrew vein, even though they contain many Hebrew elements
and forms. Covenant and memorial in particular, as well as the close relationship between them and the actions and objects that our text describes,
are absent, and are certainly well described by Smith as in the Old Testament tradition. Our text is as notably different, however, in that so many
elements that are typical of the papyri are absent from *it*. The truth of
this appears as soon as one reads a few of the admittedly magical texts.
Smith would have to say, "Before the O.T. dressing was added, the magical
dressing was removed." The many names of the god, the overemphasis
on what is to be gained from the rite, the banality or questionable morality
of much that is sought, the stress on the efficacy of the words and actions,
the exotic associations—all are absent. The core similarity that remains
may be illustrated by the following.

441. Reitzenstein speaks of the story of Joseph and Aseneth in which
the divine envoy "creates [honey] through his word and has Aseneth eat
of it", the honey being the food of immortality; and he compares this with
the union with the δαίμων πάρεδρος in *Poimandres* "[which] is achieved
by setting before him wine and food and drawing him to the couch." [50]
Actually, the Greek text has the order reversed: "σὺ δὲ τῆς χειρὸς αὐτοῦ [i.e.,

---

[50] Reitzenstein, p. 314.

of the god] λαβὼν κάθελθε καὶ κατάκλινον αὐτὸν ὡς προεῖπον· παρατίθῳ αὐτῷ ἐξ ὧν μεταλαμβάνεις βρωτῶν καὶ ποτῶν"⁵¹ Reitzenstein's inversion of the order here might suggest some kind of sexual intercourse. The word κατακλίνω can have this meaning, but it is a normal expression for sitting or reclining at table, as in 1 Sam. 16:11: "And Samuel said to Jesse, Send and fetch him, for we may not sit down till he comes." (LXX). The point is worth making, for sexual intercourse is one *means* that does not seem to have been typical of the magical rituals.

442. As for eating and drinking, the usual order in the papyri is for the petitioner to take milk, wine, honey and cakes and make an offering of these, or some of them, with incense, in order to gain the god's favor. In one case the procedure is to "Drink milk and honey before sunset and something divine will enter your heart." (Preis. 15:20). Various authors cite the love charm in the DMP in which the petitioner, a male, is told to mix a concoction of hair shavings from a man dead through violence, barley from a grave, apple seeds, blood of a worm of a black dog, blood of the petitioner himself and his semen, pounded together and mixed with a cup of wine, which is then given to the unfortunate object of his affections to drink, while with the "aforesaid parasite" bound on his arm he says seven times, among other things:

> I am Horus [there are other titles too; this one probably refers to Horus as Eros and to his escapades in punishing his father's murderer]... here... as to which the blood of Osiris bore witness to her (?) name of Isis when (the blood) was poured into this cup, this wine. Give it, blood of Osiris that (?) he (?) gave to Isis to make her feel love in her heart for him.... Give it the blood of N.... to give it to N.... in this cup, this bowl of wine today, to cause her to feel a love for him in her heart, the love that Isis felt for Osiris when she was seeking him everywhere... passion. (DMP XV 1ff).⁵²

A simpler method, still involving one's blood put into a cup of wine and given to the woman to drink, is appended, perhaps for those of more squeamish temper. Finally, Preisendanz gives an example, cited by Smith,⁵³ in which wine alone seems to have been used; at least blood is not mentioned. "A wonderful love-charm: say seven times over the cup: 'You are wine, you are not wine but the head of Athena... the entrails of Osiris, of Iao. When you enter into the entrails of NN. she will love me all her life.'" (VII, 645-651). This is reminiscent of the "τοῦτ' ἔστιν τὰ ἐμὰ σπλάγχα" from *Philemon*, discussed in 420; but nothing more than figure is suggested there.

---

⁵¹ Greek text quoted from *Zwei griechische Zauberpapyri*, trans. G. Parthey (Berlin: Königl. Akademie der Wissenschaften, 1866), p. 124.

⁵² *The Demotic Magical Papyrus of London and Leiden*, ed. F. Griffith and H. Thompson, 3 vols. (London, n. p., 1904-1908), vol. 1. Morton Smith gives most of this text on p. 122.

⁵³ See Smith, p. 111.

443. Actually, the giving by the god of some kind of heavenly food without reference to blood or any identity is more common than such examples. "If you have said the formula, Apollo will come holding a spondeion. Ask what you want. He gives recollection and on your request will give you to drink from the dish." (VII, 735-738). Similarly, "Come to me, Lord Hermes, who with you bring the food of gods and men." (VIII, 2-3). Again, quite often, food and drink is to be put before the god or angel for his own sustenance—a form of offering. (V.g., I, 85).

444. In two of the above cases actual blood is put into the wine. In another case the wine is said to be something else than blood—entrails. In the Aseneth story there is no mention of blood. In another, it may be presumed that the god (Apollo) is bringing the blood of sacrifice or the wine of offering that he has accepted and somehow made his own, though it is not said to be "his" blood. *In no case is the wine itself simply said to be blood, with no addition of blood.* Smith takes the text of 1 Cor. 11 to mean "This wine is my blood." The text that he sees as nearest to this of those presented in the papyri says, equivalently, "This wine mixed with blood is my blood." Or rather, that is the reality that founds the expression. The meaning may be somewhat different, for the wine may be nothing more than the means whereby the blood in the mixture becomes potable; so that the meaning would really be "This blood is my blood." The case of the head of Athena might just possibly have intended a mystical transformation of substance without a change of appearance, but it is far more likely that "head" and "entrails" are metonymical expressions for the power and influence of the goddess, read into the wine in metaphorical terms.

445. Considering our own text, we must remark that there is no assurance from the text itself that the wine, which is not mixed with blood, is not simply *representative* of blood. More might have been meant: the text is simply ambiguous on the point. Smith presumably sees the text as being the mere bones of an original incident or practice, and would probably assume that immediately recognizable magical accoutrements were originally present: the charms, the aim of arousing emotional attachment, the mixtures—perhaps, especially, the mixture with blood. But all this is assumption, for the presence of so many different kinds of expressions within the magical literature itself shows that it would be quite simple for anyone familiar with such literature to construct a variation using the core "body" and "blood" terminology, without using concepts that in those times would have been considered magical as distinct from merely mystical. This is the more likely because of the widely known use of sacrificial blood in various ways. The purpose of such an adaptation might well be to steal some of the magicians' thunder. "What you people have we have too, only in a genteel and spiritualized way."

446. The gentility and the spirituality are evidenced, of course, by the "window dressing". In the text itself the most forceful agents of them are "new covenant" and "memorial". In the wider Pauline context, other textual statements that might in another context be interpreted as magical take on more spiritual meaning. The "for you" is not just a boon to be gained by impounding the angelic giver in a physical and magical cocoon that forces his cooperation, but a giving of blessing or curse (in a word, of judgement) that must be referred back to a specific historical action to discern its meaning and mode of operation. So for the "my blood" and "my body". But these must not only be referred back, they must be referred upward, just as that historical action was referred upward— upward to God. Blessing is not automatic, it depends upon the Divine survey of the situation and the participants' intentionalities. This upward reference in the original event, the crucifixion, is manifest in the various analogues that the Pauline contexts mention or suggest: martyrdom in obedience to God, ransom, Akedah, sacrifice, *hilasterion*. And in special ways by special aspects of them: for sacrifice (one of the most strongly indicated analogues), by the function as sin offering, peace offering, covenant offering.

447. The covenant element is explicit in the text, and, with "memorial", gives a name to the scheme just described. Covenant traditionally involved Divine promise of judgement—favorable, to those favorably disposed. The promise was given on the Divine initiative on the occasion of incidents—also arranged directly or indirectly on the Divine initiative— like obedient service, prayer and sacrifice. It was fulfilled especially when these incidents and the servants of God associated with them were solemnly commemorated on subsequent occasions whether sombre or joyous (like the Day of Atonement or the Pasch) with accompanying invocations of the blessings of the promise. Such celebrations invariably involved cultic expressions, including sacrifice and communion, that provided ideal means to symbolize and focus the whole significance and to some extent the efficacy of the system. The term "memorial", used twice in our text in relation to an admonition to repeat just such a Christian incident, certainly has reference to such a commemoration.

11:24f,25i: " εἰς τὴν ἐμὴν ἀνάμνησιν "

448. "Ἀνάμνησις" signifies "reminder", and in the literature it and associated words, both verbs and nouns, refer to reminding-God as often as they do to reminding-man. This is as true of the words when used in covenant contexts like those described just above as in other cases; and in fact, a large percentage of the uses of the words *are* in covenant contexts. In this covenant context, the word group recalls the widespread and persistent mode of petition coupled with thanksgiving in which God is asked by his people in unison or individually to "remember your covenant promises"; a practice that simultaneously underlines the fact that the petitioners are themselves remembering them.

449. More specifically, the term, as one with "μνηόσυνον" in conveying the technical meaning of "cultic reminder" recalls a group of types and specific examples that are applicable, each in its own way, to the Christian cultic situation. To anyone familiar with Greek ways even in a moderate degree, "memorial" might have suggested a cult to the dead. Such cults occasionally developed into hero worship—an institution that could easily have been seen by Christians as preeminently suited to their own special hero, Christ. Then there was the memorial serving as a solemn memorandum to royalty, like "Demetrius' memorial to the great king". This was a secular idea that was compatible with the Hebrew idea of mediatory activity by special servants of God, and was readily linked with another area of use of nominal memorial terminology—that expressing angelic presentation to God of the prayers and offerings of the faithful. Both of the latter applications of the nominal "memorial" especially suit Paul's notion of Christ's present intercessory function, though of course in no way excluding reference to previous historical incident.

450. In the purely Hebrew tradition, indicating present remembering and reminding activity of the community, was the notion of festal celebrations and various acts and objects associated with them or with the continuing cult, as "memorials". One of these was offering in general; one particular type of offering, sacrifice. The combination of the two ideas, feast and sacrificial offering, is strongly indicated in the Eucharistic celebration: the sacrifice finding its analogue in the crucifixion, the feast including that and the recurrent communion that refers to it. Another specially evident "memorial", associated in the LXX with the relatively infrequent word "ἀνάμνησις" itself, was the institution of the showbread. At the Last Supper the twelve loaves would be seen as serving as memorials before God reminding him of the specially dedicated group who by particular privilege would consume them.

451. The same thing is true here as in the case of Paul's treatment of the crucifixion event. He does not fix that into any specific category like "sacrifice" or "hero's death" to the exclusion of other suitable analogues. Here, "memorial" does not fix on one or another particular Old Testament or Greek kind of memorial to the exclusion of others. Whatever is cogently analogous may be freely drawn on to add depth of meaning to whatever extent it in its own circumstances is similar to the Eucharistic event; and indeed, by way of contrast, to whatever extent it is dissimilar. The Eucharist is a unique memorial; and that may in fact be the precise force of the twice-used "ἐμήν". Let us give the requisite attention to this term.

" 'Εμήν"

452. Interpretation of this word may have been complicated by several factors. 1) The distinction between "μνημόσυνον" and "ἀνάμνησις" as "reminders" and "μνήμη" and "μνεία" as "rememberings" may not always have been carefully enough observed. 2) The idiom " μνείαν ποιεῖν " may have been subtly influential in the translation of our text, in which "τοῦτο ποιεῖτε " occurs in such close association with a "memory" word. In other words, it may have furthered an assumption that we are dealing with a question of mere remembering rather than reminder. 3) The fact that "μνεία" with an objective genitive can indirectly convey the notion of reminding God, as in Phil. 1:3 ("Εὐχαριστῶ τῷ Θεῷ μου ἐπὶ πάσῃ τῇ μνείᾳ ὑμῶν " = "I thank my God in all my remembrance of you"—see 352), may have led some commentators to fail to perceive valid reasons for the writer's placing still more emphasis on possession and reminding God, as by the use of a pronominal adjective rather than a genitive of possession, and by the use of a specifically "reminding" noun. 4) The fact that verbs of remembering often take the genitive may conceivably have had its own subtle influence in promoting a reading of objective genitive meaning from the text even when, as in our text, no such genitive occurs in the original.

453. There are other problems that complicate this matter—the above are mentioned simply as a preliminary to the main discussion. Obviously, no one, having had these modes of thinking proposed to him explicitly, would be likely to adopt them in considering the text. But such influences sometimes do operate from a shadowy background of semiconscious assumptions.

454. A "reminding" term like "μνημόσυνον" or " ἀνάμνησις"that has in the past been used in a reminding-God context (whether itself or in cognate forms) can be used to convey the notion of reminding-God without any additional expression of that notion like "to the Lord" or "before the Lord". We have seen a number of examples in the literature; the "reminder of sins year after year" in Hebrews 10 is a New Testament one. But when word-associations do not make the object of the reminding clear, an author might have to make use of a pronominal adjective rather than a genitive in order to safeguard intended notes both of possession and reminding. For example, in the case of the "εἰς μνημόσυνον αὐτῆς" of Mark 14:9, the writer may quite possibly have wished to portray the preaching as the woman's "memorial" in the common Greek sense of a "sign reminding about her"—a sense closely related in content to the Hebrew one of a name or progeny as "memorial". But the lack of a third person possessive adjective in Greek necessitates the use of αὐτῆς, which can also be an objective genitive when used with a word with verbal force. And in fact, the actual translations usually not only exclude the Greek "memorial" idea but even tend to obscure the "reminding" aspect and leave something like "in remembrance of her" (Jerusalem Bible) or "in memory of her" (RSV). Another case caught my attention in Philo (Quis Heres, 30) that is very much like our own, since it involves a first person, not a third, and the pronominal adjective is actually used. The Greek is: "καὶ τοῦτό μου τὸ πάθος τῆς ψυχῆς ἐστηλογράφησεν ἐν τῷ ἐμῷ μνημείῳ ὁ ἐπίσκοπος Μωυσῆς." For this the Loeb translator gives, "And the watchful pen of Moses has recorded this my soul's condition in his memorial of me." Here the term "memorial" is indeed given, but there is all the same an objective genitive. Philo uses "μνημεῖον" as the equivalent of "μνημόσυνον" in several cases— both always as "reminders" of some kind. This fits the use of the word for "tomb" so common elsewhere: the tomb does not remember, it reminds. In the context of the verb "στηλογραφέω", which literally means to write on a stele, the translation "in my memorial" seems required: if the memorial had been of stone it would have required "on my memorial". The sense of Abraham's interest in and relationship to the memorial are accurately conveyed by the pronominal adjective as against the objective "of me", which indeed sees him as an object of discussion but allows him only a distant nexus with the medium in which he is discussed. Both the Greek and the Hebrew feeling towards the memorials left to the future was that the one memorialized was somehow perpetuated by the memorial, whether it was a stone monument, a literary inscription, a name or progeny. "Of me" puts Abraham solidly in the past. Someone might point out that in De Moise I, 4 Philo speaks of the same writings of Moses he has Abraham refer to here. There he calls them "ἃς θαυμάσια μνημεῖα τῆς αὐτοῦ σοφίας", which Colson translates "the wonderful monuments of his wisdom." They are there seen as a reminder of *Moses'* wisdom and so would be *his* monument. But this refers to the whole of Moses' works, the *Quis Heres* text merely of the portion of it that refers to Abraham— part of *Genesis*.

455. Why then translate with an objective? Why indeed? We may note first that the translator makes unnecessary trouble for himself by interpolating a "his" which is not present in the Greek. This makes the second "my", which in Greek is so strongly urged by the situation and the pronominal adjective, virtually impossible in English. It would read, "This my soul's condition is his my memorial." On the other hand, a simple "in my memorial" does less than justice to Moses, whose writing is of prime interest to Philo. Something like "Moses portrayed my soul's condition when he inscribed my memorial" seems indicated.

456. There is not, of course, the same focus on the stele analogue in the Corinthians text that there is in Philo's. But the intimacy of the relationship between the subject of the memorial and the memorial itself is undoubtedly meant to be at least as close as in the case of Philo's Abraham. Strong metaphors, taken by many Christians throughout history as actual identifications, are used in the description of the symbolic materials of the memorial; and the memorial is actually commissioned and publicized by Christ. The various analogues suggested by the term "ἀνάμνησις" itself in the Pauline context certainly allow for proprietorship by the Founder, and the use of "my" stresses the institution's uniqueness, spoken of in 451. It may be emphasized that the use of "my" does not exclude the objective meaning, since the memorial is in any case concerned with the word's antecedent. Indeed, in its own way "my" really enforces that meaning. Conversely however, the objective translation, when it does not completely exclude the subjective aspects associated with "my", weakens them drastically.

457. Of the approximately 100 occurrences of "μου" in Paul, the only instances besides genitive absolutes and the special use of verbs with the genitive in which the word is translated by the RSV as an objective genitive is in the phrase "imitators of me" in Phil. 3:17, 1 Cor. 4:16; 11:1. Cases in which the associated noun clearly shows action on the ancedent of the "μου", like "witness" and "imprisonment", are translated with "my", a fact that shows the strong tendency in English, also evident in other modern languages, to read some kind of title of possession into such situations. In fact, "be my imitators" could easily be the translation in these other cases. Thus, there would have to be a special reason for translating "μου" with "ἀνάμνησις" by "of me" even if "μου" had been used. But it was not used, and the adjective "ἐμός" was, which would seem to decrease the likelihood of an exclusively objective meaning to near zero.

458. Blass and Debrunner note the relative infrequency of the pronominal adjectives in hellenistic as compared with classical times, when they were commonly used "for the emphatic possessive gen. of the person pronoun." [54] They note, however, that "'Εμος is quite frequent in Jn... but otherwise not very frequent (1 C ten times)...." [55] They state that "non-reflexive ἐμός often has little emphasis so that it is not easy to distinguish from μου." [56] We have discussed a case of emphasis in 438. In our present case, the function of "ἐμήν" is not to establish an emphasis as of "*my*" compared with "my", but to assure that the proprietory, technical, and even reminding (see 454) aspects of this *anamnēsis* are not obscured.

---

[54] F. Blass and A. Debrunner, *A Greek Grammar of the New Testament*, rev. and trans. Robert W. Funk (Chicago: University of Chicago Press, 1961), p. 149 no. 285.
[55] Ibid.
[56] Ibid.

These considerations reflect aspects of emphasis that are often not distinguished by lexicologists. There are kinds and kinds of "emphasis".

459. "Ἐμός" in Paul is translated "my" by the RSV in every case but that in our text and one other where "me" stands for the Greek "my own self" (2 Cor. 1:23). The only instance that clearly projects an objective meaning is 1 Cor. 9:3: "...my defense to those who would examine me"; but the subjective is even more strongly indicated because the emphasis is on the *response* Paul will make, not on himself as being defended. This subjective element, added to a basically objective one, is present several times when "ἐμός" is used in the New Testament, and sometimes overshadows the objective. John calls attention to this when he says, "My teaching is not mine." (7:16). His ministry is so evident that people need to be told he was originally *taught*. A less evident case is John 15:9 "As the Father has loved me, so have I loved you; abide in my love." (μείνητε ἐν τῇ ἀγάπῃ τῇ ἐμῇ). The subjective aspect appears from the comparison that is basic to the discourse, that to the vine and the branches. "As the branch cannot bear fruit by itself, unless it abides in the vine, neither can you, unless you abide in me." (15:4). They are to bear fruit "and so prove to be my disciples." (15:8). The love is an outgoing thing that will flow as long as the nexus with God through Christ (which of course is had by loving both and keeping their commandments) is maintained. "My love" is the kind of love God and Jesus both love with. The disciples' loving Christ, God, and other men is thus identically "remaining in Christ's love." The "my" emphasizes the subjective rather than the objective aspect of the love, whether by way of imitation or of location.

460. A survey of the Pauline uses of ἐμός outside the two with "ἀνάμνησις" shows in eight out of fifteen cases a clear *contrast* between the "my" and some parallel word or idea: with "your" in four cases; "God's" and "Christ's" once each; other persons(') twice. This data tends to corroborate our reading of the "my" used with "blood" in our own text in 438, where we saw it as contrasted with "animals'"; though the "ἐμός" would be justified by the principle that seems to bind the other Pauline instances of the word, namely that it is used to qualify things especially close to Paul himself. (In the "non-contrast" cases it is used with "heart", "spirit", "life", "hand", and "coming".) "My" used with "memorial" would on this principle show a close relationship of some kind between Christ and the memorial—something we have seen to be indicated already (see 456, 458). There may also have originally been some pointed contrast between this memorial and other peoples' memorials, but that is not expressed in the tradition as Paul gives it to us. (We hear of "John's baptism"—"Ἰωάννου βάπτισμα", Acts 19:3. I do not say there was a "John's memorial", but there may have been other individuals' or parties' memorials. Note, incidentally, the clear subjective meaning of "'Ιωάννου" here). As we have said, the Christian memorial is unique—like other memorials in some ways and like quite a number of memorials at that; but different from them in others. The very fact that the term "ἀνάμνησις" in context suggests the analogues means that the differences have necessarily to come to mind too, at least peripherally; this is the basis for such a contrast as "ἐμός" can indicate. The point made just above is that the contrast is not openly drawn in the text; the attention to the differences is left to the reader's own effort. He is more likely to make the effort on seeing an "ἐμός" in the text than he would be on seeing a "μου".

461. It is very easy because of some theological preoccupation or other distraction, or perhaps just from the complexity of the text, to produce a translation that diminishes the amount of denotation and/or connotation that could be read from the original text. This may have happened in Mark 14:9 and in the text from *De Moise*; it would happen in the John 15 text if a translation "abide in the love of me" were to be given. It seems to have happened in the RSV version of Rom. 11:30-31— the "contrast" principle discussed above suggests it. The Greek reads, "ὥσπερ γὰρ ὑμεῖς ποτε ἠπειθήσατε τῷ Θεῷ, νῦν δὲ ἠλεήθητε τῇ τούτων ἀπειθείᾳ, οὕτως καὶ οὗτοι νῦν ἠπείθησαν τῷ ὑμετέρῳ ἐλέει, ἵνα καὶ αὐτοὶ ἐλεηθῶσιν." The RSV translates: "Just as you were once disobedient to God but now have received mercy because of their disobedience, so they have now been disobedient in order that by the mercy shown to you they also may receive mercy." The "τούτων" is so obviously subjective that the occurrence of another pronoun in a dative construction in the next clause strongly suggests a subjective reading of some kind for *it*. But the translation not only does not give it, it associates the ὑμετέρῳ with the ἐλεηθῶσιν rather than with the ἠπείθησαν. Käsemann at least does not do the latter: he gives, "...so wurden jetzt diese über der euch (geschenkten) Erbarmung ungehorsam, damit auch sie nunmehr Erbarmung fänden." [57] He points to a chiasmus, and indeed there is one; but he seems to make the fourth member (cross-related to the "ἠλεήθητε") not the near-exact equivalent "ἐλεηθῶσιν" but the phrase "τῷ ὑμετέρῳ ἐλέει". Of this phrase he says, "Allerdings hat der Dativ nicht mehr den kausalen Sinn wie in 30b (gegen B.-D.... Bauer... Huby). Er ist dat. commodi (Dibelius...), meint also 'zugunsten'." [58] In fact, what seems indicatd not only by the syntax but by the dative form and the Pauline context is, rather literally, "Just as you were once disobedient to God but now have been had mercy on because of their disobedience, so they have now been disobedient because of your mercy, in order that they also may be had mercy on." In 11:11-12 Paul says, "But through their trespass salvation has come to the Gentiles, so as to

---

[57] Käsemann, *An die Römer*, p. 298.
[58] Ibid., p. 303.

make Israel jealous." This jealousy is precisely what will save the Jews: "in order to make my fellow Jews jealous, and thus save some of them." (11:14). They will become jealous of the salvation that has been given to the Gentiles and want to receive the same. But this is in the *future*. First they have become jealous of the salvation in another way, namely, in being resentful of the way salvation is being offered to others than themselves. Actually, Paul puts it in terms of their being "hardened" (v. 7), and of the mysterious ways of God, who "gave them a spirit of stupor" (v. 8) so that they disobeyed and opened the way for the mission to the Gentiles. Whether in terms of an initial jealousy or of this "hardening", they are in a true sense made disobedient by the giving of mercy to the Gentiles. Once this is demonstrated, we may ask how the "your mercy" of our literal translation should end up. It cannot remain in these terms, because the English phrase usually means "the mercy you show", and that is obviously not included in the meaning here. Yet something more than "the mercy shown you" is required, because the ὑμετέρῳ expresses some kind of appropriation by the individual. In v. 12 Paul speaks of "riches for the Gentiles". If "riches" or even "salvation" had been used in v. 31 instead of "mercy", there would probably be few objections to a translation "by your riches". That such an idea is possible for mercy too is implied by the RSV "have received mercy". This suggests that we simply add the word "receive" in appropriate form in order to give an adequate translation. "Just as you were once disobedient to God but now have been favored with mercy because of their disobedience, so they have now been disobedient because of your receiving mercy, in order that they also may be favored with mercy."

462. There are, of course, cases in which the objective meaning is very strong and it is not easy to see any appropriation of the kind pointed out above. Yet the appropriation may be the very thing that gave the literary punch to the passages for their original readers or hearers. L. & S. provide a number of texts like this from classical literature under the entry "ἐμός" ("with a Subst.: ....objectively.") If there is such appropriation here, of course, it is not going to be a crude material possession, but some kind of cognitive, psychological, or perhaps mystical association. One of the examples A. T. Murray translates "my marriage". ("τὸν ἐμὸν γάμον"—Od. 2,97).[59] It is not difficult to see the subjective angle here. In II.19,336 ("καὶ ἐμὴν ποτιδέγμενον αἰεὶ λυγρὴν ἀγγελίην, ὅτ᾽ ἀπαφθιμένοιο πύθηται") the same translator gives, "and with waiting ever for woeful tidings of me, when he shall hear that I am dead." But this may well be poetic irony, in that the last message from the son to the father may be that he (the son) is destroyed. "My woeful message" seems quite

---

[59] The translation is in the LCL; so for the following translations.

legitimate in such a case.   In Aeschylus Pers. 699, "Lay aside thine awe
of me" (H. W. Smyth, for "τὴν ἐμὴν αἰδῶ μεθείς") might carry the meaning, "Shake off the impression of my [a shade's] awesomeness."   Sophocles
El. 343 ("σοι τάμά νουθετήματα"), which F. Storr translates without any
pronoun, "these admonitions", may bear the meaning "warnings you make
mine".   Euripedes, Helen 364, speaks of "τὰ δ' ἐμὰ δῶρα Κύπριδος", which
the Loeb translator turns as "the gifts of Cyprus to me"; but this could
just as well be "my Cypriot gifts" because of some special sense of
attachment.   Finally, the Oedipus text (Rex, 969) has "εἴ τι μὴ τὠμῷ πόθῳ
κατέφθιθ' · οὕτω δ' ἂν θανὼν εἴη 'ξ ἐμοῦ."   Storr translates, "Unless the longing for his absent son [the speaker is that son] killed him, and so I slew
him in a sense."   If the speaker slew him "in a sense", and the longing
was what killed him, the longing is the speaker's in the same sense; i.e.,
he may be associating it, even in his father's mind, so strongly with himself
that it becomes "his" weapon (he has spoken just previously of a sword).
One cannot easily put this into English—what would be meant would be
"my presence in his mind as the object of his longing".

463. This last example, in which we put the word "object" itself
into our translation, can stand as a model for the rest.   The objective
meaning is basic, but is qualified by a subjective one, so that a translation
without something *more* than the objective fails to communicate the
whole of the original meaning.   In this case, the result is very close to
the difference between the phrases "in my memory" and "in memory of
me".   The former adds to the latter a subtle claim to part proprietorship
in the memory even as it exists in the mind of the rememberer.   It recognizes the right to a continued dignity in the one remembered that
goes even beyond the "dignity of past events" that we spoke of in Part II
relative to historical memory, being very like the special dignity associated
with leaving one's name to posterity.   The one remembered *looks forward*
to being thus perpetuated.   This is really the highest degree of the relationship between past and present in purely historical terms (there are
additional kinds of relationship, of course): it makes a conscious link
at both ends.

464. If we had in our text "εἰς τὴν ἐμὴν μνήμην", there would thus be
a most cogent reason for translating "in my memory" rather than "in
memory of me."   But we do not have "μνήμην", we have "ἀνάμνησιν", which
at the very least gives us "reminder".   The word itself, in the context of
the "τοῦτο ποιεῖτε", gives the strongest sense of that "perpetuated dignity"
just remarked on.   The rite is such as to imprint in the minds of the
participants the truth, among others, that Jesus wants it to be imprinted
there.   He is not to be relegated to the past as a mere "object" of reminding (though there would be a certain dignity here), but is to share,
as it were, in the present fellowship as its very much present author and
main subject.

Final Conclusions = Our Thesis

465. The argumentation in the preceding two paragraphs is based on a consideration of the very weakest "subjective" import of the pronominal adjective, as suggested by the texts in L. & S. When we consider the New Testament and particularly the Pauline uses, the pressure to *understand and translate* a subjective meaning along with the objective one that is undoubtedly present becomes inescapable. This would hold for "μνήμη" or "μνεία"; it holds a fortiori for "ἀνάμνησις". Further, this word as distinct from the others leaves wide open—even apart from the context—the possibility that a very strong subjective sense was intended, a true possessive. *In* the context such a possibility becomes a probability. *It is necessary to understand this and when translating to leave the possibility of the new readers' understanding it open. This can only be done by translating "ἐμήν" as "my".*

466. But additionally, *the term "ἀνάμνησις" must not be deprived of the potentialities for memorial significance that we have seen it to possess, in the given context,* by way of both general and specific denotation and connotation. A summary of meanings is given in 448-450. We may add the notion of memorial as name suggested by the appropriation expressed by "ἐμήν" and evidenced in the appellation "the Lord's Supper" itself. Also the idea of progeny; for the command could be read to convey the sense, "Do this, you (especially when you do it) are my memorial."

467. To translate "ἀνάμνησις" by "reminder" still deprives it of some of these potentialities, even though it *would* leave open the possibility that God as well as men was to be reminded. Thus, *the translation "memorial" seems indicated; and,* just as important, *this term must be explained, where the text is being explained, so as to show these wider possibilities that would have been evident to Paul himself and to so many first-century readers.* At the very least, it should not be explained so as to *exclude* such possibilities.

468. The three paragraphs just above summarize what it seems can be said about the phrase with which we are concerned. They express the thesis of the present work. The exegetical process leading up to them might perhaps serve as one model for the exegesis of certain Scriptural passages that offer difficulties because of a plurality of possible meanings—a situation that has historically often resulted in a pluralism of interpretations each trying to present itself as the sole, the "specific" meaning. As was noted earlier (412), this does not mean that a text is open to any interpretation at all. What it often will mean is that the writer left the text open to interpretation in several senses, and would have been unhappy had he known that interpreters and translators were going to deny that openness in one way or another. For our clause, which is a key element of a text extremely important in its own right, the *translation* that seems to strike the balance between these "positive" and "negative" (as they might be termed) requirements of the text is "Do this as my mmorial". The *explanation* should include the different kinds of "memorials" that we have seen the text to allow as possibilities.

469. We have not yet given specific attention to the phrase "τοῦτο ποιεῖτε" of 24e and 25g. The repetition of the command indicates that it bears on more than just the one part or the other of the tradition. And the fact that we do have "Do this" rather than "Eat this" and "Drink this" shows that, although the bread and wine and their physical handling are central to the rite, the command refers not only to them but to whatever else was done or said in accompaniment. The "εὐχαριστήσας" would be included here, of course, but in a more subtle way so would the various points we have been making about the different parts of the event and their internal and external relationships. In particular, if what is done is to be regarded as Jesus' memorial, the meaning of memorial and of Jesus' memorial as distinct from others' memorials (and perhaps even other of Jesus' memorials) will have to be used to interpret the "this" of "Do this"—an interpretation that Jesus himself presumably made in his mind (and to some extent in his accompanying words and actions) when he presided visibly at the rite, but which for his disciples then and later would require much reflection and application with respect both to the original event and to their own subsequent celebrations. Obviously, too, the "this" in repetition would include not only sameness with but some differences from the original event. Jesus' memorial in the original would have involved his reminding God and the disciples present: reminding them of God's promises, of Jesus himself and his promises, of the disciples themselves, of his and the disciples' intentionalities. In a repetition, with Jesus now in a favored position of advocacy and the original celebration now past, the same factors would occur, but now updated to include those changed circumstances as well as the present intentions and needs of the now-celebrating community. Such an inclusion would have been part of Jesus' intention when commanding the repetition, and so would be "his" in that special sense. But it would also be "his" because as in the original event he would be reminding God and God would be reminded of him: of him on Calvary, of him at the original celebration, of him now at God's right hand: all, factors that were present in the original celebration but, again, with different circumstantial relationships.

470. In paragraph 5 we stated that "Part II will also demonstrate a good probability that Paul and his readers would have adopted attitudes in these conceptual realms [those dealt with in that Part] that are in agreement with positive conclusions we shall reach in the Part, conclusions

that in turn are attuned to more specific ones relating to cult and memorial that we shall reach about Paul and his churches in Parts III and
IV." Most of the "more specific" conclusions of these latter Parts can
be reviewed fairly easily by consulting, for Part III, paragraphs 204-205,
212, 231-239, 244, 259-261, 288-292, 296-299, 313-318, 324-329, 335, and 345-
348; and for Part IV, paragraphs 351-355, 372-380, 382-384, 389-390, 396,
411-413, 422, 446-447, 448-451, 463-468. The main conclusions reached in
Part II are referred to in 177. There is no space here to draw the com-
parisons in detail, but we can at least indicate how the materials can
be used. Sacramentalism is discussed explicitly and implicitly in various
places in Parts III and IV; these references can be compared with those
given in Chapter IV of Part II. For example, a sacramental statement
about our text is made in para. 447 (in Part IV), and, for comparison, a
summary of the sacramental conclusions of Part II is given in 174-176.
Similarly for first-century interpretative and historical attitudes, compare
with Part II, Chapters I and II; for cosmological ones, with Part II,
Chapter III. More specific points should also be introduced into comparison: points like covenant, gnosticism, prayer. In general a strong
similarity will be found, so as to form a mutually corroborating set of
arguments for the probability that the views indicated were indeed those
of Paul and most of his readers. Some of the similarities have of course
been explicitly remarked on or developed in Parts III and IV themselves,
the reader will probably have detected others. But even for these the
kind of exercise suggested above should turn to the light new facets of
the material, and fortify the impression of strong similarity. The pattern,
in general, is the double converging "tapestry" one, stated in 1 Cor. in
terms of the identities of God, Jesus, Paul and the Christian community,
with the latters' celebrations of past and future salvific events (and celebrations), this parallel to the same kind of view in the first Israel. Into this
kind of picture, when the past events involve covenant promise and command, reminding-man and reminding-God fit as the spontaneous, yet traditional expression of both the humanization and the divine vitalization of
the pattern.

471. Clearly, we are now in a better position than at the beginning of this study to discuss its relationship to relevant scholarship old and new. Such a discussion will certainly clarify some questions and underline —whether by agreement or contrast—some lines of argument. Chapter II of Part I and the references to Douglas Jones in 240-244 and 253 no. 13 are presumed as the points of departure for the first of the two following chapters. The material on Brevard Childs in 181ff can be reread in connection with the actualization question; see also 421 for Marxsen's view of actualization.

Chapter I: **Reminding-God—Questioned or Overlooked**

472. Jones' positions reveal serious deficiencies. He does not recognize the near-synonymous relationship of "ἀνάμνησις" and "μνημόσυνον" throughout the literature (243); he equivalently denies the influence of the LXX on the clear development of the notion and terminology of cultic memorial in the direction of a broadening of the number of analogues that could be understood by the terms (240-242); he does not prove that the same kind of development was not manifested in the Hebrew literature as well (the subsequent studies of Childs and Schottroff suggest that it was); he does not distinguish between the Divine remembering of sin to punish (as exemplified by the "sacrifice of jealousy") and to save (as exemplified by the sin offering); and he allows himself to be influenced by a strong theological motivation that makes him see a Godward reference in 1 Cor. 11:25 as "perilous in the extreme". (244). We may add 1) He follows Jeremias in limiting the discussion of the Eucharist's *import* by assuming that its historical *origin*—supposedly a paschal celebration— imposes such a limitation when in fact it does not, even when it is accepted that the origin *was* such a celebration. 2) For the Passover analogue itself, he seems simply to pass over the fact that it was itself viewed by many as a memorial to God as well as to men, and that it was constituted in part by various specific kinds of memorials like the trumpets, offerings, priestly equipage, etc. (See 220, 227, 253, 257, 300, 317, 389ff.) 3) In the light of what we have seen of the uses of ἐμός his statement that "the most obvious meaning of our Lord's words is the straightforward one 'to call me to remembrance' " [1] [he clearly intends, "as a means to your remembering"] would, as we have said (9), puzzle a first-century reader.

473. In paragraph 10 we spoke of two poles of exegetical thinking: wildly imaginative and "exclusive". Somewhere in between is a common-sense use of analogy that has always been typical of everyday thinking, whereby words are meant to convey and are taken to mean whatever reasonable (let us note this!) things the speaker or author does not obviously exclude. Indeed, we often have to avoid the use of certain words that have come in our particular culture to have meanings that would ensure a failure of our hearers, should we use the words, to appreciate the serious things we want to say even though it is perfectly clear that we do not intend the distracting meanings. Every year half a dozen or so good English words previously in common use are for all practical purposes banned from serious future use because they are loaded with double meanings that infect the word wherever it occurs. The process of perception of alternate meanings occurs even when the alternate meanings are not disreputable. Living when and where he did, Paul was certainly sensitive to the pitfalls of language. If he had intended to exclude Hebraic cultic memorials from the readings his readers would pick up from his phrase, he could easily have taken a long step in that direction by using "μου" instead of "ἐμήν". He could have used a verbal form instead of a nominal one, and made the subject clearly the people. To suggest that he was unaware of the cultic nominal meanings is to ignore the fact that he was an educated man knowledgeable in the literature and in cultic affairs pagan and Jewish. Note that we said above "reasonable" meanings. In daily life the external situation often excludes many meanings and leaves only one acceptable. In literature more possibilities are frequently present, and they are often acceptable to the writer particularly when he deals partly in rhetoric or mysticism. Further, if he has to look over his shoulder at political or religious groups that are monitoring his efforts with a view to a possible crackdown, he may use imprecise language intentionally, in order to reach his readers with views unpopular with the establishment. Finally, as we have already seen, Paul probably abhorred the idea of having his theology frozen in its tracks before it was fully developed, or of losing valuable meaning because of exclusive focus on other meaning—even though that might be equally valuable.

Eucharist as Proclamation

474. In an article entitled "Predigt als Erzählung", Rudolf Bohren gives an example of one kind of option for theological development I think

---

[1] Jones: 188.

Paul might have wanted to keep open for himself. Referring to Dahl's view that "'to preach' corresponds less with κηρύσσειν than with ὑπομιμνήσκειν",[2] Bohren quotes Schottroff's statement that "Zkr as a concept expressing the relationship of God to men means not only a detached remembering, but an effective intervention for man who finds himself in need. The content of this remembrance is blessing and salvation."[3] He concludes,

> This all too brief summary of the conceptual history of "zkr" is very significant for the event of preaching, especially narrative preaching. Preaching in this situation cannot overlook the fact that God remembers salvifically, that he can be reminded. Before the preaching remembers men it will appeal to God's remembering. This will be so in order that human remembering may accord with God's, and may be infused by Divine salvation. In this sense preaching is the promoter of salvation: it calls to mind past and present salvation.[4]

I would suggest that Paul might have wanted the text's "memorial" to hold the possibility of explicating such a view in specific relation to cultic proclamation (see 1 Cor. 11:26c) should he or his disciples in the future get the time and occasion to develop their thinking in this area. W. M. F. Scott says that in Gregory Dix's application of some of Pedersen's thinking to the liturgy, "it is suggested that it is God to whom the work of Christ is recalled in the Eucharistic proclamation"[5]—that is, that the "proclamation" as such is to God. That is not part of the suggestion being offered here. "Proclamation" in 11:26c certainly refers to preaching to men: it is in content (and elsewhere often in form as well) "reminding-man". The point we intend is that the proclamation to men is meaningless if God is not its Sanctioner as well as its Sponsor; so that the whole event of proclamation, whether by cult or without it, must be acted out before God. The proclamation is formally addressed to men, but it is about God and Christ, so that unless it is seen as concordant with the Divine remembering of covenant promises in the manner of Bohren's statement, men's response will not only be fruitless, it will lack proper content and so not even be forthcoming; in this sense at least faith is initially and must ever remain God's prime blessing. Reminding-God, and in a cultic proclamation, the viewing of the totality of the exercise as cultic reminding-God memorial, is the perfect and obvious way to assure that the proclamation *is* seen as concordant, and indeed, to *proclaim* that necessary content; in other terms, it assures that the salvific past can be and is presently and practically actualized through the cult. *One of the most*

---

[2] Rudolf Bohren, "Predigt als Erzählung", in *Oikonomia, Heilsgeschichte als Thema der Theologie,* ed. Felix Christ (Hamburg-Bergstedt: Reich, 1967), p. 345.

[3] Bohren, p. 346, quoting Schottroff, p. 339.

[4] Bohren, p. 346.

[5] W. M. F. Scott, "The Eucharist and the Heavenly Ministry of our Lord," *Theology* 56 (1953): 43.

telling ways of preaching the meaning of the Eucharist to men—*of preaching Christ's saving death and resurrection*—*it by publicly praying the* μνήσθητι *to* God *in the Eucharistic rite with specific reference to the historic saving event and the new-covenant promises.* This makes the new *Hallel* as central in the act as the old was in the old paschal celebration, and infuses the ritual with practical meaning.

475. Paul's description of "the grace given me by God to be a minister of Christ Jesus to the Gentiles in the priestly service of the gospel of God, so that the offering of the Centiles may be acceptable, sanctified by the Holy Spirit" (Rom. 15:16), was probably written largely with initial conversion in mind, and so was not consciously applied to the Eucharistic proclamation. But the Eucharist could definitely fall within its ambit as a continued proclamation of the same gospel by the participants in the ritual act—a proclamation made principally to one another, whereby faith is as it were expressed by themselves to themselves ("until he comes"), and an oblation of self and act thereby made to God—an "offering-memorial". The Eucharist as a memorial can both suggest and focus this and other kinds of thinking that have to do with offering-memorials; it can suggest and focus, too, thinking that has to do with other cultic memorials like feasts, the songs and prayers of the assembly, the cultic symbols like wine, bread and trumpet; as well as thinking concerned with name and fame, progeny (disciples?) and the death and life of heroes. I think Paul would certainly have wanted such options to be left open. In fact, he did leave them open when he passed on the tradition of the Eucharistic institution. Considering the Pauline context, I think these are "reasonable" paths of thought that in time Paul himself might have pursued to explicit conclusions. If Jones' position were to be adopted, many of these paths would be blocked. In the case of Jeremias, there would be blocking too, but of other paths.

Jeremias' Views

476. Jeremias asserts that "the command for repetition may be translated: 'This do, *that God may remember me.*'" [6] Just what does God remember in connection with Jesus, in Jeremias' view? "...[T]he death of the Lord is not proclaimed at every celebration of the meal as a past event but as an eschatological event, as the beginning of the New Covenant. The proclamation... expresses the vicarious death of Jesus as the beginning of the salvation time and prays for the coming of the consummation." [7] He makes much of the *Maranatha*: "*As often as the death of the Lord is proclaimed at the Lord's supper, and the maranatha rises upwards, God*

---

[6] Jeremias, p. 252. His italics.
[7] Ibid., p. 253.

is reminded of the unfulfilled climax of the work of salvation 'until (the goal is reached, that) he comes'." [8]

477. Most of the force of the emphasis on the eschatological is gained from reference to Paul's phrase "until he comes". As far as it goes, the argumentation is valid. But the position definitely leaves the impression that this "New Covenant" is not really a "covenant" at all. "Covenant" absolutely requires a strong historical perspective—the reference to mutual promise *as promise*, which from the vantage point of the present, means *as past*, though of course pointing forward and incorporated into the present. This recognition of the dignity and meaning of the past is essential to the incorporation. The real basis of covenant is God's faithfulness. Without reference to past this is a featureless concept. In fact, when Jeremias relates the parousia to the now-present he implies this, for the now-present is the future's past. In place of the statement cited above (476) carrying his emphasis, we must therefore say something like *"The death of the Lord is proclaimed at every celebration of the meal as a past event that by reason of God's faithfulness relative to it, and Christ's responsive faithfulness to God in it, provided a true basis in history for the fulfilment of the Divine promises connected with it."* Christ's death on Calvary will never die in the mind of God or in the minds of men. It is God's mindfulness of it that made Jesus "Lord" (Phil. 2:9); this is the core of Paul's preaching—Jesus "crucified", a past form brought into the present. Jeremias rightly speaks of prayer for the coming of the consummation. But what happens to thanksgiving for what has already been given? The Eucharist is not *only* anticipatory thanks.

478. Rejection of the historical dimension is, unfortunately, not Jeremias' only weakness. His treatment of the "ἐμήν" is a second. With a casualness that seems almost typical of scholarly attitudes towards this word he says, "It is clear that ἐμήν represents an objective genitive." [9] For him, "The only question is: *Who* should remember Jesus?" [10] Clearly, this is a necessary question, not least for anyone who does accept the objective sense exclusively, when there is question of a word of *reminding*. We shall return to Jeremias' solution of this problem in a moment. But first, we must stress that on the basis of what we have seen of the uses of the pronominal adjective, it is put in a misleading context. Does Jeremias give any reason at all for his exclusion of subjective sense for the ἐμήν?

---

[8] Ibid. His italics.
[9] Ibid., p. 251.
[10] Ibid. His italics.

479. In fact, he accords the issue a note that says, "An objective genitive with ἀνάμνησις, μνημόσυνον is the established usage, cf. Mark 14. 9; Wisd. 16.6; Ecclus 10.17; 23.26; 38.23; 39.9; 41.1; 44.9; 45.1; 46.11; 49.1, 13; LXX, ... [an obscure reference here] I Macc. 3.7,35; 8.22; 12.53; II Macc. 6.31." [11] We have already seen these texts in our survey in Part III. With reference to the use of the genitive, we may note two specially pertinent facts. First, in no case is there a *Greek* alternative to the objective *form*— they are all in the third person. Second, in ten of the seventeen cases, the Brenton translation quite rightly gives a possessive English form: "his memorial", etc. This obviously does not eliminate the objective meaning, but it adds to it subjective meaning which as we have pointed out has to be weighed in each individual case. In nine of the instances Jeremias proposes, the μνημόσυνον is of the "name" or "progeny" types, suggesting a strong sense of appropriation of the reminder to the one who is (in these cases) principally remembered. (Incidentally, several of the instances give a clear indication of the "reminding" function of the μνημόσυνον". For example, in the 2 Mac. text: "...leaving his death for an example of a noble courage and a memorial of virtue... unto all his nation." Or 1 Mac. 8:22: "tables of brass... sent to Jerusalem, that there they might have by them a memorial of peace and confederacy." The "name" or "progeny" types are of course clearly meant to remind.)

480. Thus, the statement about "established usage" just fails to meet the point. Objective and subjective *meanings* are often indicated simultaneously. This being so, when one meets a pronominal adjective *form*, the statistics that Jeremias himself provides us would seem to suggest that in *more* than ten out of seventeen cases it will have a subjective sense whatever else it may also have. The odds will become even greater when there is clear possibility of the use of a more obvious objective form, here "μου". What "established usage" shows us is that each case must be examined for the meaning of the reminding word in its own context.

481. One of the most surprising things about Jeremias' study is that it does not really distinguish "reminding" from "remembering". In spite of references to Hebrew "reminding God", it sees this only from the point of view of "Who remembers". He intends this when he notes an example in a Nicomedian inscription in which the actual term "ἀνάμνησις" is used of a memorial foundation: "with the condition that they celebrate my ἀνάμνησις ." [12] Perrin's translation gives "my" here even though the original has "μου". His translating thus is an indication that (along with his leaving the Greek "ἀνάμνησις") underlines the presence of a technical cultic term. The text can, in fact, be understood in the sense "celebrate

---

[11] Ibid., p. 251, note 3.
[12] Ibid., p. 240.

the rite meant to remind the celebrants of me" (this of course does not express the full force of the "my" as "my memorial" would) as well as "celebrate the remembering of me". The "reminding" element was especially important in these foundations, because the founders could usually be fairly sure that without the foundation to remind, they might well be completely forgotten! Such rites can of course be called "μνήμαι", but this does not mean that the use of the term "ἀνάμνησις" would not impart a special emphasis; though of course "μνήμη" itself could pick up some "reminding" connotation from continual use as a technical term.

482. Jeremias eventually excludes the Greek kind of memorial anyway —a third kind of unjustifiable exclusion (fourth, if we call the lack of distinction between "remind" and "remember" an "exclusion"). He says, "...it is scarcely conceivable that the command for repetition should be considered as having any connection with the institution of ancient meals for the dead." [13] It is sure that such meals cannot be accepted in *all* respects as similar to the Eucharist, and never could. Jeremias' argument that the formula "εἰς ἀνάμνησιν" is not found in relation to them may be inconsequential; his pointing out that they were celebrated on the birthday and not on the death day [14] has a certain relevance. But they were in fact celebrated with the death of the founder as a central reason for their celebration, and they *were* foundations called "memorials" that owed their celebration to his wish and arrangements, and involved those close to him in life. If we add to these considerations the fact that in some cases this kind of memorial probably came to be associated with hero worship, we can see how Paul might have meant *Christ's* "memorial" to suggest to the Corinthians that they had in it something much like, but a good deal better than what the world around them had. The celebration of a dead man's memorial in the context of a belief in his resurrection has a special piquancy about it; in a sense it adds the "birthday" element—though the logical "birthday" here would be the "*dies dominica*", the day of the resurrection.

483. For most observers, of course, the most obvious "exclusion" that Jeremias makes is of the reminding of the *people*. He says, "the usual interpretation, according to which it is the disciples who should remember, is strange. Was Jesus afraid that his disciples would forget him?" [15] It may very well be that he was. But even if he was not, the frequency, intensity, persistence and manner of the remembering would certainly be of concern to him. Any adequate translation must make room for the people's remembering along with God's. Quite possibly the idea of reading two categories of rememberers simultaneously never oc-

---

[13] Ibid., p. 243.
[14] These arguments are found in Jeremias, pp. 241-243.
[15] Ibid., p. 251.

curred to Jeremias. It is true that with a restriction of the meaning of
ἀνάμνησις to "reminding-remembering" as distinct from the broader "memorial" (this restriction is a fourth—or fifth—"exclusion"), the possibility
of a diversity of analogues is greatly diminished, and the narrower meaning that is left might more easily be thought to be meant for a single
agency. Understanding the ἀνάμνησις to have not only a general "reminding" force, but to draw meaning as well from several kinds of "memorial"
analogues, we can see that it might draw from one analogue the force
to remind both God and men, perhaps Christ too; while drawing from
another the force to remind only one of these, from another that to
remind another, etc. An analogue like the loaves of proposition had as
its principal function the reminding of God about the people; but it could
remind Christ about them too; and indeed, might also be meant to remind
the people that they were never forgotten by God.

Vermes, Akedah and Jeremias

484. We have singled out C. K. Barrett as one scholar who takes
Jeremias seriously. (See 26). Another is Geza Vermes, like Dahl (see 411)
one of the more recent commentators on the analogy between the Akedah
and Christ's redeeming act. Vermes does not see the Akedah as a mere
"help" for Christians in understanding Paul's theology of Christ's death,
and certainly not as *meriting* the redemption by Christ in a strictly
"adequate" way. Rather, it is for him the basis of that Pauline theology,
and he specifically relates this view to Jeremias' thinking on the Eucharist.

485. Vermes first cites various examples of rabbinical literature that
show God being asked in liturgical prayer to remember, and in fact remembering the binding of Isaac as a reason for saving Israel. [17] He
concludes: "Rabbinic writings show clearly that sacrifices, and perhaps
the offering of all sacrifice, were intended as a memorial of Isaac's self-
oblation. Their only purpose was to remind God of the merit of him
who bound himself upon the altar." [18] He dismisses the objection that
texts like those he works from are late, [19] but even if we accept that this
narrow view of sacrifice existed in the first century C.E., it is scarcely
proven that it was representative of the "Palestinian Jew" and "Jewish
thought".[20] It is also somewhat misleading to say, "That the Pauline
doctrine of Redemption is basically a Christian version of the Akedah calls
for little demonstration",[21] since, as was remarked above, he seems to

---

16 See Geza Vermes, *Scripture and Tradition in Judaism*, Studia Post-Biblica, vol. 4,
2nd rev. ed. (Leiden: E. J. Brill, 1973), pp. 193-227.
17 See Vermes, pp. 206ff.
18 Ibid. p. 209.
19 See ibid., note 1, p. 219.
20 Ibid., p. 225.
21 Ibid., p. 219.

mean by this that Paul meant to found his theology upon the similarity of Jesus and Isaac. What Vermes' argumentation actually does is suggest some good possibilities; but based on rabbinic materials as it is, it can hardly do more. Even if we accept the centrality of the Akedah theology in some Jewish circles, its centrality for Paul is not demonstrated. On the other hand, its appropriateness would certainly have been apparent to him. The lack in his writings of specific references to the binding of Isaac as a direct redemptive analogy to Christ's dying for the Christian faithful seems to indicate either that Paul had not adverted to the analogy, that it was so commonly used already in Christian theology that he felt no advertence was necessary in his writings, or that he knew of it but did not want to overshadow other analogies of the Christian redemption by calling special attention to it. The first alternative seems unlikely; the second too, since if it held true one would expect to find some specific —even if oblique—references somewhere in the New Testament. I think Vermes might have done well to adopt in regard to Paul and Akedah the sort of conclusion he refers to relative to the meaning of the phrase "lamb of God" in the fourth gospel: "The present generally accepted opinion... recognizes in the term an amalgamation of Old Testament ideas...." [22] Akedah for Paul would be one element of such an amalgam. In fact, Vermes does adopt a conclusion like this for the New Testament in general, for he says in closing, "Although it would be inexact to hold that the... Christian doctrine of Redemption ...is nothing but a Christian version of the Jewish Akedah theology, it is nevertheless true that in the formulation of this doctrine the targumic representation of the Binding of Isaac has played an essential role." [23]

486. Likening the Jewish liturgy to the Eucharist, Vermes refers approvingly to Jeremias' thesis that it is, as he puts it, "God... whose remembrance is sought." [24] He seems of two minds whether or not to associate this with paschal liturgy as Jeremias does, asking in one place, "...would not a Paschal Eucharist be opposed to a frequent... celebration...?", [25] yet insisting on an earlier conclusion of his, [26] that Akedah was recalled at Pasch both to men and to God. [27] But he also associates it with the daily temple liturgy, and in this connection concludes, "The frequent celebration of the Eucharistic meal may, therefore, be understood as the introduction into Christianity of this other element of the Akedah theology...." [28] Vermes indicts Jeremias for a "weakness in his reasoning

---

[22] Ibid., p. 224.
[23] Ibid., p. 227.
[24] Ibid., p. 226.
[25] Ibid.
[26] See ibid., pp. 214ff.
[27] See ibid., pp. 226f.
[28] Ibid., p. 227.

because he underemphasizes the sacrificial aspect of a rite uniting, in a liturgical drama, both past and future within a continuous present." [29]   He probably has in mind here the reminding-man element of the Eucharist, which Jeremias unjustifiably rejects.   But his description of the liturgical rite seems to manifest a Caselian brand of thinking, attributing a sacrificial quality to the Eucharist on the basis of a supposed mystical dissolution of the chronological distance that separates it from Calvary.   The same idea would lie behind his statement that "the Last Supper was a ritual anticipation of the death of Jesus...." [30]   Paul would no doubt agree with the statement itself, but I think he would insist that if the Eucharist is anything more than a mere human commemoration of and dramatic reenactment of Calvary, it is so because of the reminding-God element that looks to the one Cause that alone can *effectively* dissolve such distances.   Any "sacrificial aspect" of the Eucharist would thus be more practically located by Jeremias than by Vermes, even though the reminding-man does achieve a psychological union of Eucharist with Calvary.

487. Unfortunately, most of Jeremias' other critics are as firm about excluding reminding-God as he is about reminding-men, and they exclude the range of nominal analogues too.

Christian Developments after the First Century

488. In paragraph 13 we spoke of Kosmala's statement that "We have no different witness in the Christian tradition."   What he means by this is that patristic theological thinking on the subject of the meaning of "ἀνάμνησις" in the Eucharistic formulae did not explicitly include re-minding-God—the word was explained only in terms of reminding-men. We noted (12) that the idea of sacrifice came to fulfil the Godward role in Eucharist, and that this idea in the Greek tradition had not been related to memorial as it had in the Hebrew, a good sign that the innovation was due to an increasing Greek influence on Christian attitudes rather than some kind of development from Hebrew ideas.   Personally, I doubt if there ever was an express theology of reminding-God in the Western church.   The Old Testament was used as an authority, but the appeal was directly to "sacrificial" texts.   Both Justin and *Didache* refer to the text of Malachi, "...in every place incense is offered to my name, a pure offer-ing." (1:11).   Justin quotes this and adds, "He... speaks of... us, who in every place offer sacrifices to Him, i.e., the bread of the Eucharist...." [31] In the *Didache*, the Christians are to "come together... and hold Eucharist, after confessing your transgressions that your offering may be pure... be reconciled, that your sacrifice be not defiled.   For this is that which was

---

[29] Ibid., p. 226.
[30] Ibid., p. 225.
[31] *Dialogue with Trypho* 41.

spoken by the Lord, 'In every place and time offer me a pure sacrifice....'"
(14:1-3). Besides the Malachi allusion, there is probably one here to Matt.
5:23-24, a sacrificial reference. It is unlikely that the sacrificial terminology
here and in Justin was introduced with any thought of sacrifice's being
an *example* of memorial. Justin makes mention of a flour offering in the
Old Testament ritual of cleansing of lepers, taking it to prefigure the
Eucharist, but he chooses an example that makes no mention of memorial when he could have chosen others that did. It is the offering element that suggests it to him as an interpretation of the "Do this...." Indeed,
it is offering here that interprets memorial, not vice versa. He says, "And
the offering of fine flour... was a type of the bread of the Eucharist, the
celebration of which Our Lord... prescribed, in remembrance of the suffering which He endured...." (Dial. with Trypho, 41). This is men's remembering, with no thought of God's.

489. We have already seen indications that reminding-God was part
of Paul's eucharistic thinking and prayer. (352ff). It was certainly part
of the *Didache*'s. Clement speaks of intercession for Christian transgres-
sors, "for so will they have fruitful and perfect remembrance before
God... and find compassion." (1 Clem. 56:1). The context is not especially
eucharistic, but the terminology may well reflect that of Paul. In the
light of such material, one might wonder whether perhaps the Eastern
Church in the early days developed some express theology of reminding-
God. It is an investigation we may leave to other hands, noting that even
if there was such a development, it had to deal with the idea of Eucharist
as sacrifice by the fourth century at the latest. [32]

490. Our main study has not been directly concerned with the actual
interpretation that Paul's successors in an increasingly Gentile Church
made of the materials he presented to them. Our point has been that the
reminding-God interpretation in the amplitude we have delineated was
justified (as was the reminding-men one) by the Pauline materials viewed
in the light of the milieu in which he wrote. However, it is useful to realize
what probably happened to Christian thinking about memorial in those
early years. It would seem that with the Christianization of the Gentiles
and the disruption of the existing Jewish political and religious institutions
around 70 C.E., the new Church to a great extent lost contact with the
Jewish modes of interpretation that were definitely familiar to Paul and
many of his contemporaries even though he was himself partly hellenized;
at the same time, still stronger Greek modes of thinking were ready to
move in and fill the vacuum. Paradoxically, while the Jewish ways of
thinking were lost, many of the Jewish literary materials remained available, to blend with Greek materials and thinking in the formation of the

---

[32] See Montminy, p. 390.

coming synthesis. We may call that synthesis "Catholic". It offered exciting possibilities for a new religious view of life, but it suffered from the loss just spoken of—a loss that, I feel, has never been adequately redressed. Its results are felt today in many areas, including that of the interpretation of the Pauline "ἀνάμνησις".

491. We noted in paragraph 13 that the Reformers inherited the "sacrificial" categories in their thinking about the Eucharistic memorial, even though they tended to react against them rather than embrace them. The Roman Catholic side traditionally embraced them and in fact shunned reflective reminding-God theology. Illustrative of this is the fact that two of the more influential writers on the Roman Mass, even when dealing with the "Mementos" for the living and the dead that bracket the institution formulas (though at some distance), do not even mention the fact that these are formal reminders to God.[33] The prayers begin, in both cases, with "Remember, Lord, your servants...." Their origins are probably quite old. Mme Denis-Boulet notes that "In a letter written in 416, Innocent I blames Bishop Decentius of Gubbio for having the names of the offerers read, 'before the offerings are recommended to God by the prayer of the priest.'"[34] If indeed these "recommendations" were put in terms of "Memento", there seems every likelihood that the "Μνήσμητι" of the *Didache* carried right through to our own day. Indeed, Jungmann remarks of the intercessions that are introduced by the "Mementos" (though he does not mention the fact of this introduction) that they "were embodied in the Mass as early as the second century, as borne out by Justin Martyr."[35] He proceeds to relate the significant fact that "after the fourth century at the latest... they underwent a new evolution as intercessions within the Eucharistic Prayer. [He says they had previously been a conclusion to the Liturgy of the Word.] The intention was to move the petitions closer into the most sacred zone of the sacrifice."[36] I would suggest that the distinctions between "Liturgy of the Word", "Eucharistic Prayer" and "Communion" were much less rigidly drawn in the beginning that they later came to be; in Paul's Corinth there was not even a sharp distinction between ordinary eating and the eating of the Eucharistic bread in some people's minds. The relegation of the intercessions (and reminding-God) to a place at a distance from the institution narrative or formulae may well have coincided, historically, with the development of the sacrificial emphasis, and the subsequent moving "into the most sacred zone" would reflect an untheological, practical feeling of the need for close association of these prayers with the central Eucharistic ritual.

---

[33] See Jungmann, *The Mass*; and N. M. Denis-Boulet, "The Canon or Eucharistic Prayer," in *The Church at Prayer, the Eucharist*, ed. A. G. Martimort (New York: Herder & Herder, 1973), pp. 149ff, 165.

[34] Denis-Boulet, p. 128.

[35] Jungmann, p. 196.

[36] Ibid., pp. 196-197.

492. The considerations presented in the past four paragraphs suggest the weakness of what might be called the "historical" argument for denying a potential of "reminding-God" meaning to the original Pauline "ἀμάμνησις". Had Paul or someone else made out a list of specific notes that he wanted the word to convey, there would of course have been plenty of theological development. But Paul can scarcely be expected to have been so organized in his theological views on *anamnesis*; and even had he had his ideas fully developed and categorized in his own mind, he would hardly have presented his synthesis in detail when the subject came up in an *ad hoc* manner as in 1 Corinthians. As for the next generations, they probably continued to practice reminding-God in their liturgies in the rather weak form of the "Memento", which leaves the covenant element merely implicit. But the fixing of the Godward element of the Eucharist in terms of sacrifice, by way of simple identification ("The Eucharist is a sacrifice") very soon drew attention from the reminding-God potentialities of *anamnēsis* as such. Instead of seeing sacrifice as one of the many examples of memorial, Christians came to see it as the only means to the achievement of the Lord's "memorial" command. It is somewhat ironic that even those who no longer view sacrifice in this favored light still wish to limit the possibilities of memorial.

Jungmann on 11:26-27

493. As we remarked in paragraph 23, Jungmann equivalently sees Paul's reference in 11:26-27 to proclamation of the death, as a kind of interpretation of "ἀνάμνησις". We have said that this "proclamation" is definitely to men (474). Jungmann's view would thus mean an exclusion of reminding-God meaning for "ἀνάμνησις". Verse 26 certainly does emphasize the reminding-man aspect of the word. But it does so for a definite purpose, to set up the follow-through that v. 27 represents relative to v. 22. The argumentation is: "I do not commend you [v. 22], for the Lord said this, '....' [vv. 23-25], which means that you are formally advertising your belief in his saving death each time you do what he said; and you do this again and again [v. 26]. To do what he said unworthily is thus a grave fault [v. 28]." It is that because the manner (public proclamation in cultic act and word, this constituting a solemn profession of faith), matter (the Lord's death, with all that that means), and frequency (as often as... until he comes") of the celebration are serious, and the unworthy celebration constitutes a failure to "discern" this. It means ungenuineness (v. 19) and a "despising" (v. 22) of the purpose of the community. The emphasis on the public statement makes it possible for Paul to call the public to witness against such behavior. As we stressed in 474, God's witness to such proclamation is necessarily presumed, though the proclamation is not formally directed at him. The presumption of a kind of legal thinking here on Paul's part is not gratuitous; Barrett records that "Käsemann (Essays on New Testament Themes (1964), p. 126) [sic: double round brackets] notes the accumulation of juridical and legal terms here...." [37]

494. Jungmann's interpretation takes v. 26 out of its total context and sets it in relation only to v. 25, making it in effect a mere parallel to that, a parallel in which "proclaim the Lord's death" is taken to *define* "εἰς τὴν ἐμὴν ἀνάμνησιν" The interpretation leaves the purpose of the "ὁσάκις" and "ἄχρι οὗ ἔλθη" unclear. And one would expect the "γὰρ" to go with the narrative: "When you do this, you proclaim the Lord's death, for he said...." As it is, the word, as Allo notes, "is parallel to the γὰρ of v. 23." [38] And the other two words, though they have nothing to do with a definition of ἀνάμνησις, have much to do with showing the accretion of guilt that such repeated hypocrisy would entail, thereby underlining the significance of their actions for the time when at last the Judge does come.

Hans Kosmala, Norman Hook

495. If men's witnessing is more prominent in v. 26, God's is stressed in v. 29, where Divine judgement is promised to the ones who "proclaim" unworthily. The situation is reminiscent of the Hebrews "ἀνάμνησις" text, where God is reminded of sins and salvation remains in abeyance. Kosmala seems to see a threat in this text (Heb. 10:3—see our para. 13) and argues:

> The meaning of this text is that were the servant of God no longer conscious of sin he could cease from bringing offerings, since he would be cleansed once for all; what happens instead of this is that the yearly offering for sin brings sin all the more to his attention. There is no question of God here. He always knows of sin; but it is man, who daily sins without much attention until on the Day of Atonement, through the need of bringing an offering, the sin is fully brought 'into his consciousness' in memory—since animal blood cannot remove any sin. [39]

That one purpose of the Day of Atonement, or any feast, was to remind the people, should be evident. But as Kosmala himself says, this reminding in the case of sin is a question of "all the more". The text says, "If the worshippers had once been cleansed, they would no longer have any consciousness of sin." (10:2b). The author's meaning turns precisely on the manner of getting rid of a consciousness that *cannot be got rid of* by animal sacrifices: *it keeps coming back strongly.* These offerings are

---

[37] Barrett, p. 272.

[38] E. P. Allo, *Première épitre aux Corinthiens*, 2d ed. (Paris: Librairie Lecoffre, 1956), p. 280. Allo takes "ἀνάμνησις" to mean a self-reminding by the people (see p. 279), so that his interpretation is not influenced by any desire to "save" reminding-God. He does not even consider that.

[39] Kosmala, p. 82.

those "which cannot perfect the conscience of the worshipper...." 9:9). The word could be "consciousness" here too: the people cannot by the old means become conscious of "not-sin", but must ever be plagued by a consciousness of "sin". This until some agent comes into being that can get rid of this consciousness. Again, this agency cannot be "the blood of bulls and goats...." (10:4). And the reason is that they do not please *God*. "Sacrifices and offerings thou hast not desired... in... sin offerings thou hast taken no pleasure." (10:5-6). God can take no pleasure in these, according to the author, because "in these sacrifices there is a reminder [to Him] of sin year after year." It is only a reminder to God of "not-sin" once and for all that can get rid of both the consciousness of sin the people have year after year, and the reminder of sin that their offerings to God constitute for him year after year. "Consequently, when Christ came into the world, he said.... 'Lo, I have come to do thy will, O God.'" (10:5,7). *God's* consciousness of sin has now been offset by His consciousness of Christ as "not-sin", and He moves to cleanse them of their sins. "...[T]he blood of Christ, who through the eternal Spirit offered himself without blemish to God, [will] purify your conscience...." (9:14). The author summarizes in 10:11ff:

> And every priest stands daily at his service, offering repeatedly the same sacrifices, which can never take away sins. But when Christ had offered for all time a single sacrifice for sins, he sat down at the right hand of God.... For by a single offering he has perfected for all time those who are sanctified. And the Holy Spirit also bears witness to us; for after saying, "This is the covenant that I will make with them...." then he adds, "I will remember their sins and their misdeeds no more."

He remembers no more because he is reminded no more *of sin*. And he is reminded no more because he was *once* reminded of "*not-sin*" by his own arrangement. What the Eucharistic memorial does is to remind him of this once-for-all being-reminded of *not-sin*, so as to *obviate* his ever subsequently being reminded of *sin* at this same level of reality.

496. As we have seen, Douglas Jones had a theological problem related to the Hebrews text too, but it was based on his recognition that the text does show God being reminded. Hook and Kosmala would deny this— they have another theological problem, specified by Hook when he says that "reminding" God is equivalent to "trying to induce" God. (14). It does not seem to occur to him that "reminding-God" could be a cipher for one aspect of the kind of Divine requirement that he expresses when he says that God required remembrance of the worshippers in order to "enable him to fulfil his side of the covenant relation." (Ibid.) This requirement is in one sense very close to our notion of "referent of actuality", but Hook's treatment tends towards a depersonalization of that concept by effectively disassociating from it the very reason God might require it—

because it is an expression of filial love for a Father who only "waits" to be asked in order to help. We have emphasized in several places and ways that for Paul as for earlier Jews reminding-God or other personal addresses to him would not have been understood in any way that denigrated his wisdom or power. Paul's feeling on this point would have been strong enough for him to find some explicit way of excluding remind- ing-God relative to the 1 Corinthians "ἀνάμνησις" had he felt that re- minding-God necessarily implied theurgy. He makes no such exclusion. Instead he admits various positive indications that would allow just such a meaning to be read from the word. But it cannot be expected that he or his predecessors would have had time or expertise to work out the theological specifics of an issue like this in terms satisfactory to all sub- sequent Christians. "Reminding-God" is one label on a package of valid intuitions.

497. Interestingly, Hook himself uses just such a cipher when he speaks of "enabling" God (see text in 496). With his theological back- ground, he presumably would not want to admit that God needed any kind of "enabling". He would undoubtedly call on the mystery of the Godhead in defense of his usage. That is just what Paul might have done in defense of his understanding of a "reminding-God" aspect to his " ἀνάμ- νησις" had he been challenged.

498. In the passage in which he expresses his distinction between enabling prayer and reminding-God, Hook is involved in a discussion of sacrifice in which he neither clearly distinguishes the crucifixion from the Eucharistic meal nor indicates the relationship between sacrifice and memorial. Against this background he says, "When therefore our Lord said 'Do this in remembrance of me', he wanted the Eucharist to mean to His followers all that the Passover had meant to them,"[40] concluding with the passage already referred to:

> the Godward side of the Hebrew memorial may signify two things. When it implies that God needs to be reminded, or induced to remember, then we should recognize that this is an Old Testament idea which has no place in the Christian doctrine of God. When, on the other hand, the memorial is linked with prayer, which is action on our part to enable God to exercise His grace toward us, then this is a Christian idea which belongs to the heart of sacrifice, and has its proper place in our understand- ing of the Eucharist.[41]

This seems to identify the Eucharist with "the heart of sacrifice." This would certainly have to be explained. The extent of the analogy with Passover would also have to be explained. Certainly, both Kosmala and Jeremias put overmuch emphasis on the paschal nature of the Eucharistic

[40] Hook, p. 150.
[41] Ibid.

celebration. As we have seen, the pasch is only one of the analogues suggested by " ἀνάμνησις" in the Pauline context. We agree with Jeremias when in relation to the paschal meaning he sees God as being reminded "of the unfulfilled climax of the work of salvation"; [42] with Kosmala when he sees the people being reminded of the same thing. But both God and the people were seen to be reminded of more than Christ as an analogue of the pasch: God, since he undoubtedly perceives all the meaning possible for the Eucharistic ἀνάμνησις; the people as a whole because many among them certainly knew enough about memorial to perceive more than just the paschal meaning.

499. This pluralism that Paul opts for, for himself and his readers, allows them to interpret on the basis of their own knowledge of the background of the term " ἀνάμνησις" in their literature and culture. He imposes no pressure to focus singly on the concept of pasch for the Eucharist, any more than on that of sacrifice for Calvary, though far from excluding them as analogues of the one and the other; rather, he allows the adducing of various analogues—Hebrew and Greek, Old Testament and other—in order to fill out meaning while keeping "specific" thinkers at bay. His approach is a particular instance of his philosophy, "all things to all men" (1 Cor. 9:22). As with his other concrete expressions of that principle, of course, there are limits here. But the limits cannot be demonstrated to be nearly as narrow as some theologians might wish them to be. Paul does not define, but there is a limit to the number of individual and institutional possibilities from which notes can be taken to provide meaning for his terms; just as there is a limit to the amount and quality of meaning that is applicable in each individual case.

Paul and Typical Thinking

500. In 411 we spoke of a number of analogues of Christ's death and of the fact that Paul does not make "types" of them. The same comments could be made about the analogues of memorial. Not that Paul was not willing to go as far as "type" when dealing with the Eucharist, in order to make an especially important point. Both Goppelt and McKenzie are of the opinion that the "τύπος" mentioned in 1 Cor. 10:6 includes the Eucharist as an antitype.[43] But this example and that of Adam and Christ show that Paul used explicitly "typical" terminology when dealing broadly with salvific situations. Directly involved are specifically similar termini (man [Adam] to man [Christ]; eating to eating; drinking to drinking) and a similar salvific situation. In fact, the situations in the case of the desert type and the Eucharistic antitype are at both terms a sacramental

---

[42] Jeremias, p. 253.
[43] See McKenzie, s.v. "Type, typology," and *TDNT*, s.v. "τύπος ," by Leonhard Goppelt.

communication with Christ by the church that is performed unworthily by some, thus gaining an unfavorable judgement by God. The antitype is the Eucharist in the essential Pauline context of 1 Corinthians. But Paul does not force all the individual elements of the situation into the limits of this scheme. They are free to fill out meaning by what we have called "implied simile" (411), or any other kind of figure, for that matter. It is analogy with a light hand, and has the added advantage over typical thinking of being able to make use of analogues that are outside the range of the Divinely favored body of literature Paul called "the scriptures".

CHAPTER II: **Actualization**

501. The positions adopted by Thurian and several other authors have already been discussed sufficiently in Part I, Chapter II or elsewhere. There remains one area and category that we have already met briefly (421) when we noted Marxsen's view that the celebrating church is "actualizing 'the new covenant.'" The category of "actualization" is very suitable for our own purposes for expressing the reality of the effects of past salvific actions on the church, effects related to its cultic celebrations. But there is another aspect of the topic that needs to be discussed. Brevard Childs uses this category in his theological development of his exegetical materials in *Memory and Tradition*, and he does so *without reference to the kind of actualization just described*. Our own position will be clarified and delimited by a short treatment of his development and of the whole actualization question. Such a discussion will suitably close our investigations. Fortunately, a good study has recently been done by Joseph White Groves in his dissertation *Actualization and Interpretation in the Old Testament*.[1] We could do no better than to use the fruits of his efforts as points of departure for our own reflections on the subject.

502. Groves investigates a number of authors who have used the term "actualization" in their Old Testament studies to describe various ways in which the writers and editors they studied made older traditions relevant to their own times. He finds that the authors in question discern three types of actualization: "cultic", "chronological", and what he himself calls "literary". Pointing to a "consensus... that cultic actualization... does not exist in the Bible,"[2] he questions some of the thinking behind the concept of chronological actualization or its near equivalents, and proposes to "redefine actualization in a manner that moves the content away from... chronological actualization... into literary actualization."[3] He does in fact expand and fix limits to the meaning of the third of the three types of actualization he finds in his authors, doing so on the basis of the Biblical material and the logic of their more restricted use of the term "actualization". In the light of this flexibility which he allows his own preferred concept and term, there should be no objection if we ourselves add to

---

[1] Joseph White Groves, *Actualization and Interpretation in the Old Testament*, Ph. D. Dissertation on microfiche (Yale Univ., 1979).

[2] Ibid., p. 123.

[3] Ibid., p. ii.

the category of "cultic" actualization a content that seems suggested by Old and New Testament and intertestamental texts, fits the logic of the category, and in truth fills a gap in the traditional use of "actualization" terminology.

503. Groves describes the features of the three types of actualization as follows. *Cultic*: 1) There is a re-enactment of the basic, sacred events of a community. 2) This re-enactment is dramatic. 3) This re-enactment is reality-producing. The participant experiences oneness with the god in the ceremony by partaking of the Manna [his spelling], the divine power. 4) The cultic events must be repeated. The power is of limited duration. If there is no repetition, the cosmos breaks down. 5) [The most important feature, for Groves] Cultic reenactment involves the identity of two moments in time; there is no sense of the then and now, of standing in a historic continuum; the participant feels he is experiencing the original sacred event; the time difference is dissolved.[4] *Literary*: 1) Literary actualization perceives a difference betwen two moments of time. Contrasts with cultic. 2) It manifests an awareness of the situation of the old and new moment. 3) It is applied primarily (but not exclusively) to written materials. Contrasts with cultic in this too. 4) It is not reality-producing.[5] *Chronological*: 1) Events are recognized as irreversible, once-for-all, yet immediacy is experienced by "immediate encounter", actual participation through the medium of redemptive time (this is Brevard Childs' view). "Israel truly entered into the historical situation to which the festival in question was related."[6] (This is von Rad). Martin Noth is "hard to pin down."[7] "This ambiguity [in Noth] may best be explained in the same way as for von Rad and Childs: it is an attempt to create a unique Biblical category which partakes of both cultic and literary actualization."[8] 2) Chronological actualization relates to the situation much like literary actualization. It changes and adapts the old traditions, like literary actualization, but goes a step further by speaking very particularly to crisis situations. The traditions must later be changed again. 3) It has a limited validity—is limited to one crisis. So too for cultic and literary actualization, but for different reasons. For cultic, manaistic power is gradually lost; for literary, times change. 4) Chronological actualization applies primarily (but not exclusively) to oral materials.[9]

504. Because the term "actualization" has not regularly been associated with the meanings he wishes to give to what he finally defines as "literary" actualization, Groves is lenient about expanding the definition of actu-

---

4 For these features of cultic actualization see Groves, pp. 120-121, 124.
5 For these features of literary actualization see Groves, pp. 127-128.
6 Groves, p. 131.
7 Ibid., p. 132.
8 Ibid.
9 For these features of chronological actualization see Groves, pp. 131-134.

alization to fit those meanings. But he seems to consider the question of cultic actualization to be closed, taking it as defined by use and making firm statements that would restrict further application of the term. Obviously it would be desirable to find the logic of the older use of the term "actualization" (it was originally used of cult) as well as of the newer ("literary" actualization); having done so we shall recognize that just as the genus "actualization" itself allows for diversity because of the discovery of new species or the elaboration of old, so the sub-genus "cultic" might be open to expansion or insertion. Groves defines actualization in general as contemporization and making relevant older traditional materials. He defines cultic actualization by the five features noted above, with emphasis on the fifth as the most important. He is saying that cult actualizes only by dissolving the time gap, that this dissolving is part of the specific difference that makes cultic actualization different from other actualizations. In fact, it can be shown from his own material that this is not likely to be a difference between cultic and the other two actualizations, which suggests that it might only be the difference between one kind of cultic actualization and another. Groves' failure to advert to this possibility is explicable by the fact that none of the authors he studies, with the exception of Noth, whose position we shall presently discuss, has such advertence.

505. As we saw, Groves cites a "consensus... that cultic actualization itself does not exist in the Bible." Keeping in mind that he is defining cultic actualization in part by the note "dissolving the time gap", we are prompted first to ask whether cult itself can be said to "exist in the Bible." It would be rather frivolous to say that it does not exist because the Bible itself is not cult. Certainly cult is described and advocated at length in the Pentateuch. Again, are we to say that there "is" no cult because what is described and advocated is only a literary expression and does not demonstrably represent the actual cultic picture in Israel? In other words, that we cannot reconstruct what the cult actually was? Most commentators would probably argue that what is described is the construction of the cult at the time of the writer, at least in his own circle, described etiologically. Perhaps somewhat idealized, but a good enough picture all the same. One could say this of the Eucharist in the Pauline text too. In fine, it seems quite proper to say that "there is cult in the Old Testament and the New".

506. This being so, if it is true that there is no cultic *actualization* in the Bible, it must follow that the later cult in Israel was not actualizing in any specially "cultic" way. Groves equivalently says this on the basis of von Rad's development of his ideas of actualization. Von Rad says that cultic actualization "developed into" chronological actualization, and he describes the latter as not being necessarily linked to cult except through these origins. This leaves the actual cult without any special actualizing potential—a reading that probably would have troubled the Israelite cultic participants considerably. Noth seems to have felt the need of associating a strong actualizing factor with the actual later cult; his solution is to assign the function to the same proclamation of the Word that von Rad saw at the core of his "chronological" actualization; Noth actually *calls* that "cultic actualization". Since chronological actualization does not "dissolve the time gap" by moving the subject experientially back to the original event, this understanding contradicts the definition of cultic actualization as Groves sees it. Groves' distaste for this break with existing usage is likely to distract the reader from Noth's basically sound intuition of the need to locate a special actualizing factor in the later cult.

507. Noth's principal weakness, of course, is in assigning the function to a kind of actualization that would not have fully satisfied the cultic expectations of the later Israelites and early Christians. These people were no primitives, and Noth, with the rest of the commentators, recognizes this. For the normal Jew or Christian, performing his regular cultic acts, a personal Divine power had long since displaced the primeval mana; while God's promise had replaced the primal cosmocultic laws that assured the cultic practitioners of union with the manaistic power on the occasion of their cultic exercises. But although they were no primitives, they were no selfless idealists either. They needed things, and saw God, with his power and promise, as the main Source of what they needed. Noth seems to allow them to look for only a portion of their needs. "A portion"—I would not want to deny that some of them felt faith welling up within them when they hearkened to the narrative parts of their cult, and that some of these may have thought that this faith was being *created* within them in some unique way, perhaps even the neo-orthodox way. There was a sense, perhaps mystical, of God's immediacy, and this Noth rightly emphasizes. The faith-experience gave the participants a basis for their to allow them to look for only a portion of their needs. "A portion"—I remained to invoke promise and look to fulfilment. Noth does indeed speak of promise, but when he comes to fulfilment, the faith-experience seems to be the sum of its content. The Jewish man in the street could hardly be satisfied with this "faith to faith" kind of fulfilment. For him, faith was no end in itself, but a means to many ends. Nor was his pragmatic view unjustified by the narrations: they clearly related promise to very tangible blessings like land, crops, long life, progeny; and more general ones like forgiveness, salvation, peace, honor, power. Later, immortality joined the list. Instead of relating cult to fulfilment in these practical and soul-satisfying terms, Noth passes straight on from faith to obligation. Von Rad also speaks of promise and fulfilment; *he* passes from faith to further promise: each new life-situation seems a renewal of the promise. One must seriously ask whether promise is a sufficient solution to crises that are themselves the object of previous promise. It takes either an ivory tower idealist or a sly politician to answer "Yes" to this! Certainly, promise *was* renewed, but it was in part new promise; some of the old had been fulfilled or would soon be fulfilled, partly in view of cult. This fulfilled promise was a main object of thanksgiving, of eucharist.

508. There could be mysticism in the faith experience relative to the present God. It is not likely that there was much left for the past as such. To show a sense of cultic identification with the past, commentators frequently quote the words of the Seder, "For ever after, in every generation, every man must think of himself as having gone forth from Egypt. For we read in the Torah: '...All this is because of what God did for *me* when I went forth from Egypt.'" [10] In truth, most of the force of this text for a believing Jew probably stemmed from the fact that it is Torah, the Word of the living God. It is *God's* closeness to both present and past events that makes the latter significant for my present, not any mystical closeness of mine. *He* made promises in the past that bear on this present, and is now near to do for me what in the past he did relative to previous promises bearing on the then present. Undoubtedly words like those quoted have a rhetorical effect, and can prompt an imaginative person to identify himself with past events in a dramatic sense. But the experience would become truly "mystical" only by the addition of some awareness of participation in power through channels transcending the normal emotional ones. God provides a power-link with past salvific events through his own ineffable being, but the mystical element is located in him and in the union with him now-present rather than in any other mysterious link with the past.

509. There could be mysticism relative to God; but there could also—in Jewish and Christian cult—be very little or none. The whole affair could be conducted on the basis of a severely rational understanding of God and history, an understanding that while acknowledging mystery in God as described just above, sees this as God's business and seeks no mystical relationship with him. One of the advantages of any religious system that looks to personal divinity as the main source of power is that there is room for every kind of devotee. The memorial element of cult, while not excluding the possibility of human mystical experience, does stress the rational: God's personal nature, his covenant, the historical lapse of time that brings occasion for fulfilment of covenant promise. As Noth's work suggests, it also stresses moral obligation. Such considerations are

---

[10] *Haggadah of Passover*, trans. Maurice Samuel, intr. Louis Finkelstein (New York: Hebrew Publishing Co., 1942), p. 27.

closely related to the Seder text quoted above, both in the Torah and in
the Seder itself. In Exodus the text continues: "And it shall be to you
as a sign on your hand and as a memorial between your eyes, that the
law of the Lord may be in your mouth; for with the strong hand the Lord
has brought you out of Egypt. You shall therefore keep this ordinance
at its appointed time from year to year." (Exod. 13:9-10). The following
section goes on to contemporize: the people are not satisfied with past
salvation, and ask Moses, "What have you done to us, in bringing us out
of Egypt... to die in the wilderness." (14:11-12). Moses answers: "Fear
not, stand firm, and see the salvation of the Lord, which he will work
for you today." (14:13). In the Seder the passage quoted is soon followed
by "the verse in the Torah: 'And He brought us out from thence, so that
He might bring us home, and give us the land which he pledged to our
forefathers.'" [11] And, in turn, the very realistic prayer: "Even thus, O
Lord our God, and God of our fathers, bring us ever forward in peace
to other solemn days and festivals, joyous in the building of Thy city and
happy in Thy service." [12]

510. God, his powers, his involvement with the events of the past,
present and future, his commitment to save in view of past promises as
he saved then in view of previous ones—these are the matter for cultic
or other proclamation and for the rest of what cult involves. That it
does involve more than proclamation is one clear indication of the weakness
of the neo-orthodox approach and suggests why that approach either
sidesteps the question of later cult or deals with it inadequately. Of course,
the Seder ritual uses its various elements as parts of a cultic re-enactment
—proclamation-in-act. But the elements must be examined in their own
right as well: sacrifice, the meal, the prayers and hymns, with all that
they say and imply. Similarly with the Eucharist. The very name indicates
response in a manner going beyond faith or awareness of promise, and
presumes more than mere proclamation from the side of God or man. In
turn, the term "memorial" here as with the pasch suggests that something
more than mere reflection on past salvation or promises for the future
is entailed. In the light of the history of the concept and terminology,
it suggests a personal approach by the devotee to the Source of power in
order to engage past promises for the here and now. In a word, it suggests
reminding-God. This fills in the lacuna in the genus "cultic actualization",
and in large part explains why cult went on after primitive modes of
thinking ceased or became reprehensible; why, too, it could pass over
into the Christian program.

511. If we define actualization with Groves as making the past relevant to the present, it is clear that the Eucharistic memorial as we have

---

[11] Ibid.
[12] Ibid., p. 31.

observed it contains at least two types of actualization. The reminding-men involves awareness of the elements noted in the first sentence of the preceding paragraph, and prompts the second memorial element, the reminding of God to implement here and now his commitment to save. The first step is a relatively passive awareness of relevance, the second is the first stage in actually "making relevant". Alternate or additional kinds of contemporization at the first stage might be an impression of dramatic identification with the past—relevant in the sense any deep experience is relevant—and/or the neo-orthodox concept of a Divine enkindling of faith, which thereby manifests in its very being the saving power the text proclaims. The proclamation would be Divinely faith-constituting. A special Divine influence on faith could be seen to be present in other ways; for example, as in a common scholastic view in which the faith is had before the proclamation in the form of a Divinely given potency or faculty to be engaged by the proclamation. Or, the faith might be seen as a simply natural psychological response, varying in quality and depth from case to case, to hearing the traditions. We can designate these three kinds of actualization in the following way, noting in advance that *any* "faith" response looks to salvation. 1) Merely experiential. 2) Faith-engaging. 3) Faith-producing. To these we shall presently add a fourth (see following paragraph).

512. In practice, the neo-orthodox view, represented by no. 3, does not look beyond faith to other specifics of salvation; but there is no reason intrinsic to the idea of Divine faith-constituting that would prevent its doing that. The faith-engaging view ideally looks to a further stage—to doing something to engage salvation, specify it, or engage it further. Note the distinction in our use of the term "engage": the proclamation engages faith; the faith founds acts like mental and cultic prayer to engage Divine salvific activity, whether this be seen as *further* activity or as the main object of the exercise. In Groves' terms, no. 2 is "reality producing". We may use the phrase to designate a final stage of memorial actualization [The no. 4 promised in 511: so, 4) Reality-producing], recognizing that we are speaking here of realities other than that of any ontological reality faith itself might be seen to constitute. *Memorial cultic actualization*, carried to completion, would involve at least nos. 2 and 4; though it might conceivably involve no. 3 *instead* of no. 2. It would probably include some degree of no. 1. It would differ from *primitive cultic actualization* (what Groves considers adequate to the designation "cultic actualization") in that it does not like the primitive cult look to production of reality by mystical union with the source of power; rather, it adopts a rational person-to-person approach that recognizes and indeed emphasizes the essential distinction between that source and the human who reminds. For it is an "inadequate" actualization; i.e., it depends on the pleasure of the one reminded to "remember" and provide the realities in question. Yet that will presumably not happen without the human reminder. No. 3 shows features of von Rad's "chronological actualization", and although it has a theoretical appeal, it seems difficult to demonstrate from the texts; further, as we have already noted, if taken alone its scope seems inadequate to the expectations and practice of the Israelite and early Christian believers we are interested in

513. Groves ultimately concludes that Noth has changed the definition of "cultic actualization", and sees what Noth is talking about to be much like von Rad's chronological actualization. Similarly with Claus Westermann, Hans Walter Wolf in Germany; and Douglas Jones, Ackroyd and Porteous in England. Of Childs he says:

> Childs' final formulation bears a close resemblance to that of von Rad....
> Both see the actualization of the Old Testament as a transformation of
> cultic actualization. For von Rad the transformation occurs as a result
> of the developing sense of history in Israel with its consequent secular-
> ization and rationalization; Childs, as a response to a series of unrelated
> crises. The basic difference in the two stems from their starting points.
> Von Rad's concept, beginning with a theological conception and view-
> point, remains external to the people of Israel, focusing on the word of
> God. Childs' study, stemming from his work on *zkr*, focuses on the
> internalization of the concept through memory.[13]

Groves faults Childs on several points. He claims that "The major problem is that his conclusions simply do not grow out of his data." [14] Of Childs' view that "there was an immediate encounter, an actual participation in the great acts of redemption." [15] He says, "To claim a sense of immediacy is to overstep the evidence. Certainly, when he bases this immediacy upon the creation of redemptive time he is opening himself to James Barr's criticism of a separate concept of Biblical time." [16]

Childs Speaking for Himself

514. Let us at this point return directly to Childs' *Memory and Tradition* and focus more sharply on what happens to reminding-God in his development.

515. One of the key elements in his thinking is a conclusion that he draws from a review of several of the Psalms. After saying that "the object of God's memory cannot be consistently confined to the past... [t]he great acts of the covenant continue to meet Israel in her present situation," [17] he argues:

---

13 Groves, p. 104.
14 Ibid.
15 Ibid., p. 105
16 Ibid.
17 Childs, *Memory*, pp. 41-42.

This evidence would seem to indicate that in terms of God's memory time-sequence plays a secondary role. How the great acts of the past relate to the present and the future is not seen as a problem which bears upon God's memory. His remembering is not conceived of as an actualization of a past event in history; rather, every event stems from the eternal purpose of God. Only from Israel's point of view is each remembrance past. God's memory is not a recreating of the past, but a continuation of the selfsame purpose.[18]

The two citations given here provide a distinction that Childs seems to fail to draw out to its proper conclusions, namely that between "the *object* of God's memory" [our italics] and God's *way* of remembering. Surely God is aware of the difference of Israel's past from Israel's present, and of the difference of the whole created scene (including that past and present) from himself. These are all legitimate *objects* of his "memory", however that be conceived to operate. He himself is not such an object. In other words, "memory" for God refers to his knowledge of objects for which men use "memory" language of their own knowledge. It expresses the fact that God does know man's past as well as his present, and distinguishes them as different from one another as well as from himself. He can "remember" the past quite as well as he can "remember" present Israel. And although Childs is sparing in the use of memorial terminology himself, even with regard to present Israel (perhaps he shares something of Kosmala's and Hook's fear that such language demeans God), he does talk of "God's memory" and makes statements like, "The role of the cultic memorials (*zikkāron*) was to bring Israel constantly to God's attention, which would result in his gracious aid." [19] He appears to understand "brought to God's attention" as a cipher for something like our "referent of actuality", somewhat in the way Hook uses his term "enable".

516. Childs defines actualization as "the process by which a past event is contemporized for a generation removed in time and space from the original event." [20] Now Paul, even though he might have had a vague idea of God as existing durationally, would probably have granted that no past event is contemporized *for God*. But once it is acknowledge that God knows and can even be said to "remember" past events, it becomes hazardous to make a blanket claim that he does not contemporize. It would have to be proved that he does not do so *for his creatures*, and Childs is far indeed from proving this. Indeed, just as Childs seems implicitly to allow for the legitimacy of God's memory of the past by his distinction between object of knowledge and way of knowing, he seems implicitly to allow for such contemporization. He says, "God's remembering issued in his intervention on Israel's behalf based on his previous

[18] Ibid., p. 42.
[19] Ibid., p. 85.
[20] Ibid., p. 74.

commitment to Israel." [21] There is question here of a new "intervention", but the fact is that the "previous commitment" was itself in many cases manifested by intervention. I.e., terminally speaking, there were a series of historic revelatory and otherwise salvific events in Israel's past. How God relates such events to the present interventions is not man's problem but God's, but it is clear that the Jews and Paul thought such relationships could be established by God.

517. Reminding-God in cult or out of it is linked to such contemporization or actualization as at least a necessary condition of the knowledge had by the Divine actualizer (see 170), and since the knowledge is as much his actualizing act as is the empowering of the act, the reminding-God can itself be legitimately called "actualizing". When formally "sacramentalized", with that being Divinely required as part of the condition, this would also be legitimately called "cultic actualization". Childs does not take either part of this view. Not the first part, as I see it, first because he does not explicate his distinction between object and way of knowing; and second—a parallel omission—because he does not explicate the distinction between principiative and terminal "intervention". Not the second part because he does not take the first part. In other words, then, Childs does not see a real connection through God between the present and the past event. It becomes difficult to understand how he sees anything more than an analogy of the two. He might say that seen analogy (seen by memory) stimulates the religious experience. As Groves puts it, speaking of him, "Participation in Israel's festivals arouses and incites the memory which causes her to participate in the past decisive events of her tradition. This is actualization [for Childs]." [22] But Childs wants more immediacy than this would normally be thought to provide.

518. Childs does not, of course, visualize the whole scope of the cultic event as limited to the human element. He sees God as viewing the event, and indeed mandating it. He says that "The Deuteronomist relativized the cultic tradition in conceiving of it along with the non-cultic material simply as a commandment... on which obedience could be tested." [23] Such a concept is nearly equivalent to our "referent of actuality". *But two critical differences between the positions stand out.* 1) In the fuller memorial view, the past terminal aspect of the event has a function in the present event at the Divine level but in a very true sense, though by God's generosity, *in its own right;* on the other hand, in Childs' view the past event's function in the present one is limited to the former considered only principiatively (i.e., in terms of God as its author): it is a question of God's commitment, and in this as Childs portrays it, there

---

[21] Ibid.
[22] Groves, p. 101.
[23] Childs, *Memory*, p. 79.

is really no sense of "past". At the human level, the past event for Childs seems logically to be simply a stimulus to trust, whereas for someone with the fuller concept it is seen to be somehow influential through God's use of it. The cultic actors and pray-ers are conscious of that influence and look to it as an incorporation into the Divine response to the cultic plea, so that the plea is actually in part that that influence might have effect. *There is in fact a double referent of actuality: the former event, related at the time to God's promises, and the present appeal for God's recognition of it.* "O Lord God, destroy not thy people... whom thou hast redeemed... brought out of Egypt with a mighty hand. Remember thy servants, Abraham, Isaac, and Jacob; do not regard the stubbornness of this people...." (Deut. 9:26-27). Abraham is viewed as an obedient partici-pant in the past saving action, and his obedience set off as a practical counterbalance to the disobedience that might close the way to present saving action. Similarly, Christ's death and resurrection for Paul. 2) Childs would probably allow that the sacramental and personalized aspects of cult have stimulating functions of their own, in a dramatic way. But the statement that the cultic tradition is conceived "simply as a command-ment... on which obedience could be tested" seems to lean towards formal-ism. The Godward aspect of cult is reduced to forms of address and actions that have no value except that they provide God with a knowledge of obedience. Seemingly ignored is the possibility—and indeed, consider-ing God's wisdom, the likelihood—that they are ordered because they are of value in their own right in expressing the filial relationship with God. So for the sacrificial act in the Old Testament; so, for that matter, for personal prayer.[24] In fact, these, from the human standpoint, were widely and rightly felt to be the most suitable expressions to God, and not merely culturally-indicated means of demonstrating obedience, though they demon-strated obedience too. Thus, *there was question in many cases of a double referent of actuality, present and past; and in every case, of personal approach as the main quality of referents whether present, past, or both.*

519. Of Porteous, Groves judges that his "inclusion of an obedient response by the people in the meaning of the term ['actualization'] ex-pands actualization beyond the basic meaning of the term." [25] Porteous, like Noth, was primarily concerned with obedience outside the cultic act. But obedience to the Divine mandate to perform cult obviously does have a basic function in memorial cultic actualization. In various ways it operates as a factor both in reminding man and reminding God. Further, Paul brings obedience to Divine moral demands into the Eucharist in a

---

[24] The patristic designation of the Eucharist as a sacrifice can be construed as an effort to express this same kind of vision.

[25] Groves, p. 106

special way by showing that without it Eucharist becomes hypocrisy. Consequently, such disobedience had or intended during the act would vitiate the reminding-God element of memorial actualizing. God is reminded of his covenant promises, but this automatically reminds—or should remind—everyone concerned of the covenant obligations that accompanied those promises. Porteous may have had an intuition of these relationships. But on the basis of what he actually says, one must agree with Groves' estimate that "The essence of actualization [for Porteous] lies in the act of vivifying, where the people realize the significance of the act and the nature of the demand that is made upon them." [26] Of course, one could still quite justifiably call this "actualization" if the *realization* of the need of obedient response were all that was in question. But Groves sees the response itself as falling within the denotation of the term in Porteous' mind, and that is unjustifiable.

520. We have heard Groves criticize the immediacy Childs claims for Israel's remembering of the past as an overstepping of the evidence (see 510). Childs sees this immediacy as a "bridging the gap of time and forming a solidarity with the fathers",[27] so that the term *zkr* "lost its general psychological sense to take on [this]... highly theological meaning." [28] That there was a theological actualizing frequently related to the use of memorial terminology seems evident. But it did not occur because that terminology *lost* its psychological sense; quite the opposite: it happened when that sense was intensified in prayer, cult and crisis, and urged a theological explanation. Some Israelites or Christians may have thought that on the occasion of remembering they could achieve a significant "solidarity with the fathers" by means of some mystical means other than God. But even then the means was presumably distinct from the remembering itself: remembering remained remembering and clamored to be relevant, the more so the more intense it was.

521. It is on the basis of his idea of special immediacy that Childs sees a break with the original situation in Israel, where cult was the main locus of actualization, to a new memorial development when this new kind of immediacy was had out of cult as well as within it.[29] As far as cult was concerned, it involved the "radical reinterpretation" of which we have already spoken when discussing one supposed radical change, that from "ritual minutiae" to a purer form of cult (187ff). As we then said, it is impossible to show that this was a really "radical" change. The same must be said of the other elements of change that Childs singles out.

---

[26] Ibid.
[27] Childs, *Memory*, p. 74.
[28] Ibid.
[29] See Ibid., pp. 75-76.

522. For example, after having noted that "Von Waldow has demonstrated in a most convincing manner how deeply rooted Deutero-Isaiah's message was in Israel's cultic life," [30] he says that "Memory of the past links Israel with the one great purpose of God in history which encompasses both past and future.... Israel need not turn to the past for meaning." [31] In fact, Israel generally never did stop turning to the past for meaning, even though it may have omitted past references some or even most of the time, and even though some writers may have omitted them all of the time. Certainly the Deuteronomist did not stop. Nor did Deutero-Isaiah. Granted, he says, "Remember not the former things" (43: 18), but this does not refer to God's past creative and saving acts; rather, to evil circumstances these and similar acts render passé. The past saving acts are indeed past, but are anything but passé; they are very relevant. At the very least they are a standing guarantee that Israel can expect more of the same. Not the *identical* acts, from the created angle, but *similar* ones. The author presently shows this. "Remember these things, O Jacob... and Israel.... I formed you... you will not be forgotten by me." (44:21). "These things" refers more to such present acts. But the relevance goes much further. "I formed you" is a fundamental gift in the past. God's creation is never to be forgotten either by Israel or by God, nor does it ever cease to operate. Man's memory of God's past actions adds to rather than detracts from his awareness of the unitary power of God, for the view the whole remembered biblical text gives of the multiplicity of God's interventions throws into sharp contrast man's inability to make his past powers presently realistically effective on the one side, and God's freedom from these temporal limitations on the other.

523. Childs rejects in favor of his "radical reinterpretation" the "hypothesis" that *zkr* was "employed somewhat late in Israel's history... to describe a process which had been functioning without interruption within the cult of Israel from its earliest history." [32] This is overstating the opposition's probable claims. It is only necessary to show a likelihood that the process had been functioning for some time before the Deuteronomic "reinterpretation". We have seen sufficient evidence to show that the *word* was in fact employed over a considerable span of time, and that it was applied not only to essentially the same psychological function, but —when applied theologically—in much the same theological setting throughout. "The Isaian "Remember these things" is preceded by "Remember this day...." in Exod. 13:3; by the chiding of Judg. 8:34: "The people of Israel did not remember the Lord their God, who had rescued them....";

---

[30] *Memory*, p. 79.
[31] Ibid.
[32] Ibid., p. 76.

and by the admonition in Josh. 1:13: "Remember the word which Moses the servant of the Lord commanded you, saying, 'The Lord your God is providing you a place of rest....'"

524. The "redemptive time" that Groves criticizes is explicitly stated by Childs not to be a "timeless idea or a non-historical ground-of-being." [33] Rather, it is a "quality of time." [34] Unfortunately, he does not define time. However, certain things he says make it seem that he *is* taking it to be a measure of events: "redemptive time" would then be Israel's way of looking at redemptive events. "How?", then, would be the main question. Childs seems in *Memory and Tradition* to say that Israel sees the original event somehow actually present in the now-event in some way other than mere concurrence of natural effects or psychological memory or any combination of these—standing here not in its past dignity or in results really distinct from it, but in a modernized version of itself that the past event has now really *become*. If this is a correct reading, I doubt if it follows from any questioning on Childs' part of the possibility of reconstructing a previous historical event—the possibility we discussed in 58, 61, 66, 69. Whence, then? No one would deny that past salvific events have repeatedly been reinterpreted inside the Bible and out of it in the sense that analogies are seen between the past and present, and the eternal sameness of God invoked to bring about here and now effects analogous to those known to have been had in the past. In this process the story may receive new dress and applications, but there usually remains a clear historical core in which the pastness of the event and the distinctness of the Divine interventionary element are clearly defined. "God saved Israel from the Egyptians" keeps coming through. When, without clear reference on his part to analogy, we read in Childs that "The biblical events have the dynamic characteristic of refusing to be relegated to the past," [35] and "[this] means more than that the influence of a past event continued to be felt in successive generations," [36] we might somehow get the uneasy feeling that God, who is specifically included in Childs' considerations, has to be offered the past created event in an already strongly "unitarized" form in order for him, unitary as *he* is, to be able to intervene in the present. This would be much different from saying, as I think Paul would say of Christ's resurrection, that the *effects* of the past event remain in existence within the same personal identity so that in that sense (as well as in the memorial one) the event can be said to be perpetuated. At any rate, it seems necessary to stress that the real point of the Godward reference in cult or out of it seems to be to recognize in

---

[33] Ibid., p. 84.
[34] Ibid.
[35] Ibid., p. 88.
[36] Ibid., p. 83-84.

a practical way that creature—whether event or person—in *unable* by itself to bridge the time gap in any completely satisfying way, either by going backwards or by bringing forwards; and that God, by reason of his being Creator and unlimited by durational flow, can do it and wants to be asked to do it. The Godward reference does not minimize the created time-gap, it maximizes it, so that it may overcome it.

525. In *Memory and Tradition* Childs is treating of the developments of and from cult. Past traditions are dealt with with a view to their function in encounters with God in the present. These encounters are studied not from any revelatory man-from-God aspect but from the way that they open upward to God, as in their manifesting obedience. In other words, Childs is concerned with one kind of *use* made of past traditions. In his more recent work, he has approached the same traditions from another standpoint, studying both the measures taken by the tradents to contemporize the traditions, and additionally, the reasons for accepting them as authoritative. His reason for seeking out the reasons is expressed in an article written in 1972, when he complains that "We have difficulty hearing in [the Bible]... the word of God...." [37] His response then was that "The formation of the Christian canon was that process by which the early church, testifying to the authority of its traditions, set some apart as Sacred Scripture." [38] Again, in 1978 at the beginning of an article, he says that the historical-critical methodology has not solved the problem of the Bible as an authoritative force in the formation of the Christian life.[39] His response is a development of the earlier one. He argues that the canonical editors contributed to an aggregation of texts that lay claims to constitute an ongoing and authoritative witness to "the experience of Israel, as the addressee of God's judgement and redemption." [40] In this process, "one concern which is expressly mentioned is that a tradition from the past be transmitted in such a way that its authoritative claims be laid upon all successive generations of Israel." [41] It is not merely that the text was authoritative in its original setting, and should now be recognized as having been such; but that it retains authority for the times beyond that setting. This would be true, no doubt, should the original situation recur, should that be possible; but more importantly, the text can be understood as applying in more general or extended contexts than the original through the medium of generalizations or extensions evidenced in subsequently-formed treatments of the tradition. Childs speaks of

---

[37] Brevard S. Childs, "The Old Testament as Scripture of the Church," *Concordia Theological Monthly* 43 (1972): 711.

[38] Ibid.

[39] See Brevard S. Childs, "The Canonical Shape of Prophetic Literature," *Interpretation* 32 (1978): 47.

[40] Ibid., pp. 53-54.

[41] Brevard S. Childs, *Introduction to the Old Testament as Scripture* (Philadelphia: Fortress, 1979), p. 78.

"God's perspective" giving a hope beyond the historical perspective of the prophet (in this case, Amos).[42] This reference to God, plus others to Divine influence, indicates that Childs sees the biblical editors as conscious of participating in a Divinely-guided process. He says, "Israel registered the word of the prophets along with its own reception and saw in both the Spirit of God at work."[43]

526. In dealing with the *means* whereby this program was implemented, Childs selects various examples of literary devices that the writers used to show the continuing applicability of the old texts—various *methods* of "extending and generalizing". He speaks of such means as "actualization", as in the following.

> It is an axiom of many redactional critics that the layering within a biblical book derives from a desire to 'update' an original tradition. While this description occasionally applies, the canonical approach offers a very different model of interpreting the growth of multilayered texts. The major issue turns on how one understands the process by which a biblical text is actualized.... the hermeneutical task of actualizing past traditions for each successive generation lies at the heart of the process. Theological reflection on its actualization has been built into the structure of the canonical text.... Little wonder that once the text has been anchored in the historical past by 'decanonizing' [by critical methodology], the interpreter has difficulty applying it to a modern religious context.[44]

This is the sense of "actualization" whose methods Groves describes when he says, for example, of Isaiah 36-39:

> These chapters function as a literary connective on the semantic level of metaphor and image.... A shift to metaphor... dehistoricizes the underlying themes of the material. As a result, the traditions in Isa. 36-39 are actualized for all subsequent generations... all situations of exile and restoration. We may describe the contemporization encountered here as actualization through metaphor.[45]

527. But Childs' deeper concern still seems to be not *how* but *why* the traditions continue to be considered relevant. This appears in the statements in the text cited in our previous paragraph: "The major issue turns on how one understands the process by which a biblical text is actualized.... Theological reflection on [the past tradition's] actualization has been built into the structure of the canonical text." The term "actualization" is here applied to the means, but the "major issue" is the theological reflection *on* this actualization. From what we have heard Childs say, we can judge that the basic question is "Why accept as relevant today formulations made in long defunct situations?" And the

---

[42] See Childs, "The Canonical Shape," p. 49.
[43] Ibid., p. 53.
[44] Ibid., p. 49.
[45] Groves, p. 244.

answer, "Because they make authoritative claims on our acceptance, and the Spirit in us recognizes the claims as just."

528. Since the theological reflection has been "built into the... text", it would be quite proper to call this reflection itself "actualization", for it certainly fulfils Childs' definition of actualization as "the process by which a past event is contemporized...." (See 516). It is not the *literary* process, but a theological one that has been incorporated in the literary expressions. Such actualization might be called "legitimizing". It would include various kinds of normative or legal pressures for acceptance, whether from God, from the state, from human religious authorities, or from strong convention. It gives the readers reason, authorization, or motivation for taking a text as relevant.

Pertinent Thoughts on Literary Actualization

529. It should be clear that we have been primarily concerned in this study with what we have called "memorial cultic actualization". (512). But in demonstrating the likelihood that Paul was concerned with it too, we have pointed out the probability of a Pauline use of analogues that would in itself be a form of literary actualization. I refer to the phenomenon of "implied simile" designated by that name in 411 and 500. By Paul's use of it, traditions, texts, or other sources of knowledge about formerly (and perhaps also presently) prevalent concepts, institutions and practices like ransom, martyrdom, sacrifice, Akedah, mercy-seat, scapegoat, etc. become relevant as sources of meaning in explaining the crucifixion; ones like hero-cult, royal memoranda, festal celebrations, some kinds of cultic memorials, sacrificial communion, "name" and progeny serve in the same way for the Eucharist. The method is especially useful for painting a wide spectrum of meaning and avoiding restriction of meaning to one or a very few specific analogues.

530. Among other ways, Groves speaks of contemporization through metaphor, allusion, and parallels.[46] A "parallel" is a kind of analogue. We have also noted that metaphor is a strong form of analogy. Groves discusses analogy briefly in an early section on von Rad, remarking that for the latter "all Old Testament typology is analogical thinking,"[47] that typology "focuses upon the historical kerygma of Israel's faith and its prefiguration of Christ;[48] also that "integrally related to typology... is a scheme of promise and fulfilment."[49] It seems evident that where biblical typology is understood as completed by a later analogue, there is an actu-

---

[46] See Groves, pp. 226ff.
[47] Groves, p. 45. On p. 46 he adds that for von Rad, "Allegory is also analogical thinking."
[48] Ibid., p. 47.
[49] Ibid.

alization to whatever extent promise-fulfilment is related to the completion. Such relevance would be more than merely literary, since it would involve either Divine intervention or at least a mystic aura by way of a sensibility of Divine foreknowledge and perhaps planning. This can of course be true of any kind of literary actualization: the content may actualize in a manner different from that of the container.

531. Figures like allegory, typology, simile and metaphor would involve analogy as an actualizing factor. Allusion would be one way of engaging the analogy, this stressing the author's influence rather more than the word we used earlier a number of times, "connotation". Groves is certainly correct in saying that such a process need not be reflective.[50] It should of course be realized that other literary means than figures of speech can actualize: simple or extended declarations, imperatives, various literary forms, etc.

A Schema of Actualization

532. We may summarize what we have said about actualization, placing in one column some aspects of agencies of relevance, in another, the nature of the relevance achieved. This will be no exhaustive picture, of course, but only some factors that seem more directly suggested by Groves' study and our own. The factors in A and B may overlap and combine vertically, both within A and within B, and between them. For example, traditions may be incorporated into Godward ritual; while ritual itself may also serve for proclamation. (See 474ff). The factors in the second column under A may be related to various of those in Col. I under A; those under B to various of those in Col. I under B.

I) *Process of making the past relevant*

    A) Manward
       1) Source
          a) God directly, as by inspiration of a prophet
          b) Human beings, perhaps as instruments of God

       2) Form
          a) By literary forms like legends, historical narratives, parables, sayings, proverbs, etc.
          b) By rhetorical devices like declaration, imperative, question, condition, suggestion, connotation, allusion, etc.

II) *Nature of relevance to the communicatee*

    A) 1) The experience (of being communicated with) as such
       2) Religious faith as somehow supernatural
       3) The residue of experience and faith
       4) Addition of, deepening of rational meaning
       5) Impressions of need, advantage, special obligation, propriety, or other motivations following on the above

---

[50] See Groves, p. 229.

c) By figures of speech

d) By staging and sacramentalization (over and above the material signing element in literary expressions)

3) Content

Any of the above (under "form") may be used to communicate information, sense of participation, promise, threat, conventional pressures, etc.

B) Godward

1) Memorial = reminding-God
   a) Prayer without the formality of cult
   b) Judaeo-Christian cult
   c) Demonstration of faith and/or obedience

2) Non-memorial
   a) Primitive cult, operating by mystic union with manaistic power
   b) Hellenistic-type mystery cult, operating by mystical union with divinity
   c) Theurgy, magic

B) 1) The cultic experiences as such
2) Retention of shared power
3) Forgiveness, salvation, blessings of different kinds

This scheme can be supplemented by that given in para. 170 on the "purpose and mode of operation of prayer and liturgical celebrations". In terms of actualization, I, A. 2 involves what might be called "artistic" actualization, with I, A, 2, a, b and c "literary" actualization. "Legitimizing" actualization would fall under I, A, 3 and II, A, 4.

533. The presence of prayer as a type of memorial actualization may be noted specially. We have remarked this equivalently several times, and at some length, with regard to Paul in particular and the Hebrews and Christians in general. Groves remarks when listing difficulties in Childs' position that the exile was the only extended time in Israel's history when she was without organized cult.[51] We may safely say she was never without prayer, and much of this was certainly, at least in later years, memorial in thought and expression. Formally memorial prayer is, in fact, a linguistic person-to-person expression of reminding-God memorial thinking. It is commonly associated with physical gesture, and the fact underscores the possibility of viewing and partly defining cult as the *formalizing* of

---

[51] See Groves, p. 104.

both the linguistic and the gesticulatory elements of reminding-God. This scheme naturally calls to mind the distinction between the linguistic and non-linguistic elements of proclamation in the Eucharist (see 475). As we said, proclamation is reminding-man. Carried to completion, cult blends both the linguistic and the gesticulatory elements of reminding-man and reminding-God. It is not a question of cult's being physical action plus proclamation, but of cultic memorial's usually having both physical and linguistic elements, and of cultic proclamation's having them too. Cult takes the proclamatory element and makes it the basis for reminding God. When complete, cult adds prayer to proclamation and joins the dramatic action played out before men to elements directed towards God. "When complete": ideally vocal prayer would be involved, but it seems clear that as long as the reminding-God *intention* is present, and as long as there is dramatic action done, in part, with that intention, vocal expression of it is a matter of excellence rather than essence. One might speak of adding "prayer or the spirit of prayer". It is harder to think of a speechless "proclamation", but pantomime can communicate.

534. How does the Eucharist fit into our schema? Knowledge of it on man's part is attributed to Christ as source, which presumably means that God himself is the ultimate source. Paul and others also contribute to the transmission. Several forms among or like those mentioned are used to gain comprehension of the meaning of the transmission: among them direct quotation, declaration, narrative, imperative, implied simile, metaphor, metonymy. These transmit meanings seen directly and by analogy, fostering perceptions of moral obligation, promise, threat, etc. Especially because of the Divine origin, and because the tradition includes Christ's own words, some kind of supernatural faith-experience might be thought to be involved. The experiences would all leave their psychological traces. Paul also spells out some practical implications of the tradition.

535. But the main relevance for Paul's Christians would probably come from the anticipated Divine response to the personal element of the Godward movement, from reminding-God. The Eucharist is cult, which as Groves says looks to "reality production". The ultimate source of the realities is God, but a link is made, in the historical context, with the mediating activity of Jesus. The Eucharist of course demonstrates faith and obedience to Christ's imperative (see I, B, 1, c in the schema), but that obedience itself recognizes a call by God and Christ to personal relationship, filiation and even friendship. Personal communication is the *first kind* of obedience God wants here. This Divine call is the real reason for the expectation of salvation. The salvation looked for is freedom from the power of sin, blessings both temporal and eternal, in addition to renewed faith and renewed promise.

A Final Statement

536. This chapter has shown that the category "actualization" is suitable in several ways for our purposes, and suggested that there are important lacunae in the views various scholars have taken of what fits into the category and how much fits in each case. The chapter and the previous one both locate our endeavors more exactly in the spectrum of scholarship and by comparison and contrast throw useful light on various aspects of our final basic conclusions as stated in paras. 465-470. The reader wishing to review those conclusions briefly is asked to to turn to those paragraphs.

Bibliography

I: Texts and Translations

The Ante-Nicene Fathers. Edited by Alexander Roberts and James Donaldson. New York: Charles Scribners Sons, 1899. Vol. 1: *The Apostolic Fathers—Justin Martyr—Irenaeus.*

Apocalypsis Henochi Graece, Fragmenta. Edited by M. Black. Leiden: E. J. Brill, 1970.

Apocrypha and Pseudepigrapha of the Old Testament in English. Edited by R. H. Charles. 2 vols. Oxford: Clarendon Press, 1913.

The Authorized Daily Prayer Book. Edited by Joseph H. Hertz. Rev. ed. New York: Bloch, 1948.

The Bible, Revised Standard Version. 2d ed. New York: American Bible Society, 1971.

Biblia Hebraica. Edited by Rudolf Kittel. 14th ed. Stuttgart: Württembergische Bibelanstalt, n.d.

Biblia Sacra iuxta Vulgatam Clementinam. 5th ed. Madrid: Biblioteca de Autores Cristianos, 1977.

The Complete Works of Flavius Josephus. Translated by William Whiston. Philadelphia: John E. Potter, n.d.

The Dead Sea Scriptures. Translated with notes by Theodor H. Gaster. 3rd revised ed. Garden City, New York: Anchor Press/Doubleday, 1956.

The Demotic Magical Papyrus of London and Leiden. Edited by F. Griffith and H. Thompson. 3 vols. London: n.p., 1904-1908.

The Ethics of the Talmud: Sayings of the Fathers. Edited, translated with commentary by R. Travers Herford. New York: Schocken Books, 1962.

Greek Religious Thought. By F. M. Cornford. (Includes translations). New York: J. M. Dent and Sons, 1923.

The Greek Versions of the Testaments of the Twelve Patriarchs. Edited by R. H. Charles. 3rd ed. Oxford: University Press, 1966.

Greek Votive Offerings. By W. H. D. Rouse. (Contains Greek votive texts). Cambridge: University Press, 1902; reprinted 1976.

Haggadah of Passover. Translated by Maurice Samuel, introduction by Louis Finkelstein. New York: Hebrew Publishing Co., 1942.

Hellenistic Religions. Edited by Frederick C. Grant. Indianapolis: Bobbs-Merrill, 1953.

Jamblique Les Mystères D'Égypte. Translated by Édouard des Places. Paris: Société D'Édition 'Les Belles Lettres,' 1966.

Later Greek Religion. By Edwyn Bevan. (Includes translations). London: Dent, 1927.

The Loeb Classical Library. London: William Heinemann Ltd; Cambridge, Mass.: Harvard University Press.

The Mishnah. Translated by Herbert Danby. Oxford: University Press, 1933.

The Nag Hammadi Library. Edited by James M. Robinson. New York: Harper and Row, 1957.

The New Testament. Translated by James A. Kleist and Joseph L. Lilly. Milwaukee: Bruce, 1956.

Novum Testamentum Graece. Cum apparatu critico curavit Eberhard Nestle, novis curis elaboraverunt Erwin Nestle et Kurt Aland. 25th ed. Stuttgart: Württembergische Bibelanstalt, 1963.

Papyri Graecae Magicae. Edited and translated into German by Karl Preisendanz. 2 vols. Leipzig, Berlin: B. G. Teubner, 1928-31.

The Prayer Book. Translated and edited by Ben Zion Bokser. New York: Hebrew Publishing Co., 1957.

Les Psaumes de Salomon. Translated into French by J. Viteau. Paris: Letouzey et Ané, 1911.

The Scroll of the War of the Sons of Light against the Sons of Darkness. Edited and commented on by Yigael Yadin, translated by Batya and Chaim Rabin. Oxford: University Press, 1954.

Septuaginta. Edited by Alfred Rahlfs, editio minor. Stuttgart: Deutsche Bibelstiftung, 1935.

The Septuagint Version of the Old Testament, with an English Translation, and companion volume, *The Apocrypha, Greek and English*. Translated by Sir Lancelot C. . Brenton. New York: Harper and Bros.; London: Samuel Bagster and Sons, 1851. These two volumes have recently been combined and reprinted (Grand Rapids: Zondervan Publishing House, eighth printing, 1980.)

The Thanksgiving Hymns. Translated by Menahem Mansoor. Leiden: E. J. Brill, 1961.

The Zadokite Documents. Translated by Chaim Rabin. Oxford: Clarendon Press, 1954.

Zwei griechische Zauberpapyri. Translated by G. Parthey. Berlin: Königl. Akademie der Wissenschaften, 1866.

II: Works Quoted or Referred to by Name

Allo, E. P. *Première épitre aux Corinthiens*. 2d ed. Paris: Librairie Lecoffre, 1956.

Barr, James. *Biblical Words for Time*. Studies in Biblical Theology no. 33. Naperville, Ill.: Alec R. Allenson, 1962.

Barrett, Charles Kingsley. *A Commentary on the First Epistle to the Corinthians*. New York: Harper and Row, 1968.

Bauer, Walter. *A Greek-English Lexicon of the New Testament and Other Early Christian Literature*. Translated and adapted by William F. Arndt and F. Wilbur Gingrich from the 4th ed. of the German (1952). Chicago: The University of Chicago Press, 1957.

Betz, Johannes. *Die Eucharistie in der Zeit der griechischen Väter*. 2 vols. Freiburg: Herder, 1961.

Bevan, Edwyn. *Later Greek Religion*. London: Dent, 1927.

Blass, Friedrich, and Debrunner, Albert. *A Greek Grammar of the New Testament and Other Early Christian Literature*. Translated and revised by Robert W. Funk from the 9th-10th German edition. Chicago: The University of Chicago Press, 1961.

Boer, see de Boer.

Bohren, Rudolf. "Predigt als Erzählung." *Oikonomia, Heilsgeschichte als Thema der Theologie*. Edited by Felix Christ. Hamburg-Bergstedt: Reich, 1967. Pp. 345-359.

Bokser, Ben Zion, trans. and ed. *The Prayer Book*. New York: Hebrew Publishing Co., 1957.

Bridgehouse, Donald. "Dom Odo Casel." *Downside Review* 75 (1957), 140-148.

Bromiley, Geoffrey M., see Kittel, Gerhard.

Büchler, Adolph. *Studies in Sin and Atonement* in the rabbinic literature of the first century. Library of Biblical Studies, editor Harry M. Orlinsky. New York: KTAV Publishing House, 1967. First published 1927.

Büchsel, F. *TDNT*, s.v. "λύω."

Bultmann, Rudolf. *History and Eschatology.* New York: Harper and Row, 1957.

————. *History of the Synoptic Tradition.* Revised edition, translated by John Marsh. New York: Harper and Row, 1963.

————. "The Idea of God and Modern Man." Translated by Robert W. Funk. *Translating Theology into the Modern Age.* Vol. 2 of Journal for Theology and the Church. Edited by Robert W. Funk. New York: Harper and Row, 1965. Pp. 85-95.

————. *Jesus Christ and Mythology.* New York: Charles Scribner's Sons, 1958.

————. *Theology of the New Testament.* Translated by Kendrick Grobel. 2 vols. New York: Charles Scribner's Sons, 1951-55.

Calloud, Jean. *Structural Analysis of Narrative.* Translated by Daniel Patte. Philadelphia: Fortress Press, 1976.

Chenderlin, Fritz. "Man's Finality in Shankara's Vedantism." *Divus Thomas* 78 (1975), 376-406.

Childe, Vere Gordon. *What is History?* New York: Henry Schuman, 1953.

Childs, Brevard S. "The Canonical Shape of Prophetic Literature." *Interpretation* 32 (1978), 46-55.

————. *Introduction to the Old Testament as Scripture.* Philadelphia: Fortress, 1979.

————. "The Old Testament as Scripture of the Church." *Concordia Theological Monthly* 43 (1972), 709-722.

————. *Memory and Tradition in Israel.* London: SCM Press, 1962.

Clements, R. E. "The Meaning of Ritual Acts in Israelite Religion." *Eucharistic Theology Then and Now.* Editor not named. London: S.P.C.K., 1968. Pp. 1-14.

Collingwood, Robin George. *The Idea of History.* Oxford: Clarendon, 1946.

Conzelmann, Hans. *1 Corinthians.* Translated by James W. Leitch from *Der erste Brief an die Korinther,* 1st ed. [Göttingen: Vandenhoeck & Rupprecht, 1969]. Philadelphia: Fortress Press, 1975.

Cornford, F. M. *Greek Religious Thought.* New York: J. M. Dent and Sons, 1923.

Cullman, Oscar. *Christi and Time.* Revised edition, translated by Floyd V. Filson. Philadelphia: Westminster, 1964.

Dahl, Nils Alstrup. "The Atonement—an Adequate Reward for the Akedah?" *The Crucified Messiah and Other Essays.* Reprinted from *Neotestamentica et Semitica, Studies in Honor of Matthew Black,* edited by Ellis and Wilcox (Edinburgh: T. & T. Clark Ltd., 1969). Minneapolis: Augsburg, 1974.

————. *Jesus in the Memory of the Early Church.* Minneapolis: Augsburg Publishing House, 1976.

Dan, Joseph. *Encyclopaedia Judaica,* s.v. "Sacrifice," second section.

Daube, David. *The New Testament and Rabbinic Judaism.* London: The Athlone Press, 1956.

de Boer, P. A. H. *Gedenken und Gedächtnis in der Welt des alten Testaments.* Stuttgart: Franz Delitzsch-Vorlesungen, 1960.

de la Taille, Maurice. *The Mystery of Faith.* 2 vols. New York: Sheed and Ward, 1940.

Denis-Boulet, N. M. "The Canon or Eucharistic Prayer." In *The Church at Prayer, the Eucharist.* Edited by A. G. Martimort. New York: Herder and Herder, 1973. Pp. 131-170.

DeVries, Simon. *Yesterday, Today and Tomorrow.* Grand Rapids: William B. Eerdmans, 1975.

Dodds, E. R. *The Greeks and the Irrational*. Berkeley: University of California Press, 1951.

Doty, William G. *Contemporary New Testament Interpretation*. Englewood Cliffs, New Jersey: Prentice-Hall, 1972.

Dillon, Richard D., and Fitzmyer, Joseph A. "Introduction" to "Acts of the Apostles," *JBC*, 45:3.

Encyclopaedia Judaica. 16 vols. New York: Macmillan, 1972.

Faley, Roland J. "Leviticus." *JBC*, 4:34.

Fitzmyer, Joseph A. "Pauline Theology." *JBC*, 79:86.

Fuchs, Ernst. *Das Urchristliche Sakramentsverständnis*. Bad Cannstatt: R. Müllerschön Verlag, 1958.

Gadamer, Hans-Georg. *Philosophical Hermeneutics*. Edited and translated by David E. Linge. Berkeley: University of California Press, 1976.

————. *Truth and Method*. New York: Seabury Press, 1975.

————. *Wahrheit und Methode*. Tübingen: Mohr, 1960.

Gardiner, Patrick, ed. *Theories of History*. Glencoe, Ill.: The Free Press, 1959.

Gnilka, Joachim. *Das Evangelium nach Markus*. 2 vols. Neukirchen-Vluyn: Benziger Verlag and Neukirchener Verlag, 1978.

Goppelt, Leonhard. *TDNT*, s.v. " ποτήριον " and " τύπος."

Grant, Frederick C., ed. *Hellenistic Religions*. Indianapolis: Bobbs-Merrill, 1953.

Groves, Joseph White. *Actualization and Interpretation in the Old Testament*. Ph. D. Dissertation on microfiche. Yale University, 1979.

Guthrie, W. K. C. *The Greeks and Their Gods*. Boston: Beacon, 1950.

Harrison, Jane Ellen. *Themis*. Cambridge: University Press, 1927.

Heidegger, Martin. *Sein und Zeit*. Tübingen: Max Niemeyer, 1963.

Heinemann, Joseph. *Prayer in the Talmud*. New York: Walter de Gruyter, 1977.

Hermann, Johannes. *TDNT, s.v.* " ἱλάσκομαι."

Hertz, Joseph H. *The Authorized Daily Prayer Book*. Revised edition. New York: Bloch, 1948.

Hook, Norman. *The Eucharist in the New Testament*. London: The Epworth Press, 1964.

Huber, Carlo E. *Anamnesis bei Plato*. München: Pullacher Philosophische Forschungen, 1964.

Huesman, John E. "Exodus." *JBC*, 3:32.

Jeremias, Joachim. *The Eucharistic Words of Jesus*. Translated by Norman Perrin from *Die Abendmahlsworte Jesu*, 3rd ed. [Göttingen: Vandenhoeck & Ruprecht, 1960] with author's revisions to July, 1964. New York: Charles Scribner's Sons, 1966.

The Jerome Biblical Commentary. Edited by Raymond E. Brown, Joseph A. Fitzmyer, Roland E. Murphy. Englewood Cliffs, New Jersey: Prentice-Hall, 1968.

The Jerusalem Bible. Garden City, New York: Doubleday, 1966.

Jones, Douglas. " ἀνάμνησις in the LXX and the Interpretation of 1 Cor. XI. 25." *Journal of Theological Studies* 6 (1955), 183-191.

Jungmann, Josef A. *The Mass*. Translated by Julian Fernandes, edited by Mary Ellen Evans. Collegeville, Minn.: Liturgical Press, 1975.

Käsemann, Ernst. *An die Römer*, 2d rev. ed. Tübingen: J. C. Mohr [Paul Siebeck], 1974.

Kittel, Gerhard, ed. *Theological Dictionary of the New Testament*. Translated from *Theologisches Wörterbuch zum Neuen Testament*, and edited, by Geoffrey W. Bromiley. 10 vols. Grand Rapids, Michigan: Wm. B. Eerdmans, 1964.

Kittel, Rudolf, ed. *Biblia Hebraica*, 14th ed. Stuttgart: Württembergische Bibelanstalt, n.d. (9th ed., 1954).

Kleist, James A. and Lilly, Joseph L., translators. *The New Testament*. Milwaukee: Bruce, 1956.

Koehler, Ludwig, ed. *Lexicon in Veteris Testamenti Libros*. Leiden: E. J. Brill, 1958.

Kosmala, Hans. "'Das tut zu meinem Gedächtnis'." *Novum Testamentum* 4 (1960), 81-94.

Liddell, Henry G., and Scot, Robert, compilers. *A Greek-English Lexicon*. 9th ed. revised and augmented by Henry Stuart Jones and Roderick McKenzie, with a supplement. Oxford: Clarendon Press, 1968.

Lietzmann, Hans. *Mass and Lord's Supper*. Translated by Dorothea H. G. Reeve. Leiden: E. J. Brill, 1964.

Linge, David E., ed., trans. *Philosophical Hermeneutics*. With extensive introduction by editor. Berkeley: University of California Press, 1976.

Marsh, John. *The Fullness of Time*. New York: Harper and Brothers, 1952.

Marxsen, Willi. *The Lord's Supper as a Christological Problem*. Translated by Lorenz Nieting from *Das Abendmahl als christologisches Problem* [Gutersloh: Gerd Mohn, 1963]. Philadelphia: Fortress Press, 1970.

McKenzie, John L. *Dictionary of the Bible*. Milwaukee: Bruce, 1965.

Michel, O. *TDNT*, s.v. "μιμνήσκομαι," "μνήμη."

Milgrom, Jacob. *Encyclopaedia Judaica*, s.v. "Kipper."

Montminy, Jean-Paul, "L'offrande sacrificielle dans l'anamnèse des liturgies anciennes." *Revue des sciences philosophique et théologique* 50 (1966), 385-405.

Morford, Mark and Lenardon, Robert. *Classical Mythology*, 2nd ed. New York: David McKay Co., 1977.

Neunhauser, Burkhard. "The Mystery Presence." *Downside Review* 76 (1958), 266-273.

Nickelsburg, George W. E. Jr. *Resurrection, Immortality, and Eternal Life in Intertestamental Judaism*. Cambridge, Mass.: Harvard University Press, 1972.

O'Callaghan, Denis. "The Theory of the 'Mysteriengegenwart' of Dom Odo Casel, A Controversial Subject in Modern Theology." *Irish Ecclesiastical Review* 90 (1958), 246-262.

O'Neill, Colman E. "The Mysteries of Christ and the Sacraments." *Thomist* 25 (1962), 1-53.

Pagels, Elaine Hiesey. *The Gnostic Paul*. Philadelphia: Fortress Press, 1975.

Pedersen, Johs. *Israel*. 2 vols. London: Oxford, 1926.

Piper, Otto A. "The Lord's Supper in New Testament Perspective." *Journal of the Interseminary Movement of the Southwest*, ed. James C. Laing. Enid, Oklahoma: Interseminary Movement Press of the Southwest, 1962. Pp. 5-17.

Prümm, Karl. *Religionsgeschichtliches Handbuch*. Rome. Päpstliches Bibelinstitut, 1954.

Rainey, Anson. *Encyclopaedia Judaica*, s.v. "Sacrifice," first section.

Reitzenstein, Richard. *Hellenistic Mystery-Religions*. Translated by John E. Steely from *Die hellenistischen Mysterienreligionen*. 3rd ed. [Stuttgart: B. G. Teubner, 1926]. Pittsburgh: The Pickwick Press, 1978.

Robinson, James M., ed. *The Nag Hammadi Library*. New York: Harper and Row, 1977.

——. "The Sacraments in Corinth." *Journal of the Interseminary Movement of the Southwest*, ed. James C. Laing. Enid, Oklahoma: Interseminary Movement Press of the Southwest, 1962. Pp. 21-32.

Rouse, W. H. D. *Greek Votive Offerings*. Cambridge: University Press, 1902; reprinted 1976.

Ruef, John. *Paul's First Letter to Corinth*. First published Penguin Books Ltd., 1971. Philadelphia: Westminster Press, 1977.

Sanders, E. P. *Paul and Palestinian Judaism.* London: SCM Press, 1977.

Sanders, James A. *Torah and Canon.* Philadelphia: Fortress Press, 1972.

Schoeps, Hans J. *Paul.* Translated by Harold Knight from *Paulus: Die Theologie des Apostels im Lichte der jüdischen Religionsgeschichte.* [Tübingen: J. C. B. Mohr, 1959]. Philadelphia: Westminster Press, 1961.

Schottroff, Willy. *'Gedenken' im alten Orient und im alten Testament.* Revised edition. Neukirchen-Vluyn: Neukirchener Verlag, 1967.

Schweizer, Eduard. *The Lord's Supper.* Translated by James M. Davis. Philadelphia: Fortress Press, 1967.

————. *TDNT*, s.v. "σῶμα."

Scott, W. M. F. "The Eucharist and the Heavenly Ministry of our Lord." *Theology* 56 (1953), 42-50.

Skehan, Patrick W., MacRae, George W., and Brown, Raymond E. "Texts and Versions." *JBC* 69:52.

Smith, Morton. *Jesus the Magician.* San Francisco: Harper and Row, 1978.

Soulen, Richard N. *Handbook of Biblical Criticism.* Atlanta: John Knox Press, 1976.

Suarez, Francisco. *Disputationes Metaphysicae.* Hildesheim: Georg Olms Verlagsbuchhandlung, 1965; reprinted from Paris edition of 1866.

Taille see de la Taille.

Terrien, Samuel. *The Elusive Presence.* San Francisco: Harper and Row, 1978.

Thurian, Max. *The Eucharistic Memorial.* In two parts. Translated by J. G. Davies. Richmond, Virginia: John Knox Press: Part I 1960; Part II 1961.

Vermes, Geza. *Scripture and Tradition in Judaism.* Studia Post-Biblica, vol. 4. 2d rev. ed. Leiden: E. J. Brill, 1973.

Wagner, G. *Das religionsgeschichtliche Problem von Römer 6, 1-11.* Zürich: Zwingli Verlag, 1962.

Webster's Third New International Dictionary. Chicago: G. and C. Merriam Co., 1971.

Williams, Sam K. *Jesus' Death as Saving Event, the Background and Origin of a Concept.* Harvard Dissertations in Religion 2. Missoula, Montana: Scholars Press, 1975.

Zeivin, Ze'ev. *Encyclopaedia Judaica,* s.v. "Food."

III: Some of the Other Works Consulted

Allmen, Jean-Jacques von. *The Lord's Supper.* Richmond, Virginia: John Knox Press, 1969.

Aulén, Gustaf. *Eucharist and Sacrifice.* Translated by Eric H. Wahlstrom. Philadelphia: Muhlenberg Press, 1958.

Aune, David E. "The Phenomenon of Early Christian 'Anti-Sacramentalism'". *Studies in New Testament and Early Christian Literature.* Leiden: E. J. Brill, 1972.

Baneth, Eduard, translator and commentator. *Mishnajot.* Basle: Victor Goldschmidt Verlag, 1968.

Barnes, Harry Elmer. *A History of Historical Writing.* Norman, Oklahoma: University of Oklahoma Press, 1937.

Barr, James. *Old and New in Interpretation.* New York: Harper and Row, 1966.

Benoit, Pierre, ed. *The Breaking of Bread.* New York: Paulist Press, 1969.

Blank, Sheldon H. "Men Against God: The Promethean Element in Biblical Prayer". *Journal of Biblical Literature* 72 (1953), 1-13.

Bloch, Marc. *The Historian's Craft.* New York: Random House, 1953.

Bornkamm, Günther. *Early Christian Experience*. New York: Harper & Row, 1969.

Botte, B. "Problèmes de l'Anamnèse". *Journal of Ecclesiastical History* 5 (1954), 16-24.

Craig, Clarence Tucker, and Short, John. "The First Epistle to the Corinthians". *The Interpreter's Bible*, vol. 10. New York: Abington Press, 1953.

Cullmann, Oscar. *The Early Church*. Edited by A. J. B. Higgins. Philadelphia: Westminster Press, 1956.

Dalmais, I. H. *Introduction to the Liturgy*. Translated by Roger Capel. Baltimore: Helicon Press, 1961.

Danielou, Jean. *The Bible and the Liturgy*. Notre Dame, Indiana: University of Notre Dame Press, 1956.

Diezinger, Walter. *Effectus in der Römischen Liturgie*. Bonn: Peter Hanstein Verlag GMBH, 1961.

Donagan, Alan and Donagan, Barbara. *Philosophy of History*. Toronto: Macmillan, 1965.

Drower, Ethel S. *Water into Wine*. London: John Murray, 1956.

Eliade, Mircea. *Cosmos and History*. Translated by Willard R. Trask. New York: Harper & Row, 1959.

———. *Patterns in Comparative Religion*. Translated by Rosemary Sheed. London: Sheed & Ward, 1958.

Engnell, Ivan. *A Rigid Scrutiny*. Translated and edited by John T. Willis with the collaboration of Helmer Ringgren. Nashville: Vanderbilt University Press, 1969.

Faivre, B. "Eucharistie et mémoire". *La nouvelle revue théologique* 90 (1968), 279-290.

Feneberg, Rupert. *Christliche Passafeier und Abendmahl*. München: Kösel Verlag, 1971.

Fiorenza, Elisabeth Schüssler, ed. *Aspects of Religious Propaganda in Judaism and Early Christianity*. Notre Dame, Indiana: University of Notre Dame Press, 1976.

Hadas, Moses. *Hellenistic Culture*. Morningside Heights, New York: Columbia University Press, 1959.

Gerken, Alexander. *Theologie der Eucharistie*. München: Kösel-Verlag, 1973.

Harrison, Jane. *Prolegomena to the Study of Greek Religion*. 3d ed. Cambridge: University Press, 1922; Meridian Books, 1955.

Héring, Jean. *The First Epistle of Saint Paul to the Corinthians*. 2d ed. Translated by A. W. Heathcote and P. J. Allcock. London: Epworth Press, 1962.

Higgins, A. J. B. *The Lord's Supper in the New Testament*. Chicago: Henry Regnery Co., 1952.

Hull, John M. *Hellenistic Magic and the Synoptic Tradition*. London: SCM Press, 1974.

Hurd, John Coolidge, Jr. *The Origin of I Corinthians*. New York: Seabury Press, 1965.

Kessler, Charles Louis. *The Memory Motif in the God-Man Relationship of the Old Testament*. Ph. D. dissertation on microfilm. Northwestern University, 1956.

Lehman, Helmut T., ed. *Meaning and Practice of the Lord's Supper*. Philadelphia: Muhlenberg Press, 1961.

Lietzmann, Hans. *An die Korinther I*. Tübingen: J. C. B. Mohr, 1907.

Marshall, Howard, ed. *New Testament Interpretation*. Grand Rapids, Mich.: Wm. B. Eerdmans, 1977.

Martin-Achard, Robert. "Souvenir et Mémorial selon l'Ancien Testament". *Revue de théologie et de philosophie* 15 (1965), 302-310.

Metzger, Bruce M. "Methodology in the Study of the Mystery Religions and Early Christianity". *Historical and Literary Studies*. Leiden: E. J. Brill, 1968.

Moll, Helmut. *Die Lehre von der Eucharistie als Opfer*. Koln-Bonn: Peter Hanstein Verlag GMBH, 1975.

Neuenzeit, Paul. *Das Herrenmahl*. München: Kösel-Verlag, 1960.

Pannenberg, Wolfhart, ed. *Revelation as History*. Translated by David Granskou. New York: Macmillan, 1968.

Rahner, Karl. *The Church and the Sacraments*. New York: Herder and Herder, 1963.

Robertson, Archibald, and Plummer, Alfred. *First Epistle of St. Paul to the Corinthians*. 2d ed. Edinburgh: T. & T. Clark, 1914.

Rordorf, W., et al. *L'Eucharistie des premiers Chrétiens*. Paris: Éditions Beauchesne, 1976.

Sandvik, Bjørn. *Das Kommen des Herrn beim Abendmahl*. Zürich: Zwingli Verlag, 1970.

Schmithals, Walter. *Gnosticism in Corinth*. Translated by John E. Steely. Nashville: Abingdon Press, 1971.

Schweizer, Eduard. *Beiträge zur Theologie des neuen Testament*. Zürich: Zwingli Verlag, 1970.

Speyr, Adrienne von. *Korinther I*. Einsiedeln: Johannes Verlag, 1956.

Sykes, Marjorie H. "The Eucharist as 'Anamnesis'". *The Expository Times* (1960), 115-118.

Vermes, Geza. *Jesus the Jew*. New York: Macmillan, 1973.

Weiss, Johannes. *Der erste Korintherbrief*. Göttingen: Vandenhoeck & Ruprecht, 1925.

Wendland, Heinz-Dietrich. *Die Briefe an die Korinther*. Göttingen: Vandenhoeck & Ruprecht, 1964.

Indices

Passages

N.B.: Numbers to right refer to paragraphs, not pages.

Old Testament

Genesis	Para.		Para.		Para.
		20:14,24	197	*Numbers*	
4:25	188	23:13	213	3:41,45	410
5:2	188	24:4ff,7	436	5:15	213,221,232
5:3	200	28:11-12	222		233,235,244
8:1	213	28:11	232	5:18ff	221
8:21	436	28:21,35	253	5:27ff	235
8:28	200	28:23	222	9:9	213
9:4	189,405	29:18	425	10:2ff	253
9:16	213	29:19	436	10:8,10	227
11:4	51	30:12,16	222	10:9	213,233
12:2	51	30:14,16	409	15:28,30	201
15:—	436	30:16	232	16:13	201
17:—	436	30:35	239	16:39-40	222
17:10	151	32:6	370	16:41ff	201
19:29	211	36:14	222	18:12	436
22:15	436			18:19	239
26:25	436	*Leviticus*		25:12	436
28:13ff	197	1:5,15	236	31:54	222,232
28:18-22	197	1:9,13	425		
30:22	211	1:9	236	*Deuteronomy*	
31:54	436	2:1-2,9-10,16	221	4:7	290
		3:13,16	239	4:21,23-24	382
Exodus		3:9,16-17	236	5:15	212[bis]
2:22-25	436	5:5-6	235	7:18	211,228
3:15	184,218	5:7	201	8:2	211
6:4	436	5:11ff	401	8:10	348
7:12	367	5:11-13	221,235	8:18	211
12:12	367		236,244	9:7	211
12:14-15	220	5:16-24	201,212	9:26-27	518
12:27	389	6:1-6	201,212	9:27	211
13:3	523	6:16-18	221	11:26ff	382
13:8-10	220	16:28, 30	403	12:6-14	192
13:9-10	509	23:24	220	12:31	194
13:13	215	24:6-8	227	15:15	211
14:11-13	509	24:7	237,239	16:2-3	211
16:36	339		240,243	16:5	389
17:14	225	24:8	418	16:12	211
19:5	151	26:2-6	382	24:11,20,22	211
19:7	436	26:40-46	202,211	25:17	211

Old Testament Apocrypha and Pseudepigrapha
(Order and nomenclature as in R.H. Charles)

Subjects, Authors, Editors, Greek Words, etc.

N.B.: Numbers refer to paragraphs, not pages.

Entries within quotation marks usually indicate the occurrence of the given word or phrase in the paragraph numbered. Investigation of synonyms and associated ideas will often unearth appropriate passages. Most entries having to do with God will be found under "DIVINE".

(in Judaism); 316 (& memorials);
318 (heavenly ministers); 367; 381
n. 3; 443, 446 (in magical papyril);
449

animal see brute

"anthropological" thinking & God 76;
79; 81

anthropomorphism (see also theomorphism) 76ff; 79; 81 (Paul &; Philo &);
120 (implied); 176 (in relationship
with God?); 338 (Philo &)

anticipation see hope, prospect

apocalypse 318 (& memorial)

apocrypha 180 (state of question); 246ff;
313-14; 315 (cult strong in); 324 (&
Qumran); 342 (& Nag Hammadi)
(statistics on) 350 (state of question)
(on scale of memorial thinking)

Apollo 328 (omniscient)

apostle 356; 359; 369

apotheosis 269; 273; 279; 294 (& he-
roization)

appropriation 457 ("some title of possession"); 458 ("proprietorship"); 460
("things close to") ("close relationship"); 461 (exegesis of Rom. 11:30-
31; 463; 469; 479

Aquinas 141 (substance-accident)

arbitrariness of gods 268; 275

archaeology 55

aristocracy of the gods 274

Aristophanes 294

Aristotle 328 (& "ἀνάμνησις")

ark of covenant 317; 397, 399 (its cover
is mercy seat)

arrogance (see also *hubris*) 393 (relation
to dissension)

artist 64

"artistic actualization" 532

Asian religion (see mystery cults) 273

astrology 267; 272

Atonement see Day

atonement [mostly when term is used]
(see also *Akedah*, propitiation, sin
offering, expiation, forgiveness, sacrifice, etc.) 125 (day of); 199; 200;
201; 202 n. 41; 205 (E. P. Sanders
on); 333; 403; 409 ("atonement
money") (Hebrew word) (idea related
to ransom & mercy seat); 411 n. 26
(*Akedah* as); 485

author see text

authority of Scripture 525; 527 (Childs
&)

authorization (see also authority Divine
Mandate) 456 (of a memorial); 464
(of Eucharist by Jesus)

autonomy see dignity

Avinu Malkenu 332

azkarah 14 (Hook on); 206 (Schottroff
on); 240; 497

Baal 188 (Elijah &); 193 (Hosea &)

baby [example of learning] 56

"backward" against flux see flux

Bagster 210 n. 51

"banality" 440 (of magical papyri)

baptism 374 (& Eucharist related for
Paul?); 378

Barr, James 92; 102; 113; 116 (& the
Gk view); 513

Barrett, C. K. 26 (takes Jeremias
seriously); 27, 29 ("specific" thinking
by); 384; 425 (& "flesh"); 484

Barth, K. (see also analogical thinking)
165 (his position implied: Divine "un-
necessitating")

beatitude see immortality, resurrection, etc.

"bearing" sin 403-4

"because" 374

becoming 42ff

"before" God 197; 352, 353 (in Paul);
389; 454

Behm, J. 208

being 43ff (Gadamer, Descartes, Plato
&)

belief see faith

benedictions see blessings

Bethel 197

betrayal 389 (of Christ)

"between events" 77; 82; 106

Betz, J. 25; 144ff

bias, theological see theological

biblical criticism 525-6

biblical view (see also Paul, OT) 79
(theomorphic); 92 (& time); 95 (of
time); 97 (of event); 100 (of time
quite modern) (& memory); 101
(practical, not philosophical); 102
(of time not a "container" view); 103
(& God's action); 106 (& time) (&
Divine action); 173

binding see *Akedah*

birthday 482

bitterness 429

admits for trumpets); 261 (summary of OT & apocrypha); 313ff (summary of pseudepigrapha); 324 (strong in Qumran) (God can remember sin to forgive); 325 (NT summary) (what, in NT); 330 (*Zikhronot*); 331 (*Amidah*); 332 (*Avinu Malkenu*); 391 (in *Hallel*); 396 (God "regarding" Christ as *hilasterion*); 432 (none of sin, in new covenant) (this a cipher for "new covenant" scheme); 472; 484ff (Vermes, Jeremias &); 495 (of sin in Heb. 10:3) (of covenant in Heb. 10:11ff); 510 (matter of cult); 515 (Childs &) (object of, manner of distinguished); 516 (implications of)

Response to prayer see D. Remembering, small case prayer

Revealing 78; 79; 83 (about future); 106; 124 (where made); 132; 138 (& cult); 525 (not the point in Childs' *Memory & Tradition*); 532; 534 (of Eucharist)

Right 409; 410 (implied)

Sadism? 152

Sameness see D. Timelessness

Sanctioner 473

Spaciality 114

Spirit 103 (Paul &); 111: 155 (Intercessor); 158 (& prayer); 159-160; 161 (power of how operative) (& prayer); 173; 175; 360; 364 (criterion of salvation, with Christ); 431 (freedom in); 525, 527 (Childs &)

"Sponsor" 474-5

"Tapestry" 132

Tendency to Act 206 (in Schottroff)

Threat see D. Wrath

Timelessness 130; 131; 522; 524

Transcendence 79 n. 20; 104-106; 113; 120 ("tension"); 130 (implied); 131-132; 149 (& prayer); 162ff (implied); 195 (& spiritualization of cult); 197; 290-291; 292 (& "Condescension"); 497; 508-9; 522

Truth 84

"Unitary" Power 522; 524

"Un-necessitating" 165

Vengeance see D. Wrath

Will 155 (prayer &)

Wisdom 371 (& glory to God); 496; 518

Witness (see also D. Attention) 23; 493

Works (see also D. Action & references) 212, 259 (remembered)

Wrath 15; 202 n. 41 (& land); 206 (Schottroff on); 209; 216 (μνησικα-κέω); 381 (implied); 382; 429 ("cup"); 434; 472; 532-3

Dodds, E. R. 264-5

dog (example) 40 n. 39; 41

dogma 78; 82; 268 (Gks &) 269; 393; 408 ad finem (implied)

δῶρον 238

"Do this...." 12; 328 (implied); 466; 469; 488 (& sacrifice, in early patristic thinking); 498 (Hook on)

Doty, W. 76 (& Bultmann)

doubt 53

doxologies 159

dramatic quality 503 (of cultic actualization); 508; 511

dreams 264

drinking 413 (at Pasch); 415; 426; 441ff (in magical rites); 469 (no "Drink this....")

drugs 170 (& cult)

drunkenness 387

dualism 163

Dupont-Sommer, A. 321

duration 45, 49, 89 (& meaning); 70; 92 (Cullmann &); 93 (& time); 94ff; 95 (& intersection); 96 (how expressed); 113ff (God as); 131 (summary) (God &); 141f (Casel &, in Mass); 145 (ancients' view of); 173 (in summary); 516 (durational gap—Childs implies); 524

duress 409 (bis)

"dynamism" 69b; 83; 106; 184 (Childs' type, & other)

eating (see also communion, Eucharist, food, bread) 413 (at pasch); 422 (Conzelmann &); 426; 441ff (in magical rites); 469 (no "Eat this...."); 491 (sacred & other at Corinth)

Ebeling, G. 35

ʾebhed 150

ecstasy 264; 271

ecumenism 19 (Thurian &)

editor 188 (bis)

effect (see cause-effect, blessing, ef-